Richard Palliser

the Bb5 Sicilian

a dynamic and hypermodern opening system for Black

Gloucester Publishers plc   www.everymanchess.com

First published in 2005 by Gloucester Publishers plc (formerly Everyman Publishers plc), Northburgh House, 10 Northburgh Street, London EC1V 0AT

Copyright © 2005 Richard Palliser

The right of Richard Palliser to be identified as the author of this work has been asserted in accordance with the Copyrights, Designs and Patents Act 1988.

All rights reserved. No part of this publication may be reproduced, stored in a retrieval system or transmitted in any form or by any means, electronic, electrostatic, magnetic tape, photocopying, recording or otherwise, without prior permission of the publisher.

British Library Cataloguing-in-Publication Data
A catalogue record for this book is available from the British Library.

ISBN 1 85744 397 7

Distributed in North America by The Globe Pequot Press, P.O Box 480, 246 Goose Lane, Guilford, CT 06437-0480.

All other sales enquiries should be directed to Everyman Chess, Northburgh House, 10 Northburgh Street, London EC1V 0AT
tel: 020 7253 7887 fax: 020 7490 3708
email: info@everymanchess.com
website: www.everymanchess.com

Everyman is the registered trade mark of Random House Inc. and is used in this work under licence from Random House Inc.

EVERYMAN CHESS SERIES (formerly Cadogan Chess)
Chief advisor: Garry Kasparov
Commissioning editor: Byron Jacobs
General editor: John Emms

Typeset and edited by First Rank Publishing, Brighton.
Cover design by Horatio Monteverde.
Production by Navigator Guides.
Printed and bound in the US by Versa Press.

CONTENTS

BIBLIOGRAPHY

Books

A Startling Chess Opening Repertoire, Chris Baker (Everyman 1998)
Anti-Sicilians: A Guide for Black, Dorian Rogozenko (Gambit 2003)
Beating the Anti-Sicilians, Joe Gallagher (Batsford 1994)
Easy Guide to the ♗b5 Sicilian, Steffen Pedersen (Everyman 1999)
Encyclopaedia of Chess Openings Volume B (4th edition, Sahovski Informator 2002)
Meeting 1 e4, Alex Raetsky (Everyman 2002)
Sicilian Defence: Moscow variant 1 e4 c5 2 ♘f3 d6 3 ♗b5+ ♘c6, Milan Skoko (Best Chess Editions 1998)
Sicilian Defence: Moscow variant 1 e4 c5 2 ♘f3 d6 3 ♗b5+ ♘d7, Milan Skoko (Best Chess Editions 1999)
Nunn's Chess Openings, John Nunn, Graham Burgess, John Emms & Joe Gallagher (Everyman 1999)
Secrets of Chess Defence, Mihail Marin (Gambit 2003)
Sicilian Defence 8: Moscow Variation 1 P-K4 P-QB4 2 N-KB3 P-Q3 3 B-N5+, L.M.Pickett (The Chess Player 1976)
The Anti-Sicilian: 3 ♗b5 (+), Yuri Razuvayev & Aleksander Matsukevich (Batsford 1984)
The Chess Advantage in Black and White, Larry Kaufman (Random House 2004)

Periodicals

CHESS, *Chess Informant*, *New in Chess Magazine* and *New in Chess Yearbook*

DVDs, CDs and Websites

Bashing the Sicilian with ♗b5: volumes one and two, Murray Chandler (Bad Bishop 2003)
Mega Corr 3, (ed.) Tim Harding (Chess Mail, 2003)
Mega Database 2005 (ChessBase, 2004)
The Week in Chess, *Chess Today* and *ChessPublishing.com*

PREFACE

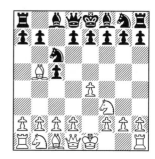

The popularity and success of the Sveshnikov Sicilian, as championed by Kramnik and Leko, has seen interest in the Rossolimo variation (1 e4 c5 2 ♘f3 ♘c6 3 ♗b5) soar amongst the elite in recent years. A variation which was once considered as a playable alternative to 3 d4, but one which was much less theoretical and critical, has now become almost as important as the Open Sicilian after 2...♘c6. The two antagonists of Brissago may have only rarely employed 3 ♗b5 themselves, but the move has often been ventured in this millennium by Adams, Anand, Grischuk, Morozevich and Shirov, while even Kasparov has turned to it on occasion.

Taking into account all of the recent developments in the Rossolimo was a challenging task, but I do hope that this book presents an up-to-date picture of its theory. Likewise the latest state of play in the Moscow variation (1 e4 c5 2 ♘f3 d6 3 ♗b5+) is given, while I've also aimed to challenge the view that the check on b5 is just rather dull. Some lines after it are quite drawish, but the move should appeal to creative players, as well as just to positional ones, with Glek and Rublevsky certainly having enjoyed much success with it.

Having over 40,000 games with the ♗b5(+) Sicilian on my databases has meant that very complete coverage wasn't possible. However, the current state of play in all of the main variations is supplied, while I've especially examined recent trends and ideas for both sides, as well as variations slightly neglected by earlier sources, especially 3...d6, 3...e6 and the currently fashionable 3...♘f6 in the Rossolimo.

Thanks are due to Adam Collinson, Scott Fraser, John Hodgson, Gawain Jones and Peter Wells for their analytical suggestions, and to Chris Duggan, Carsten Hansen, Paul Hopwood, Sean Marsh and Norman Stephenson for locating some very useful material. Once again the team at *Everyman* worked wonders, with the editing, patience and support of John Emms and Byron Jacobs being greatly appreciated.

Richard Palliser,
Harrogate,
September 2005.

INTRODUCTION

The Moscow Variation:
An Undeserved Reputation

As a staunch 2...d6 Sicilian player, I would place 3 ♗b5+ as White's best try for an advantage after 2 ♘f3 should he wish to avoid all of the theory associated with 3 d4. However, the Moscow variation does not enjoy the best of reputations in certain quarters. Many Black players complain that the check is dull or drawish, but that is surprisingly often just because they have actually suffered against it. White can certainly play rather carefully after the check, but he does have a number of different possible set-ups and ideas; many of which contain a fair amount of bite, as a talented young Ukrainian grandmaster recently found out.

V.Malakhov-A.Areshchenko
Aeroflot Open, Moscow 2005

1 e4 c5 2 ♘f3 d6 3 ♗b5+ ♗d7 4 ♗xd7+ ♕xd7 5 0-0 ♘f6 6 ♕e2 ♘c6 7 ♖d1!?

Fittingly first played by Rossolimo in 1950, this rare move has recently begun to stage a small revival. White's idea is that after 7...g6 8 c3 ♗g7 9 d4 cxd4 10 cxd4 d5, the black bishop will be misplaced on g7, although simply 7...e6 is quite playable. Areshchenko, however, has a more aggressive idea in mind.

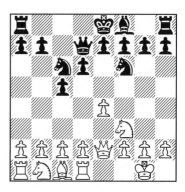

7...♕g4?! 8 d3 ♘e5 9 ♘bd2 e6?

Too slow. Black underestimates the potential danger to his own king. If 7...♕g4 is to be resuscitated then 9...♘h5!? could be tried, but 10 ♕f1, intending an exchange on e5 and then ♘c4, looks good for White as does even 10 h3!? ♘f4 11 hxg4 ♘xe2+ 12 ♔f1.

10 h3! ♕h5 11 d4!

Opening the centre to rapidly activate the white pieces, and already Black is in serious danger.

11...♘xf3+ 12 ♘xf3 cxd4?! 13 e5!

Even stronger than recapturing on d4 as Malakhov fully exploits the initiative.

13...dxe5 14 ♕b5+ ♘d7 15 ♖xd4 ♖d8

15...0-0-0 was the last chance, but after 16 ♗e3 the black monarch's days would have been numbered in any case. In the game the huge pin along the a4-e8 diagonal now decides.

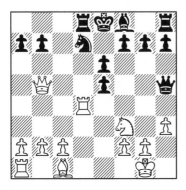

16 ♖xd7! ♖xd7 17 g4 1-0

Contemporary Exponents of the Moscow

As with any opening, those who employ the Moscow variation in their repertoire should keep an eye open for recent games from its leading practitioners. Apart from Vladimir Malakhov, there are several leading grandmasters who make regular use of the check: Michael Adams, Vladimir Baklan, Viktor Bologan, Igor Glek, Viorel Iordachescu, Eduardas Rozentalis, Zhang Zhong and especially 'Mr ♗b5' Sergei Rublevsky.

Each time in the course of this book that we encounter a new defence for Black we will meet the leading antagonists of that particular variation, such as Sergei Tiviakov and Veselin Topalov for 3...♘c6. That block, along with its cousin 3...♘d7, sees Black attempt to avoid the supposedly sterile positions which can arise after 3...♗d7 should White be happy with a draw. However, both knight moves are, as John Nunn puts it so well in *NCO*, 'certainly more risky than 3...♗d7 and in a way play into White's hands'. As we will see, both 3...♘c6 and 3...♘d7 are fighting defences to

the check and White must be prepared to play creatively and often fairly aggressively against them if he wishes to fight for the advantage.

Key structures

3...♗d7 remains by far Black's main defence to the Moscow variation after which both sides have some key choices to make over which pawn structure will be contested. Should White opt for a set-up with c3 and d4 then Black is usually best advised to counter with ...d5, after which a French structure arises. Black has usefully already exchanged his light-squared bishop, but White can still hope to turn his space advantage into a kingside attack.

R.Kasimdzhanov-V.Topalov
FIDE World Championship, Tripoli 2004

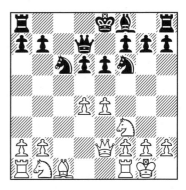

White's strong centre even gives him ideas here of an e5 or d5 push, and so Black must immediately challenge it.

9...d5! 10 e5 ♘g8!? 11 ♖d1 ♘ge7 12 ♘c3 ♘c8

In the Advance French this knight would often head towards the kingside. Here though it isn't needed to blunt a white light-squared bishop, while Black must be quite careful if he breaks with ...f6. Then e6 can easily become rather weak, and so Topalov instead prefers to look for play on the queenside.

13 ♗e3 ♘b6 14 b3 ♖c8 15 ♕b2!

White enjoys slightly the better development and so Kasimdzhanov wisely improves his pieces. This not so much prevents an annoying ...♗a3, as prepares to re-route the c3-knight towards more active duties on the kingside.

15...♗e7 16 ♘e2 0-0 17 ♘f4 ♖c7 18 ♕e2 ♖fc8 19 ♘e1!

For the time being Topalov is restrained on the queenside, but he will gain play there at some point, especially due to his control of the c-file. However, before Black can generate a breakthrough, Kasimdzhanov pushes him on to the defensive.

19...♕d8 20 ♕g4 ♘d7 21 ♘ed3 ♘f8 22 g3 ♗a3 23 ♘h5 ♘g6 24 h4!

Topalov has defended well over the past few moves and now intends to begin exchanges with ...♘b4. However, White has retained a pleasant advantage for his kingside play is more potent than Black's down the c-file. Kasimdzhanov now kept control well and eventually advanced his g-pawn en route to gaining a serious advantage.

Topalov's response to the attack on his f6-knight was a little unusual. Instead Black normally exploits the opportunity to advance his knight to e4, although Topalov may have felt that after 11 ♘bd2 the position could easily become rather drawish, especially with multiple exchanges down the c-file not unknown in this line. White can instead play more critically with 11 ♗e3 ♗e7 12 ♘e1, threatening to trap the e4-knight after 13 f3, but Black has then scored quite well of late after advancing his f-pawn.

G.Souleidis-A.Naiditsch
Julian Borowski, Essen 2002

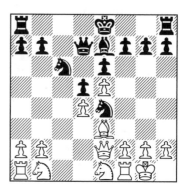

12...f5

Giving the knight an escape square, but 12...f6 is more popular. The main idea is to force White to advance his f-pawn to defend e5, such as with 13 f3 ♘g5 14 ♘d3 0-0 15 ♘d2 ♘f7 16 f4 when 16...f5 is similar to 12...f5. However, there is the important difference that White no longer has access to the f4-square. 12...f6 has been believed to be the more accurate move, but that's not so clear. At any rate White now fails to make any use of the f4-square.

13 f3 ♘g5 14 ♘d3 0-0 15 ♘c3 ♘f7 16 ♔h1?! ♖ac8 17 ♖g1

White lacks a good plan, but perhaps he should just have challenged on the c-file, possibly after f4, waiting to see if Black could make any progress. Advancing the g-pawn fails to disturb Naiditsch at all and actually just lands up creating weaknesses.

17...♘h8! 18 g4?! ♘g6 19 g5 ♘a5 20 ♕f2 b5 21 h4?

It was the last chance for 21 f4, although Black has already made major inroads on the queenside.

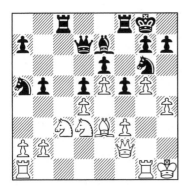

21...f4!

An excellent positional pawn sacrifice. At a stroke Black prevents White from gaining a bind and lots of space with h5 and ♘h4, while also gaining the f5-square. The f4-pawn will eventually drop off, but then White will simply come under pressure down the f-file.

22 ♗c1 b4 23 ♘e2 ♕b5! 24 ♖d1 ♖f5 25 ♗xf4

This could be criticised, but Souleidis has been completely outplayed over the past dozen moves and is already struggling to breathe.

25...♖cf8 26 ♕g3 ♘c4 27 b3?

Cracking under pressure and losing material to a neat tactic. White could have battled on with 27 ♖ab1, but 27...♕a6 would then have left White completely bottled up and with his a-pawn dropping off.

27...♘b2! 28 ♘xb2 ♕xe2

Now the pressure down the f-file nets a piece to cap an impressive display from the young German.

29 ♖d2 ♕a6 0-1

White Plays c4

As Malakhov has shown, White doesn't these days only play c3 or c4 after 3...♗d7, with the fianchetto of his queen's bishop yet another possible set-up. However, playing c4 is rather popular and is well on the way to replacing the older idea of c3 and d4 as the main line of the Moscow variation. Black doesn't have to allow White to carry out d4, but he often does after which it is he who has a choice of structure. Of course whether Black opts for an ...e6 or for a ...g6 set-up does not alter the fact that White has opted for a Maróczy Bind, but here we will use that term to generally refer to ...g6 positions, with ...e6 ones being classified as Hedgehogs.

Setting up a Hedgehog position will not suit everyone, especially as this can become a tricky breed of Hedgehog for Black. He is a little less cramped without the light-squared bishops on the board, but without them has lost some important dynamism while White can manoeuvre more freely within his own camp. Black can still aim for the key ...b5 and ...d5 breaks, but he must watch out for a rapid kingside attack.

L.Psakhis-M.Maki Uuro
Isle of Man Open 1999

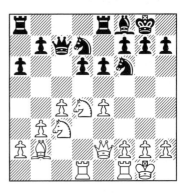

The black bishop on f8 helps to neutralise a rook lift to g3 and so Psakhis instead advances in the centre.

14 f4

In a normal Hedgehog this would be rather double-edged, but the absence of light-squared bishops is clearly here in White's favour. Black lacks pressure against e4, while the white position is very harmonious.

14...♖ab8 15 ♔h1 h6?!

Maki Uuro rather lacks counterplay, but weakening the kingside is unsurprisingly not a great idea.

16 ♖d3 d5?

The ideal break, but unfortunately for Black this is badly timed, although it wasn't at all easy either for him to break with the alternative ...b5.

17 cxd5 exd5 18 e5! ♕a5 19 ♘f5

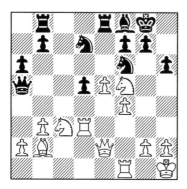

Perhaps the Finn underestimated the strength of White's attack. The e5-pawn certainly cuts the black camp in two, in a rather Kasparovian manner, after which the experienced ex-Soviet grandmaster makes no mistake on the kingside.

19...♘b6 20 ♕d1! ♘e4 21 ♘xh6+! 1-0

and Black resigned as 21...gxh6+ 22 ♘xe4 would have been followed by a decisive doubling on the g-file.

A more popular response to White's attempt to set up a central clamp is for Black to fianchetto his king's bishop. Then he can play the position along the lines of the Accelerated Dragon, rerouting the queen from d7 to a5 in preparation of supporting the ...b5 break. Traditionally, moving the queen from d7 has been considered necessary for that is not the most natural of squares for her in a Sicilian. However, Black has recently been making good use of the queen's position on d7 with ...e6, angling for a quick ...d5 break.

A.Delchev-V.Ivanchuk
European Ch., Silivri, 2003

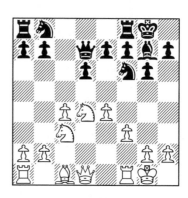

10...♖c8!

Played with a specific idea in mind. Previously Black would have completed his development with 10...♘c6 when 11 ♗e3 a6 12 a4 e6 leads to a dynamically unbalanced, but roughly level, position as we'll see in Chapter Five.

11 b3 d5!

A strong novelty which exploits White's vulnerable pieces down the a1-h8 diagonal to fully equalise.

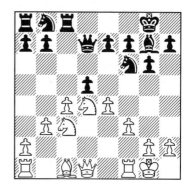

12 exd5

White has nothing better as 12 e5 ♘e8 13 ♘xd5 e6 14 ♘c3 ♗xe5 is at least fine for Black, especially after 15 ♘de2? b5! as in the game G.Vescovi-A.Areshchenko, Moscow 2004.

12...♘xd5 13 ♘xd5 e6! 14 ♗e3

White must lose the piece back, although here 14 ♗h6!? is a more critical try, but then practice has shown that 14...exd5 15 ♗xg7 ♔xg7 16 ♘b5 dxc4 17 ♘d6 ♖d8 also fully equalises.

14...exd5 15 cxd5

There is now nothing wrong with the simple recapture 15...♘xd5, but Ivanchuk prefers a different way to regain the pawn and to fully equalise.

15...♘a6 16 ♖c1 ♖xc1 17 ♕xc1 ♘b4 18 ♕d2 ♘xd5 19 ♘e2 ♕e7 ½-½

The Rossolimo Variation and Nicolas Rossolimo

H.E. Bird and Elijah Williams both employed 2 ♘f3 ♘c6 3 ♗b5 at the great London tournament of 1851, but the move is named after the Kievan born Nicolas Rossolimo (1910-75). Rossolimo was never quite in the world's elite, although he did represent France and the USA in several Olympiads, and it was his sparkling victories with 3 ♗b5 in the late forties which brought the variation to a wider audience.

N.Rossolimo-Romanenko
Salzburg 1948

1 e4 c5 2 ♘f3 ♘c6 3 ♗b5 g6

Rossolimo generally intended rapid development after 3 ♗b5 as another game of his shows: 3...e6 4 0-0 ♘f6?! 5 ♖e1 d5 6 exd5 ♘xd5 7 ♘e5 (7 d4! looks like a better way to a pleasant advantage) 7...♕c7 8 ♕f3?! ♗d6! 9 ♘xc6 bxc6?? (dropping a piece whereas 9...0-0 10 ♘xa7 ♖xa7 11 h3 b6 would have been quite attractive for Black) 10 ♕xd5 ♗xh2+ 11 ♔h1 0-0 12 ♕h5! and 1-0 in N.Rossolimo-C.Kottnauer, Bad Gastein 1948.

4 0-0 ♗g7 5 ♘c3!?

White places quick development ahead of trying to build a big centre with c3 and d4, while this variation later appealed to a young

Morozevich.

5...♘f6 6 ♖e1 ♘d4?

Too ambitious and a rather illogical follow-up. Instead, as Razuvaev and Matsukevich point out, Black had to play 6...0-0 when 7 e5 ♘e8 8 ♗xc6 dxc6 9 d3 ♘c7 10 ♘e4 ♘e6 actually transposes to a position we will shortly consider in Benjamin-Ni Hua.

7 e5!

White wanted to make this advance in any case, but now it serves to severely disrupt Romanenko's development.

7...♘g8

Presumably Black had intended to buy his knight a square here with 7...♘xb5 only realising at the last moment that it actually loses to 8 exf6 ♘xc3 9 fxg7! (Razuvaev and Matsukevich).

8 d3 ♘xb5 9 ♘xb5 a6

Rather provocative, but the major oversight has already been made. Razuvaev and Matsukevich suggest 9...♘h6, but after 10 ♗g5 0-0 11 ♘d6 the black position remains truly horrendous.

10 ♘d6+!

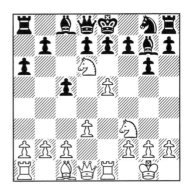

Now 10...♔f8 would have left Black very cramped and severely behind in development; Romanenko prefers to go down in flames.

10...exd6?! 11 ♗g5 ♕a5 12 exd6+ ♔f8 13 ♖e8+!

Continuing in style as White can even introduce his queen into the attack with tempo.

13...♔xe8 14 ♕e2+ ♔f8 15 ♗e7+ ♔e8

Alternatively Black could have preferred to be have been murdered with many of his army still asleep after 15...♘xe7 16 ♕xe7+ ♔g8 17 ♘g5.

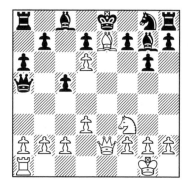

16 ♗d8+!

The coup de grâce to a very attractive display from Rossolimo.

16...♔xd8 17 ♘g5 1-0

A Line Suited not only to the Very Positional Player

The Rossolimo can be viewed as quite a positional line against 2...♘c6, especially if White then doubles the black pawns on c6. However, White must often proceed quite dynamically after that, while he doesn't have to exchange on c6 and can instead prefer an approach based on quick central play. Thus 3 ♗b5 appeals to a wide range of players with its current leading advocates including, on top of those who are also exponents of 2...d6 3 ♗b5+: Vladimir Akopian, Laurent Fressinet, Alexander Grischuk, Luke McShane, Alexander Morozevich and Ruslan Ponomariov, along with even Alexei Shirov, Emil Sutovsky and Peter Svidler; three players certainly not known for their timidity!

Black should thus be careful if he tries too hard to avoid a positional struggle. Along with 3...♘f6, 3...♘a5 is currently fairly fashionable, but not all White players will mind then trans-

posing to an Open Sicilian type position after a quick d4. Should Black wish to play creatively and to quickly reach an unbalanced position then 3...e6 deserves serious attention. This has been employed in recent years by Alexei Shirov and Garry Kasparov, although the world number one has suffered defeats with it against Akopian and Rublevsky. After 3...e6 4 0-0 ♘ge7 White can aim for rapid development and a favourable Open Sicilian with a quick d4, or he can follow Adams' lead and prefer to take over the centre with c3 and d4. 4 ♗xc6 is also a pretty valid option when the position often becomes rather dynamic and can even quickly flare up.

E.Sutovsky-H.Nakamura
Pamplona 2003

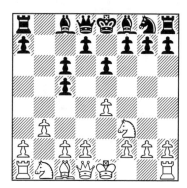

Now Black often chooses 5...♘e7 6 ♗b2 ♘g6, when he intends ...f6 and ...e5, while control of e5 is usually rather important in this line. Nakamura's choice is highly committal for Black will be severely hampered by his doubled c-pawns, unless he can gain some rapid activity.

5...d5!? 6 ♕e2 ♘e7 7 ♗a3 ♘g6

Thus the knight unravels to its best square, but Sutovsky doesn't panic in the face of Black's imminent kingside demonstration.

8 0-0 ♕a5 9 ♗b2 ♗d6!?

Continuing in aggressive vein, whereas blunting the powerful bishop with 9...f6 would have been more normal. Black must of course though try to avoid closing the centre for after 9...d4?! 10 e5! ♗a6 11 d3 ♗e7 12 ♕e4 (Ftacnik) White would enjoy a pleasant edge. Black's queenside is crippled in the long run, while White also enjoys a useful space advantage on the kingside.

10 ♗xg7!?

As Sutovsky explains in *New in Chess*, using Caesar's famous declaration, there was nothing wrong with 'the sane 10 e5 ♗e7 11 d3, but alea iacta est!'

10...♘f4 11 ♕e3 ♖g8! 12 e5 ♘xg2! 13 ♕h6!

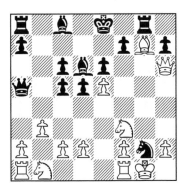

and the board was in flames. We really have no option but to later return to this fascinating position and encounter as we will in Game 55.

The Main Line Rossolimo with 3...g6

This remains Black's most popular response to 3 ♗b5 and has a pretty good and sound reputation. White traditionally has looked to play in the centre with 4 0-0 ♗g7 and then 5 ♖e1 or 5 c3 and such systems remain popular, although both sides must also always bear in mind the possibility of an exchange on c6.

J.Benjamin-Ni Hua
China-USA match, Shanghai 2002

White has just exchanged on c6 and now

capitalised on his space advantage to increase the pressure on the black position.

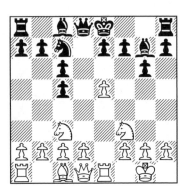

9 ♘e4! ♘e6 10 d3 0-0 11 ♗e3 b6 12 ♕d2

Black is a little passive here, but is fairly solid. However, it is important that he aims to challenge White's grip and so here 12...f5! is the way to go, forcing White to exchange off his e5-bridgehead as we'll see in Chapter Ten (see Game 76).

12...♘d4?! 13 ♘xd4 cxd4

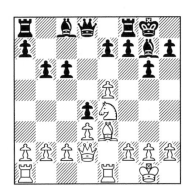

14 ♗h6!

Ni Hua has ironed out his structure, but these doubled c-pawn positions are more complex than just that. Black may be solid, but he must also maintain some dynamism in his position. The exchange on d4 has robbed his position of that as too will the exchange on g7, which also serves to weaken the black kingside.

14...c5?!

Quite possibly after Rabinovich's suggestion of 14...♗xe5! 15 ♗xf8 ♕xf8 White is still objectively better, but Black had to try that to change the trend of the game.

15 ♕f4 ♗b7 16 ♗xg7 ♔xg7 17 b3 ♕d5 18 ♕g3!

White's space advantage allows him to advance on the kingside and so he prepares f4, while Black lacks any real counterplay and must try to defend as accurately as possible.

18...♖ad8

Ni Hua decides to counter White's plan by advancing his own f-pawn, but he must prepare that for 18...f5 19 exf6+ exf6 20 ♘d6, followed by 21 ♖e7+, would have been pretty painful.

19 ♖e2 f5!? 20 exf6+ exf6 21 ♖ae1 ♗c6 22 f4! ♖de8?! 23 f5!

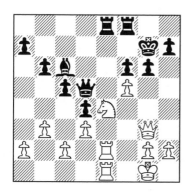

Reopening the queen's dark-square influence and leaving Black facing serious difficulties as he tries to desperately prevent a decisive rook invasion on e7. Indeed Ni Hua now immediately cracked with 23...♕e5?, losing material after 24 ♘d6 ♕xe2 25 ♘xe8+.

Associated with the rise in popularity of the Rossolimo has been the immediate exchange on c6, when 4...dxc6 is the more respectable recapture. Black will usually then clamp down on the centre with ...e5, when he enjoys the long-term advantage of the two bishops and can hope to expand on the kingside. White thus needs to exploit his slightly better development, and he can do that by opting for either a b4 or for an f4 break; two plans which Black must try to be ready for.

R.Ponomariov-V.Kramnik
Linares 2003

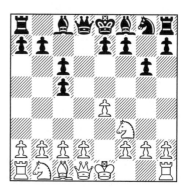

5 d3 ♗g7 6 h3 ♘f6 7 ♘c3 ♘d7 8 ♗e3 e5 9 ♕d2

White has developed quickly and harmoniously, but must find a way to open up the solid black position. Of course doing so will involve opening the position for the black bishop-pair, which explains why White often likes to prefix the f4-break with ♗h6 and an exchange of bishops. Black can now continue very solidly with 9...♕e7, ...f6 and ...♘d7-f8-e6, but instead Kramnik prefers a more ambitious approach.

9...h6!?

Preventing the desired exchange of bishops, which also slightly weakens the black kingside, at the cost of a delay in castling. However, this isn't such a bad delay for White must keep his queen on d2 to prevent castling, but that in turn prevents the f3-knight from being redeployed to c4. In a position like this White mustn't just focus on the b4 and f4 breaks, but he must also aim to find good roles for his knights which currently, as Marin explains in his superb *Secrets of Chess Defence*, 'don't yet have any stable outposts'.

10 0-0 ♕e7

11 a3

A very natural plan, but unfortunately for Ponomariov, Kramnik is ready with an ingenious idea. Undoubling the c-pawns with b4 may at first sight appear a little strange, but White needs to open paths to attack down. If he can force a pawn exchange on b4 then he suddenly acquires strong pressure down the a-file. Black, however, would prefer not to have to prevent b4 with ...a5, as then a4, followed by ♘f3-d2-c4, severely cramps his queenside and exploits the weaknesses on a5 and b6.

11...♘f8! 12 b4 ♘e6

Improving the knight and keeping the position closed in a modern manner of which John Watson would approve. Opening the position with Black lagging in development would be much more likely to favour the white knight-pair than the black bishops. Furthermore, after 12...cxb4? 13 axb4 ♕xb4? 14 ♗xa7 White threatens to win an exchange and

14...b6 15 ♖fb1 (Marin) would already leave White with a huge advantage.

13 ♘a4

White has no desire to exchange on c5 for then he would have failed in his objective to open the queenside. He really needs to force an exchange on b4 to obtain sufficient open lines, and so increases the pressure against the c5-pawn.

13...b6!

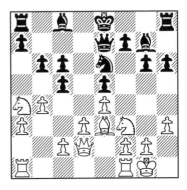

This is Kramnik's big idea which, in this instance, appears to neutralise White's plan of a3 and b4. White's problem is that he has been unable to open queenside lines after all, as 14 bxc5 b5! keeps them closed and then 15 ♘c3 f5! leaves Black with a useful initiative and good chances on the kingside.

14 ♘h2?! f5

Black is still not fully developed, but, with White stymied on he queenside, decides that he can already advance on the kingside. In the game he quickly obtained an excellent position after 15 f3 f4 and we'll see more of this fashionable variation in Chapter Nine.

CHAPTER ONE

3...♘c6:
Connecting Both Variations

1 e4 c5 2 ♘f3 d6 3 ♗b5+ ♘c6

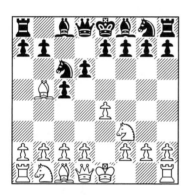

An uncompromising response to the check which has been championed by grandmasters known for their fighting chess: Veselin Topalov, Sergei Movsesian, Sergei Tiviakov and Andrei Kharlov. Of course this position also often arises after 2 ♘f3 ♘c6 3 ♗b5 d6, while the resulting positions are rather complex. White is usually forced to make an unbalancing concession, such as ceding the two bishops, if he wishes to construct his classical centre with c3 and d4. He doesn't have to aim for that, but there is no easy route at all to a white advantage, while play tends to be more aggressive than in the 3...♗d7 lines.

4 0-0

For a long time most ♗b5 exponents simply castled here and then went down one of the main lines. However, in recent years White has begun to investigate the alternatives; to a small extent 4 c3 and especially 4 ♗xc6+ bxc6 5 0-0. This certainly leads to some rather unbalanced positions, while White will hope to gain the advantage by breaking with c3 and d4 and we examine this approach in Games 1–3.

4...♗d7

4...♗g4 drifts in and out of fashion. However, since Adams smashed Tiviakov with it in the 1994 PCA Candidates, it's been pretty rare. Black players still avoid 5 h3 ♗h5 6 c3 ♕b6 (6...a6 may well be better, although then 7 ♗xc6+ bxc6 8 d4 cxd4 9 cxd4 ♘f6 10 ♗g5! looks like a pleasant edge with 10...♘xe4? impossible due to 11 ♕c2) 7 ♘a3! a6 8 ♗a4 ♕c7 9 d4 b5 10 ♘xb5! axb5 11 ♗xb5 0-0-0 12 b4 with a huge attack for the piece.

5 ♖e1

Already White is at an important cross roads. Play normally continues down the main line with 5 c3 ♘f6 6 ♖e1 a6 (or 5 ♖e1 ♘f6 6 c3 a6) when, as we will see, White dictates the course of the struggle with 7 ♗xc6!?, 7 ♗a4 or 7 ♗f1. Some sources have, however, recommended that Black flick in ...a6 on move 5, after which White may no longer be able to reach his desired set-up. Thus 7 ♗f1 players should avoid 5 c3 a6, while 7 ♗a4 ones should employ a 5 c3 move order as 5 ♖e1 a6 rules out a retreat to a4. However, while 5 c3 a6 appears to be a sensible choice, 5 ♖e1 a6?! looks rather risky, albeit so long as White is happy to reach a favourable Open Sicilian type position after 6 ♗xc6 ♗xc6 7 d4 as we'll see Sutovsky do in Game 4.

5...♘f6 6 c3

The main move, but recently 6 h3!? has become quite fashionable as White hopes to avoid too much theory while also setting Black new tasks to solve. The b5-bishop will drop back to f1 when, compared with the main line, its d7-counterpart lacks a good square, and this positional approach is the subject of Games 5-7.

6...a6

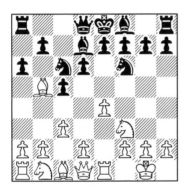

7 ♗f1

The most popular move of recent years, although with the gambit 7 ♗xc6!? ♗xc6 8 d4 White can still hope to catch Black out. However, Black is theoretically fine as we'll see in Ivanchuk-Topalov (Game 8). Instead with 7 ♗a4 White adopts a different mindset as he hopes to manoeuvre Black away from a Sicilian structure, into one reminiscent of the Ruy Lopez. Many players will try to avoid that fate with the 7...c4 of Sutovsky-Hamdouchi (Game 9), while 7...b5 8 ♗c2 e5 is covered in

Psakhis-Gallagher (Game 10).

7...♗g4

Just like Black's two previous moves, this is pretty standard these days and again leaves White at a junction.

8 d3

The fashionable continuation after which White intends to only hassle the bishop once he is ready to recapture with a knight on f3. However, an immediate 8 h3 ♗xf3 9 ♕xf3 has often led to a small White edge in practice (as in Sutovsky-Tiviakov, Game 11), although Black players not so keen on a fairly slow game there after 9...g6 can instead prefer 8...♗h5!?. Whereas 8 h3 has maintained a pretty consistent level of following, the much sharper 8 d4!? is fairly rare these days unlike in the 1990s. Then 8...cxd4 9 cxd4 ♗xf3!? 10 gxf3 d5 11 e5 reaches an interesting and unbalanced position in which 11...♘h5, intending ...e6, ...g6, and probably ...♘g7-f5, is a good practical response and has done fairly well in practice, but 11...♘d7 12 e6! fxe6 13 ♗h3 gave White good compensation in Zhang Zhong-Ni Hua, Yongchuan 2003.

8...e6 9 ♘bd2 ♗e7 10 h3 ♗h5 11 g4

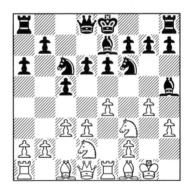

The only way to make progress and now White can net the bishop-pair, while Black remains pretty solid and hopes to demonstrate that White has overextended on the kingside, as we will investigate in Game 12 (Morozevich-Akopian).

1 e4 c5 2 ♞f3 d6 3 ♗b5+ ♞c6 4 ♗xc6+ bxc6 5 0-0

Having doubled Black's c-pawns one might expect White to simply develop, intending to later exploit his structural advantage. However, by playing too slowly White risks leaving himself without a plan while Black takes over the centre and then the initiative after ...e5. Thus White usually aims to open the centre with c3 and d4 when his superior development may well allow him to exert pressure against c6 and d6.

5...e5

Traditionally the main line, but this certainly commits Black to having to play pretty aggressively at any early stage. Instead 5...♞f6 is a little careless as it allows 6 e5!, while 5...♗g4 is the subject of Game 3.

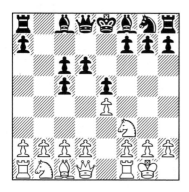

6 c3

Preparing to quickly blast the centre open, while once again it's risky for White to play too slowly. 6 ♖e1 is useful, but then 6...g5! (a recurring theme, while clearly now 7 h3? h5 only helps Black) 7 d3 doesn't look like too appetising a position for White and 7...g4 8 ♞fd2 ♞e7, intending 9...♞g6 with a kingside bind, is awkward for him.

6...g5?!

Optimism and hope may have been in the air at Prague, but Polgar was under pressure having lost the first game of this mini-match; hence this aggressive choice. However, this thrust is too weakening and Kasparov powerfully and classically responds by opening the centre. She should thus have preferred 6...f5!?, the subject of our next game, or the relatively solid 6...♞f6. However, White can still then play aggressively should he wish and 7 d4!? (instead 7 ♖e1 is fairly well met by Akopian's 7...♗g4, although 8 d4!? cxd4 9 cxd4 exd4!? 10 ♕xd4 ♗xf3 11 gxf3 ♗e7 12 e5! wasn't so comfortable for Black in O.Salmensuu-V.Akopian, Linares 2001; however, he should have earlier strong-pointed e5 with 9...♕c7 or have now opted for 12...♞d5!? (Akopian) when 13 exd6 ♕xd6 14 ♕xg7 is the only way to try and trouble Black, but then simply 14...♕g6+! 15 ♕xg6 hxg6 appears to supply full compensation for the pawn) 7...exd4 (critical, while Black should avoid 7...♞xe4?! 8 ♖e1 f5 9 dxe5 d5 10 ♕a4 when his e4-steed doesn't fully prevent White's pressure with c4 imminent)

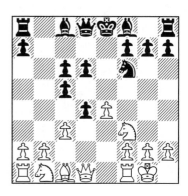

8 ♖e1!? (Nisipeanu's sacrificial idea which aims to breathe new life into 7 d4 as White has been struggling after 8 cxd4 ♞xe4 9 ♖e1 d5) 8...dxc3 reaches a sharp and important position where Nisipeanu and Stoica's suggestion of 9 ♕a4!? (9 ♞xc3 ♗e7 10 e5 dxe5 11

♕xd8+ ♗xd8 12 ♘xe5 ♗e6!, preparing to meet 13 ♗e3 with 13...♗c7, saw Black equalise in L.Nisipeanu-M.Parligras, Curtea de Arges 2002) 9...cxb2 10 ♗xb2 deserves serious attention; White is two pawns down, but 11 e5 is next up and Black must tread carefully, although he does have 10...♗e7 11 e5 dxe5 12 ♘xe5 0-0! when 13 ♘xc6 ♗d7 14 ♘xe7+ ♕xe7 15 ♖xe7 ♗xa4 16 ♗xf6 gxf6 17 ♘c3 ♗c6 will probably lead to a draw.

7 d4! g4 8 ♘fd2 cxd4 9 cxd4 exd4 10 ♘c4! c5

Polgar decides that she might as well have a pawn for her suffering, while instead 10...♗g7 11 ♗f4 ♗e6 12 ♘xd6+ ♔f8 13 ♘d2 ♘e7 14 ♘b3 ♕b6 15 ♖c1 simply gave White a large advantage in S.Rublevsky-A.Stripunsky, Kazan 1995.

11 ♖e1!

Eyeing up the black king and preparing to open the position to exploit White's superior development.

11...♗e6 12 ♘ba3 ♗e7 13 e5!

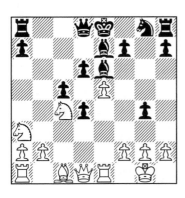

13...d5 14 ♘d6+! ♔f8

Criticised by Kasparov, although one can easily appreciate why Polgar didn't like the look of 14...♗xd6 15 exd6 ♕xd6 when she would have been very weak on the dark-squares; something which Kasparov's 16 b4! then neatly exploits.

15 ♗f4 h5 16 b4!

Destroying the black centre and winning

back the gambited pawn after which White retains a strong bind on the position while Polgar struggles to coordinate her ragged position.

16...c4 17 ♕xd4 h4 18 ♘ab5 ♖h5 19 ♕e3

Being a rapid game, it would be surprising if White were to convert his large advantage flawlessly, but the world no.1 does begin to drift around here, with one good option simply being 19 ♘xa7!? ♗xd6 20 exd6 ♕d7 21 ♗e3 (Psakhis) when White's queenside pawns should decide.

19...♕d7 20 ♘d4 ♗d8! 21 ♕d2 ♘e7 22 b5 ♘g6 23 ♘c6 c3 24 ♕c1

White has two colossal knights, but Polgar has resisted well thus far although now she becomes too ambitious in her bid for counterplay.

24...g3?! 25 fxg3 hxg3 26 ♗xg3 ♗b6+ 27 ♔h1 ♔g7 28 ♕xc3

The g3-bishop holds the kingside together and White is now two pawns up, but there's still no forced winning line in sight.

28...♖ah8 29 ♖f1 ♔g8 30 ♖ae1?! f5! 31 exf6 ♕h7 32 f7+

Having lost control a little one would expect White to calm prefer 32 ♘d4! ♖xh2+ 33 ♔g1, but Kasparov has seen something flashy.

32...♗xf7

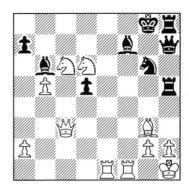

33 ♕xh8+?!

An impressive idea, but objectively this does throw away White's advantage and allow Black right back into the game. Instead White should have calmly sacrificed the bishop to block the h-file, according to Kasparov, whereupon 33 ♗h4! ♖xh4 34 h3 should be winning for White due to his huge pressure against f7 and the black monarch.

33...♘xh8 34 ♘e7+ ♔f8 35 ♘ec8?

Kasparov has just a rook for the black queen, but he does have a fair amount of pressure and is much better coordinated. Now he should have maintained his impressive compensation with 35 ♘ef5 rather than allow the extra queen into the game...

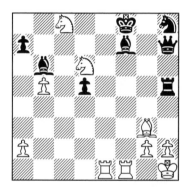

35...♕d3?

...except that Polgar chooses the wrong way. Instead 35...♗c5! 36 ♖e8+ ♔g7 37 ♖e7 ♕d3! looks rather good for Black and would have completed a quite remarkable turn-around.

36 ♖f3 ♕c2?

She should at least have threatened to capture on h2 with 36...♕d2, and after this second mistake White quickly regains his material and is left with an easy win as both players blitzed out their remaining moves.

37 ♘xf7 ♘xf7 38 ♘d6 ♕g6 39 ♖xf7+ ♕xf7 40 ♘xf7 ♔xf7 41 ♖e5! ♖xe5 42 ♗xe5 d4 43 ♔g1 ♔e6 44 ♗b8 ♔d5 45 ♔f1 ♔c4 46 ♔e2 d3+ 47 ♔d1 ♔xb5 48 h4 a5 49 ♗e5 ♗f2 50 h5 ♗e3 51 ♗g7 1-0

Game 2

V.Belikov-S.Halkias

Cappelle la Grande Open 2002

1 e4 c5 2 ♘f3 d6 3 ♗b5+ ♘c6 4 ♗xc6+ bxc6 5 0-0 e5 6 c3 f5

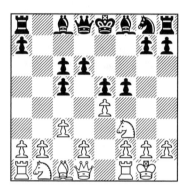

7 exf5

The main move, but 7 d4!? is a sharp and critical alternative when 7...fxe4 (alternatively Black can exchange a doubled c-pawn but lose some central control with 7...cxd4 8 cxd4 fxe4 when 9 ♘g5!? remains critical, whereas 9 ♘fd2 ♕b6! 10 ♘xe4 ♕xd4 11 ♕h5+ g6 12 ♕f3 shouldn't give White enough activity and compensation after Prudnikova's12...♗f5!) 8 ♘g5 d5! (ambitious and best whereas 8...exd4?! 9 ♘xe4 ♗e7 10 ♖e1! ♗f5 11 ♗g5 gave White the initiative in V.Komliakov-A.Grischuk, Nizhnij Novgorod 1998 when Black could find nothing better than to suffer after 11...♗xg5!? 12 ♘xd6+ ♔f8 13 ♘xf5 ♕d5 14 ♕g4!) 9 dxe5 ♗e7 10 f4!? (supporting the g5-knight whereas 10 e6 ♘f6! reveals Black's main idea and then 11 ♘f7 ♕c7 12 ♘xh8 ♗xe6 13 f4 g6 14 ♘a3 0-0-0 gave him superb compensation for the exchange in P.Velicka-S.Movsesian, Czech Republic 1999) 10...g6! (wisely preventing the check and preparing to ask the knight if it really wants to retreat unaesthetically to h3) 11 ♕a4 ♕b6 12 c4!? (boldly sacrificing the knight for a strong pawn chain, although this doesn't fully convince) 12...h6 13 cxd5 hxg5 14 d6 c4+ 15 ♔h1 g4! (reminding the white monarch that it is a little vulnerable down the half-open h-file) 16 g3 e3 17 ♘c3 e2! 18 ♘xe2 ♗e6 19 ♘c3 ♗d8 and Black had cleverly untangled and stood clearly better, despite White's enterprising play, in E.Miroshnichenko-S.Movsesian, Panormo 2002.

7...♗xf5

Allowing the pawn to live with 7...♘f6?! is certainly a risky business and then 8 d4 e4 9 ♘g5! was awkward for Black in D.Marciano-J.Lautier, Besancon 1999; 9...♗xf5 10 f3! quickly opens the position to White's advantage, but the game's 9...d5 10 f3 h6 11 ♘e6 ♗xe6 12 fxe6 ♗d6 13 fxe4 dxe4 14 ♗e3! 0-0 15 ♘d2 also favoured White.

8 ♖e1 ♗e7

Wisely blocking the e-file which 8...♗d3?! doesn't achieve after 9 ♖e3! when 9...c4 10 ♘e1 ♗f5 11 ♘a3 picks off the c4-pawn.

9 d4 cxd4

Avoiding the trick 9...e4?! 10 dxc5! when Black must clearly avoid 10...exf3 11 cxd6, although instead 10...dxc5 11 ♕xd8+ ♖xd8 12 ♘e5 ♖d6 13 ♗e3 ♖e6 14 ♘c4 ♘f6 15 ♘bd2 may be no more than an edge for White as Black can gain some counterplay based around his control of d5 after 15...♘d5, as in M.Savic-N.Bojkovic, Belgrade 2001.

10 cxd4 e4

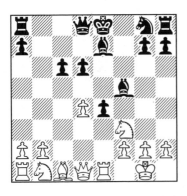

11 ♘g5!?

Certainly more active than 11 ♘fd2?! ♘f6 12 ♘c3 d5 when White can quickly come under kingside pressure and then 13 f3 ♕b6! 14 ♕a4 ♗b4 15 ♘xd5?! ♘xd5 16 fxe4 0-0! 17 exd5 ♕xd4+ 18 ♔h1 ♗h3! 19 ♖g1 ♖ae8 20 ♘f3 ♗xg2+ 21 ♖xg2 ♖e1+ and 0-1 in B.Lalic-A.Shchekachev, Metz 1998 was a crushing miniature.

11...d5

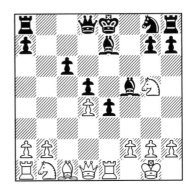

12 f3!

Correctly sacrificing the knight as after 12 ♘c3 ♘h6! White lacks a good move as Black has prepared to meet 13 f3 with Halkias' 13...♗xg5 14 fxe4 ♗g4!.

12...♗g6

Now White can gain three dangerous pawns for the piece and so 12...♗xg5 13 fxe4 ♗h4! should be preferred when Halkias analyses in *Informator* 14 g3 (or 14 exf5+ ♗xe1 15 ♕xe1+ ♕e7! 16 ♕c3 ♘f6! 17 ♕xc6+ ♔f7 which also calls White's idea into question) 14...♗xe4!? 15 ♕h5+ ♔f8 16 ♕xh4 ♕xh4 17 gxh4 ♘f6 18 ♗f4 ♔f7 and, although there are opposite-coloured bishops, Black holds the edge due to his better structure and control of e4.

13 fxe4 ♗xg5 14 ♗xg5 ♕xg5 15 exd5+ ½-½

Here a draw was agreed, although White may well be better after capturing on c6 next after which he can force through d5 when the pawns are rather strong, while the black king is also far from happy.

Game 3
S.Rublevsky-I.Smirin
Russia v World Rapidplay, Moscow 2002

---

1 e4 c5 2 ♘f3 d6 3 ♗b5+ ♘c6 4 ♗xc6+ bxc6 5 0-0 ♗g4

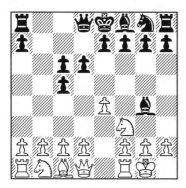

6 c3

Still aiming to take over the centre, although 6 d3 is White's usual choice when Black can opt for an ...e5 set-up or for 6...♘f6 when 7 ♘bd2!? (developing slowly and negating the pin whereas 7 ♗g5 ♘d7!? 8 ♘bd2 f6 9 ♗h4 e5 10 ♘c4 ♗e7 11 ♘e3 ♗e6, intending ...d5, gave Black a good game in V.Ivanchuk-V.Topalov, Wijk aan Zee 2003) 7...♘d7 has been favoured by Tiviakov and Cheparinov. After 8 h3 ♗h5 9 c3 (the 9 b3!? e6 10 ♗b2 f6 11 ♕e1 ♗e7 12 ♘h2! ♗f7 13 f4 of J.Magem Badals-S.Tiviakov, Bled 2002 deserves attention and looks like a more dangerous set-up) 9...e6 10 ♕a4?! ♕c7 11 ♖e1 ♗e7 12 d4 0-0 the pressure against f3 was already awkward for White in A.Skripchenko-V.Babula, Saint Vincent 2002.

Another option for White is 6 h3 ♗h5 when 7 d3 transposes to lines considered after 6 d3, but the ambitious 7 e5!? has recently received some testing. Gelfand opted for the solid 7...e6 (against Shirov at Dortmund 2002), but

critical is 7...dxe5 when I wonder if Shirov would really have continued with 8 g4!?, instead of claiming slower structural compensation after 8 ♖e1. Here 8 g4 e4 has been assessed by Yudasin as favouring Black and it may well, although the position is certainly messy and the players wimped out with a draw after 9 gxh5 exf3 10 ♘c3 ♘f6 11 ♕xf3 ♖c8 in R.Rabiega-M.Palac, Dresden 2002.

6...♘f6

Instead 7 ♖e1 e5 transposes to a line we considered after 5...e5 6 c3 ♘f6 7 ♖e1 ♗g4 (see the note to Black's sixth in Game 1), but Rublevsky prefers a less common course.

7 d3 e5 8 h3 ♗h5 9 ♗g5 ♗e7 10 ♘bd2 0-0 11 ♖e1 ♖b8 12 ♕c2 ♘d7!

Freeing his position with exchanges, while also preparing counterplay.

13 ♗xe7 ♕xe7 14 d4

The only real break to try, but Rublevsky never gains more than a nominal edge.

14...cxd4 15 cxd4 ♗xf3 16 ♘xf3 c5! 17 dxe5 ♘xe5 18 ♘xe5 ♕xe5 19 b3 ♖b4!

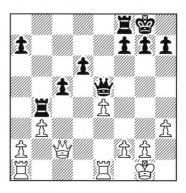

Akopian may have an extra pawn island, but he is active enough and now held the draw without too much difficulty:

20 ♖ad1 ♖e8 21 f3 h6 22 ♕f2 ♖b6 23 ♖d5 ♕c3 24 ♖ed1 ♖e6 25 ♖5d3 ♕e5 26 ♕d2 ♖g6 27 ♔h1 ♕e7 28 ♖d5 ♖e6 29 ♖c1 ♖b4 30 ♖c3 ♔h8 31 ♖cd3 ♖b6 32 ♖e3 ♔g8 33 ♕d3 ♖e5 34 ♖e2 ♖e6 35 f4 ♕f6 36 ♖f5 ♕e7 37 ♖d5 ♕f6 38 ♖f5

♕e7 39 ♖d5 g6 40 e5 ½-½

Game 4
E.Sutovsky-V.Grebionkin
EU Internet Ch. (blitz) 2003

1 e4 c5 2 ♘f3 ♘c6 3 ♗b5 d6 4 0-0 ♗d7 5 ♖e1 a6?!

A rather clever, but probably too clever, move order idea as Black hopes to avoid the fairly positional nature of the play in the ♗a4 lines (as could occur after 5...♘f6 6 c3 a6 7 ♗a4).

6 ♗xc6 ♗xc6 7 d4!

Transposing to an Open Sicilian-type position and hoping to exploit White's lead in development. Black must especially beware the e1–rook which enables White to meet ...e6 with some rather dangerous ♘d5 sacrificial ideas.

7...cxd4 8 ♕xd4!

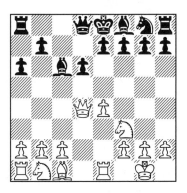

This appears to be stronger than the usual 8 ♘xd4, while it is also more thematic as White hopes to quickly blast Black away. Now after 8...♘f6 the position has some similarities to the line 1 e4 c5 2 ♘f3 d6 3 d4 cxd4 4 ♕xd4!? ♘c6 5 ♗b5 ♗d7 6 ♗xc6 ♗xc6, except that the combination of 0-0 and ♖e1 appears more useful than that of ...♘f6 and ...a6; a nudge which has certainly cost Black some time and quite possibly too much time.

8...♘f6 9 ♘c3 e6?!

One adherent of 8 ♕xd4 is the ever creative Joel Benjamin who has both played it and recommended it in an article for *www.jeremysilman.com*. He now points out that 9...g6? is too slow due to 10 e5! dxe5 11 ♕xe5 ♗g7 12 ♗h6! with a crushing position as 12...♗xh6 13 ♖ad1 leaves Black unable to satisfactorily defend his queen and to cover f6. However, Black's best defence is probably 9...e5!?, giving up control over d5 to slow down the white initiative. Najdorf players may find such a move quite easily, but not everyone hit by 8 ♕xd4 will probably enjoy playing such a potentially weakening advance. Furthermore, after 10 ♕d3 ♗e7 11 ♗g5 Black still remains under some pressure with, for example, 11...♕c7 12 ♖ad1 ♖d8 being too slow due to 13 ♘h4!. Instead he must find 11...0-0 12 ♖ad1 ♕b6! 13 b3 ♕c5 which restricted White to just a small edge after 14 ♘d2! (heading for e3 via f1) in V.Iordachescu-O.Chernikov, Dresden 2003.

10 ♘d5! ♗xd5

This fails to keep lines closed, but 10...♗e7 11 ♘xe7 ♕xe7 12 e5! dxe5 13 ♘xe5 h6 14 ♘xc6 bxc6 15 ♕c3 also left White clearly better in J.Benjamin-D.Vigorito, Philadelphia 2004, with ♗e3-c5 just one of Black's worries. However, neither does accepting the temporary sacrifice help; 10...exd5 11 exd5+ ♗e7 12 dxc6 bxc6 13 ♗f4 and Black remains under heavy pressure as 13...0-0 runs into 14 ♖xe7!.

11 exd5 e5

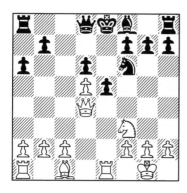

12 ♘xe5! ♗e7

Meekly giving up material instead of facing some strong pressure after 12...dxe5 13 ♕xe5+ ♔d7 14 ♗f4 ♕b6 15 ♕f5+ ♔d8 16 d6! when White's superior development and king position should quickly prove decisive.

13 ♘f3 0-0 14 ♗g5

White has retained much the better position, as well as being a pawn to the good, and now went on to win this blitz game with some ease:

14...h6 15 ♗f4 ♖c8 16 c4 ♘d7 17 ♖ac1 ♗f6 18 ♕d2 ♕b6 19 b3 a5 20 ♗e3! ♕b4?! 21 ♕xb4 axb4 22 ♗f4 ♘c5 23 ♗xd6 ♘d3 24 ♗xf8 1-0

Game 5
S.B.Hansen-S.Tiviakov
North Sea Cup, Esbjerg 2002

---

1 e4 c5 2 ♘f3 ♘c6 3 ♗b5 d6 4 0-0 ♗d7 5 ♖e1 ♘f6 6 h3

White's aim is to be able to retreat his bishop to f1 and then to expand with c3 and d4, while Black suffers from the problem that his light-squared bishop lacks a good square.

6...a6

Driving the bishop to a square it is happy to go is not strictly necessary. This is, however, Black's most popular choice, although many may prefer one of the alternative set-

ups which will be examined in the next two games.

7 ♗f1

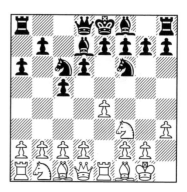

7...♘e5!?

A common idea in this line by which Black aims to counter White's plan of c3 and d4 by exchanging knights. However, this isn't forced and instead 7...e6 transposes after 8 c3 to 6...e6 7 c3 a6 8 ♗f1 (see Game 7), while 7...g5!? is rather radical, but such g-pawn advances have been fashionable of late. However, after 8 d4! g4 9 d5 gxf3 (7...g5!? still deserves more tests, but it may well be the case that 9...♘e5!? is actually superior after which 10 ♘xe5 dxe5 11 hxg4 ♗xg4 12 f3 ♗d7 13 ♗e3 ♕c7 14 ♕d2 h5! led to a very complex struggle, in which Black's prospects on both flanks shouldn't leave him worse, in E.Vasiukov-L.Gutman, Tbilisi 1979) 10 dxc6 ♗xc6 11 ♕xf3 e6 12 ♘c3 ♗e7 13 ♗f4 Black might enjoy an extra centre pawn, but he cannot make any use of it for some time. Furthermore, he must proceed carefully over the next few moves and thus I prefer White in this unbalanced position and certainly 13...♖g8 14 ♖ad1 ♗g6 15 a3! ♕c7 16 b4 left White better with a useful queenside initiative in M.Adams-H.Hamdouchi, Tripoli 2004.

Those happy to handle Lopez positions as Black can though opt for 7...e5 when 8 c3 ♗e7 9 d4 ♕c7 (strong-pointing e5 in Chigorin Spanish style) 10 a4 0-0 11 ♘a3 (11 dxe5!? dxe5 12 ♘a3 ♘a5 is also fine for Black due to 13 ♘c4 ♘xc4 14 ♗xc4 b5!) 11...cxd4 12 cxd4 exd4! 13 ♘xd4 ♖fe8 gave Black good counterplay in A.Motylev-A.Grischuk, St Petersburg 1998.

8 a4

Aiming for a queenside clamp, but White also has good chances of gaining the advantage with 8 ♘xe5!? dxe5 9 b3, taking aim at e5 which can no longer be covered by ...g6 and ...♘d7.

8...♘xf3+ 9 ♕xf3 e6

Tiviakov evidently didn't mind the resulting queenside clamp and indeed it probably isn't too problematic. Nevertheless, as the ...d5-break doesn't work out well, Black should give serious consideration to keeping open ...b5 options with Psakhis' 9...b6!?.

10 d3 ♗c6 11 ♘d2 ♗e7 12 a5! 0-0 13 ♘c4

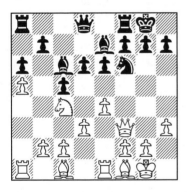

13...♘d7

It is Black's next which is questionable and indeed it's hard to believe that he should be more than a little worse here. He is very solid, but does lack active counterplay and so must manoeuvre carefully as he did in Smirin-Lautier, European Team Ch., Leon, 2001 with 13...♕c7 14 ♗f4 ♖ad8 15 ♕d1 ♘d7! 16 ♗g3 ♘e5 17 ♘d2 ♘g6! 18 c3 ♗f6 and White was getting nowhere.

14 ♕g3 d5?! 15 exd5 ♗xd5?! 16 ♗f4 ♗h4 17 ♕g4 ♗f6 18 c3

Blunting the bishop and leaving Black, who must have wished he hadn't allowed a5, struggling for counterplay while White can easily improve his pieces.

18...♖e8 19 ♘d6! ♖e7 20 ♘e4 ♗xe4?!

Quite possibly the decisive mistake, even though Black still looks rather solid after this. However, he cannot hold up an e5-advance for ever after which the white pieces, which have a far greater scope than their counterparts, can begin a decisive attack against the black monarch. Perhaps Tiviakov didn't sense the danger until too late, and herein lies one of the dangers behind such deceptively quiet moves as 6 h3, while instead he had to avoid improving Hansen's structure, beginning with 20...♖e8!.

21 dxe4 ♗e5 22 ♗e3 ♖c8 23 ♖ed1 ♗b8 24 f4! ♕c7 25 e5 ♖ce8 26 ♗c4 ♕c6 27 ♗f2!

Forcing a weakness and already heralding the end.

27...f6!

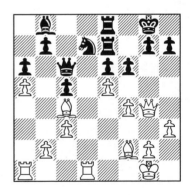

28 ♖xd7!

Now White crashes through and this proves to be stronger than 28 ♖d3 when 28...fxe5 29 ♗h4 ♖f7 30 f5 ♘f8! enables Black to continue resisting, whilst White must keep an eye open for ...e4 and ...♕c7 ideas.

28...♖xd7 29 exf6 ♖f7 30 ♗h4 ♔f8

This doesn't halt the powerful white bishops from dismantling the black position, but even after Psakhis' suggested 30...♕e4!? White would have retained a large advantage in the ending with 31 f5! ♕xg4 32 hxg4 gxf6 33 ♗xe6 ♔g7 34 ♗xf7 ♔xf7 35 ♖d1.

31 fxg7+ ♖xg7 32 ♗g5! ♕e4 33 ♗h6 ♖ee7 34 ♖d1! ♗c7 35 ♗xe6!

Finishing a fine game and a lovely attack in style as now 35...♕xe6 36 ♗xg7 would have seen White emerge two pawns ahead with a crushing position. Tiviakov prefers to grab, but unsurprisingly that does nothing to halt the deadly attack.

35...♗xa5 36 ♗d5 ♕g6 37 ♕c8+ ♖e8 38 ♕xc5+ ♖ee7 39 ♗xg7+ 1-0

Game 6
J.Shaw-A.Collinson
British League 2003

---

1 e4 c5 2 ♘f3 d6 3 ♗b5+ ♘c6 4 0-0 ♗d7 5 ♖e1 ♘f6 6 h3

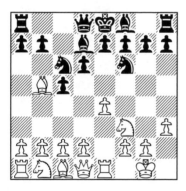

6...g6

The best point to fianchetto as after 6...a6 7 ♗f1, the white bishop is no longer vulnerable to ...a6 prods or to ...♘e5 ideas. However, an immediate 6...♘e5 is an important alternative which again sees Black hoping for exchanges, although White can try to force them on his own terms:

a) 7 ♗xd7+ ♘fxd7 8 b3! g6 9 ♘xe5 dxe5 10 ♗b2 ♗g7 11 f4! (necessary as otherwise Black is fairly comfortable and will reroute his knight to c6 or to e6) 11...e6?! (this doesn't prevent 12 f5 and so Black should consider 11...0-0 when 12 f5 is consistent, but Black can then begin counterplay with 12...c4!?) 12 ♘a3 0-0 and now the aggressive 13 f5! exf5 14 exf5 gxf5 15 ♘c4 gave White excellent compensation for the pawn in Kveinys-Glek, Bonn 1994 after which 15...f4 16 ♘xe5! ♘xe5 17 ♖xe5 ♗xe5 18 ♕g4+ ♔h8 19 ♗xe5+ f6 20 ♗c3 was a deep and fairly promising exchange sacrifice.

b) Adams has preferred 7 a4!? when 7...♘xf3+ (Topalov's choice and probably best, although 7...a6 is playable; Black's idea is to meet 8 ♗f1 with 8...♘xf3+ 9 ♕xf3 ♗c6, but critical is 8 ♗xd7+!? ♘fxd7 9 ♘xe5 ♘xe5 and now 10 d4!? is a fighting alternative to Adams' more restrained choice of 10 d3 g6 11 ♘c3 ♗g7 12 f4) 8 ♕xf3 a6 9 ♗xd7+ ♘xd7 10 b3 g6 11 ♗b2 e5 12 ♕d3 ♗e7 13 ♘c3 0-0 left Black a touch worse but very solid in M.Adams-V.Topalov, Wijk aan Zee 2001. Instead of 14 a5 ♘f6 15 ♖f1 ♖c8 when even 16 ♘d5 didn't lead anywhere, White could try Boersma's suggestion of 14 ♖f1!?, although then 14...♘f6 15 f4 exf4! 16 ♖xf4 ♘h5 17 ♖f3 ♗f6 challenges the long diagonal and should defend.

Black must though take care not to be too ambitious against 6 h3, such as with 6...♘d4?! when 7 ♗xd7+ ♕xd7 8 ♘xd4! cxd4 9 c3 dxc3 10 ♘xc3 e6 11 d4 gave White a pleasant edge in N.Short-M.Petursson, Tilburg (rapid) 1992.

7 c3 ♘e5

Black doesn't mind an exchange on e5 when, especially due to the now weakening c3, he will gain good pressure down the d-file and thus White tends to prefer to trade bishops. However, 7...♘e5 isn't forced and instead 7...♕b6!? hopes to gain a tempo against the bishop, while 7...♗g7 is playable, not fearing an exchange on c5 although 8 d4 0-0 9 a4!? cxd4 10 cxd4 d5 11 exd5! offers White chances of an edge. However, rather than strengthen the white centre with 11...♘xd5 12 ♘c3 ♘xc3 (or 12...♘cb4 13 ♗c4 e6 14 ♗xd5, intending 14...exd5 15 ♕b3) when 13 bxc3 ♖c8 14 ♗g5 leaves White better, Black should give serious consideration to 11...♘b4!? when 12 d6 exd6 rather resembles ...g6 Panov lines, but does appear to be quite playable for him.

8 ♗xd7+ ♘fxd7!

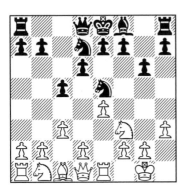

9 d4

9 ♘xe5 dxe5 still doesn't really lead anywhere for White who must now go 10 d3 as 10 d4?! exd4! 11 cxd4 ♗g7 leaves the white centre exposed and then 12 d5 0-0 saw Black go on to exploit his dark-square control and queenside play in L.McShane-R.Pert, British League 2004.

9...♘xf3+ 10 ♕xf3 ♗g7

This position already appears pretty acceptable for Black who has sufficient pressure against the white centre which he can keep in check.

11 e5!?

Probably too ambitious, although 11 ♗e3 0-0 12 dxc5 dxc5 13 ♕e2 ♕c7 14 ♘d2 ♖fc8 15 f4 c4! also didn't cause Black any real problems in Y.Visser-S.Tiviakov, Dutch Ch. 2004.

11...dxe5 12 dxe5 ♘xe5! 13 ♕xb7 0-0

Already this is a little problematic for White due to his lack of development.

14 ♗g5?! ♕b6 15 ♕xb6 axb6 16 b3 ♖a7?!

Simply 16...h6! 17 ♗e3 ♖fd8 (Collinson) would have been rather good for Black due to the weaknesses of c3 and d3. After that let off, and with some precise defence, Shaw now held the draw:

17 a4 c4 18 bxc4 ♘xc4 19 ♖xe7 ♖xe7 20 ♗xe7 ♖e8 21 ♘a3! ♗xc3 22 ♖c1 ♘b2 23 ♖xc3 ♖xe7 24 ♖b3 ♘xa4 25 ♖b4 ♖a7 26 ♘c4 ♔g7 ½-½

Game 7

A.Kveinys-J.Markos

Bled Olympiad 2002

1 e4 c5 2 ♘f3 d6 3 ♗b5+ ♘c6 4 0-0 ♗d7 5 ♖e1 ♘f6 6 h3 e6

6...a6 7 ♗f1 e6 8 c3 is an equally common route to the position reached at move eight and was actually how Kveinys-Markos began.

7 c3

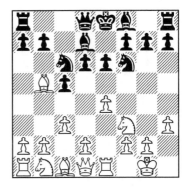

7...a6

Black should seriously consider 7...d5!? here, although this has been surprisingly rather rare in practice, perhaps due to 8 d3 (8 exd5 ♘xd5 9 d4 cxd4 10 ♘xd4 ♘xd4 11 ♗xd7+ ♕xd7 12 ♕xd4 ♘f6! – Avrukh – is clearly nothing for White) 8...♗e7 9 ♘a4!, preparing e5 as 9 e5? ♘xe5! simply lost a pawn in Odeev-Veingold, Bled Olympiad 2002. However, it's not clear that e5 is such a problem as after 9...h6!? (9...♕a5 10 ♗g5 dxe4 11 dxe4 ♘e5 12 ♗c2! ♘xf3+ 13 ♕xf3

♗c6 14 ♘d2 ♕c7 15 ♘c4 left White with the edge and attacking chances on the kingside in J.Timman-B.Avrukh, Apeldoorn 2004) 10 ♘bd2 ♕c7 11 e5 (the only consistent idea) 11...♘h7 the black position appeared quite playable in Chen Fan-Wang Yue, Jinan 2005. White now had to advance with 12 d4 as 12 ♘f1 ♗g5! would have begun to undermine e5, but his lack of full development remained a problem. Chen tried to rectify that with 12...cxd4 13 ♘xd4!? (13 cxd4 ♘b4! would have swapped off the bad French bishop and begun counterplay for Black), but then 13...♘xd4 14 ♗xd7+ ♕xd7 15 cxd4 ♘f8, heading for g6, didn't give White anything.

8 ♗f1 ♗e7 9 d4 cxd4

It appears best to accept a French structure as otherwise White can easily gain a pleasant edge, as he did after 9...e5 10 d5 ♘a7 11 a4! 0-0 12 a5 in A.Kveinys-J.Maiwald, Bonn 1995, when ♘xe5 ideas were on the cards.

10 cxd4 d5! 11 e5 ♘e4

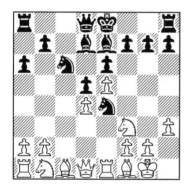

12 ♗d3!

This currently appears promising and is certainly better than an immediate 12 ♘bd2 when 12...♘xd2 13 ♗xd2 ♖c8 14 ♕b3 b5 15 ♖ac1 0-0 16 ♕e3 ♕b6 17 ♗d3 f5! 18 exf6 ♗xf6 left Black with a good Tarrasch French position in F.Pierrot-V.Topalov, Moscow 2001.

12...♘g5

Trying to undermine d4, whereas Kveinys

and Sakalauskas rightly don't trust Black's compensation after 12...♘b4 due to the strong and forcing 13 ♗xe4 dxe4 14 ♖xe4 ♗c6 15 ♖g4!.

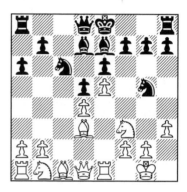

13 ♘bd2! ♕b6

White is well placed to meet this, but finding an improvement is rather tough with, for example, 13...♖c8 not impressing as then Black can no longer castle queenside as he really needs to.

14 ♘xg5 ♗xg5 15 ♘b3! h6!?

Giving up a pawn to be able to go long, while White had covered d4 as 15...♗xc1 16 ♕xc1 ♘xd4? 17 ♕e3 wins the pinned knight, and instead 16...0-0 looks pretty risky in view of 17 ♕g5!.

16 ♕g4 0-0-0 17 ♗xg5 hxg5 18 ♕xg5 ♔b8 19 ♖ac1

By this point White clearly holds a large advantage and Kveinys now effectively converted his advantage and managed to gain a strong attack:

19...♔a7 20 ♕e3 ♖h4 21 ♖c3! ♘a5 22 ♖ec1 ♘xb3 23 ♖xb3 ♕xd4 24 ♖c7! ♗c6 25 ♕c1 ♕a4 26 ♖a3 ♖c4 27 ♗xc4 ♕xc4 28 ♖c3 1-0

Game 8
V.Ivanchuk-V.Topalov
Melody Amber (Blindfold), Monaco 2003

---

1 e4 c5 2 ♘f3 ♘c6 3 ♗b5 d6 4 0-0 ♗d7

5 ♖e1 ♘f6 6 c3 a6 7 ♗xc6!? ♗xc6 8 d4

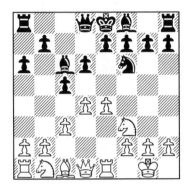

8...♗xe4

After 8 d4, Black already faces a big decision; whether or not to exchange on d4, and not doing so has been the more popular of late. However, 8...cxd4 9 cxd4 ♗xe4 remains playable when 10 ♘c3 d5!? has gained some recent attention, and is more challenging and probably slightly better than the solid 10...♗xf3 11 ♕xf3 e6. Here 11 ♗g5 (the rare 11 ♘e5!? is probably more critical and was played in the strongest clash in this line; Black being roughly level in an unclear position in H.Hamdouchi-A.Dreev, Gibraltar 2005 after 11...e6 12 ♕b3! ♗e7! 13 ♕xb7 ♕c8 14 ♕b3 0-0) 11...e6 12 ♗xf6 gxf6 13 ♘xe4 (White should regain his pawn as after 13 ♘d2? ♗g6 14 h4 h5 he cannot get anywhere on the kingside and 15 ♘f1 ♗g7 16 ♘g3 f5! 17 ♕f3 ♔f8 18 ♘ce2 ♕xh4 was superb for Black in J.Becerra Rivero-M.Suba, Balaguer 1997) 13...dxe4 14 ♖xe4 ♕d5 15 ♖e3 ♗d6 has been tested a few times and isn't fully clear, but Black appears to hold the edge due to his bishop and to the weakness of d4, and so we may well see more of 11 ♘e5!? in the future.

9 ♗g5 ♗d5!

Refusing to exchange the bishop until White has played c4 and this is clearly critical. Instead 9...d5 has received a fair amount of testing, but Black should exchange first on d4 if he wishes to play like this as 10 dxc5! e6 11

♗xf6!? gxf6 12 ♘bd2 ♗xf3 13 ♕xf3 ♗xc5 14 c4! dxc4 (acquiescing to the desired opening of further lines, although 14...♗e7 15 ♖ad1! also leaves Black under some pressure) 15 ♖ad1 ♕e7 16 ♘e4 left Black unable to find anything better than to give up an exchange after 16...f5 17 ♕c3 in S.Arkhipov-M.Muhutdinov, Nabereznye Chelny 1993.

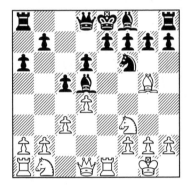

10 c4

In view of Topalov's strong novelty, White should probably prefer to play the complex positions arising after 10 ♘bd2. Then 10...e6 11 c4! (the best move order as 11 ♗xf6?! ♕xf6 12 c4 ♗xf3 13 ♘xf3 ♕d8! neutralises the check on a4 and leaves White struggling for compensation) 11...♗xf3! (Black must be prepared to return the bishop as 11...♗c6?! 12 d5! ♗d7 13 ♘e4 leaves him facing severe pressure) 12 ♕xf3 cxd4 13 ♗xf6! (taking the chance to weaken the black structure) 13...gxf6 14 ♕xb7 reaches a critical position. White has regained his pawn and retains slightly the better development and king position, but the black central pawn mass should not be underestimated. The position isn't clear, but White doesn't appear to have any advantage, while dynamic black players should be quite happy here. After 14...♗g7 (14...♗e7!? 15 ♕c6+ ♔f8 16 ♘f3! e5 17 ♘h4 ♖c8 18 ♕f3 gave White reasonable enduring compensation in M.Sebag-Bu Xiangzhi, Cannes 2004) 15 ♕c6+ ♔e7! the black pawns certainly perform an excellent job of keeping the white pieces under control and Black has scored well in practice, although the position remains unclear.

10...♗xf3 11 ♕xf3 cxd4 12 ♕xb7 ♖c8!

Utilising a key point behind 9...♗d5!; namely to exchange the black b-pawn for the white d-pawn. Black is now very comfortable after an exchange of queens due to his central control, but avoiding that doesn't leave White too well placed either.

13 ♕f3 e5!

A strong novelty which logically makes immediate use of Black's extra centre pawns. Instead 13...e6 14 ♗xf6 gxf6 has turned out well for White after both 15 ♘d2!? and 15 ♕xf6.

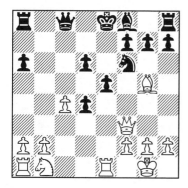

14 ♘d2?

Now White struggles against the black pawn mass and so he simply had to try 14 ♗xf6 gxf6 15 ♕xf6 ♖g8. Unlike after 13...e6, d4 is not en prise here, whilst the black position is pretty dynamic and fairly comfortable. Still this could do with a test as matters aren't so clear after 16 ♘d2 ♖b8 (possibly best as 16...♕e6 17 ♕f3 ♖b8 18 b3 ♗h6 19 ♖ad1 doesn't fully convince for Black, while an immediate 16...♗g4? allows 17 ♖xe5+! dxe5 18 ♕c6+) 17 b3 (White would prefer to sacrifice this, but 17 ♘e4!? ♖g6 18 ♕h8 ♕xc4 isn't especially convincing) 17...♕g4, although White must try to avoid an exchange of

queens, as one would allow Black to start strongly rolling with ...f5.

14...♘d7! 15 ♘b3 f6 16 ♗d2 ♗e7 17 ♕e2 ♘b6 18 ♖ac1 ♖a7 19 f4 0-0 20 c5!?

The only try to dent the black camp, but now Topalov gets to force a good ending.

20...dxc5 21 fxe5 fxe5 22 ♕xe5 ♕f5! 23 ♘xc5 ♕f2+ 24 ♔h1 ♕xd2 25 ♕e6+ ♔h8 26 ♕xb6 ♗xc5 27 ♕xc5 ♖af7!

The key point behind the exchanging combination. Black will emerge a pawn ahead and went on to instructively convert:

28 h3 ♕xb2 29 ♖cd1 ♕xa2 30 ♕xd4 ♕b3 31 ♕d5 ♖f1+! 32 ♖xf1 ♖xf1+ 33 ♔h2 ♕b8+ 34 ♕d6 ♖f8 35 ♕xb8 ♖xb8 36 ♖a1 ♖a8 37 ♖a5 ♔g8 38 ♔g3 ♔f7 39 ♔f4 ♔e6 40 ♔e4 ♔d6 41 h4 ♖a7! 42 g4 ♔c6 43 ♔d4 ♔b6 44 ♖g5 a5 45 ♔c3 a4! 46 ♔b2 ♔c6 47 ♖h5 g6 48 ♖g5 ♖b7+ 49 ♔a3 ♖b5 0-1

> ## Game 9
> ## E.Sutovsky-H.Hamdouchi
> *Gibraltar Masters 2005*

1 e4 c5 2 ♘f3 ♘c6 3 ♗b5 d6 4 0-0 ♗d7 5 ♖e1 ♘f6 6 c3 a6 7 ♗a4

A much less violent option than the exchange on c6 and now White hopes to steer the game into Lopez-like channels.

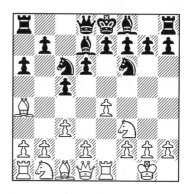

7...c4

With the 7...b5 8 ♗c2 e5 of Game 10

Black must be happy to play the black side of a Spanish position, whereas Hamdouchi wishes to deter White from his plans. This sensible riposte prevents White from immediately setting up a strong centre and now the battle usually hinges around the clamping c4-pawn.

8 ♗c2

Best and usual these days for the simple reason that after 8 d4 cxd3 9 ♕xd3 White's pieces aren't particularly well placed for the resulting Open Sicilian type position. The bishop on a4 is a little misplaced and come become vulnerable, as can the queen on d3, while it's actually far from easy for White to implement a strong Maróczy Bind.

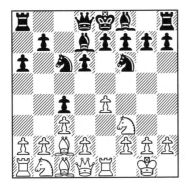

8...e5!

With d4 restrained, Black is happy to claim space in the centre, while the alternatives haven't been holding up so well of late, such as 8...♖c8 9 b3 b5 10 a4!? (rare, but deserving of further attention) was seen in L.Webb-Jo.Hodgson, London (rapid) 2003, when even the superior 10...cxb3 11 ♗xb3 ♘a5 12 axb5 ♘xb3 13 ♕xb3 ♗xb5 14 ♘a3 appears to favour White, such as after 14...♗c6 15 d3 e6 16 ♘c2!.

9 d3!?

Rare, but not illogical as the black d-pawn is now backward, although 9 b3 remains the main test. Now 9...cxb3!? (an interesting novelty, although the older 9...b5 also remains

possible and has been used by Khalifman; 10 ♘a3 ♘a5! 11 bxc4 bxc4 12 ♖b1 ♗e7 13 ♗a4 0-0 14 ♗xd7 ♕xd7 didn't cause Black any problems in A.Zapolskis-A.Khalifman, Liepaya (rapid) 2004) 10 axb3 ♗g4! is a promising idea to exploit White's slow play. Black has only relinquished some of his control over d4 and will hope to make good use of his rapid development, such as by breaking with ...d5. I.Smirin-B.Avrukh, Israeli Team Ch. 2002 continued 11 d3 (White must build slowly as 11 d4 ♗xf3! would force him to recapture with the pawn) 11...♗e7 12 ♘bd2 0-0 13 h3 ♗h5 14 ♘f1 d5! and Black was already pretty comfortable. Smirin logically pressed ahead on the kingside, although after 15 g4 ♗g6 16 ♘g3 ♖c8 17 ♗b2 Black could have seized a good position and blunted the white bishop-pair with Avrukh's 17...d4!.

9...cxd3 10 ♕xd3 h6!

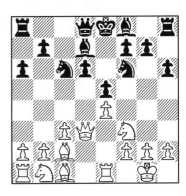

An idea which we will see more of in the 3...♘d7 lines; Black prevents White from increasing his control over d5 with ♗g5xf6 and challenges him to find a good alternative plan.

11 ♘bd2 ♗e6 12 ♘c4 ♖c8 13 ♘e3 ♗e7 14 ♘h4!?

The logical move was 14 ♘d5, but then Black can, and probably should, just ignore the knight, although 14...♗xd5 15 exd5 ♘b8 is also quite playable for him as he is solid and possesses a useful central majority. Instead this attempt with 14 ♞h4!? to pressurise the black kingside is easily repulsed.

14...g6! 15 ♞f3 ♚f8 16 ♞d5 ♚g7

White might currently control d5, but Hamdouchi is ready to exchange there and appears to have a pretty reasonable Najdorf in any case. Sutovsky now did his best to unbalance the struggle, but Black was never in any real danger:

17 ♞xf6 ♚xf6 18 ♚b3 ♛e7 19 ♚e3 ♚xb3 20 axb3 ♛e6! 21 b4! ♞e7 22 ♖ed1 ♖hd8 23 ♖a5?! d5! 24 exd5 ♞xd5 25 ♖xd5 e4 26 ♖xd8! exd3 27 ♖8xd3 ♛a2 28 ♖3d2 a5 29 bxa5 ♛xa5 30 h3 ½-½

Game 10
L.Psakhis-J.Gallagher
Pula Zonal 2000

---

1 e4 c5 2 ♞f3 d6 3 ♚b5+ ♞c6 4 0-0 ♚d7 5 c3 ♞f6 6 ♖e1 a6 7 ♚a4 b5 8 ♚c2

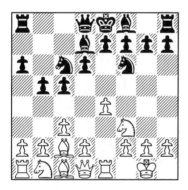

8...e5

Black isn't yet committed to playing along Lopez lines as 8...c4 would still transpose to the previous game, but he should avoid 8...♖c8?! when 9 a4! g6 10 axb5 axb5 11 d4! cxd4 12 cxd4 exploited White's superior development to gain a very comfortable edge in M.Adams-R.Kasimdzhanov, Tripoli 2004.

Tiviakov's favoured 8...♚g4!? does though remain a valid alternative when 9 h3 (White should consider building more slowly with 9

d3!? e6 10 ♞bd2 ♚e7 11 h3 ♚h5 12 ♞f1, although it remains a moot point as to whether his bishop is better off on c2 than on f1, and 12...0-0! 13 ♞g3 ♚g6 14 ♞h4 ♞d7 15 ♞xg6 hxg6 16 ♚e3 d5 17 ♞e2 ♞b6! already gave Black the edge, due to White's passivity, in A.Bisguier-G.Kacheishvili, Las Vegas 2003) 9...♚xf3 10 ♛xf3 g6 11 a4 ♖b8! (wisely ceding the a-file as 11...♚g7?! 12 axb5 axb5 13 e5! was rather strong in W.Watson-A.Kharlov, Porz 1993) 12 axb5 axb5 13 ♞a3!? (critical whereas 13 d3 ♚g7 14 ♚e3 ♞d7! 15 ♖d1 ♛c7 16 ♛e2 b4! gave Black at least sufficient queenside counterplay in V.Jansa-S.Tiviakov, Echternach [rapid] 2000) 13...♞d7! (clearing the diagonal for the bishop and also avoiding 13...♚g7? 14 ♞xb5! ♖xb5 15 e5) 14 ♛e2 ♛b6 15 ♚d3 c4 16 ♚c2 ♞c5! (superior to routinely developing with 16...♚g7 when 17 d3! cxd3 18 ♚xd3 is awkward for Black as Tiviakov has experienced) 17 d3 cxd3 18 ♚xd3 ♞xd3 19 ♛xd3 ♚g7 20 ♚e3 ♛b7 and Black had held b5, leading to equality in the game S.Reshevsky-L.Christiansen, Jacksonville 1981.

9 a4!?

A logical queenside strike, but it is Psakhis' strong follow-up which deserves to gain more supporters. Instead White should avoid 9 d4 cxd4 10 cxd4 ♚g4!, but he can also build more slowly after 9 h3.

9...♚e7 10 ♞a3!

The queen's knight would normally head for the kingside via d2 and f1, but Psakhis first increases the pressure on b5, knowing full well that the knight can still make the journey, just via c2 and e3 instead.

10...0-0 11 d3 ♖b8 12 axb5 axb5 13 h3 ♕c7?!

Rather compliantly allowing White to increase his control over d5 with ♗g5. Thus Black should have preferred 13...h6! with a tough struggle in prospect, but also one in which Black can consider strengthening his kingside with the standard ...♖e8, ...♗f8 and ...g6.

14 ♗g5 h6 15 ♗xf6! ♗xf6 16 ♘b3!

Now White can improve his knight and Psakhis supplies a model Lopez lesson.

16...♘e7 17 ♘c2 ♗c6 18 ♘e3 g6

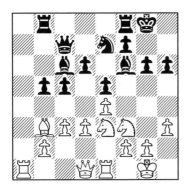

19 h4! ♗g7?

After this the white plan to soften up the black kingside succeeds as he gains control over f5. Thus, as Psakhis' notes observe, it was essential to fight with 19...h5! when White can proceed slowly or rush ahead with the critical, but not totally clear, 20 g4!? hxg4 21 ♘xg4 ♗g7 22 ♘g5.

20 h5 g5 21 ♘d2 ♔h8 22 g4! ♕d7 23 ♕f3 ♗b7 24 ♘df1 d5?

An understandable bid to break out in this grim position, but this had to be prepared as Gallagher now struggles to gain any real compensation.

25 ♗xd5! ♘xd5 26 exd5 b4 27 ♘g3 bxc3 28 bxc3 e4 29 dxe4!

Retaining control as Black can never grab an exchange for then his kingside would promptly collapse, but the white knights are set to dominate the board in any case.

29...♗xc3 30 ♖ac1 ♗e5 31 ♘gf5 ♖bc8 32 ♘c4 ♗f4 33 ♘b6 ♕c7 34 ♘xc8 ♗xc8 35 ♕c3+ 1-0

Game 11
E.Sutovsky-S.Tiviakov
European Team Ch., Leon 2001

---

1 e4 c5 2 ♘f3 ♘c6 3 ♗b5 d6 4 0-0 ♗d7 5 ♖e1 ♘f6 6 c3 a6 7 ♗f1 ♗g4 8 h3

The general consensus appears to be that White is better off including 8 d3 and 9 ♘bd2 before dealing with the g4-bishop, although he still has chances to out manoeuvre Black and to gain an edge after 8 h3.

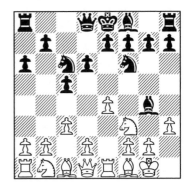

8...♗xf3

Ceding the bishops for quick and simple development. Instead Black should only retreat with 8...♗h5!? if he is happy to meet 8 d3 with 8...e6; a line which White could now transpose to with 9 d3 when there is little better than 9...e6. However, keeping the bishop is considered risky in view of 9 d4!?; a timely change of gear, although 9...cxd4 10 cxd4 ♗xf3! 11 gxf3 d5! (best, while Black has frequently suffered after 11...g6 when, for example, Xu Yuhua-A.Kosteniuk, Moscow 2001 continued 12 d5! ♘b8 13 ♕b3 ♕c7 14 ♗e3 ♘bd7 15 ♖c1 ♕b8 16 ♘a3 and Black was already under considerable queenside pressure) 12 ♘c3! e6 13 ♗g5 ♗e7! (this looks like the optimum way for Black to allow the position to open up as 13...dxe4 14 d5! exd5 15 ♗xf6! ♕xf6 16 ♘xd5 is somewhat more awkward for him) 14 ♗xf6!? ♗xf6 15 exd5 ♘xd4 16 ♖e4! ♘f5 17 dxe6 0-0! saw Black fully neutralise the initiative in R.Perez-L.Bruzon, Santa Clara 1999 and it's not clear that White can easily improve after 11...d5!.

9 ♕xf3 g6

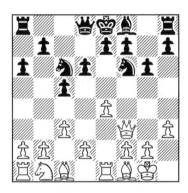

10 ♕d1

Black's pieces coordinate fairly well after the fianchetto, while he will aim to make good use of all of them by advancing with ...b5-b4. White can, and must, aim to get his pawn to d4 in reply, blunting the fianchettoed prelate and taking some of the life out of the black camp. The immediate queen retreat has received the most attention, but more modest set-ups should not be underestimated as no less a player than Kasparov has demonstrated:

a) 10 d3 ♗g7 11 ♗e3 0-0 12 ♘d2 ♘d7 13 ♕d1 b5 14 a3 should probably just be met by the older and sensible 14...e5!, keeping an eye on the key d4- and f4-squares, whereas 14...♖b8 ran into the direction changing 15 f4! e6 16 ♘f3 d5 17 e5 f6 18 d4 when White had suddenly gained lots of space in G.Kasparov-

M.Petursson, Reykjavik (rapid) 2004, although now Black should probably have tried to keep lines fairly closed with 18...c4!?.

b) 10 ♘a3!? ♗g7 11 ♘c2 ♘d7 12 ♕d1 brought Glek some success before he switched to 10 ♕d1. Here the standard 12...♕b6 appears to disrupt Black's coordination more than White's, and so simply 12...0-0!? deserves a test when 13 d4 cxd4 14 cxd4 ♕b6! reaches a critical position, when 15 d5!? ♘a5 certainly doesn't make it easy for White to untangle.

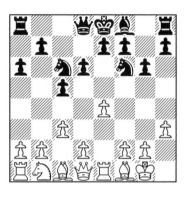

10...♗h6!?

Preventing d4 for the time being, while in general Black is happy to see an exchange of bishops. Putting the bishop on g7 instead isn't so bad, but it can then be blunted by pawns on c3 or d4, while White would then enjoy the bishop-pair. Here, as in many other positions, the advantage of the white bishop against the black knight is much less once the bishop is no longer operating as part of a bishop-pair. True, the f1–prelate can still exert some pressure against the black queenside, but White must always now beware being left with a bad bishop.

11 ♘a3 0-0 12 ♘c2

Continuing a by now familiar plan, while avoiding the problematic 12 d4?! ♗xc1 13 ♖xc1 cxd4 14 cxd4 d5!, further restricting the white prelate.

12...e5! 13 g3

Delaying d4 for a move, but with Black having sensibly increased his dark square control, it cannot be left too long. Instead an immediate 13 d4 should be met by 13...♗xc1 14 ♖xc1 cxd4! 15 cxd4 ♕b6 (Tiviakov), when we can again see that, despite or even because of the exchange of the bishops, Black enjoys good dark-square play. However, keeping the bishops on is rather slow and 13 ♘e3 ♗g7 14 d3 ♕d7 15 g3 ♖ad8 16 ♗g2 ♔h8 17 h4 ♘e7! didn't give White anything in G.Sax-S.Movsesian, Rabac 2004.

13...b5?! 14 d4!

Tiviakov's last was rather careless as now this is strong for White can gain a potential queenside target, while ...♕b6 is no longer so potent.

14...♗xc1 15 ♖xc1 ♔g7?! 16 d5 ♘e7 17 a4! ♕d7 18 ♕e2! ♖ab8 19 ♘a3 bxa4 20 ♘c4 ♘e8

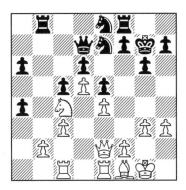

21 f4?!

With straightforward play White has gained the advantage and given both his minor pieces good roles, but he should now have aimed to win back his pawn and then to press ahead on the queenside after 21 ♖a1.

21...f6 22 ♗g2?! ♘c8! 23 ♖f1?! ♕b5

White isn't going to get anywhere on the kingside and this mini-plan is remarkably misguided. Tiviakov has seized his chance to gain the queenside initiative and how Sutovsky must now have been regretting let the a4-

pawn live.

24 ♖f2 ♘b6 25 ♗f1 ♕xc4 26 ♕xc4 ♘xc4 27 ♗xc4 ♘c7 28 ♖a1 ♖fe8! 29 ♖e2 f5!

The bishop may already be bad, but opening the position leads to the collapse of the white centre and to further weaknesses.

30 ♖xa4 exf4 31 gxf4 ♖xe4 32 ♖xe4 fxe4 33 b4 cxb4 34 cxb4 ♖b6 35 ♔f2 ♔f6 36 ♔e2 ♔f5 37 ♔e3 h6 38 h4 h5 39 ♗b3 a5 40 ♖xa5 ♖xb4 41 ♗a4 ♖xa4!

Now Black will have three pawns for the exchange and Tiviakov's technique was more than up to scratch:

42 ♖xa4 ♘xd5+ 43 ♔d4 ♘xf4 44 ♖a2 ♘e6+ 45 ♔c4 ♔e5 46 ♖a5+ ♔f4 47 ♖a1 ♘c5 48 ♖f1+ ♔e5 49 ♖f7 ♘e6 50 ♖d7 e3 51 ♔c3 d5 52 ♖e7 ♔d6 53 ♖e8 d4+ 54 ♔d3 ♔d5 55 ♔e2 ♔e5 56 ♔f3 ♔f6 57 ♖h8 ♘g7 58 ♖d8 ♘f5 59 ♔e2 ♔e5 60 ♔d3 ♔f4 61 ♖f8 ♔g3 62 ♖f6 ♘xh4 63 ♔e2 g5 64 ♖f1 ♘g2 65 ♖g1 h4 0-1

Game 12

A.Morozevich-V.Akopian

Russia v World Rapidplay, Moscow 2002

---

1 e4 c5 2 ♘f3 ♘c6 3 ♗b5 d6 4 0-0 ♗d7 5 ♖e1 ♘f6 6 c3 a6 7 ♗f1 ♗g4 8 d3 e6

This leads to some rather complex positions, but has been the main choice of most leading 3...♘c6 exponents of late. However, 8...g6 is still possible and taste may well determine whether Black prefers the more straightforward play after it, albeit at the cost of the bishop-pair. V.Bologan-S.Halkias, Moscow 2003 was though now a model performance from White: 9 ♘bd2 ♗h6 10 h3 ♗xf3 11 ♘xf3 ♗xc1 12 ♕xc1! (rare, but strong as White exploits the weakened kingside dark squares) 12...e5 13 ♕h6 ♘d7 14 ♘d2! ♕e7 15 ♘c4 b5 16 ♘e3 ♕f8 17 ♕h4 ♕e7 18 ♕g3 and White held the edge.

9 ♘bd2

Preparing to recapture with the knight, although 9 h3 is also seen when 9...♗h5 10 ♘bd2 ♗e7 takes us back to the main line, but an immediate 10 g4?! ♗g6 11 ♘h4 appears premature due to 11...d5! when e4 is a little tender and after 12 g5 ♗h5 13 ♕b3 c4 14 dxc4 dxc4! 15 ♕xc4 ♘d7 16 ♕d3 h6! Black had an excellent position in E.Sutovsky-G.Rechlis, Israeli Team Ch. 2003.

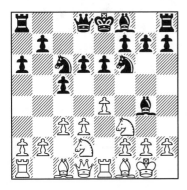

9...♗e7

It is noticeable that Topalov has long tried to avoid this, with 9...♘d7!? being his latest idea after which 10 h3 ♗h5 11 g4 ♗g6 12 d4 (the only real try for the advantage with White no longer able to make headway on the kingside with ♘h4) 12...cxd4 13 cxd4 ♗e7 (but not 13...e5?! 14 d5 ♘cb8 15 b4! and White's extra space proved awkward in V.Anand-V.Topalov, Dortmund 2001) 14 d5 ♘ce5 produces a finely balanced position which certainly deserves to be explored. Black is very solid and, although White has the central space, he must be pretty careful not to be left overextended and behind in development. V.Bologan-S.Movsesian, Sarajevo 2004 continued 15 ♘xe5 dxe5 16 ♘f3 (16 ♘c4 0-0 17 d6?! ♗h4 18 ♗g2 leaves d6 more of a weakness than a strength after 18...♖c8) 16...♖c8 17 ♗g2 (Black was also very equal after 17 b3 exd5 18 ♕xd5 f6 19 ♘h4 ♘c5! 20 ♕xd8+ ♖xd8 21 ♘f5 ♗xf5 22 exf5 ♘d3 in Zhang Zhong-V.Topalov, Wijk aan Zee 2004) 17...exd5 18 exd5 ♗d6! when the blockade on

d6 left the position roughly level.

10 h3 ♗h5 11 g4

11 a3 is pretty rare these days, compared to in the nineties, quite possibly just because after 11...d5 12 g4 ♗g6 13 ♘h4 dxe4 14 ♘xg6 hxg6 15 ♘xe4 Black shouldn't actually be worse due to his solid position and to the weakness of f4.

11...♗g6 12 ♘h4 ♘d7! 13 ♘g2!

Fashionable and challenging as White simply prepares to launch his f-pawn. Instead 13 ♘xg6 hxg6 hasn't done especially well for White, although the resulting positions are still pretty rich and unclear, when 14 f4!? (instead, having been highlighted by Pedersen, it's surprising that 14 ♘b3!? hasn't been tested more, although with the knight out on the queenside, Black might well be happy to lose a tempo with 14...♗g5!?, provoking 15 f4 ♗h4 16 ♖e2 g5!) 14...♗h4 15 ♖e2 g5 has received some high-level tests and then 16 ♘f3?! (although 16 f5 ♘de5 17 ♖e3 0-0 18 ♗g2 b5! 19 ♘f3 ♘xf3+ 20 ♖xf3 b4 didn't lead anywhere for White in V.Potkin-Geo.Timoshenko, Ismailia 2004) 16...gxf4 17 ♘xh4 ♕xh4 18 ♗xf4 e5! 19 ♗h2 ♘f8 20 a3 ♘e6 favoured the knights over the bishops, due to the weak white kingside, in D.Sadvakasov-A.Grischuk, Poikovsky 2005.

13...e5?!

This has been played a fair few times, but White's next, eyeing up the vulnerable d5- and f5-squares, appears to favour him, especially with Black struggling for counterplay. Thus Black should instead prefer one of the alternatives:

a) 13...0-0 14 f4 h6 is the solid choice after which 15 ♕f3 (or 15 ♘f3 ♗h7 16 f5 ♘de5! 17 ♘f4 ♘xf3+ 18 ♕xf3 ♗g5 19 ♕d1 ♖e8 20 ♗g2 g6! and Black had no complaints at all in D.Reinderman-S.Tiviakov, Wijk aan Zee 2000) 15...♗h7 16 ♕g3 ♔h8 17 ♘f3 ♕c7 18 ♔h2 ♖ae8 was finely poised in G.Vescovi-S.Movsesian, Bermuda 2004. As the game showed, the black position is pretty resilient and it's far from clear that he is objectively any worse, especially with both the f5 and g5 breaks being rather doubled-edged.

b) 13...h5!? is a fighting response, although I'm not overly keen on the black position after 14 ♘f4! hxg4 15 ♘xg6 fxg6 16 ♕xg4 ♔f7 (M.Labollita-L.Liascovich, Buenos Aires 2002) when it appears easier for White to improve both his pieces and his kingside chances.

14 ♘e3!

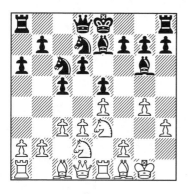

14...h5!?

A natural attempt to gain counterplay, but the fianchettoed bishop will cover everything

from g2, while 14...♗g5 15 ♘dc4 ♗xe3 16 ♗xe3 ♕e7 17 ♗d2 h5 18 ♗g2 also didn't convince in P.Wells-P.Tomcsanyi, Hungarian Team Ch. 1998 and after 18...f6 19 ♘e3 ♗f7 20 d4! White had seized the initiative.

15 ♘f5 hxg4 16 hxg4 ♗xf5 17 exf5!

It's hard not to agree with Kaufman here, whose superb one volume repertoire work, *The Chess Advantage in Black and White,* we will be hearing more of later, that White is better, while his pieces are certainly much the easier to improve and coordinate.

17...♗g5 18 ♗g2 ♔f8 19 ♘e4 ♗xc1 20 ♖xc1 ♘f6 21 ♘xf6 gxf6

Psakhis' commentary also mentions 21...♕xf6 22 ♕b3! ♘d8 23 d4! when the position opens up to favour White's more actively placed pieces.

22 ♖e3 ♕b6 23 ♖b1! ♔e7 24 b4!? cxb4 25 d4

Opening lines against the black monarch and Morozevich now handles the initiative superbly, before his pieces eventually over-run their counterparts:

25...a5 26 a3 ♖a7 27 dxe5 dxe5 28 g5! fxg5 29 ♕g4 f6 30 ♕c4! ♘d8 31 ♖d3 ♖h4 32 ♕g8 ♖f4 33 ♖b2 ♘f7 34 ♖bd2 1-0

Summary

Theory hasn't always been especially kind to 3...♘c6, but it does appear to be a good choice for those keen to reach an unbalanced position against 3 ♗b5+, while of course the variation can also be reached via 2 ♘f3 ♘c6 3 ♗b5 d6. Black appears to be in reasonable shape in the main lines and so the aggressive 4 ♗xc6+ and the positional 6 h3 may well continue to grow in popularity. 5...♗g4 and 5...e5 6 c3 f5!? appear quite playable against the former, while 6...g6 and 6...e6 appear best against the latter.

Those intending to fight with this line as Black must remember they are also ready for 4 d4 cxd4 5 ♕xd4, while it appears prudent not to employ the 5 ♖e1 a6?! move order. Black does though have a number of reasonable lines against the 7 ♗xc6 ♗xc6 8 d4!? gambit, with 8...♗xe4 9 ♗g5 ♗d5 continuing to hold up well. Instead 7 ♗a4 remains a good psychological choice against very aggressively minded players, but White probably has better chances for an advantage with 7 ♗f1. After 7...♗g4, 8 h3 ♗h5 may now be playable, but the main lines arising after 8 d3 e6 continue to produce some very rich and complex positions in which the better prepared player will often do well. Do though expect to see more of Topalov's 9 ♘bd2 ♘d7!?.

1 e4 c5 2 ♘f3 d6 3 ♗b5+ ♘c6 (D)
4 0-0
> 4 ♗xc6+ bxc6 5 0-0
>> 5...e5 6 c3
>>> 6...g5 – *Game 1*; 6...f5 – *Game 2*
>> 5...♗g4 – *Game 3*

4...♗d7 5 ♖e1 ♘f6
> 5...a6 – *Game 4*

6 c3
> 6 h3 (D) 6...a6 – *Game 5*
>> 6...g6 – *Game 6*; 6...e6 – *Game 7*

6...a6 7 ♗f1
> 7 ♗xc6 – *Game 8*
> 7 ♗a4
>> 7...c4 – *Game 9*; 7...b5 8 ♗c2 e5 – *Game 10*

7...♗g4 (D)
> 8 h3 – *Game 11*; 8 d3 – *Game 12*

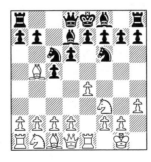

3...♘c6   *6 h3*   *7...♗g4*

CHAPTER TWO

3...♘d7:
Bold and Dynamic

---

1 e4 c5 2 ♘f3 d6 3 ♗b5+ ♘d7

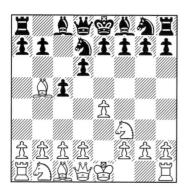

Another uncompromising response to the check after which it is very hard for White to kill the game off should he so desire. Furthermore, many of the resulting positions are pretty complex, although there is also no doubt that 3...♘d7 is a much more risky approach than 3...♗d7. Still Black should be happy to play the resulting positions which are often reminiscent of the Open Sicilian and so it's not surprising that the variation has appealed to Viktor Bologan and to Joe Gallagher; leading exponents of the black cause along with Farrukh Amonatov, Vladislav Nevednichy and Evgeny Vorobiov.

4 d4

If White doesn't desire to reach an Open Sicilian type position, and even a fairly positional version of one, then he should seriously consider the popular idea of 4 c3!?, especially as 4 0-0 ♘gf6 5 ♖e1 a6 6 ♗f1 hasn't been considered promising for some time. With 4 c3, White hopes that the game will take on Lopez characteristics after 4...♘gf6 5 ♕e2 a6 6 ♗a4 e5 7 0-0 ♗e7 8 d4 b5. Svidler has shown that Black can play that way, but we will focus on his alternatives in Game 13.

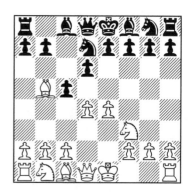

4...♘gf6

Black's most common move order, although if he wants to play one of the fashionable ...♗xd7 lines then he should consider preferring 4...cxd4 5 ♕xd4 a6 6 ♗xd7+ ♗xd7

---

as he did in Baklan-Gallagher (Game 19). This form of capture has been doing quite well of late, unlike the older preference for ...♘xd7, although it's still fairly early days for the idea.

5 ♘c3

White has a major alternative here in the shape of 5 0-0 which is a sacrifice, but 5...♘xe4 is rather risky as Andrew-Ellison (Game 14) reveals. 5 0-0 is Rublevsky's current choice and it does allow White to meet 5...cxd4 6 ♕xd4 e5 with 7 ♕d3 h6 8 c4!? (see Game 15). Again though Black might prefer 6...a6!? 7 ♗xd7 ♗xd7 which we'll see Rublevsky tackling in Game 16, while the risky 6...g6!? is also possible, but then the forcing 7 e5 dxe5 8 ♕xe5! ♗g7 9 ♖e1 e6 10 ♕d6 a6 11 ♗f1 ♕e7 12 ♕xe7+ ♔xe7 13 ♘bd2 left White slightly better in S.Rublevsky-Ye Jiangchuan, Moscow 2004.

5...cxd4

The main alternative is 5...a6 6 ♗xd7+ ♘xd7 (essential as neither 6...♗xd7 7 dxc5! ♕a5 8 cxd6 ♘xe4 9 ♕d5! nor 6...♕xd7 7 0-0 cxd4 8 ♘d5! ♘xd5 9 exd5 ♕g4 10 ♖e1! – Obukhov – with strong pressure against e7, are particularly satisfactory for Black) which was all the rage in the mid-nineties. However, 7 0-0 leaves Black struggling after 7...e6 8 ♗g5 ♕c7 9 d5! (Game 17) and with 7...cxd4 (Game 18).

6 ♕xd4

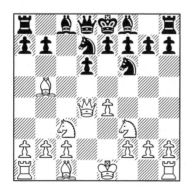

6...e5

Set-ups with 6...e6 have been rather unfashionable since the seventies, although White must proceed pretty accurately to gain an advantage with 7 ♗g5 ♗e7 (or 7...a6!? 8 ♗xd7+ ♗xd7 9 0-0-0 ♗e7 10 e5! dxe5 11 ♘xe5 ♗c6 12 ♘xc6 bxc6 13 ♕xd8+ ♖xd8 14 ♖xd8+ ♗xd8 15 ♖d1 – Kaufman – with a small edge for White in the endgame) 8 e5! dxe5 9 ♘xe5 0-0 10 ♘xd7 ♘xd7 11 ♗xe7 ♕xe7 12 0-0-0 ♘f6 13 ♖he1 (Polugaevsky) when he has a pretty pleasant position.

However, ...g6 set-ups have received some recent attention and after 6...g6 White hasn't got anywhere with an immediate 7 e5 and so should prefer to use his superior development with 7 ♗g5! ♗g7 8 0-0-0 0-0 and only then opt for 9 e5!. After 9...dxe5 10 ♘xe5 the black queen must flee the d-file, but 10...♕a5 11 ♘c4! is still quite awkward for her and then 11...♕c7 12 ♗f4! ♕c5 13 ♗e5! b6 14 ♗xd7! was I.Glek-B.Kohlweyer, Vlissingen 2002. Glek now felt that Black had to try 14...♕xd4, although then 15 ♗xd4 ♘xd7 16 ♘d5! e5 17 ♗c3 ♔h8 18 ♗b4 would still have left White much better.

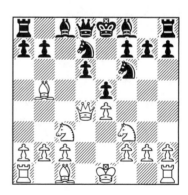

7 ♕d3 h6

The structure is now the same as in many Najdorf lines and, while White is ahead in development, his f3-knight and b5-bishop aren't optimally placed.

8 ♗e3

The main move, but we will consider some

other set-ups in Game 20, while in the main line Black has recently found some new ideas to challenge the notion that White has a pleasant and easy edge as we'll discover in Game 21.

Game 13
H.Nezad-S.Zagrebelny
Asian Ch., Doha 2003

1 e4 c5 2 ♘f3 d6 3 ♗b5+ ♘d7 4 c3 ♘gf6 5 ♕e2 a6

Kicking the bishop and gaining the option to expand with 5...b5 is both useful and normal. Instead Leonid Yudasin, a leading 4 c3 exponent along with Joel Benjamin, Jaan Ehlvest and Evgeny Miroshnichenko, has demonstrated that an immediate 5...g6?! is rather suspect when the forceful 6 0-0 ♗g7 7 d4 0-0 8 e5! ♘e8 is rather good for White after just 9 ♗g5 or the more aggressive 9 e6! of L.Yudasin-B.Kreiman, New York (rapid) 2003.

6 ♗a4

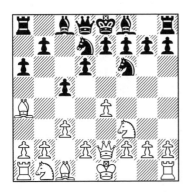

6...c4!?

Critical and, just like in the 7 ♗a4 c4 line of the 3...♘c6 variation, Black does his best to prevent White from getting his pawn to d4. Here though the move is actually a sacrifice, albeit, as the game reveals, one which should really be declined. Black has, however, also tried a number of other set-ups:

a) 6...e6 7 0-0 ♗e7 8 d4 b5! 9 ♗c2 ♗b7 may appear a little misguided at first sight as Black has allowed White his strong centre. Black's hypermodern set-up is though playable; he will hope to gain counterplay on the queenside or down the c-file, while aiming to keep White tied down defending his centre. However, after 10 a4!? 0-0 11 ♗g5! (the pressure against b5 and down the h4-d8 diagonal is now a little awkward for Black, even if not immediately threatening) 11...h6 12 ♗h4 ♕c7 13 ♖e1 cxd4 14 cxd4 ♖ac8 15 ♗d3! White's fine play left him better, with Black lacking counterplay and with a queenside weakness, in E.Miroshnichenko-D.Stets, Alushta 2001.

b) 6...g6!? is fairly natural and sees Black hoping to force a sharpening of the struggle.

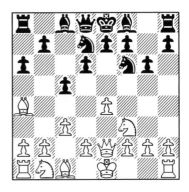

Unsurprisingly it's thus appealed to Nakamura and after 7 0-0 ♗g7 8 d4 b5 9 ♗c2 0-0 10 e5!? (committal, but the only real way to trouble Black) 10...♘e8 11 ♗g5 dxe5 12 dxe5 ♘c7! 13 ♕e4 ♖b8 14 ♕h4 ♖e8, intending 15...♘e6, Black was able to defend in I.Labib-H.Nakamura, Linares 2003, although White then shouldn't have given up his bishop on g5.

c) 6...b5 7 ♗c2 e5 may appear to play into White's hands, but it is playable should Black be happy with a closed game. White has struggled to prove an advantage after 8 d4 ♗e7 9 0-0 0-0, such as with 10 ♖d1 (10 a4!? ♗b7 11 d5 is probably the best try) 10...♕c7

11 a4 ♗b7 when White was a long way from occupying d5, while Black had sufficient counterplay on the queenside and against e4 in A.Delchev-P.Svidler, Calvia Olympiad 2004.

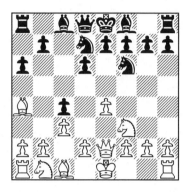

7 ♗xd7+?

Avoiding getting the queen trapped after 7 ♕xc4?? b5 8 ♕c6 ♖b8 and attempting to refute Black's last, but Zagrebelny was no doubt actually rather happy to see this. Instead White can consider 7 0-0!? e5 8 ♗c2 ♕c7 9 a4, intending to pressurise c4 as in S.Rocha-E.Van den Doel, Lisbon 2000, although Black might prefer the more ambitious 7...b5!? 8 ♗c2 ♘e5, aiming to support c4 and to clamp down on d3.

Preparing b3 with 7 ♗c2 has actually been White's most common choice when 7...♕c7!? (or more simply 7...b5 8 b3 cxb3 9 axb3 e5! and then 10 0-0 ♗e7 11 d4 ♕c7 12 ♘h4 ♘b6 was roughly balanced in V.Komliakov-I.Kurnosov, Serpukhov 2002) 8 0-0 ♘e5! quickly led to a complex position in J.Benjamin-J.Sarkar, New York 2004 after 9 ♘xe5 dxe5 10 b3! cxb3 11 axb3 ♗d7. Black was well placed to meet 12 d4?! with 12...exd4 13 cxd4 ♖c8 and so Benjamin preferred 12 ♗a3 ♖c8 13 f4!? exf4 14 e5 with compensation for the pawn, although now 14...♘d5 would have been critical. Instead White could launch his f-pawn a move earlier with 12 f4!? when 12...exf4 13 d4 again sees the strong

white centre grant him some compensation, although Black does have 13...e5!, intending 14 dxe5 ♘g4 15 ♗xf4 ♘xe5! 16 ♕h5 ♕c5+ 17 ♔h1 ♘g4.

7...♗xd7 8 ♕xc4

The only consistent follow-up, although Black's extra light-squared bishop now immediately makes itself felt.

8...♗b5! 9 ♕d4 e5 10 ♕e3

After this Zagrebelny's initiative continues to grow as he boots the white queen around. However, if instead 10 ♕b4 then Black simply has 10...d5 11 ♕b3 ♘xe4, regaining the pawn with a great position and intending 12...♘c5.

10...♘g4 11 ♕g5 ♕c8!

Black could even exchange queens here and still retain a strong initiative, but Zagrebelny wants to continue to exploit the hapless white lady.

12 d4 ♗e7! 13 ♕d2

A grim retreat after which Black gets to open more lines, but 13 ♕xg7?? ♕c4 would have been all over on the spot.

13...f5! 14 ♕c2 fxe4 15 ♕xe4 ♘f6 16 ♕c2 e4 17 ♘g5 ♗d3

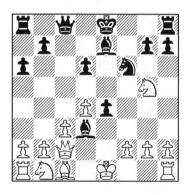

18 ♕b3?

Having been unable to develop anything for the past ten moves, White must have been feeling like a punch-bag and unsurprisingly doesn't put up the most resistance. However, his position was hardly to be envied after 18

♕d1 ♕f5 19 ♘a3 0-0, intending a crushing 20...♘g4.

18...♕g4!

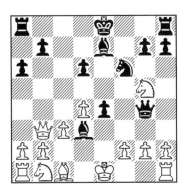

Fittingly finishing White off on his vulnerable light squares, while the black monarch can easily flee the spite checks.

19 ♕f7+ ♔d7 20 f3 ♕xg2 0-1

Game 14
D.Andrew-D.Ellison
England 2002

---

1 e4 c5 2 ♘f3 d6 3 ♗b5+ ♘d7 4 d4 ♘gf6 5 0-0!? ♘xe4?!

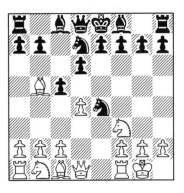

Of course the proof of the pudding is in the eating, but this, despite some recent grandmaster testing, simply appears incredibly risky.

6 ♖e1!

Rare, but direct and dangerous, although the more common 6 ♕e2 is also quite challenging for Black.

6...♘ef6 7 dxc5! dxc5

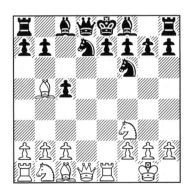

8 ♘g5!?

White goes on to win in style after this, but the best course is probably the similar 8 ♗c4!? e6 9 ♘g5! as in V.Baklan-J.M.Degraeve, Belgian Team Ch. 1996, when after 9...♗e7 (and not 9...h6? 10 ♘xf7! ♔xf7 11 ♗xe6+ ♔g6 12 ♕d3+! mating – Lane) 10 ♗xe6 0-0 (Black could consider 10...fxe6!? 11 ♘xe6 ♕b6 12 ♕e2 ♘g8!, although this looks incredibly risky, but 13 ♕g4 ♘f8! may defend and so perhaps White should simply settle for the also fairly dangerous 13 ♗f4!?) 11 ♕e2 ♘b6! 12 ♗xc8 ♘xc8 13 ♘c3 White was certainly better, although Black was still in the game.

8...e6

Instead 8...a6? 9 ♗c4 e6 isn't possible due to 10 ♘xf7!, but critical is the very provocative 8...h6!. Now retreating certainly doesn't give White more than enough compensation, and he would prefer to sacrifice with 9 ♘xf7!? when 9...♔xf7 10 ♗c4+ ♔e8 11 ♕d3 ♕c7 12 ♘c3 a6 is critical. White is a piece down, but his superior development along with the vulnerable black monarch offers him some practical compensation, although it's not so easy to prevent Black from unravelling with ...♘e5 or after 13 ♕g6+ ♔d8 14 ♖d1 ♕e5!.

9 ♕e2 ♗e7 10 ♘c3 a6?

Andrew exploits this in style and although 10...0-0 11 ♘xe6 would have been clear cut, 10...h6! 11 ♘xe6 fxe6 12 ♕xe6 wouldn't have been. Once again White has some compensation for the piece, but his main problem is that after 12...♔f8 13 ♗c4?! ♕e8 14 ♗f4, unlike in the game, Black has the rather strong 14...♘b6! available.

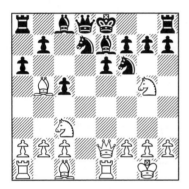

11 ♘xf7!! ♔xf7 12 ♕xe6+ ♔f8 13 ♗c4 ♕e8 14 ♗f4 ♘b8

White was fully developed and ready to crash through on d6 and e7 in any case, but this does allow a lovely combination. However, neither would 14...♘g8!? 15 ♖ad1 ♘df6 have survived due to 16 ♕b6! (J.Littlewood) when Black is in zugzwang after 16...♘d7 17 ♕c7, while 16...♘c6 fails to 17 ♖d8+! ♘e8 18 ♕xc6 bxc6 19 ♗d6.

15 ♕d6! ♘c6

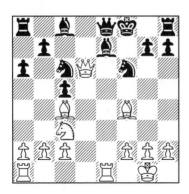

16 ♖xe7!! ♘xe7?!

Allowing a rapid and neat finish, but the main point of Andrew's beautiful combination was 16...♕xe7 17 ♖e1! ♘e8! (17...♕xd6? 18 ♗xd6+ ♘e7 19 ♖xe7 wins easily as the raking bishops are far too strong) 18 ♕d1!, as John Littlewood's excellent notes in *Chess-Moves* observed. White intends to reroute the queen to h5 and Black lacks a defence, such as 18...♕d7 (or 18...♕f6 19 ♘d5 ♕g6 20 ♗e3! ♘d4 21 ♗xd4 cxd4 22 ♕e2 – Littlewood – and Black cannot satisfactorily cover e7 as 22...♕e6 23 ♕f3+ ♘f6 24 ♕a3+ is crushing) 19 ♕h5 (threatening to mate with 20 ♖xe8+! ♕xe8 21 ♗d6+ ♘e7 22 ♕f3+) 19...g6 20 ♗h6+ ♘g7 21 ♕xc5+ ♘e7 22 ♕e5 ♖g8 23 ♕f6+ completes the rout; the white queen and bishops are simply far too strong whereas the extra black rook never gets a look in.

17 ♕xf6+! gxf6 18 ♗h6 checkmate

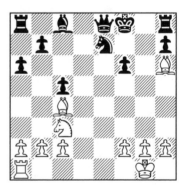

A lovely miniature, although 8 ♗c4 might well be objectively the best way to a white advantage.

Game 15
S.Rublevsky-A.Fedorov
Russian Team Ch. 2000

---

1 e4 c5 2 ♘f3 d6 3 ♗b5+ ♘d7 4 d4 ♘gf6 5 0-0 cxd4 6 ♕xd4 e5 7 ♕d3 h6

Just as had White played ♘c3 rather than castling, this is prudent whereas 7...♗e7 8

♗g5 0-0 9 ♗xd7! (taking control of d5) 9...♘xd7 10 ♗xe7 ♕xe7 11 ♘c3 gives White a pleasant edge, even after 11...♘c5 12 ♘d5 ♕d8 13 ♕e3 f5! 14 ♘xe5! f4 15 ♕a3 ♘xe4 16 ♘f3 ♗e6 17 ♖ad1 as in G.Sarakauskas-R.Sebe Vodislav, La Fere 2004.

8 c4!?

Clamping down on d5, and having this option is one of the key ideas behind preferring 5 0-0 to 5 ♘c3.

8...♗e7 9 ♘c3 0-0

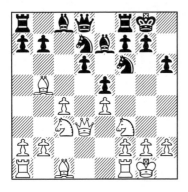

10 ♗xd7

This doesn't really lead anywhere and so White should seriously consider not rushing to claim d5, with the rare 10 ♗e3!? being more flexible. Then 10...a6 11 ♗a4 ♘b6 (Black must develop and 11...♕a5?! is hit by 12 b4! when 12...♕xb4?? 13 ♗xd7 ♗xd7 14 ♖fb1 ♕a5 15 ♗b6 traps the queen, while 12...♕c7 13 ♖ac1 ♘b6 14 ♗b3 ♗g4 15 ♘h4! ♔h8 16 h3 ♗c8 17 ♖fd1 was excellent for White in S.Belkhodja-V.Epishin, Nimes 1991) 12 ♗c2!? ♗e6 is critical, but White may well retain the edge in the Old Indian type position arising after 13 ♘d5! ♘bxd5 14 cxd5 ♗d7 15 ♕b3, although here Black does have 15...b5!?, intending 16...♕b8-b7.

10...♗xd7 11 ♗e3

Rublevsky later tried 11 ♖d1!? a6 12 c5!? dxc5 13 ♗xh6! when the bishop was immune due to 13...gxh6 14 ♘xe5 ♗g4 15 ♕g3 ♗d6 16 f4! (Rublevsky). Instead S.Rublevsky-

Z.Efimenko, Moscow 2003 continued 13...♕c7 (it might well have been better to gain space immediately with 13...c4!? when presumably Rublevsky intended 14 ♕e2 when the bishop still can't be captured, whereas 14 ♕d2? gxh6 15 ♕xh6 ♘g4! 16 ♕h5 ♗f6 17 ♘d5 ♗g7 18 h3 ♘h6 19 ♘xe5 ♗e8 successfully defended in M.Wilder-J.Fedorowicz, New York 1979) 14 ♗g5 ♗e6 15 ♗xf6 ♗xf6 16 ♘d5 ♗xd5 17 exd5 (preparing to bring the knight to e4) 17...c4! 18 ♕e4 ♖fd8 and now the vigorous 19 g4! g6 20 h4! gave White the advantage.

11...a6

Very similar is 11...♗e6!? 12 b3 a6 when 13 a4 ♕a5 14 ♘d2 ♖ac8 15 ♖fd1 ♘d7! 16 ♘f1 f5 17 exf5 ♗xf5 18 ♕d5+ ♕xd5 19 ♘xd5 ♗d8 gave White d5 but no advantage, and Peng Xiaomin-Xu Jun, Beijing 2000 was shortly drawn.

12 a4 ♗e6 13 a5 ♖c8 14 b3 ♘d7! 15 ♘d5

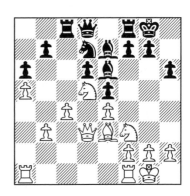

15...♕e8!

Avoiding 15...f5? 16 exf5! ♖xf5 17 ♘d2! ♗f8 18 ♘e4 (Rublevsky) when White gets his second knight to a superb square, but now he lacks a good plan with 16 ♘xe7+ ♕xe7 17 ♖fd1 easily repelled by 17...♖c6.

16 ♖fd1 ♗d8 17 ♘d2 ♔h7 18 f3

Instead White could have continued to improve his knight with 18 ♘f1!?, although then 18...♘c5! 19 ♗xc5 ♖xc5 20 b4 ♖c8 21 ♘fe3

♕c6 still doesn't appear to favour him. Black has good counterplay down the c-file and will finally start to break with ...g6 and ..f5.

18...g6 19 ♘c3 ♗e7!

Fedorov has impressively restrained himself from making a premature ...f5 break, and Rublevsky now decided that there was simply no way past the rock solid black position.

20 ♘d5 ♗d8 ½-½

Game 16
S.Rublevsky-V.Bologan
Poikovsky 2003

---

1 e4 c5 2 ♘f3 d6 3 ♗b5+ ♘d7 4 d4 ♘gf6 5 0-0 cxd4 6 ♕xd4 a6 7 ♗xd7+ ♗xd7!?

With Black not doing so well of late after 7...♘xd7 8 ♘c3 e6 (see Neelotpal-Paragua), this alternative recapture has become fairly popular. Black remains quite flexible after it and, although he will usually follow up with ...e6, he can sometimes also consider instead...e5 or ...g6.

8 ♗g5

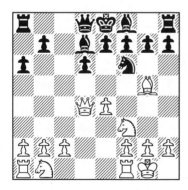

8...e6

Natural whereas the Rauzeresque 8...h6 9 ♗xf6 gxf6 has been condemned ever since Ivanchuk crushed Kasparov after 10 c4 e6 11 ♘c3 at Linares 1991. However, instead of Kasparov's dynamic 11...♖c8 12 ♔h1 h5!? 13 a4 h4 14 h3 ♗e7 when 15 b4! slightly fa-

voured White, Hracek has recently preferred to simply develop and 11...♗e7 12 ♖fe1 ♖c8 13 a4 ♕c7 14 b3 ♕c5! 15 ♕d2 h5! was fine for Black in P.Velicka-Z.Hracek, Opava 2000. However, White can pose more problems than that, such as with 12 ♕d3!?, intending ♖ac1 and then trying to advance with b4, or ♘d4 and then f4-f5.

9 ♘bd2!

Flexible and strong; Rublevsky realises that from c3 the best that the knight can do is really just to sacrifice itself on d5, and instead he exploits its late development to pressurise d6.

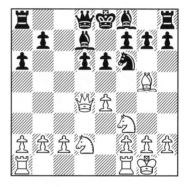

9...♗c6!

Bologan counters well and this was a prepared improvement over 9...♗e7 10 ♘c4 ♗b5 11 ♗xf6! gxf6 12 a4! ♗xc4 13 ♕xc4 ♖c8 14 ♕b3 ♕c7 15 ♘d4 which was pretty good for White in E.Maljutin-S.Shipov, Minsk 1993.

10 ♘c4

Natural, but now Black gets to demonstrate the main point behind his last move. Instead he would also have been fine, due to his bishop-pair, in the ending after 10 ♗xf6 ♕xf6 11 ♕xf6 gxf6 12 ♘d4 ♗h6. However, Rublevsky later attempted to improve with 10 ♖ad1!? when 10...♗e7 11 ♘c4 0-0 (11...b5!? is also possible and then 12 ♗xf6 gxf6 13 ♘e3 isn't clear; it's not easy for either side to play especially actively, while White needs to improve his pieces, such as with ♕d3, ♘d4 and then possibly c4) 12 ♖fe1! d5! 13 exd5 ♘xd5 14 ♕e5!? ♗xg5 15 ♘xg5 saw Black produce the howler 15...b5??, allowing 16 ♘xe6+ fxe6 17 ♕xe6+ ♔h8 18 ♕xc6, in S.Rublevsky-E.Vorobiov, Krasnoyarsk 2003, but instead 15...♕f6!? (Psakhis) or 15...♕e7 would have keep White's small edge under control.

10...b5

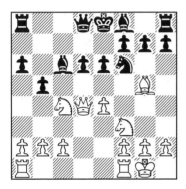

11 ♗xf6

Again this is a little compliant and, evidently also dissatisfied with 10 ♖ad1!?, Rublevsky turned to the critical 11 ♘b6!? in his most recent outing against 7....♗xd7. Then Black had to try 11...♖b8 12 ♘d5 exd5 13 exd5 ♗b7 14 ♖fe1+ ♔d7, which offers White good compensation, although not definitely anything more than that. White should probably continue with 15 c4, aiming to open lines as quickly as possible, but this is still a far better prospect for Black than the 12...♗e7? 13 ♘xe7 ♕xe7 14 ♖ad1 h6 15 ♗xf6 gxf6 16 ♖fe1 ♖d8 17 ♕d2 of S.Rublevsky-N.Misailovic, Budva 2004 when Black was much worse due to his severe structural difficulties and lack of any counterplay.

11...♕xf6! 12 ♘xd6+ ♗xd6 13 ♕xd6 ♗xe4

Now Black threatens 14...♕e7 when he would even stand slightly better due to his advantage of bishop over knight. Rublevsky is thus forced to play actively to maintain the

balance, but he is more than up to the task.

14 ♖fd1! ♖d8!

Wisely avoiding 14...♕e7? 15 ♕e5 and 14...♗xf3? 15 gxf3 ♕xf3 16 ♕d7+ ♔f8 17 ♕d6+! ♔e8 18 ♖d3 ♕b7 19 ♖e1 (Bologan) with a huge attack for White.

15 ♕a3 ♗b7 16 c4!

Rublevsky has whipped up an initiative from nowhere, but Bologan now doesn't panic and instead correctly focuses on getting castled.

16...♗xf3! 17 gxf3 ♕g5+ 18 ♔h1 bxc4 19 ♕xa6 0-0 20 ♕xc4 ♖d2!

White has managed to win a pawn, but the weakness of his kingside along with Black's activity, means that Bologan enjoys full compensation for it.

21 ♕c3!?

A radical way to deal with the active black rook, but the ever creative Rublevsky has seen a way to win the black queen!

21...♖xf2 22 ♖g1 ♕h6 23 ♖xg7+! ♕xg7 24 ♖g1 ♕g6! 25 h4!

The queenside pawns aren't far enough advanced for White to have any winning chances and so, by preventing Black from improving his kingside structure, White creates the option of a perpetual check.

25...♖d8 26 h5 ♕xg1+ 27 ♔xg1 ♖e2 28 ♔f1 ♖h2 29 ♔g1! ♖xh5!?

Trying to win, although the players shortly reach an impasse which neither can break.

30 a4 ♖a8 31 ♕c6 ♖ha5 32 b3 h5 33 ♔f2 ♔g7 34 ♕c3+ ♔g6 35 ♕c2+ ♔g7 ½-½

Game 17
A.Kornev-E.Vorobiov
Suetin Memorial, Tula 2002

1 e4 c5 2 ♘f3 d6 3 ♗b5+ ♘d7 4 d4 ♘gf6 5 ♘c3 a6 6 ♗xd7+ ♘xd7 7 0-0

This position can also arise via 5 0-0 a6 6 ♗xd7+ ♘xd7 7 ♘c3, while now Black doesn't have to keep the tension and we will deal with 7...cxd4 next in Neelotpal-Paragua.

7...e6

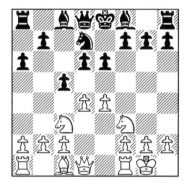

8 ♗g5!

White has been doing rather well with this of late and it certainly appears more promising than the older 8 dxc5 ♘xc5 9 ♗g5. Also possible is an immediate 8 d5!? and White hopes that such a policy will restrict the black bishops. However, first inserting 8 ♗g5 ♕c7 does make it harder for Black to develop and 8 d5 ♘f6!? 9 dxe6 ♗xe6 10 ♖e1!? ♗e7 11 ♗g5 0-0 12 ♗xf6 ♗xf6 13 ♘d5 g6 14 c3 ♗g7 saw d5 and the knights give White certainly no more than a small edge in J.Votava-Y.Yakovich, Stockholm 2000, when Black responded well with ...b5 and ...♖a7-d7 before actively pressing ahead on the queenside.

8...♕c7

The main counter to the fashionable 8

♗g5, but now White gains a pleasant edge and so Black should consider the risky alternatives:

a) 8...f6 9 ♗e3 (and not 9 ♗h4?! h5!) 9...♗e7! 10 d5 e5 leaves Black a little cramped, but also pretty solid. Furthermore, it's not so easy for White, who must keep an eye on the ...b5 and ...f5 breaks, to find a good plan here and he could really do with his pawn being on c4. D.Prasad-V.Gashimov, Dubai 2004 continued with the natural 11 a4 0-0 12 ♘d2! b6 13 ♘c4 ♖b8 14 g3, preparing f4, but after 14...♖e8! White should have changed plans with Psakhis' 15 g4!?, aiming to run Black out of counterplay right across the board.

b) 8...♗e7!? doesn't have a good reputation and weakening d6 like this looks a little suspect, but after the theoretically approved 9 ♗xe7 ♕xe7 10 dxc5!? dxc5 (and not 10...♘xc5? 11 ♕d4 0-0 12 ♖fd1 ♖d8 13 b4 when d6 falls) 11 e5 0-0 12 ♘e4 (White should prefer 12 ♕d3!? b5 13 ♖ad1 ♖d8 14 ♕e4, still with chances for an edge), Black was able to fully neutralise the grip on d6 with 12...♖d8! (so that ♘d6 will be countered by ...♘xe5!) 13 ♕c1 b5 14 h4 ♗b7 15 ♕e3 c4 16 ♖fe1 ♗xe4 17 ♕xe4 ♘c5 in D.Popovic-A.Kovacevic, Petrovac 2004.

9 d5!

Closing the position and making it tough for Black to develop and to gain counterplay.

9...e5 10 a4!

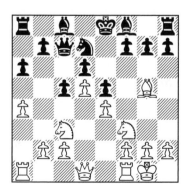

10...h6

With e7 no longer a good square for his dark-squared bishop, Black must fianchetto it, although he doesn't have to prefix that with 10...h6. Instead 10...g6 11 ♘d2 ♗g7 12 ♘c4 ♘b6 13 ♘a3!? h6 14 ♗h4 0-0 transposes back to our main game. However, White doesn't have to keep the knights on, although that does set a devious trap, and 13 ♘xb6 ♕xb6 14 a5! ♕c7 15 ♕d2 was also rather pleasant for White in I.Glek-N.Belichev, Cappelle la Grande 1998. Now 15...♗d7 would have been met by the aggressive 16 f4, but after 15...0-0 16 ♘a4! f5 17 ♘b6 ♖b8 18 f3 White, who intended c4 and then b4, had an excellent version of a King's Indian.

11 ♗h4!

Keeping the bishop pointing at the key e7-square, whereas 11 ♗e3 would allow Black to unravel with 11...♗e7 12 ♘d2 and then 12...♘f6, intending 13...0-0, 14...♘h7 and 15...♗g5, or even with an immediate 12...♗g5!?.

11...g6

Instead 11...b6!? may prevent a5, but then 12 ♘d2 g6 13 ♘c4 ♗g7 14 ♖a3! (an instructive rook lift) 14...♖b8 15 ♖b3 f6! 16 ♗g3! prepared f4, although Black remained pretty solid, but passive, in Lim Yee Weng-P.Kotsur, Aden 2002.

12 ♘d2 ♗g7 13 ♘c4 ♘b6 14 ♘a3!?

He could also still play a la Glek with 14 ♘xb6 ♕xb6 15 a5 ♕c7 16 ♕d2 when if Black wants to prevent both 17 ♘a4 and 17 f4 (which would still be the answer to 16...♗d7), then he only has the ugly 16...g5 17 ♗g3 ♗d7 available.

14...0-0?

Falling for the well disguised trap, but Vorobiov is by no means the only player to have done so. Instead Black must delay castling with 14...♗d7! 15 a5 ♘c8 when 16 ♘c4 b5 (R.Fontaine-D.Feletar, Novi Sad 2003) 17 axb6 ♘xb6 18 ♘a5 ♘a4!? 19 ♘xa4 ♕xa5 20 b3 ♕b4 21 f3 (Feletar) may be an improve-

ment on 14...0-0, but this still looks rather pleasant for White as Black will struggle to gain effective counterplay on the kingside, while 21...c4? fails to 22 ♗e1! ♕b7 23 bxc4 ♕c7 24 ♗f2!.

15 a5 ♘d7

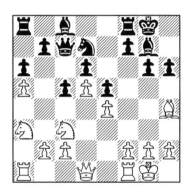

16 ♗e7! ♕xa5

Black had no option but to lose the exchange as 16...♖e8 would have been met by the crushing 17 ♘ab5!! axb5 18 ♘xb5 ♕b8 19 ♗xd6 and the black queen is trapped. Instead Black tried 16...b5 in V.Bhat-Wang Yue, Shanghai 2002 when White converted his extra material fairly easily after 17 axb6 ♘xb6 18 ♗xf8 ♗xf8 19 b3! f5 20 ♘c4.

17 ♘c4! ♕c7 18 ♘xd6 ♖d8 19 ♘cb5 1-0

Black had seen enough and 19...♕b6 20 ♕f3! was completely crushing, such as with 20...♘f6 21 ♗xf6 ♖xd6 22 ♘xd6 ♕xd6 23 ♗xg7 ♔xg7 24 ♕c3.

Game 18

D.Neelotpal-M.Paragua

Alushta 2004

1 e4 c5 2 ♘f3 d6 3 ♗b5+ ♘d7 4 d4 ♘gf6 5 ♘c3 a6 6 ♗xd7+ ♘xd7 7 0-0 cxd4

Gallagher discussed this in his 1994 work, but by the time he came to write the Moscow section for *NCO* he considered it dubious. Black does avoid the d5 idea of the previous game, but at the cost of furthering White's already useful lead in development.

8 ♕xd4

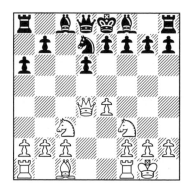

8...e6

Black has tried to resuscitate 8...cxd4 with 8...♕b6!?, but this isn't especially convincing, although 9 ♘d5 ♕xd4 10 ♘xd4 ♖b8 doesn't lead anywhere for White. Instead 9 ♗e3! ♕xd4 10 ♗xd4 e6 11 a4! demonstrates that the exchange of queens has merely served to remove much of the dynamic potential from the black camp. Furthermore, Black still experiences developmental difficulties and in E.Rozentalis-R.Kempinski, Zakopane 2000, White maintained control with 11...f6 12 ♘d2! g5 13 ♘c4 ♘e5 14 ♘b6 ♖b8 15 f3 ♖g8 16 ♔h1! ♗e7 17 g3 ♘d7 18 ♖ad1 ♗d8 19 ♘c4 ♗c7 20 ♗a7! ♖a8 21 ♗e3 ♔e7 when Black had been outplayed and after 22 f4! White could finally open the position up to favour his superbly placed pieces.

9 ♗g5

A popular move, but probably not best. Instead 9 ♖d1!, a move recommended by both Gallagher and Kaufman, is strong. White intends to simply take aim at d6 after 9...f6 (even worse is 9...♕c7? which led to a massacre after 10 ♗f4!! e5 11 ♘d5 ♕b8 12 ♕c3 exf4 13 ♘c7+ ♔d8 14 ♘xa8 ♕xa8 15 e5 ♗e7 16 exd6 ♗f6 17 ♕c7+ ♔e8 18 ♖e1+ ♔f8 19 ♖e7! in V.Tkachiev-A.Suhendra, Jakarta 1996, while after 11...♕c6 12 ♗xe5! dxe5 13 ♘xe5

♕d6 14 ♘c4 ♕c6 15 ♘db6 White would have regained his material with interest) 10 b3 (although 10 a4 ♕c7 11 ♗e3 ♗e7 12 a5 ♘e5 13 ♘xe5! dxe5 14 ♕a4+ ♗d7 15 ♕a2! is also pretty good for White who went on to convert his superior structure after 15...♖c8 16 ♘a4 ♗xa4 17 ♕xa4+ ♕c6 18 ♕xc6+ ♖xc6 19 c3 in J.Shaw-H.Hamdouchi, Gibraltar 2003) 10...♕c7 11 ♗a3. In T.Oral-F.Janz, 2nd Bundesliga 2002, White stuck to that aim with 11...♘c5 12 b4! ♘d7 13 b5 when 13...♘c5 14 ♖ab1 ♗e7 15 b6 ♕c6 16 ♕c4, threatening 17 ♘d4 ♕d7 18 ♗xc5 dxc5 19 ♘f5, gave him a great position.

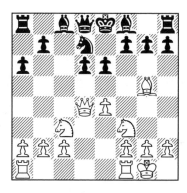

9...f6! 10 ♗e3

Keeping the bishop active whereas after 10 ♗h4 ♘e5! it's not especially easy for White to play around the knight, although then 11 ♘d2!?, intending simply f4, deserves serious attention. Instead 11 ♕d1 ♕c7 12 ♘xe5?! dxe5 13 ♕h5+ g6 14 ♕e2 ♗e7 15 f3 0-0 16 ♗f2 b5! gave Black the initiative in Zhang Zhong-E.Pigusov, Beijing 1997.

10...♕c7 11 a4 ♗e7?!

Too slow and there was no hurry to develop with this. Instead after 11...♘e5! Black would have had a reasonable position, with the bishop able to be developed more actively after 12 ♘xe5 dxe5 13 ♕b6 ♕xb6 14 ♗xb6 ♗d7 15 ♖fd1 ♗b4!.

12 a5! 0-0 13 ♕d3 ♘e5 14 ♘xe5 dxe5?! 15 ♗b6

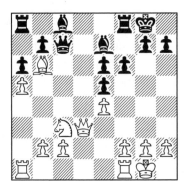

15...♕c6

The queen gets harassed here, but, as Psakhis points out, 15...♕d7 16 ♖fd1 ♕xd3 17 ♖xd3 ♔f7 18 ♖ad1 would also have been horrendous for Black who cannot free his queenside.

16 ♖a4! ♖f7 17 ♖c4 ♕d7 18 ♖d1 ♗f8?

Exchanging on d3 was still incredibly grim and so Black prefers to end the game immediately as now 19 ♕e2 ♕e7 20 ♖d8 picks up the c8-bishop for starters.

19 ♕e2 1-0

Game 19
V.Baklan-J.Gallagher
Isle of Man Open 2004

---

1 e4 c5 2 ♘f3 d6 3 ♗b5+ ♘d7

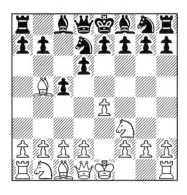

4 d4

In Rublevsky-Bologan we examined the idea (after 4 d4 ♘f6 5 0-0 cxd4 6 ♕xd4 a6 7 ♗xd7) of recapturing with the bishop on d7, but that popular idea can also be implemented earlier as we will now explore. Indeed it's impossible for White to avoid ...♗xd7 lines, unless he opts for 4 c3 when his bishop can retreat to a4 after ...a6. Instead 4 0-0 isn't a highly recommended move order as Black can, and probably should, cut down White's options with 4...a6!? 5 ♗xd7+ ♗xd7. Now 6 d4 cxd4 7 ♕xd4 transposes to the note to White's seventh in our main game, but castling so early is a little inflexible, while Black can also consider 6 d4 ♗g4!?.

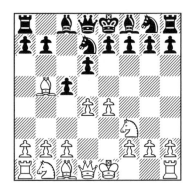

4...cxd4

Ensuring that Black can get the ...♗xd7 option in, rather than have to rely on White meeting 4...♘gf6 with Rublevsky's 5 0-0. The problem is that after 5 ♘c3 a6 6 ♗xd7+, 6...♗xd7?! is no longer any good due to 7 dxc5! ♕a5 8 cxd6! ♘xe4 9 ♕d5! and Black lacked compensation for the pawn in V.Bobolovich-J.Murey, USSR Team Ch. 1967.

However, an immediate 4...a6!? deserves attention when 5 ♗xd7+ ♗xd7 6 ♘c3 cxd4 7 ♕xd4 avoids the option (7 ♗g5!?) which Baklan now employs. This has been considered slightly suspect for Black due to 6 dxc5 ♕a5+ 7 ♘c3 ♕xc5 8 ♗e3 ♕a5 9 ♕d5! and White had seized the initiative in A.Adorjan-

L.Ljubojevic, Wijk aan Zee 1972. However, recently Black has been doing fairly well with the much more solid 6...dxc5, such as 7 ♘c3 e6 8 ♗f4 ♘e7! 9 ♕e2 ♘g6 10 ♗g3 ♗e7 11 h4 h5 12 0-0-0 b5 was pretty unclear, but roughly level, in Z.Hracek-C.Lutz, Calvia Olympiad 2004.

5 ♕xd4 a6 6 ♗xd7+ ♗xd7

7 ♗g5!?

Critical and very interesting as White intends to take play back into Rublevsky-Bologan after 7...♘f6 8 0-0, although Black now has some independent options which exploit the bishop's being on g5. 7 ♘c3 is though an important alternative and, of course, White might have to play this position if he meets 4...a6!? with 5 ♗xd7+ ♗xd7 6 ♘c3. However, here Black has often been employing 7...e5!? of late (a central strike which the crafty 7 ♗g5!? prevents) when play tends to transpose, after 8 ♕d3 h6 into lines often reached via 6...e5, but with White having exchanged on d7 much earlier than he would usually like to.

Black has an important alternative after 7 ♘c3 in 7...♘f6, but 8 ♗g5 h6 9 ♗xf6 gxf6 slightly favours White. 10 ♘d5 is now the main move, but also promising is 10 0-0-0!? ♖g8 11 g3 simply asking Black how he intends to develop. He should probably opt for ...e6 and ...♗e7, which White will aim to counter with ♕d2, ♘d4 and f4-f5, retaining

an edge, while 11...♗g7 12 ♕d3 ♕a5 13 ♘d4! f5? 14 exf5 ♗xd4 15 ♕xd4 ♕xf5 16 ♖he1 left White nicely centralised and much better after 16...♗e6 17 ♕b6 in D.Pavasovic-N.Alfred, Ljubljana 2002.

7 0-0 also has its supporters, but can be said to be less challenging than 7 ♗g5!? and 7 ♘c3 and so White should perhaps avoid 4 0-0 (due to 4...a6). It's probably not best for Black to now take play back into Rublevsky-Bologan with 7...♘f6 8 ♗g5, while 7...e5 8 ♕d3 h6 9 c4 b5!? 10 ♘fd2! is considered to favour White. Instead an interesting option is 7...♗g4!? 8 ♕d3 ♘f6 when White has struggled and after 9 c4 ♖c8 10 b3 g6 11 ♘c3 ♗g7 12 ♘d4 0-0 13 f3 ♗d7 Black had a perfectly acceptable version of the Accelerated Dragon in M.Oratovsky-B.Gelfand, Belgrade 1999.

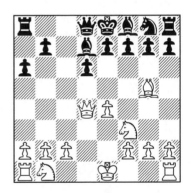

7...h6

Not the only way to avoid playing 7...♘f6 and instead Stocek has preferred 7...f6!?. Here though 8 ♗d2!? ♕c7 9 ♘a3! ♖c8 10 ♖d1 was a deep and promising set-up from White in T.Oral-J.Stocek, Luhacovice 2003. The idea is to quickly pressurise d6 after 10...e6 and so Stocek preferred to continue in offbeat vein with 10...g6 11 0-0 ♘h6, but now Psakhis' 12 ♖fe1 ♗g7 13 ♕d5! would have favoured White. 14 ♘d4! is the answer to even 13...♗g4, while 13...♗c6 14 ♕e6 ♗d7 15 ♕b3 ♘f7 16 ♘d4 is still a pleasant edge for White.

8 ♗h4

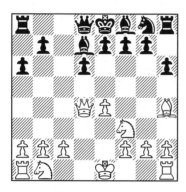

8...♕a5+!

Rare, but this appears to be a good anti-dote to 7 ♗g5!?. With the white bishop now a little offside, Black realises that he will gain a good version of the ...e5 lines. Instead 8...♘f6 is also quite playable, albeit rather double-edged when 9 ♗xf6 (9 ♘c3 is well met by the dynamic 9...g5! 10 ♗g3 ♗g7 as Black had already realised by the early seventies) 9...gxf6 10 ♘c3 ♖g8 11 ♘d5! f5! 12 0-0-0 ♖g4 was unclear and led to a sharp tussle in Z.Medvegy-A.Adly, Cairo 2003.

9 ♘c3 e5

10 ♕d3

White might prefer the more aggressive 10 ♕d5!?, although then 10...♕b4! 11 ♘xe5 ♗e6 12 ♘d3 ♕xc3+ 13 bxc3 ♗xd5 14 exd5 ♗e7 gave Black full compensation for the pawn, in

view of the weakness of c3 and d5, in R.Hasangatin-V.Babula, Czech Team Ch. 2004.

10...♖c8 11 ♘d2 g5!

Reducing the bishop's influence and allowing Black to develop his kingside.

12 ♗g3 ♘f6 13 h4!

The only way to trouble Gallagher, but as Baklan cannot now get anywhere against d6 or down the h-file, this position appears to be fine for Black.

13...♖g8 14 hxg5 hxg5 15 ♘b3 ♕c7 16 0-0-0 b5 17 a3 ♕c4! 18 ♕xc4 ♖xc4 19 f3 ♗e6 20 ♘d2 ♖c6 21 ♘f1! g4!

Gaining sufficient counterplay before White gets a knight to d5 and now the position remains dynamically equal, while it's not long before Baklan realises that he lacks any way to make an impression on the compact black camp.

22 ♔b1 gxf3 23 gxf3 ♗e7 24 ♗e1 ♔d7 25 ♘e3 ♖cc8 26 ♗h4 ½-½

Game 20
R.Scherbakov-E.Vorobiov
Russian Ch. Qualifier, Tomsk 2004

---

1 e4 c5 2 ♘f3 d6 3 ♗b5+ ♘d7 4 d4 ♘gf6 5 ♘c3 cxd4 6 ♕xd4 e5 7 ♕d3

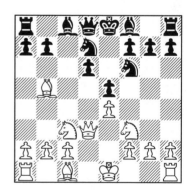

7...h6

Wise, whereas 7...♗e7?! 8 ♗g5 0-0 9 ♗xd7! gives Black a choice of evils:

9...♗xd7!? 10 ♗xf6 ♗xf6 11 ♕xd6 doesn't give him enough for the pawn, while 9...♕xd7 10 ♖d1! ♖d8 11 ♗xf6 ♗xf6 12 ♘d5 was also pretty good for White in S.Rublevsky-A.Minasian, Krasnodar 1997.

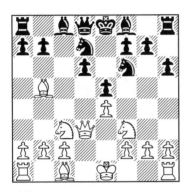

8 ♘d2!?

Eyeing up d6, although White's most popular choice is 8 ♗e3, preparing to exchange off bishop for knight on c5 or b6, after which White hopes that Black will be hindered by being left with a bad bishop and we'll consider that approach next. Instead 8 h3!? and intending to follow up with g4 is White's most aggressive choice, and is a favourite of one of England's most recent IMs, Gary Quillan. Then 8...a6 9 ♗xd7+ ♗xd7 is critical when Quillan has preferred 10 ♗e3, against which Black should still continue with 10...♗e7 11 g4 ♖c8, angling for a later exchange sacrifice. An immediate 10 g4 ♖c8! 11 g5?! is though premature with Black not having played ...♗e7 and then 11...hxg5 12 ♗xg5 ♗e6 13 0-0-0 ♕a5! gave Black a strong attacking position in G.Charleshouse-J.Stocek, Coventry 2005 which continued with the thematic 14 a3 ♖xc3! 15 bxc3 ♕xa3+ 16 ♔d2 ♕a4! 17 ♗xf6 gxf6 18 ♔e1 ♗c4 19 ♕e3 ♕xc2 20 ♘d2 ♗h6 when White was already in deep trouble.

8...♗e7!

Rightly not worrying too much about the d-pawn. Instead Black has often preferred

8...a6 9 ♗xd7+ ♗xd7 10 ♘c4 ♗e6 of late, but then the older 11 ♗e3! remains quite testing.

9 ♘c4 0-0

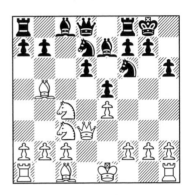

10 ♗e3

8...♗e7 has been holding up well recently, while here 10 ♘xd6? clearly fails to 10...♘c5. However, 10 ♗xd7 ♗xd7! 11 ♘xd6?! is also too greedy whereupon 11...♕c7 12 ♘f5 ♗xf5 13 exf5 e4! 14 ♘xe4 ♕e5 15 f3 ♖ad8 gave Black excellent activity and compensation in L.Yudasin-G.Kasparov, European Club Cup, Ljubljana 1995

10...♕c7

Leaving both the c4-knight and the b5-bishop a little short of squares.

11 ♗a4 ♖d8 12 0-0 ♘c5! 13 ♗xc5 dxc5

White would usually welcome this recapture, but here he is not well placed to exploit d5.

14 ♘d5!?

The alternative was 14 ♕g3 ♗e6! 15 ♕xe5 ♕xe5 16 ♘xe5 ♗d6 17 ♘f3 ♘g4 with good compensation for the pawn due to the well-placed black bishops, while White's remains badly offside.

14...♘xd5 15 exd5 a6! 16 ♖ad1! b5

Forcing White's next after which the exchanges quickly lead to complete simplification and a draw:

17 d6 ♗xd6 18 ♘xd6 ♗e6 19 ♕e4 bxa4 20 ♕xe5 ½-½

Game 21
M.Kazhgaleyev-A.Fedorov
Aeroflot Open, Moscow 2003

1 e4 c5 2 ♘f3 d6 3 ♗b5+ ♘d7 4 d4 ♘gf6 5 ♘c3 cxd4 6 ♕xd4 e5 7 ♕d3 h6 8 ♗e3 ♗e7 9 ♗c4

White is at an important junction. This prevents Black from getting in ...b5, but Fedorov shows that Black still doesn't have to castle. 9 0-0 is the main alternative when 9...a6 (9...0-0 10 ♗c4 ♘b6 11 ♗b3 ♗e6 is not especially accurate as now both 12 ♘d2!? and 12 ♘h4 are promising for White) 10 ♗c4 ♕c7 11 a4 ♘c5 (or 11...0-0) is the solid, but slightly better for White, old main line. Instead Black can though prefer 10...b5!?, transposing to the note to White's tenth.

9...a6!?

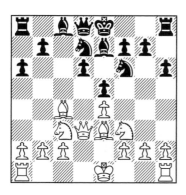

10 a4

Preventing ...b5 whereas 10 0-0 gives Black a choice:

a) 10...♕c7 is the traditional choice when 11 a4 ♘c5 (or 11...0-0 12 ♘d2 ♖b8!? 13 a5 ♘c5 14 ♕e2 ♗e6 15 ♗xe6 and 15...♘xe6 16 ♖a4 left White slightly better in M.Adams-P.Svidler, New Delhi 2000, but that was a better choice than 15...fxe6?! which allows White to make further progress with 16 ♕c4 and 17 ♗xc5) 12 ♗xc5! ♕xc5 13 ♘d5!? ♘xd5 14 ♕xd5 is a new approach from Glek,

but Black then remains solid if a little worse. Instead 13 ♘h4!? ♗e6 14 ♗a2! ♗xa2 15 ♖xa2 was J.Shaw-J.Rowson, Edinburgh 2000, which is now rather well known and to understand much more about this sort of position, and especially the 'bad' black dark-squared bishop, readers are referred to page 76 of the enjoyable and thought-provoking *The Seven Deadly Chess Sins*.

b) 10...b5!? 11 ♗d5 (11 ♗b3 ♗b7 12 ♘d5?! ♗xd5 13 ♗xd5 ♘xd5 14 ♕xd5 0-0 didn't give Black any problems at all in G.Mohr-B.Gelfand, Portoroz 2001, while 12 a4!? b4 13 ♕c4 0-0! 14 ♕xb4 ♖b8 15 ♕c4 ♘xe4! 16 ♘xe4 d5 was also fine for Black in J.Zeberski-P.Bobras, Poraj 2003) 11...♖b8 12 ♗a7 ♘xd5 13 ♘xd5 ♖b7 doesn't currently appear to favour White, and Amonatov has twice shown that 14 ♗e3 (14 ♘xe7 ♕xe7 15 ♗e3 ♘f6 16 ♘d2 0-0 17 ♘b3? ♗e6 18 ♘a5 ♖c7 19 ♗d2 d5! saw Black achieve his ideal break, which left him clearly better, in Ye Jiangchuan-A.Fedorov, Belfort 1999) 14...♘f6! 15 ♘xf6+ ♗xf6 16 ♖fd1 0-0 17 ♘d2 ♗e6 gives Black at least sufficient counterplay.

10...♘b6!?

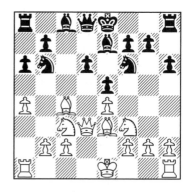

A promising idea and now Black gains time to develop his queenside, but 11 ♗xb6 ♕xb6 (eyeing the potential weaknesses of b2 and b4) 12 0-0 ♗e6 is also fine for Black.

11 ♗b3 ♗e6 12 a5 ♘bd7

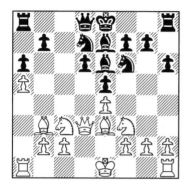

13 ♗xe6

This isn't especially effective, but the only real alternative was 13 ♘d5 when 13...♗xd5 14 ♗xd5 ♘xd5 15 ♕xd5 ♕c7 16 0-0 ♕c6! (Fedorov) is fine for Black.

13...fxe6 14 ♕c4 ♔f7 15 h3 ♕c8 16 ♕b3 ♕c6! 17 ♖a4

Logically aiming to pressurise b7, although now a5 becomes weak, whereas after 17 ♘d2, Black should still consider 17...♖hb8!, intending to try to open the queenside himself with ...b5.

17...♘c5 18 ♗xc5 ♕xc5 19 0-0 ♖hb8!

Again ...b5 is threatened and this forces White's hand.

20 ♖b4 ♕xa5 21 ♖xb7 ♘d7 22 ♖d1 ♕c5 23 ♘d2 ♖xb7 24 ♕xb7 ♖a7 25 ♕b3 ♖c7

Black should be quite happy with this roughly level position, while he has successfully kept the white knights at bay. White

shouldn't be in too much trouble here, but Kazhgaleyev now embarked on a risky plan to win the Black a-pawn after which Fedorov instructively outplayed him, while utilising much of the dynamism within the black position:

26 ♕a4?! ♗h4! 27 ♕xa6? ♗xf2+ 28 ♔h1 ♔e7 29 ♘f3 ♘f6 30 ♕d3 ♖c6! 31 ♖a1 ♘h5! 32 ♖a6? ♖xa6 33 ♕xa6 ♕e3 34 ♘d1 ♕c1 35 ♕d3 ♗c5 36 g4 ♘f4 37 ♕d2 ♕xd2 38 ♘xd2 ♘xh3 39 ♔g2 ♘g5 40 c3 d5! 41 b4 ♗a7 42 c4 dxc4 43 ♘xc4 ♘xe4 44 ♘xe5 ♔d6 45 ♘d3 e5 46 ♔f3 ♔d5 47 ♘e1 ♗d4 48 ♘c2 ♘g5+ 49 ♔e2 ♘e6 50 ♘ce3+ ♔e4 51 ♘f2+ ♔f4 52 ♘d3+ ♔g3 53 b5 e4 54 ♘b4 ♘f4+ 55 ♔d2 ♔f3 56 ♘bc2 ♗c5 57 ♘f5 ♘e6 58 ♘ce3 ♘d4 59 ♘h4+ ♔f2 60 ♘d1+ ♔g3 61 ♘g6 ♘xb5 62 g5 h5 63 ♘e3 ♘d6 0-1

Summary

This remains an excellent choice for the fighting player looking to counter the Moscow. It can be especially recommended to Najdorf and Classical players happy to play 4 d4 ♘f6 5 ♘c3 cxd4 6 ♕xd4 e5 7 ♕d3 h6 which has often been a little unfairly condemned by theory. The ...♘xd7 lines aren't in good shape these days, but Black players not wishing to play ...e5 should jump on the ....♗xd7 bandwagon.

4 c3 is a fairly respectable option for White, but if he is happy to play the main lines then he should probably prefer 4 d4 ♘f6 5 0-0 to 5 ♘c3. The e4-pawn is effectively then taboo, while White also gains some promising options after both 5...cxd4 6 ♕xd4 e5 and 6...a6 7 ♗xd7+ ♗xd7. Both those lines are though still quite playable for Black, although he may wish to give serious thought to playing ...a6, intending ....♗xd7, as early as he can, such as immediately after both 4 d4 and 4 0-0.

1 e4 c5 2 ♘f3 d6 3 ♗b5+ ♘d7 *(D)*

4 d4

        4 c3 – *Game 13*

4...♘gf6

        4...cxd4 5 ♕xd4 a6 – *Game 19*

5 d4

        5 0-0 *(D)*

                5...♘xe4 – *Game 14*

                5...cxd4 6 ♕xd4

                        6...e5 – *Game 15*; 6...a6 – *Game 16*

5...cxd4

        5...a6 6 ♗xd7+ ♘xd7 7 0-0

                7...e6 – *Game 17*; 7...cxd4 – *Game 18*

6 ♕xd4 e5 7 ♕d3 h6 *(D)*

        8 ♘d2 – *Game 20*; 8 ♗e3 – *Game 21*

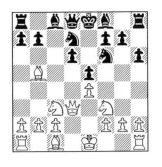

3...♘d7   *5 0-0*   *7...h6*

CHAPTER THREE

3...♗d7 4 ♗xd7+ ♘xd7: An Underrated Line

1 e4 c5 2 ♘f3 d6 3 ♗b5+ ♗d7 4 ♗xd7+ ♘xd7

Despite being endorsed in Steffen Pedersen's 1999 work, this variation is rather unfashionable. Indeed from the 52 games of Rublevsky's with the Moscow variation which I could trace since the beginning of 2000, Mr ♗b5+ has faced 4...♘xd7 just once. This unpopularity might well be due to the fact that after 4...♘xd7 White can force a Hedgehog position, and many 2...d6 players may not be happy to patiently defend such positions. Those happy to counterattack from a Hedgehog base should though find 4...♘xd7 a playable option and it continues to attract a number of faithful followers: chiefly Igor No-

vikov, but also Nick De Firmian, John Fedorowicz, Danny King and Yannick Pelletier.

However, White isn't forced to exchange on d7 and can instead prefer 4 a4!?; a former favourite of Gurgenidze's and Larsen's, whilst its current leading exponent is the Irish IM, Gavin Wall. With 4 a4 White declares that he is happy to avoid theory and just to play chess, although the move is not completely harmless and Black should especially beware opening the a-file with an exchange on b5. After 4...♘c6 5 d3 g6 6 0-0 ♗g7 7 ♘bd2! ♘f6 8 ♘c4 0-0 9 ♖e1 White is happy to exchange his light-squared bishop in return for the b6-square, while he also may break with e5, and 9...d5! 10 exd5 ♘xd5 11 c3 a6 12 ♗xc6 ♗xc6 13 a5 ♕c7 14 ♘fe5 ♗b5 15 ♕f3 ♖ad8 was roughly level in G.Wall-A.Shirov, British League 2005.

Returning to 4...♘xd7:

5 0-0

White can also prefer 5 c4 ♘gf6 6 ♘c3 when 6...e6 7 d4 cxd4 8 ♘xd4 returns play to Hedgehog lines, while after 6...g6 7 0-0 ♗g7 White doesn't have to go 8 d4, but can prefer the direct 8 d3!? 0-0 9 ♘g5!, intending to launch the f-pawn as we consider in Ehlvest-Sadvakasov (Game 22). Such an approach should not be taken lightly and is currently

White's most popular way of handling the 4...♘xd7 variation, although he often prefers to omit c4 from his set-up.

5...♘gf6

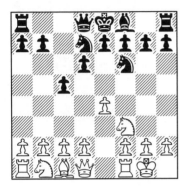

6 ♕e2

If White is determined to avoid a Hedgehog and isn't convinced by the d3 and ♘g5 lines, then following up 6 ♖e1 or 6 ♕e2 with c3 is the alternative. However, the resulting French-type positions are fairly comfortable for Black as we'll see in Games 23 and 24. Instead 6 d3!? is the fashionable choice, again simply intending ♘g5 and f4, and we'll examine this dangerous approach in Morozevich-Khalifman (Game 25).

6...e6

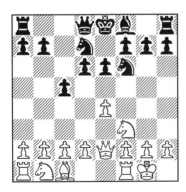

7 b3

Fianchettoing before entering the Hedgehog structure, although White can also prefer

the move order 7 d4 cxd4 8 ♘xd4 ♗e7 (8...a6 9 c4 g6!? deserves consideration) 9 c4 0-0 10 b3 as Rublevsky has done. However, this allows Black some independent options, such as 10...♕b6!? 11 ♗b2 ♖fe8! is a useful Hedgehog move which enables the bishop to drop back to f8 and helps to support ...d5, and also specifically here as it continues to prevent 12 ♘c3, unlike 11...♖ac8?! when 12 ♘c3! ♕xd4? 13 ♘d5! would be embarrassing.

7...♗e7 8 ♗b2 0-0

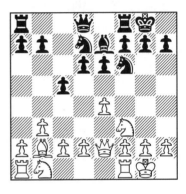

9 c4

Erecting the bind before breaking with d4 as after an immediate 9 d4, 9...d5!? is a little awkward and 10 ♘bd2 ♖c8 11 e5 ♘e8 12 c4 ♘c7 13 g3 ♘b6! left the white centre under a bit of pressure in A.Heinz-Z.Efimenko, Bad Wiessee 2002.

9...a6

Instead the solid 9...e5 is a playable option, albeit one usually slightly more pleasant for White. 10 ♘c3 ♘e8 sees the black knight head for e6, while the f3 one will go to e3 and 11 ♘e1 ♘c7 12 ♘c2 has been assessed as favouring White, but after 12...♗f6 13 ♘e3 ♘e6 14 g3 g6! 15 ♕d3 ♘d4 16 ♘cd5 ♗g7 White has no advantage and after 17 f3 G.Hernandez-H.Mecking, Calvia Olympiad 2004 was agreed drawn.

10 d4

Delaying this with 10 ♘c3 isn't too effective in view of 10...♘e5! when an exchange of knights would cripple the d-pawn and give Black good central control, but 11 ♖ad1 ♘xf3+ 12 ♕xf3 b5! 13 d4 didn't give White anything and a draw was agreed here, before Black exchanged on d4 and c4, in P.Zarnicki-J.Gallagher, Bled Olympiad 2002.

10...cxd4 11 ♘xd4

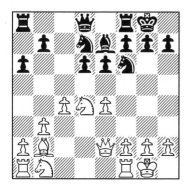

This is the main line of the 4...♘xd7 Hedgehog. The position is unbalanced and which side to favour really comes down to personal taste and experience of such positions; see Fressinet-Polgar (Game 26).

Game 22
J.Ehlvest-D.Sadvakasov
World Open, Philadelphia 2003

---

1 e4 c5 2 ♘f3 d6 3 ♗b5+ ♗d7 4 ♗xd7+ ♘xd7 5 c4!?

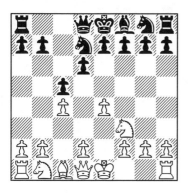

5...♘gf6

Allowing White to later choose between going in for a Hedgehog or preferring the d3, ♘g5 and f4 approach. Those wishing to cut across White's plans should seriously consider 5...♘e5!? when Black hopes to clamp down on d4 by bringing a knight to c6. 6 0-0 is then the Kaufman suggested repertoire, but after 6...e6 7 d3 (or 7 ♘c3 ♘e7 8 ♘e1 g6 when 9 f4 ♘5c6 10 d3 resembles the main game, but with the key difference that the black king's knight is not on f6) 7...♘e7 8 ♘e1 (White's only real plan is to expand with f4) 8...♘5c6! 9 ♗e3 g6 10 ♘c3 ♗g7 White could find nothing better than 11 ♘f3 in Z.Jasnikowski-R.Akesson, Polanica Zdroj 1981. 11 f4 would have been more consistent, but after 11...♘d4 the opening clearly hasn't been a success for White. Black has a very harmonious set-up worthy of a Closed Sicilian, with his knights well coordinated.

6 ♘c3 g6

Heading for a fianchetto with White apparently going to break with d4, but Black can also prefer 6...e6 7 0-0 ♗e7 when Kaufman's recommendation is 8 d4 cxd4 9 ♘xd4, reaching Hedgehog lines, while 8 d3!? 0-0 9 ♘g5 transposes to a position which Benjamin has favoured and which we deal with in Game 25 (after 6 d3 e6 7 c4!?).

7 0-0 ♗g7 8 d3! 0-0 9 ♘g5!

As Kaufman correctly observes 'this amateurish-looking move is actually quite strong here'. By avoiding opening the position with d4, White makes it much harder for Black to gain counterplay. Indeed Black's set-up now appears a little passive and he could really do with the queen's knight being on c6, which would allow him to exploit the d4-square and to achieve more from the ...b5 advance.

9...h6 10 ♘h3 e6

Kaufman has employed his own recommendation – a sure sign that this position is quite promising for White – although his opponent preferred to counter in the centre.

However, after 10...e5!? 11 g3! ♘e8 12 f4 f5 13 ♔h1 ♔h7 14 ♕e2 ♘c7 the accurate 15 exf5! gxf5 16 fxe5 dxe5 17 ♕g2 ♖b8 18 ♗e3 ♕e8 19 g4! broke up the hanging pawns and favoured White in L.Kaufman-I.Bendich, Philadelphia 2003.

11 f4

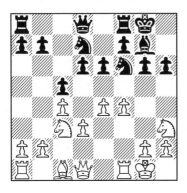

11...♕b6?!

The queen achieves little on c6 and is a long way from the defence of the kingside. Thus Black had to begin arranging ...b5 with 11...a6, although Ehlvest still feels, as his *New in Chess* notes reveal, that White's kingside play leaves him with 'a lasting positional advantage'.

12 ♘f2 ♕c6 13 ♕f3 ♔h7 14 ♗e3 ♘e8

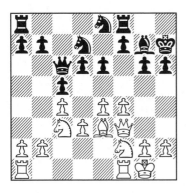

15 f5!

Essential and strong; White must advance before Black sets up a harmonious position

and halts him with 15...f5!. Now though the attack quickly gains momentum with the king's knight demonstrating that it is well placed on f2, as it can come to g4 or to e4 to increase the pressure.

15...exf5 16 ♕h3! ♘ef6

Trying to shore up his kingside, although 16...fxe4? would have been the critical test of White's play. Both players were no doubt aware though that after 17 ♗xh6! the attack is incredibly dangerous, such as 17...♖h8 18 ♘fxe4 ♔g8 (or 18...f5 19 ♘d5! ♗xh6 20 ♘e7 ♕b6 21 ♘xf5! with a mating attack) 19 ♖xf7! ♘e5 20 ♕e6! ♘xf7 21 ♘d5 (Benjamin) is crushing with the queen and knights combining very well.

17 exf5 ♘e5 18 ♘fe4 ♘eg4 19 ♗d2 ♖ae8 20 ♖f4!

Sadvakasov is grimly clinging on, but now his position becomes very critical as Ehlvest invites his remaining rook to the kingside party.

20...h5 21 ♖af1 ♔g8 22 ♕h4 ♘xe4 23 ♘xe4 d5

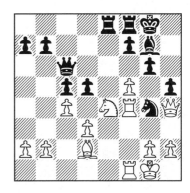

24 f6!

Black's only hope was to break in the centre, but now the attack can crash through in style.

24...♗h8 25 ♖xg4

After this Black could restrict White to a large advantage with 25...dxe4 and so Ehlvest should have preferred the more accurate 25 cxd5! ♕xd5 26 ♖xg4, intending 26...hxg4 27 ♘g5 and 26...♕xd3 27 ♕xh5 ♕xe4 28 ♗h6 (Kaufman) which is winning easily enough. Sadvakasov though misses his chance and White quickly wraps up an impressive attacking display.

25...♖xe4? 26 dxe4 hxg4 27 cxd5 ♕a4 28 ♕xg4 ♖e8 29 ♗c3 b5 30 d6 b4 31 e5! ♕c6 32 d7 ♖d8 33 e6 1-0

Game 23
J.Slaby-K.Jakubowski
Polish U20 Ch., Poraj 2003

---

1 e4 c5 2 ♘f3 d6 3 ♗b5+ ♗d7 4 ♗xd7+ ♘xd7 5 0-0 ♘gf6 6 ♖e1 e6

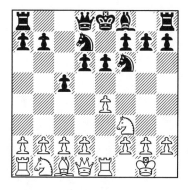

7 c3

Setting up a pawn centre, although White could still prefer the Maróczy approach. However, he has committed his rook to e1 rather earlier than usual and, for example, E.Mirzoeva-A.Timofeev, Dubai 2002 continued 7 c4 ♗e7 8 ♘c3 0-0 9 d4 cxd4 10 ♘xd4 ♖c8 11 b3 a6 12 ♗b2 ♕a5 13 ♕d2 ♖fe8 14 ♖ad1 ♗f8! and Black had a reasonable position.

White could also prefer to begin with 7 d4 cxd4 8 ♕xd4, but then 8...♗e7 9 c4 0-0 10 ♘c3 a6 11 ♕d3?! ♖c8 12 b3 ♘e5! was an instructive way to exploit the absence of a bishop on b2 in S.Vokarev-K.Sakaev, Russian Team Ch. 2003. 13 ♕e2 b5! would have ex-

ploited White's problems down the c-file, although Black was still pretty happy with 13 ♘xe5 dxe5, increasing his central control and still allowing him to meet 14 ♕f3 with 14...b5!.

7...♗e7

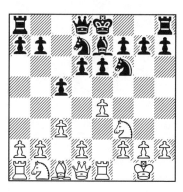

8 d4 cxd4

Heading for a French position is simplest, although Black can also prefer 8...0-0!? which is also fine for him and, for example, 9 e5!? ♘e8 10 ♘bd2?! cxd4! 11 cxd4 dxe5 12 dxe5 ♘c5 gave Black a good c3 Sicilian, despite the knight's being back on e8, with d3 weak in I.Glek-I.Novikov, Korinthos 2000.

9 cxd4 d5 10 e5 ♘e4 11 ♘bd2

11 ♖e2!? ♕b6 12 ♘e1 threatens to trap the knight, but if White wants to play like this he should opt for 6 ♕e2 e6 7 c3, and here 12...f6! 13 f3 ♘g5 14 ♗e3 fxe5 15 dxe5 ♕a6! 16 ♘d3 ♘f7! 17 f4 ♘h6 18 ♘c3 ♘f5 saw Black's thematic play gain the advantage in V.Arapovic-D.Komljenovic, Augsburg 1991

11...♘xd2 12 ♗xd2 ♕b6

Now White has 13 ♕a4 and so Black should first prefer to castle and 12...0-0 13 ♕b3 (13 ♖c1 ♕b6 would transpose to our main game) 13...♕b6! 14 ♕a4 ♘b8! thematically improved the knight in R.Van Kemenade-R.Palliser, York 2002. White should now have sat tight though as after 15 ♗g5?! ♗xg5 16 ♘xg5 ♘c6 17 ♘f3 Black could have grabbed with 17...♕xb2!? when 18 ♖ab1 ♕c3

19 ♖xb7 ♖ab8 gives him the advantage due to the weakness of d4 and the white back rank.

13 ♖c1 0-0

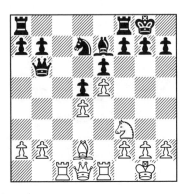

14 ♖c3

Black would also have been fine after 14 ♕a4! ♘b8!, but chasing the queen to a6 doesn't help White as she still exerts awkward pressure from there.

14...♖ac8 15 ♖b3?! ♕a6 16 ♗g5

White's only hope in this variation is to attack on the kingside, but such a plan rarely succeeds and, despite being rated over 2350, Slaby gets nowhere.

16...♗xg5 17 ♘xg5 h6 18 ♘h3 ♖c4! 19 ♘f4 ♖fc8 20 h4 ♘f8!

Covering the kingside and it wasn't long before Black's pressure down the c-file told:

21 ♖g3 ♕a5 22 ♘h5 ♘g6! 23 ♖f1 ♖c1! 24 ♕xc1 ♖xc1 25 ♖xc1 ♕d2 26 ♖c8+ ♔h7 27 ♖f3 ♕xd4 28 ♘g3 ♘xe5 29 ♖b3 b6 0-1

Game 24
V.Nevednichy-C.Balogh
Nagykanizsa 2003

---

1 e4 c5 2 ♘f3 d6 3 ♗b5+ ♗d7 4 ♗xd7+ ♘xd7 5 0-0 ♘gf6 6 ♕e2 e6 7 c3 ♗e7 8 d4 cxd4

Again Black can also prefer to keep the tension with 8...0-0 when 9 ♖d1, exploiting one of the advantages of 6 ♕e2 over 6 ♖e1, is

the best try for an advantage. After 9 ♖d1 Black should consider continuing to wait with 9...♖c8 or 9...♕c7!? as the French option is no longer so good. However, 9...cxd4 remains the most popular move, but then 10 cxd4 d5 11 e5 ♘e4 12 ♘e1! favours White. The e4-knight is now in danger of being trapped, while Black lacks counterplay and 12...f6? (although even 12...h6!? 13 ♘d3 ♘b8! 14 ♕g4 ♔h8 15 ♘f4 ♘c6 16 ♘c3! ♘xc3 17 bxc3 ♗g5 18 ♖d3 saw White, who is slightly better here, continue to press despite the exchanges in S.Arkhipov-P.Leko, Lippstadt 1993) 13 f3 ♘g5 14 exf6! ♗xf6 15 ♗xg5 ♗xg5 16 ♕xe6+ ♔h8 17 ♕xd5 left Black clearly with insufficient compensation for his pawns after 17...♕e7 18 ♘c3 ♖ae8 19 ♘c2 ♗f4 20 ♕h5! ♘f6 21 ♕h3 ♕f7 22 g3 in A.Kovalev-J.Gallagher, European Team Ch., Plovdiv 2003.

9 cxd4 d5 10 e5 ♘e4

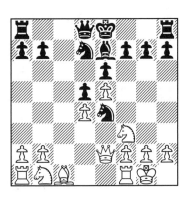

11 ♘e1

Once more making good use of the absence of a rook on e1, while again 11 ♘bd2 doesn't lead anywhere, but does have a rather drawish reputation. However, Black can certainly play this French position on and after 11...♘xd2 12 ♗xd2 ♕b6 13 ♕d3 h6! (a noteworthy idea to prevent White from gaining any kingside play as he would have done after 13...0-0 14 ♗g5!) 14 ♖fc1 0-0 15 ♕c3 ♘b8! 16 b4 ♘c6 17 ♖ab1 ♖ac8, White surprisingly underestimated the effectiveness of the queen after 18 b5? ♘xe5! 19 ♕xc8 ♘xf3+ 20 gxf3 ♖xc8 21 ♖xc8+ ♔h7 22 ♗e3 e5! and Black won without any real difficulties in V.Sanduleac-L.Ftacnik, Calvia Olympiad 2004.

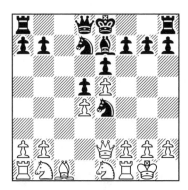

11...f5?!

Enabling the knight to retreat, but even if Black wants to fix the structure he should still first flick in 11...♕b6! when 12 f3? runs into 12...♕xd4+ 13 ♗e3 ♕xe3+! 14 ♕xe3 ♗c5, while after 12 ♗e3 Black has gained the useful extra option of 12 ...f6!?. However, the solid 12...f5 is fine for Black as practice has shown that White can't easily exploit the f4-square and 13 f3 ♘g5 14 ♘c3 0-0 15 ♘d3 ♘f7 16 ♔h1 ♖ac8 17 ♖g1 was seen in P.Ricardi-A.Hoffman, Buenos Aires 1995. This has been assessed as favouring White, but Ricardi later employed 12...f5 himself, while here White's only hope is to open the kingside. However, Black is very solid there and after 17...g5!? 18 g3 a6 19 h4 h6! 20 ♖g2 ♔g7, 21 g4 f4 22 ♗xf4!? gxf4 23 ♘xf4 was certainly no more than an interesting sacrifice. Black now collapsed after 23...♘h8, whereas 23...♗xh4! might have left White struggling with 24 ♕d3 well met by 24...♘fxe5!.

12 exf6! ♗xf6 13 ♘c3!

Exploiting the lack of cover of e6 to weaken the black structure through a series of exchanges.

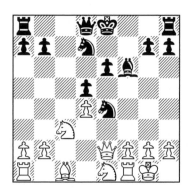

13...♗xd4 14 ♘xe4 dxe4 15 ♕xe4 ♘c5 16 ♕c2! 0-0

Black struggles for a good follow-up after this, but there wasn't anything better with 16...♖c8 17 ♘f3 ♗f6 18 ♗e3! b6 19 ♖ad1! ♕c7 20 b4 ♘d7 21 ♕d3 just one way for him to quickly get into trouble.

17 ♘f3

17...♖xf3!?

Aiming for active counterplay, although this isn't objectively enough. However, White would also have defended after 17...♘d3 18 ♖d1 ♖xf3 (or 18...♗xf2+!? 19 ♔f1 ♘b4 20 ♕e2! ♗d4 21 ♕c4 ♘c6 22 ♗e3 winning) 19 gxf3 ♘e5 20 ♕e4! ♕f6 21 ♔g2, while Balogh understandably didn't like the look of 17...♖c8 18 ♘xd4 ♕xd4 19 ♗e3 with a very pleasant position for White in view of his superior minor piece and structure.

18 gxf3 ♕d5?

Now White consolidates quite easily and 18...♕h4! would have been somewhat more testing, although 19 ♖d1 b6! 20 ♗e3 (20 ♕e2 ♖f8! 21 f4! e5 22 ♗e3 ♘e6! isn't so clear) 20...♗e5 21 f4 appears to defend after 21...♗xf4 22 ♗xf4 ♕xf4 23 ♕e2 ♖f8 24 ♕e3 ♕g4+ 25 ♔h1 (and not 25 ♕g3 ♕e2! with sufficient activity for Black, while then 26 b4 ♘e4 27 ♕g2 ♘d2 forces a draw) and Black doesn't have quite enough, such as 25...♕f5 26 b4 ♘e4 27 f4 ♕xf4 28 ♕xf4 ♖xf4 may give him two pawns for the exchange, but after 29 ♖d7 White is active and stands better.

19 ♗e3 e5 20 ♗xd4 exd4 21 ♖ac1! ♕g5+ 22 ♔h1 ♕f4 23 ♕c4+ ♔h8 24 ♕d5!

Defending his kingside, which Balogh has failed to further dent, and now the d-pawn soon drops off due to some back-rank tactics.

24...♘d3 25 ♖c4 ♕d2 26 ♖xd4 ♘xf2+ 27 ♖xf2! 1-0

> ### Game 25
> ## A.Morozevich-A.Khalifman
> *Russian Cup Final, Samara 1998*

1 e4 c5 2 ♘f3 d6 3 ♗b5+ ♗d7 4 ♗xd7+ ♘xd7 5 0-0 ♘gf6 6 d3

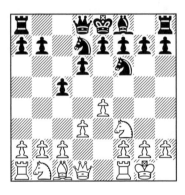

Instead 6 ♕e2 e6 7 d3 transposes back to our main game, but 6 ♕e2 enables White to meet 6 ♕e2 g6 with 7 c3 and central expansion.

6...e6

Despite Glek's preference for a 6 ♕e2 move order, White has done quite well against 6...g6!? here with 7 ♘g5!? when 7...♗g7 8 f4 0-0 9 c4!? h6 10 ♘h3 e6 11 ♘c3 transposes to Ehlvest-Sadvakasov. However, White can also just let Black press ahead on the queenside and 9 ♔h1!? b5 10 ♕e2 ♕c7 11 ♘d2! (exploiting the undeveloped queenside to race the knight straight over to the kingside) 11...b4 12 g4 a5 13 ♕g2 a4 14 ♖b1! (stepping out of the way of 14...a3) 14...♘b6 15 ♘df3 h6 16 ♘h3 ♘fd7 17 g5! h5 18 f5 ♔h7 19 ♘f4 gave White a very strong attacking position and he shortly broke through with a sacrifice on h5 in P.Kotsur-A.Motylev, Tula 1999.

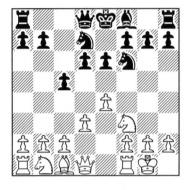

7 ♕e2

This flexible move keeps White's options open and helps to reduce any counterplay. Instead 7 ♘c3 ♗e7 8 ♘g5 isn't so effective due to 8...d5 or to 8...h6 9 ♘h3 g5!? 10 f4 g4 11 ♘f2 ♖g8! when Black had avoided the routine ...0-0 in favour of active counterplay in J.Zeberski-K.Jakubowski, Polish Team Ch. 2004. Instead 7 ♘g5 h6 8 ♘h3 ♗e7 9 f4 c4! is a little awkward for White and so Benjamin has tried 7 c4!?, simply continuing with Ehlvest's plan even without Black having given away a kingside target with ...g6. This deserves further attention although Black can gain some counterplay, while 7...♗e7 8 ♘c3 0-0 9 ♘g5 h6 10 ♘h3 ♘e5 11 f4 ♘c6 12

♔h1 (J.Benjamin-J.Sarkar, New York [rapid] 2004) 12...d5! 13 e5 ♘e8 (Benjamin) reaches a fairly tense position. White would like to make some use of his h3-knight and to press ahead on the kingside, but an exchange on d5 doesn't fully convince. Thus he could try 14 f5!? when 14...♘xe5 15 ♗f4 ♘c6 16 fxe6 fxe6 17 ♕g4 ♖f6 18 ♖ae1 ♘d4 19 ♗e5! gives White reasonable attacking compensation for the pawn.

7...♗e7 8 ♘g5! h6

Practice has shown that Black is advised to find a way not to go short, but a number of players continue to underestimate the white set-up and 8...0-0 9 f4 ♘e8 10 ♘c3 ♘c7 11 ♗d2 ♗xg5 (Black doesn't have to take up the challenge, but otherwise his queenside play looks rather slow after Glek's 11...b5 12 ♖ae1 b4 13 ♘d1 ♘b5 14 c3!? bxc3 15 bxc3 ♖b8 16 ♕h5!, increasing the pressure against h7 and f7) 12 fxg5 (simply intending to double on the h-file; hence Black's next) 12...f6 13 gxf6 ♖xf6 14 ♗f4! e5 15 ♗g3 ♖xf1+ 16 ♖xf1 ♕e7 17 ♘d1!, followed by bringing the knight to f5, saw White retain a pretty useful edge in I.Glek-Y.Pelletier, European Ch., Silivri 2003.

9 ♘h3

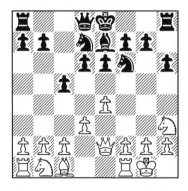

9...♕c7!?

Khalifman wants to whisk his king away to the queenside; a plan which isn't so bad, although Black has subsequently tried a number of alternatives:

a) 9...0-0 could be said to be castling into it, but after 10 f4 ♖e8! White must be aware that he needs pieces to attack with. Thus 11 ♘d2-f3 is sensible, whereas 11 g4!? ♗f8! 12 g5 hxg5 13 fxg5 ♘h7 14 g6 fxg6 15 ♕g2 ♗e7 16 ♘f4 ♗f6! 17 ♘xg6 ♘e5 18 ♘f4 ♕e7 saw the black minor pieces successfully defend the kingside in V.Bhat-J.Donaldson, San Francisco 2000.

b) Preventing f4-f5 with 9...e5?! is not, however, advisable as after 10 f4 exf4 11 ♘xf4 the very active king's knight is already back at the heart of the action and 11...0-0 12 ♘c3 ♘e5 13 ♘cd5 ♘eg4 14 c4 ♘xd5 15 ♘xd5 ♘f6 16 ♘e3! left White much better due to the weakness of f5 and the black kingside in I.Glek-J.Werle, Bussum 1999.

c) 9...g5!? is an intriguing idea we've met before when 10 f4!? or 10 c4 ♕c7 11 f4!? is critical, whereas 11 ♗e3 ♘e5 12 f3?! 0-0-0 13 ♘d2 ♘c6 14 ♖ac1 ♖dg8 15 ♔h1 ♖h7 16 ♘b3 e5! didn't lead anywhere for White in S.Videki-J.Palkovi, Austrian Team Ch. 2004.

10 f4 0-0-0 11 c4 ♘b8 12 ♗e3 ♘c6 13 ♘d2!

Once again the knight is better off away from c3, and by coming to f3 helps to challenge for control of the key d4-square. Morozevich now intends to press ahead with a3 and b4 and so Khalifman has to respond actively.

13...♘d7! 14 a3! f5 15 ♖ab1 ♘f6 16

♔h1!

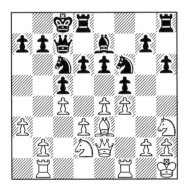

Remaining alert to Black's aims and enabling the bishop to retreat to safety on g1.

16...♘g4 17 ♗g1 ♗f6 18 b4 ♘d4 19 ♕d1

The position is fairly complex, but still slightly in White's favour due to his queenside prospects. Khalifman could now have tried 19...g5, but the white kingside is very solid while the h3-knight covers f4. Thus Black prefers to improve his pieces, relying upon the current strength of his knights; one of which at least must be challenged and is.

19...♕c6 20 ♘f3! g6 21 a4! ♖hg8 22 a5 ♔b8

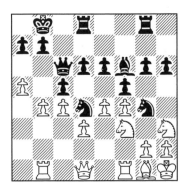

23 e5!

A strong blow which undermines the d4-knight and serves to open lines to assist Morozevich's queenside pressure.

23...dxe5 24 bxc5 ♘xf3?

Winning a pawn, but at too high a cost to the black queenside. However, finding a defence was not so easy with, for example, 24...exf4 25 ♘xf4 g5 26 ♘h5! ♗h8 27 h3! ♘xf3 28 ♕xf3 ♕xf3 29 gxf3 ♘e5 30 a6 ♖d7 31 d4! being another way for White to gain a dangerous initiative.

25 ♕xf3! ♕xf3 26 gxf3 ♖xd3 27 fxg4 ♖xh3 28 c6 ♖g7 29 fxe5! ♗d8

29...♗xe5 30 ♖fe1 ♗f4 31 ♖xe6 would have been rather strong, but pushing up to b6 doesn't save Khalifman for long.

30 a6 b6 31 c5 ♖a3 32 cxb6 axb6 33 ♗xb6 ♗xb6 34 ♖xb6+ ♔a7 35 ♖b7+! ♖xb7 36 axb7 ♔b8 37 ♖d1 1-0

Game 26
L.Fressinet-J.Polgar
Enghien les Bains 2003

1 e4 c5 2 ♘f3 d6 3 ♗b5+ ♗d7 4 ♗xd7+ ♘xd7 5 0-0 ♘gf6 6 ♕e2 e6 7 b3 ♗e7 8 ♗b2 0-0 9 c4 a6 10 d4 cxd4 11 ♘xd4

11...♖c8

Black hopes that the rook will prove useful here, with the pressure down the c-file assisting a successful ...b5 or ...d5 break. However, this doesn't have to be played immediately and Black can, and quite possibly should, prefer to first decide where to deploy his queen:

a) 11...♕b6!? again prevents 12 ♘c3 and,

just as in our previous game, is a little awkward for White to meet. Then 12 ♖d1 enables 13 ♘c3, but White wouldn't usually want the king's rook here, and 12...fe8 13 ♘c3 ♖ad8! (preparing to play in the centre, while White continues to sort out his position) 14 ♔h1 ♘e5! (a key Hedgehog strategy for Black is to tempt the white pawns forward; such a plan must be well calculated, but here Ftacnik has realised that an advance of the f-pawn doesn't really help White, but does create weaknesses) 15 f4?! ♘g6 16 f5 (or 16 ♘f3 e5!) 16...exf5 17 exf5 ♗f8 18 ♕f1 ♘e5 19 h3 d5! and Black had achieved his main break and was left with the better and more harmonious position in S.Movsesian-L.Ftacnik, Prague (blitz) 1999.

b) 11...♕c7 12 ♘c3 ♖fe8 also sees Black keep open the option of employing the queen's rook on c8 or d8 depending on how aggressively White plays.

Then 13 ♖ad1 ♗f8! (exploiting the white queen's being on e2 to threaten 14...d5, while 13...d5? doesn't yet quite work due to 14 cxd5 exd5 15 ♘f5! dxe4 16 ♘xe4! which is rather strong and neatly exploits the pressure down the long diagonal, as 16...♘xe4 17 ♖xd7! ♕xd7 18 ♕g4 wins the black queen) 14 f4!? ♖ad8 15 ♔h1 g6 reaches a tense position. This whole variation often hinges around whether White can achieve a successful e5-break as, due to the absence of light-squared bishops, playing on the queenside is rarely on

for c4 becomes too weak.

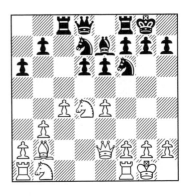

12 ♘c3 ♕c7 13 ♖ad1 ♖fe8 14 ♔h1 ♗f8 15 f4

Both sides have developed consistently with their overall approaches and we are now at a critical juncture with Black needing to find a way to deal with 16 ♘f3 and 17 e5.

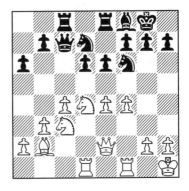

15...♕a5?!

The queen continues to cover e5 from here, but Fressinet is happy to sacrifice his e-pawn after which the queen is not too happy on a5. However, Black should here avoid the tempting break 15...e5?! due to 16 ♘f5! exf4 17 ♖xf4 when 17...♘e5 18 ♕d2 keeps up the pressure and favours White. Probably Black's best is simply not to panic with De Firmian's calm 15...h6!? (usefully preventing the f3-knight from leaping to g5) 16 ♘f3 ♖ed8!. Then 17 e5 dxe5 18 fxe5 ♘e8 (covering d6)

19 ♘e4 ♘c5! prepared exchanges and was fine for Black after 20 ♘g3 ♖xd1 21 ♖xd1 ♗d8 22 ♗d4 a5! in R.Fontaine-N.De Firmian, Stockholm 2004.

16 ♘f3 ♖ed8 17 e5! dxe5 18 fxe5 ♘g4 19 ♘g5! ♘dxe5!

Black must try to exchange rooks, while 19...♘gxe5? 20 ♕e4! would have been rather strong as after 20...g6 (or 20...f5 21 ♕h4 ♘f6 22 ♘xe6 ♖xd1 23 ♘xd1! and White is much better) there is the thematic sacrifice 21 ♘xf7! ♘xf7 22 ♕xe6 ♘de5 23 ♘d5! ♖c6 24 ♘e7+ ♗xe7 25 ♕xe7 (Psakhis) when White's colossal pressure ensures that he will regain the piece while maintaining a crushing position.

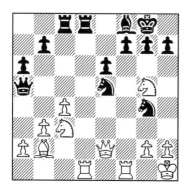

20 ♘d5

Continuing to play for the attack, although the simpler 20 ♘xf7!? ♖xd1 21 ♘xd1! ♘xf7 22 ♕xg4 ♖e8 23 a3 would have left White with a pretty pleasant advantage.

20...exd5?!

The exchanges don't help Black and so she should have tried to change the course of the struggle with 20...♕xa2!, intending 21 ♕c2 ♘g6 22 ♖a1 ♕xa1 23 ♗xa1 ♖xd5 with reasonable compensation for the queen.

21 ♗xe5 ♘xe5 22 ♕xe5 ♖c7

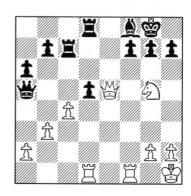

23 cxd5?!

Here Kaufman's 23 ♕f4! was much stronger when f7 falls and Black is close to being lost after 23...♗b4 24 ♖xd5 ♖xd5 25 cxd5 ♕b6 26 ♘xf7 due to the extra d-pawn and to the kingside threats. In the game Fressinet does force some kingside weaknesses, but Polgar defends strongly and in the end it's White who's left having to force the draw:

23...♖e7 24 ♕f5 g6 25 ♕h3 f5! 26 d6 ♖ed7 27 g4 f4! 28 ♘e6 ♖e8 29 g5! ♖xd6! 30 ♘xf8 ♖xd1 31 ♕xh7+ ♔xf8 32 ♕h8+ ♔f7 33 ♕f6+ ♔g8 34 ♕xg6+ ♔f8 35 ♕h6+ ♔g8 36 ♕g6+ ♔f8 37 ♖xd1 ♖e1+ 38 ♖xe1 ♕xe1+ 39 ♔g2 ♕e2+ 40 ♔h3 f3 41 ♕f5+ ♔e7 42 ♕f6+ ♔d7 43 ♕f7+ ♔d6 44 ♕f4+ ♔c6 45 ♕c4+ ♔b6 46 ♕d4+ ♔c6 ½-½

Summary

Those happy to play the Black side of the Hedgehog should give this slightly under-rated defence serious consideration. Black's eleventh move options in Fressinet-Polgar reveal that he shouldn't fear the main line when White selects a Hedgehog structure. Instead c3 and d4 isn't a promising plan, while the fashionable path for White involves d3 and ♘g5, and there's no reason to see why this won't continue to grow in popularity. However, it will be interesting to see how a 4...♘xd7 connoisseur like Novikov responds to such a direct approach and Black has gradually begun to fight back against it, such as by countering with the aggressive ...g5.

1 e4 c5 2 ♘f3 d6 3 ♗b5+ ♗d7 4 ♗xd7+ ♘xd7 *(D)*

5 0-0

      5 c4 – *Game 22*

5...♘gf6 6 ♕e2

      6 ♖e1 – *Game 23*

      6 d3 *(D)* – *Game 25*

6...e6 7 b3

      7 c3 – *Game 24*

7...♗e7 8 ♗b2 0-0 9 c4 a6 10 d4 cxd4 11 ♘xd4 *(D)* – *Game 26*

      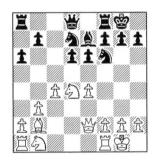

    4...♘d7   *6 d3*   *11 ♘xd4*

CHAPTER FOUR

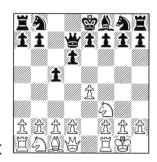

3...♗d7 4 ♗xd7+ ♕xd7: 5 0-0 and Quick Development

1 e4 c5 2 ♘f3 d6 3 ♗b5+ ♗d7 4 ♗xd7+ ♕xd7

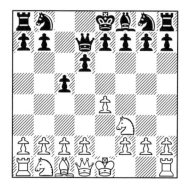

Recapturing with the queen is the most popular response to the Moscow, although Black does have to be prepared to play a number of structures after it; most notably French-type positions and Maróczy Bind ones. It has been Garry Kasparov's main choice in recent years, while it has also been heavily used by Najdorf expert Boris Gelfand and by leading Dragon exponents, Kiril Georgiev and Chris Ward. 5 c4 is the subject of our next chapter, while here we will solely focus on the older

5 0-0

which can be the prelude to some aggres-

sive play.
5...♘c6

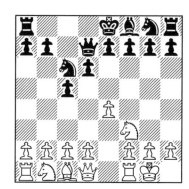

6 c3

Keeping White's options open, whereas 6 ♖e1 ♘f6 7 c3 is fine for Black due to the 7...e6 8 d4 cxd4 9 cxd4 d5! of Game 27. Instead 7 b3 (the subject of Game 28) is more challenging when Black can allow a Hedgehog position after 7...e6 or prefer 7...g6. If White wants a French structure then 6 ♕e2 ♘f6 7 c3 gives him more options than 6 ♖e1 and this has recently been employed by Rublevsky, as he did in Game 29.

7 ♖d1!? has recently received some attention and may well be set for more after it was advocated by Kaufman. The Introduction

revealed 7...♕g4 to be misguided here and instead Black usually responds with the natural 7...e6 (7...e5 8 c3 ♕g4!? also merits further attention) when 8 c3 d5 is fine for him. However, 8 d4!? reveals the main point behind 7 ♖d1 when 8...cxd4 9 ♘xd4 ♗e7 reaches a Hedgehog position. Here ...d5 is fairly easy to contain, but Black should be objectively fine so long as he doesn't rush to exchange knights when d6 can quickly be targeted, and 10 c4 0-0 11 ♘c3 should be compared with Game 33 of the next chapter.

6...♘f6 7 d4!?

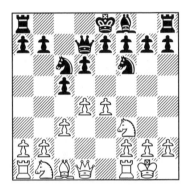

7...♘xe4

White's last brought about the Bronstein Gambit which has received an injection of new ideas in recent years, especially from Baklan and Glek. Indeed Black often now seeks to avoid the gambit altogether by preferring the move order 5...♘f6!?. After that White can stay in the realms of Games 27-29 by defending his e-pawn, or opt for the critical 6 e5!? as he does in Game 30.

With interest in 5 c4 starting to wane, this gambit continuation may well be set to gain more grandmaster adherents. Black doesn't have to accept the gambit, but he doesn't gain too easy a life by declining it here: 7...cxd4 8 cxd4 d5 9 e5 ♘e4 (Black has fared better in practice with 9...♘g8!?, although then 10 ♕e2! e6 11 ♖d1 transposes to the note to Black's tenth in Game 29) 10 ♘e1! h6 (10...f6

also enables the knight to retreat, but again isn't too appealing for Black and after 11 f3 ♘g5 12 ♗xg5! fxg5 13 f4! gxf4 14 ♘d3 e6 15 ♘xf4 0-0-0 16 ♘c3 practice has confirmed that White's space advantage and pressure against e6 grants him a fairly pleasant edge) 11 f3 ♘g5 12 ♗e3 e6 13 ♘c3 ♗e7 14 ♘d3! heads for f4 and then h5, or to c5 should Black go long or try 14...f5?! 15 exf6 ♗xf6.

8 d5 ♘e5

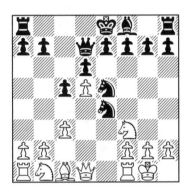

9 ♖e1

The modern way of playing the Bronstein Gambit, while Black's eighth move alternatives and the older 9 ♘xe5 dxe5 10 ♖e1 are discussed in Game 31. There we also examine what happens if Black meets 9 ♖e1 by critically hanging on to the pawn with 9...♘xf3+ 10 ♕xf3 ♘f6.

9...♘f6!?

Attempting to return the pawn like this has gained some attention of late, especially in Glek's games as we'll see in Game 32.

> ### Game 27
> ## O.De la Riva Aguado-S.Karjakin
> *Pamplona 2004*

1 e4 c5 2 ♘f3 d6 3 ♗b5+ ♗d7 4 ♗xd7+ ♕xd7 5 0-0 ♘f6 6 ♖e1 ♘c6 7 c3 e6

Just as in the 4...♘xd7 variation, heading for a French structure is the most reliable response for Black.

8 d4

White has also preferred to try and out-manoeuvre Black here with 8 d3; a plan which emphasises that the French positions arising after 8 d4 cxd4 9 cxd4 d5 aren't too problematic for Black. However, neither objectively is 8 d3 a problem for him and after 8...♗e7 9 ♘bd2 0-0 10 ♘f1 ♖fd8 11 ♘g3 ♘e5! Black prepares to exchange off a potential kingside attacker. White can keep his knight, but 12 ♘g5! c4! 13 d4 ♘d3 14 ♖e2 b5 15 ♘f3 b4 again gave Black good queenside play, and he certainly wasn't worse at this stage, in A.Morozevich-E.Najer, Russian Ch., Krasnoyarsk 2003.

8...cxd4 9 cxd4 d5

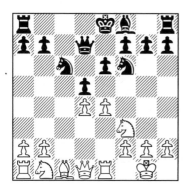

10 e5

There have been countless games with 6 ♖e1 and 7 c3 and White has tried just about every plan, but is yet to find any route to an advantage. He can also opt for an IQP position here with 10 exd5!? ♘xd5 11 ♘c3 or with 10 ♘c3 dxe4 11 ♘xe4, but Black is fairly comfortable in both cases and, after the latter, 11...♘xe4 12 ♖xe4 ♗e7 13 ♕e2 ♕d5! 14 ♗f4 0-0 15 a3 ♖ac8 16 ♖e1 ♖fd8 already left Black slightly for choice in H.Ahamed-K.Sundararajan, Udaipur 2000.

10...♘e4

If Black has some French experience or is desperate to keep more pieces on the board then 10...♘g8!? should be considered. However, after 11 a3 ♘ge7 12 ♘c3 Black should avoid 12...♘g6 13 h4! when White gains the advantage on the kingside, in return for 12...♗c8!?, intending ...♘b6, ...0-0-0, ...♔b8 and ...♘c8.

11 ♘bd2 ♘xd2 12 ♗xd2 ♗e7

This position should be compared with similar ones reached in the last chapter. Black's knight is already on c6 here, but his queen is less active. Thus Black should consider ...♕d7-d8-b6 or try to exploit her current position by playing for ...f6. White can again aim to press forwards on either flank, but objectively Black is fine and this whole line is just rather dull. Indeed the best equaliser might actually be 12...♗b4!? when 13 ♖c1 ♗xd2 14 ♕xd2 0-0 15 ♖c2 ♖fc8 16 ♖ec1 h6!, intending 17...♘e7 and exchanges down the c-file, was completely equal in N.Jakupovic-O.Cvitan, Sarajevo 1998.

13 ♖c1 0-0

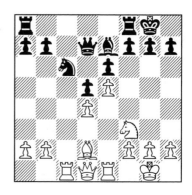

14 ♖c3

Preparing to swing over to the kingside, although Karjakin is never too troubled there. However, neither has 14 ♗g5 led to any advantage, while 14 a3?! ♖fc8 15 ♖c3 ♕d8 16 ♖d3 b5! notably took advantage of the newly created white queenside weakness to give Black the edge in R.Jenetl-S.Nadyrhanov, Krasnodar 2000.

14...♖ac8 15 a3 a6 16 ♖d3!?

Keeping pieces on while the b4-square is

now covered, but Black can instead prepare to exploit the weakness of c4 and to gain some pressure down the b-file.

16...♛d8! 17 h4 ♘a5 18 ♘g5

18 h5 would have been met by 18...h6! when White cannot easily increase the kingside pressure, whereas the game now ends in an attractive perpetual as Karjakin has no wish to be mated down an open h-file.

18...h6 19 ♘h3 ♚h7 20 ♘g5+! ♚g8! 21 ♘h3 ♚h7 22 ♘g5+ ½-½

Game 28
M.Adams-V.Anand
Dortmund 2001

---

1 e4 c5 2 ♘f3 d6 3 ♗b5+ ♗d7 4 ♗xd7+ ♛xd7 5 0-0 ♘c6 6 b3 ♘f6 7 ♖e1

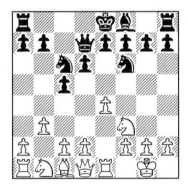

7...g6!?

Contesting the diagonal, although Black also has 7...e6 when play doesn't have to lead to a Hedgehog. Indeed Black appears to be able to equalise with 8 ♗b2 (or 8 c4 e5!? 9 d3 g6 10 ♘c3 ♗g7 11 a3 0-0 12 ♖b1 ♘h5! with good kingside counterplay in S.Johannessen-K.Lie, Asker 2000; having the knight on c6 makes ...e5 more effective than it is after 4...♘xd7) 8...♗e7 9 d4 cxd4 10 ♘xd4 d5!, while 9 c4 can again be met by 9...e5. Instead 9...0-0 10 d4 cxd4 11 ♘xd4 reaches a Hedgehog position in which Black is a little less flexible than were his queen on d8 and c6-

knight on d7. Even here breaking with ...d5 isn't easy to achieve and 11...♖fd8 12 ♘c3 a6 13 a4! clamps down on both breaks and prepares to meet 13...d5 with 14 cxd5 exd5 15 e5, while 13...♘e8 14 ♘c2! ♘c7 15 ♘e3 ♗f6 16 ♛h5 ♗d4 17 ♖ad1 ♖ac8 18 ♖d2 left Black a little cramped and White building up some pressure down the d-file in M.Adams-B.Lalic, Southend 2000.

8 c3!

Wisely switching plans with Black committed to a fianchetto, whereas 8 ♗b2 ♗g7 9 c4 e5! gives Black fairly easy play and a clear plan. Then 10 a3 0-0 11 d3 ♘e8 12 ♘c3 should probably just be met by 12...f5!?, as Black can always later challenge d5, rather than by an attempt to fight on the queenside with 12...♘c7 (supporting ...b5 and possibly heading for e6) 13 ♖b1 ♖fb8 as in E.Rozentalis-K.Landa, Chalkidiki 2002.

8...♗g7 9 d4 cxd4 10 cxd4 d5! 11 e5 ♘e4

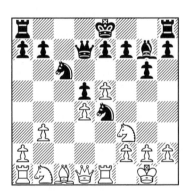

12 ♗b2

White can also challenge with 12 ♘bd2 when Karjakin has been happy to continue solidly with 12...♘xd2 13 ♗xd2 0-0, intending 14...♖fc8 and 15...♘d8, although Black can also be more ambitious with 12...♘c3!? when 13 ♛c2 ♘b5 14 ♛c5! ♘c7! (heading for the key e6-square from where the knight covers a number of important squares) 15 ♘f1 0-0 was P.Leko-G.Kasparov, Dortmund 2000. After

16 ♕c3 the position was roughly level, but also rather unbalanced after 16...f6!? 17 ♗b2 ♘e6 18 ♖ad1 ♖ac8 19 ♕d2 f5 20 h3 h6.

12...0-0 13 ♘bd2

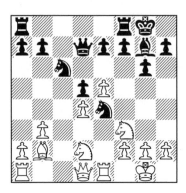

13...♘xd2

Black must be fairly patient in this line, while his bishop can always be improved via f8 or h6. Instead 13...f5?! is a fairly common mistake and is too ambitious due to 14 exf6 ♘xd2 15 ♘e5! when 15...♘xe5 16 dxe5 exf6 17 e6! ♕d6 18 ♕xd2 ♖fe8 19 ♕e3 left Black under pressure from the e6-pawn in L.Christiansen-Cu.Hansen, Reykjavik 1998.

14 ♕xd2

Yudasin had previously assessed this as favouring White, but Adams is never able to make any real progress on the kingside, while Anand gains sufficient queenside play and eventually activates his bishop.

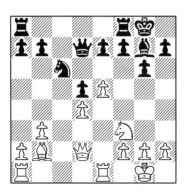

14...♖fc8 15 h3 ♘d8! 16 ♖ac1 ♘e6 17 ♗a3 ♗f8 18 ♘h2 ♖xc1 19 ♖xc1

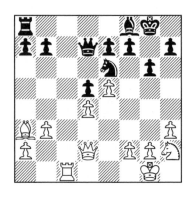

19...a5!

Taking some space and preparing to open the a-file, although 19...♖c8 20 ♖xc8 ♕xc8 21 ♘g4 ♕c6 22 ♘e3 b6 23 ♕d1 f5! previously hadn't really given White anything in M.Adams-L.Ftacnik, Bundesliga 1999.

20 ♘f1 a4 21 ♗b4 axb3 22 axb3 h5 23 ♕d3 ♗h6! ½-½

Game 29
S.Rublevsky-D.Sadvakasov
Poikovsky 2005

---

1 e4 c5 2 ♘f3 d6 3 ♗b5+ ♗d7 4 ♗xd7+ ♕xd7 5 0-0 ♘c6

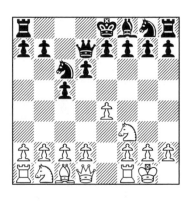

6 c3

If Black had to continue with 7...e6 then

White would be more flexibly placed following up 6 b3 ♘f6 with 7 ♕e2 than with 7 ♖e1, but after 7...g6! 8 ♗b2 ♗g7 Black is fine and the white queen is actually a little misplaced. Black can capitalise on its position with a timely ...♘h5 and 9 d4?! ♕g4! 10 ♖e1 (but not 10 dxc5?? ♘h5! when the huge threat of 11...♘f4 wins the b2-bishop, while 10 e5?! ♘d5 leaves the white centre under pressure) 10...cxd4 11 h3 ♕h5 12 ♘xd4 ♕xe2 13 ♖xe2 ♘d5! saw him gain a small but useful initiative in Ye Jiangchuan-S.Atalik, Beijing 1997.

6...♘f6 7 ♕e2

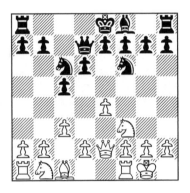

7...e6

Now we reach a more complex French position than those arising after 7 ♖e1, while recently Black has begun experimenting here with 7...♕g4!?. The idea is to force favourable exchanges after 8 ♖e1 with 8...♘e5! and so critical is 8 d3 ♘e5 9 ♘bd2 ♘h5! 10 d4! ♘f4 11 ♕b5+, but so far White hasn't been able to prove any advantage here. Then 11...♔d8!? (radical, but 11...♘c6 12 ♘e1 0-0-0 13 ♘b3! gives White some queenside pressure) 12 ♘e1!? (those of a nervous disposition might prefer to force an immediate draw with 12 g3 ♘h3+ 13 ♔g2 ♘f4+ 14 ♔g1) 12...♘ed3 13 f3 ♕g5 14 ♘b3! ♘xe1 15 g3 turned out well for White in S.Rublevsky-A.Volokitin, Russian Team Ch. 2004. However, Black can improve with 14...♘e2+! 15 ♔h1 ♘dxc1 (threatening 16...♘g3+ and perpetual) 16 ♘xc1! ♘g3+! 17

hxg3 ♕h6+ 18 ♔g1 ♕e3+ 19 ♖f2!? ♕xe1+ 20 ♕f1 ♕xf1+ 21 ♖xf1 cxd4 22 cxd4 e6 (Golubev) which should be fine for him as, despite White's space advantage, he is very solid.

8 d4 cxd4 9 cxd4 d5!

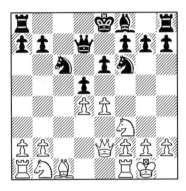

10 e5 ♘e4

One advantage of White's set-up is that he can now meet 10...♘g8!? with 11 ♖d1! and then, as we saw in the Introduction, the accurate 11...♘ge7 12 ♘c3 ♘c8 13 ♗e3 ♘b6 14 b3 ♖c8 15 ♕b2 ♗e7 16 ♘e2! gave White the advantage in R.Kasimdzhanov-V.Topalov, Tripoli 2004.

11 ♗e3!

Just as had Black recaptured on d7 with the knight, this is the most critical as White covers d4 in preparation for ♘e1.

11...♗e7 12 ♘e1

White can also begin with 12 ♖d1 so that after 12...0-0 13 ♘e1 he has the option of later returning the knight to f3, without first blocking in the f1-rook. Then 13...f6 (or 13...f5 14 f3 ♘g5 15 ♘d3 ♘f7 16 ♘c3 and now Black should have continued with 16...♖ac8, whereas 16...g5?! 17 g3 ♘h8 18 f4 g4 19 ♘c5 halted Black on the kingside and gave White a pull in J.Gallagher-R.Loetscher, Swiss Team Ch. 2004) 14 f3 ♘g5 15 ♘c3 ♘f7! 16 f4 ♖ac8 17 ♗f2 ♘h6 18 ♖d3 fxe5 19 fxe5 ♘f5 saw Black make excellent use of his king's knight to gain a pretty reasonable position in D.Barua-M.Sadler, Hastings 1993/4.

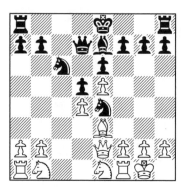

12...f6!?

As we witnessed in the Introduction, Black doesn't have to play so dynamically and 12...f5 13 f3 ♘g5 14 ♘d3 0-0 15 ♘c3 ♖ac8 (15...♘f7 16 ♔h1?! ♖ac8 17 ♖g1 ♘h8! was the course of Souleidis-Naiditsch) 16 h3 ♘f7 17 g4 ♘h8! was very solid for Black in S.Rublevsky-S.Karjakin, Moscow 2004.

13 f3 ♘g5 14 ♘d3 0-0

Black can also begin with 14...♘f7 when 15 ♗f2 ♘f7 transposes to our main game, whereas 15 exf6?! ♗xf6 leaves d4 more vulnerable than e6 and then 16 ♘c5 ♕e7 17 ♕d2?! ♘d6 18 ♘a3 ♘f5 19 ♘b3 ♕b4! was excellent for Black in J.Cooper-R.Palliser, Yorkshire League 2005.

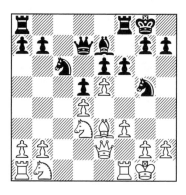

15 ♗f2!?

Covering e5, while Rublevsky's new twist

in this line is that he doesn't mind a pawn exchange on e5 and so he won't rush to meet ...♘f7 with f4.

15...b6

Rublevsky had previously faced an immediate 15...♘f7 when 16 ♖d1 f5!? 17 h4 ♖ac8 18 ♘c3 b6 19 ♘f4 saw him make good use of the f4-square in S.Rublevsky-A.Motylev, Bastia (rapid) 2004, although after 19...♘h8! 20 ♖ac1 ♘g6 21 ♘xg6 hxg6 22 f4 ♔f7! 23 g3 ♘a5 Black didn't have any problems and so ...f5 may well be the way to go, especially if exchanging on e5 turns out not to be too promising after 15 ♗f2!?.

16 ♘c3 ♘f7 17 ♖ac1 ♖ac8

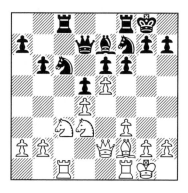

Sadvakasov's problem is that it's not so easy for him to press ahead on the queenside without f4 having been played. After that his knight would cover the kingside, whilst his other pieces ensure sufficient play on the other wing. As Black must now gain some counterplay, he feels it's necessary to exchange on e5, but Rublevsky maintains a small pull after this.

18 ♖fd1 fxe5 19 dxe5 ♘h6 20 ♕d2 ♘a5! 21 ♘e2! ♘f5 22 ♖xc8 ♖xc8 23 ♖c1 ♖xc1+ 24 ♕xc1 ♗f8?!

This leaves Black very solid and does give the knight a retreat-square, but it is a little passive. Still White's control of d4 and mobile kingside pawn mass gave him slightly the more pleasant position in any case, and

Rublevsky now instructively put those advantages to good use:

25 b3! ♞c6 26 ♛c3 ♞a5 27 h4! g6 28 g4 ♞e7 29 ♛d2 h6 30 ♗e3 ♚h7 31 h5! gxh5 32 ♞ef4 hxg4 33 ♞h5 ♛c7 34 fxg4 ♞ac6 35 ♞f6+ ♚g6 36 ♞e8 ♛b8 37 ♛h2! ♚f7 38 ♞d6+ ♚g8 39 ♛h5 ♗g7 40 ♛f7+ ♚h8 41 ♞e8 ♗xe5 42 ♗xh6 1-0

Game 30
V.Nevednichy-I.Nikolaidis
European Ch., Silivri 2003

---

1 e4 c5 2 ♞f3 d6 3 ♗b5+ ♗d7 4 ♗xd7+ ♛xd7 5 0-0 ♞f6!? 6 e5!? dxe5 7 ♞xe5

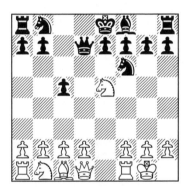

7...♛c8

The safest square for the queen from where she cannot be hit by ♞c4 (unlike 7...♛d6) nor by ♗f4 (as 7...♛c7 can), although this is a little passive. However, 7...♛c7!? is also quite playable when 8 d4 (the only try for the advantage as, for example, 8 ♞c4 ♞c6 9 ♞c3 e6 10 d3 ♗e7 11 a4 0-0 12 ♗d2 ♖ad8 13 ♖e1 ♞d5! was fine for Black in V.Nevednichy-C.Balogh, Miskolc 2004) 8...cxd4 reaches a critical and fairly sharp position. Then 9 ♗f4 (9 ♛xd4!? has scored well, although usually because Black has often eschewed the sensible 9...♞c6! 10 ♞xc6 ♛xc6 and then the dynamic 11 ♗g5 ♞e4 12 ♗h4 ♖d8! 13 ♛xa7 g5! 14 ♗g3 ♗g7 with good counterplay and compensation in

A.Vydeslaver-V.Karpman, Israeli Team Ch. 2002) 9...♛b6 10 ♞d2 gives White some initiative for the pawn, although after 10...♞c6! 11 ♞dc4 ♛c5 12 ♛f3 e6 13 ♖ad1 ♖d8! 14 ♖fe1 ♗e7 15 ♛b3, rather than 15...♛b4 16 ♞xc6 bxc6 17 ♞e5 ♖c8 when 18 ♛g3! turned out well for White in A.Volokitin-V.Ivanchuk, Warsaw (rapid) 2002, Volokitin's notes suggest that the active and precise 15...b5! 16 ♞xc6 ♛xc6 17 ♞e5 ♛b6 18 a4 ♖d5! would have left White struggling a little.

Black can also keep his queen centralised with 7...♛d6 as Rogozenko has advocated.

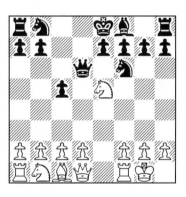

However, White has been doing fairly well of late with 8 ♛e2! (8 d4 appears sharper, but after 8...♛xd4 9 ♛e2 Rogozenko's still untested 9...♛e4! 10 ♛b5+ ♞bd7 11 ♞xd7 ♞xd7 12 ♞c3 ♛b4! appears to leave White struggling for compensation, while after 8 ♞c4 all three queen retreats are quite playable, but simplest appears to be 8...♛d8!? which allowed Black to fully equalise with 9 ♞c3 e6 10 d3 ♗e7 11 ♗f4 ♞c6 12 ♛d2 0-0 13 ♖ae1 ♞d5! in A.Alavkin-S.Ionov, Samara 2000) 8...♞bd7 (and not 8...♞c6? 9 ♛b5!) 9 ♞c4 ♛c6 10 ♞c3 when f4 is on the cards. After 10...e6 11 f4!? g6 (the dynamic 11...♗e7!? 12 f5 0-0 13 fxe6 fxe6 14 ♖e1 b5! might well be better as 15 ♞a5 ♛c7 16 ♛xe6+ ♚h8 17 ♛c6 ♗d6! gives Black plenty of compensation for the pawn, while 15 ♛xe6+ ♛xe6 16 ♖xe6 ♚f7 17 ♖xe7+ ♚xe7 18 ♞xb5 ♞b6 19 ♞e3

♔d7 20 d3 ♖ae8 wasn't a fully convincing exchange sacrifice from White in C.Bauer-R.Kempinski, Bad Zwesten 2004) 12 f5! gxf5 13 ♖xf5 ♖g8 14 ♖f3 ♗e7 15 a4! Black was very solid, but the strong c4-knight and pressure down the f-file left White slightly for choice in A.Volokitin-L.Dominguez, Esbjerg 2002.

Returning to the marginally most popular move, 7...♕c8:

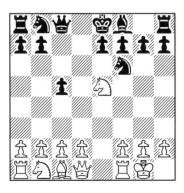

8 ♕f3!

Preventing ...♘c6, and again making active use of the white queen is the most challenging idea. Instead 8 d4 e6! 9 ♘c3 ♘c6 appears to be fine for Black and after 10 ♗e3 ♗e7 11 ♘xc6 ♕xc6 12 dxc5 ♗xc5 13 ♗xc5 ♕xc5 14 ♕f3 ♕b6 15 b3 0-0 16 ♘e4 ♘xe4 a draw was agreed in M.Adams-D.King, Southend 2000.

8...♘bd7

Trying to unravel through exchanges and this is more accurate than 8...e6 9 d3! ♘bd7 10 ♘c4 ♘b6 11 ♗f4! ♘fd5 (or 11...♘xc4 12 dxc4 ♗e7 13 ♘c3 0-0 14 ♖ad1 with a useful grip on the position) 12 ♗e5 when White was better in E.Sutovsky-S.Karjakin, Pamplona 2003. However, fianchettoing is quite playable and 8...g6!? 9 ♖e1 ♗g7 10 d3 0-0 11 ♘c3 ♘a6! (heading for b4, whereas Psakhis' 11...e6 12 ♗g5 ♘fd7 wouldn't have solved Black's problems as his kingside is vulnerable after 13 ♘g4!) 12 ♘c4 ♘b4 13 ♖xe7!? ♘xc2 14 ♖b1 ♖e8 15 ♖xe8+ was seen in E.Sutovsky-

A.Romero Holmes, Pamplona 2003 when 15...♕xe8?! 16 ♗g5 favoured White, but it's hard to believe that Black should be in too much trouble after 15...♘xe8! due to his control of d4.

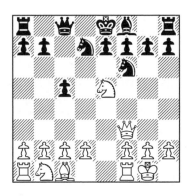

9 ♘c4 e6 10 ♘c3

Now 10 d3 can be met by 10...b5!, although White can still focus his attention on the vulnerable d6-square.

10...♗e7 11 d3

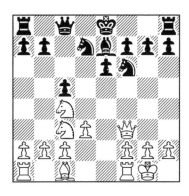

11...0-0

Black should probably be less compliant with 11...♘b6!? when 12 ♗f4!? ♘bd5 13 ♗g3 deserves attention, whereas 12 ♘a5 ♘bd5! 13 ♘xd5 ♘xd5 14 c4 ♘b4 15 ♕xb7 ♕xb7 16 ♘xb7 a5!? wasn't clear in J.Degraeve-A.Naiditsch, Belgian Team Ch. 2003, while Black would also have been fine after simply 16...♘xd3.

12 ♗f4 ♘b6 13 ♘d6 ♗xd6?!

Surprisingly Topalov has also ceded the bishop-pair like this, but 13...♛d7! looks like a clear improvement as the b-pawn is immune due to 14 ♛xb7? ♘h5! and 14 ♘xb7? a5, while 14 ♘de4 ♘bd5 also seems to be fine for Black after 15 ♗e5 ♘xc3 16 ♗xc3 ♘d5.

14 ♗xd6 ♖e8 15 ♖fe1 ♘bd5 16 ♘e4! ♘xe4 17 dxe4 ♘b4 18 ♖e2!

Preparing to double on the d-file and, having dominated that file, Nevednichy now exploited his dark-square advantage to thematically lever open the black kingside:

18...♛c6 19 ♛g3 f6 20 c3 ♘a6 21 e5! f5 22 ♖d1 ♖ad8 23 ♖ed2 ♖d7 24 h4! ♖ed8 25 h5 ♘c7 26 h6 g6 27 ♛g5 ♘e8? 28 ♗xc5! 1-0

Game 31
R.Pfretzschner-J.Forsberg
correspondence 1992

---

1 e4 c5 2 ♘f3 d6 3 ♗b5+ ♗d7 4 ♗xd7+ ♛xd7 5 0-0 ♘c6 6 c3 ♘f6 7 d4 ♘xe4 8 d5

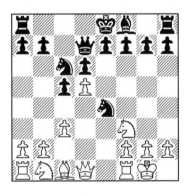

8...♘e5

The most active and popular move; the alternatives give White a fair amount of pressure, although they may appeal to ardent materialists:

a) 8...♘d8 9 ♖e1 ♘f6 10 ♗g5 ♘g8!? was slightly dismissed by Kaufman, but has been used by Sakaev and Georgiev and is quite logical as Black avoids permanent damage to his position, unlike after 10...e6 11 ♗xf6 gxf6 12 ♘h4!. After 10...♘g8!?, 11 b4!? h6 12 ♗e3! cxb4 13 ♗d4!? ♘f6 14 ♗xf6 gxf6 15 cxb4 ♗g7 16 ♘bd2 gave White good and long lasting compensation, especially due to the weakness of f5, in I.Glek-S.Klimov, Russian Ch., Krasnoyarsk 2003.

b) 8...♘b8 9 ♖e1 ♘f6 10 ♗g5 also gives White good pressure down the e-file, although Black is fairly solid. Then 10...♘a6 11 c4 0-0-0!? 12 ♘c3 ♚b8 13 a3 ♖c8 14 ♛e2 h6 was the critical course of D.Bronstein-L.Masic, Tbilisi 1969. Polugaevsky now recommended 15 ♗xf6! gxf6 16 b4!? and this certainly appears to give White good queen-side pressure, especially if Black grabs, such as with 16...cxb4 17 axb4 ♛g4 18 c5! ♖g8 19 g3 ♘xb4 when 20 c6! is excellent for White who threatens 21 ♖eb1 and 22 ♖a4.

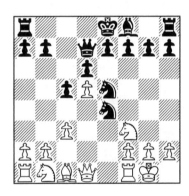

9 ♖e1!

The modern handling of the position and this has generally superseded the older 9 ♘xe5 dxe5 10 ♖e1 when 10...♘f6 transposes to our next illustrative game, but 10...♘d6! 11 ♖xe5 g6 has been considered more problematic for White. After 12 ♖e1 ♗g7 13 ♗g5! Black can't immediately castle, while 13...♘f5 (and not 13...f6?! 14 ♗f4 0-0 15 ♘d2 ♘f5 16 c4! ♖ad8 17 ♘b3 b6 18 ♛e2 when e6 had been badly weakened in M.Lazic-S.Estremera

Panos, Genova 2004) 14 ♘a3 should probably just be met by 14...♖d8, intending to go short when the position is roughly level and 15 d6 ♕xd6 16 ♕a4+ ♕c6 isn't problematic for Black.

9...♘xf3+

Keeping the pawn, while we will deal with Black's attempt to return it with 9...♘f6!? next in Glek-Stefansson.

10 ♕xf3 ♘f6

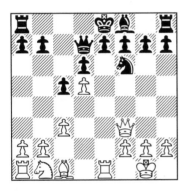

11 ♘a3!?

Heading for c4 to put pressure on d6 should Black break with ...e6 or ...e5, although White more usually increases his clamp and space advantage with 11 c4.

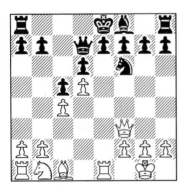

Then 11...e5 (Black should try this as 11...0-0-0 doesn't solve his problems when White can launch an attack with 12 b4!? or prepare that with 12 ♘c3 g6 13 ♖b1 when

13...♕f5 14 ♕xf5+! gxf5 15 ♗g5 didn't see the queen exchange helping Black at all in J.Gallagher-V.Gashimov, Calvia Olympiad 2004) 12 dxe6 fxe6 13 ♗g5 ♗e7 14 ♘c3 reaches a critical position in which Black is under some pressure.

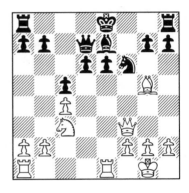

White has recently been scoring well after 14...0-0 (14...h6!? has been considered more accurate, intending to cover e6 after 15 ♕h3 with 15...♔f7, while 15 ♗xf6 0-0! 16 ♕h3 ♗xf6 17 ♕xe6 ♕xe6 18 ♖xe6 ♖ae8 is also fine for Black; 15 ♗h4 0-0 16 ♕h3 g5! was suggested by Adams when 17 ♗g3 e5! 18 ♕xh6 ♕f5 threatens ...♖f7-h7 and Black had no problems at all in J.Degraeve-J.Balcerak, 2nd Bundesliga 2002, but White can try 17 ♕xe6+!? ♕xe6 18 ♖xe6 ♔f7 19 ♖ae1 ♖fe8 20 ♗g3, albeit only transposing to the next note) 15 ♕h3 h6 16 ♕xe6+! ♕xe6 17 ♖xe6 ♔f7 18 ♖ae1 as exchanging all the rooks doesn't lead to too a simple draw for Black. Then 18...♖fe8 19 ♗h4 ♗f8?! (19...g5! is a clear improvement as White mustn't be allowed to gain too much kingside space and 20 ♗g3 ♗f8 21 ♖xe8 ♖xe8 22 ♖xe8 ♘xe8 should be defensible, although the weakness of d6 and d5 offers White a tiny edge) 20 ♖xe8 ♖xe8 21 ♖xe8 ♘xe8 22 f4! ♗e7?! 23 ♗xe7 ♔xe7 24 ♔f2 h5 25 ♔f3 ♔e6 26 h3 g6 27 g4 hxg4+ 28 ♔xg4! saw White gain a clearly better ending in V.Baklan-A.Vouldis, European Team Ch., Plovdiv 2003.

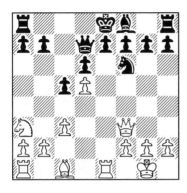

11...0-0-0

Now Black struggles a little for counterplay and White can mount a queenside attack. Thus 11...e6 12 dxe6 fxe6 13 ♗g5 ♗e7 has usually been preferred when 14 ♖ad1 gives White some compensation and pressure, but not enough for an advantage, although Glek has generally preferred this over 11 c4. After 14...0-0-0 15 ♘c4 ♖hf8 16 ♛e3 ♘d5!? 17 ♛xe6 ♛xe6 18 ♖xe6 ♘xc3! 19 ♗xe7 ♘xd1 20 ♗xd8 ♖xd8 21 ♖e2 the black knight was trapped in I.Glek-E.Najer, Russian Team Ch. However, Black will acquire some very mobile queenside pawns for it and it appears that he has at least sufficient compensation in this fascinating ending after 21...d5 22 ♘a3 c4 23 ♖d2 ♘xb2 24 ♖xb2 a6! 25 ♖d2 ♔c7 26 f4 b5.

12 ♗g5! h6

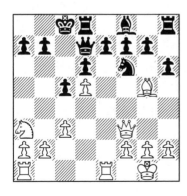

13 ♗xf6 gxf6

Now Black struggles to do anything and he later improved with 13...exf6! when 14 b4 f5 15 ♖ab1 g6 16 ♘c4 ♗g7 activates the bishop, although White retains some pressure after 17 bxc5 dxc5 18 ♖ed1!. However, Black then defended well with 18...♛a4! 19 ♛d3 ♖he8 20 ♖b5 ♗xc3! in R.Pfretzschner-D.Baramidze, German Ch., Heringsdorf 2000 when 21 ♖xc5+ ♔b8 22 ♘e3 ♗e5 23 ♛b1 b6 24 ♖c4 retained compensation but no more.

14 b4! cxb4

14...♖g8 15 ♛e3! ♛g4 16 g3 would have sidestepped any potential kingside counterplay, but now the queenside opens as Pfretzschner has played for.

15 ♘c2! bxc3 16 ♘d4

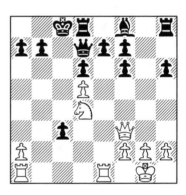

16...♛c7

16...♔b8? 17 ♘c6+! bxc6 18 dxc6 ♛c7 19 ♖ab1+ ♔a8 20 ♖b7 ♛a5 21 c7 would have been rather strong, but Black cannot beat off the attack for long with just his queen in the defence.

17 ♖ac1 ♛a5 18 ♖xc3+ ♔b8 19 ♖b1 ♔a8 20 ♖a3 ♛c5 21 ♘b5 ♛c2 22 ♖xa7+ ♔b8 23 ♖a8+! 1-0

Game 32
I.Glek-H.Stefansson
North Sea Cup, Esbjerg 2002

1 e4 c5 2 ♘f3 d6 3 ♗b5+ ♗d7 4 ♗xd7+

♕xd7 5 0-0 ♘c6 6 c3 ♘f6 7 d4 ♘xe4 8 d5 ♘e5 9 ♖e1 ♘f6!?

A fairly popular idea; Black aims to avoid coming under pressure, unlike when he hangs on to the extra pawn, while he hopes that while White regains the pawn on e5 he has time to develop his kingside after ...e6.

10 ♘xe5 dxe5

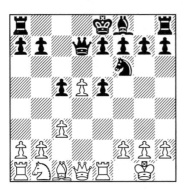

11 c4!?

Glek's preference and with this White decides that he doesn't need to immediately regain the pawn, although 11 ♖xe5 has also had a number of recent outings. Then 11...e6 12 c4 0-0-0 13 ♘c3 ♗d6 14 ♖e1 exd5 reaches a critical position. White has recently been preferring 15 ♘xd5!? ♕f5 (15...♘xd5 16 cxd5! ♖he8 17 ♖xe8 ♖xe8 18 ♗e3 ♖e5 19 ♖c1! ♔b8 20 g3 maintained the d-pawn and kept a small edge for White in S.Nadyrhanov-R.Bigaliev, Moscow 1995) 16 ♗e3, although here Black is fairly active and appears to be able to hold the balance with 16...♖he8! 17 h3 (instead 17 b4? has been recommended by some annotators, but then 17...♘g4! is rather embarrassing when 18 h3 ♘xe3 19 ♖xe3 ♖xe3 20 fxe3 ♕e5 is rather good for Black, while 18 g3? ♖xe3! forced immediate resignation in P.Zarnicki-A.Ramirez, Buenos Aires 2003) 17...♘xd5 18 cxd5 ♔b8!. This position isn't clear and Bronstein Gambit adherents may well like its unbalanced nature, although d5 is rather vulnerable and White should be

careful how he continues on the queenside as 19 b4 ♗c7! 20 ♕a4 ♕xd5 21 ♖ac1 ♕d7 fully equalised in P.Hokkanen-A.Shneider, Halkidiki 2002.

11...e6

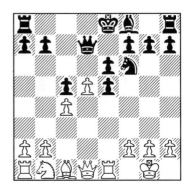

12 ♘c3

Glek soon gains a favourable position and indeed 12 ♘c3 appears promising, but, perhaps dissatisfied by 12 ♘c3 0-0-0, he later turned to 12 dxe6!? and it will be interested to see if he repeats this as 12...fxe6! (maintaining good central control) 13 ♕e2 0-0-0 14 ♘c3 ♕d3 15 ♕xd3 ♖xd3 16 ♖xe5 ♔d7 17 h3 ♗d6 18 ♖e2 ♖e8 19 ♔f1 ♔c6! didn't give White anything in I.Glek-G.Jones, Porto San Giorgo 2003.

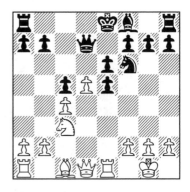

12...♗e7?!

The bishop is rather passive here, while Stefansson soon experiences some tactical problems down the e-file. Thus Black should prefer 12...0-0-0 when 13 ♖xe5 ♗d6 transposes to 11 ♖xe5, but White can and should prefer 13 ♗g5! when 13...h6 14 ♗h4 ♗e7 15 ♖xe5 ♗d6! (15...♘xd5 16 cxd5 ♗xh4 17 ♕g4 ♗f6 18 dxe6 fxe6 19 ♖xc5+ gives White a small, but clear edge due to the weakness of e6 as Kaufman points out) 16 ♖e1 g5!? was seen in I.Glek-E.Leriche, French Team Ch. 2003 and now 17 ♗g3 ♗xg3 18 hxg3 exd5 19 ♕f3 didn't cause Black, who could even consider 19...d4!?, any real problems. Thus Kaufman has suggested 17 ♕f3! when 17...♘xd5 18 cxd5 gxh4 19 dxe6 fxe6 20 ♖ad1 appears to favour White. Black enjoys some open lines, but his ruined structure, which ♕h3 will help to target, appears to be the most important feature of the position.

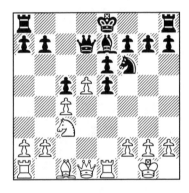

13 ♖xe5 exd5 14 ♗g5 d4

Now White regains his pawn with a large advantage and so perhaps Black should just

have accepted losing a tempo with 13...♗d6!? on his last turn. However, by this point the d-file had to be closed as both 14...dxc4? 15 ♕xd7+ ♔xd7 16 ♖d1+ and 14...0-0? 15 ♘xd5 ♘xd5 16 ♖xe7! would have dropped a piece.

15 ♘e4!

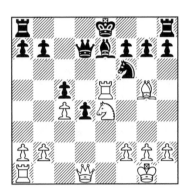

15...0-0-0

Now the white knight reaches the ideal d3-square after which Glek can increase the pressure at his leisure on the queenside and down the e-file, but 15...0-0 16 ♗xf6 gxf6 17 ♘xc5 ♕c6 18 ♖xe7 ♕xc5 19 ♖xb7 would also have left White with a large advantage.

16 ♘xc5 ♕c7 17 ♘d3 ♔b8 18 c5 ♗a8 19 ♕f3 ♖d7 20 ♖ae1 ♗d8 21 ♘b4!

Preparing to open the queenside and, faced with a well coordinated white army, Stefansson was unable to resist for long:

21...♕c8 22 c6 bxc6 23 ♘xc6 ♕b7 24 a4 d3 25 ♗d2 ♖d6 26 ♖c1 a6 27 b4! ♘d7 28 ♖f5 f6 29 b5 1-0

Summary

It's not hard to see why 4...♕xd7 remains Black's main defence to 3 ♗b5+ as he's very solid after it and it's not so easy for White to pose him problems. Despite some recent interest from Rublevsky, 6 ♕e2 ♘f6 7 c3 should be fine for Black after 7...e6 8 d4 cxd4 9 cxd4 d5, although the sharp 7...♕g4!? will probably gain further attention. Those seeking to avoid the Bronstein Gambit as White should explore 6 ♖e1 ♘f6 7 b3, although 7...g6 is currently holding up well for Black. The b3-option can also be used against 5...♘f6, whereas after that fashionable move all three options for the black queen remain viable against the sharp 6 e5!?.

The Bronstein Gambit has been enjoying a renaissance of late, with Black unable to gain a good position by declining it. After 9 ♖e1 ♘f6, Glek's 10 ♘xe5 dxe5 11 c4!? currently appears promising and so Black should prefer 9...♘xf3+ 10 ♕xf3 ♘f6. Then 11 ♘a3!? deserves further exploration, while Black should be able to hold the draw with a little accuracy after 11 c4 despite Baklan's best efforts.

1 e4 c5 2 ♘f3 d6 3 ♗b5+ ♗d7 4 ♗xd7+ ♕xd7 5 0-0 *(D)*
5...♘c6

    5...♘f6

        6 ♖e1 ♘c6

            7 c3 – *Game 27*; 7 b3 – *Game 28*

        6 ♕e2 ♘c6 7 c3 – *Game 29*

        6 e5 *(D)* – *Game 30*

6 c3 ♘f6 7 d4 ♘xe4 8 d5 ♘e5 9 ♖e1 *(D)*

    9...♘xf3+ – *Game 31*

    9...♘f6 – *Game 32*

    5 0-0   *6 e5*   *9 ♖e1*

CHAPTER FIVE

3...♗d7 4 ♗xd7+ ♕xd7: 5 c4 and the Maróczy Bind

1 e4 c5 2 ♘f3 d6 3 ♗b5+ ♗d7 4 ♗xd7+ ♕xd7 5 c4

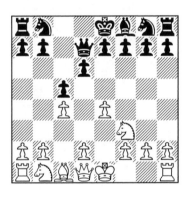

Constructing a Maróczy Bind and bringing about the Sokolsky variation. This attempt to slowly strangle the life out of the black position received a new lease of life in the late nineties when White realised that he didn't have to rush his bishop to e3 after 5...♘c6 6 ♘c3 ♘f6 7 d4 cxd4 8 ♘xd4 g6. Instead attention turned to the prophylactic retreat 9 ♘de2, preventing Black from freeing his position through a timely exchange on d4 and enabling the bishop to be more actively deployed on g5.

5...♘c6

Black's standard response as he prepares to contest the important d4-square, although he can also begin with 5...♘f6. Instead 5...♕g4?! 6 0-0 ♕xe4 does win a pawn and so might put some very positional players off 5 c4, but after 7 d4! the position is opening up. White enjoys very promising compensation due to his better development, while he will gain further tempi against the black queen, and thus 5...♕g4 is rare nowadays.

6 ♘c3

Rublevsky's preferred move order, but White can, and probably should, aim to avoid a number of sidelines with 6 d4 cxd4 7 ♘xd4 ♘f6 8 ♘c3. Then 8...♕g4 is Game 34, while 8...g6 9 f3 ♗g7 10 ♘de2 will lead to Games 37 and 38, and 10 ♗e3 to Game 35. Meanwhile after 6 d4, 6...♕g4?!, intending to equalise with 7 0-0?! ♘xd4!, is again too risky and then 7 d5! ♕xe4+ 8 ♗e3 ♘d4 9 ♕a4+ b5?! 10 ♕a6 ♘c2+ 11 ♔d2!? (11 ♔d1 is also very promising) 11...♕d3+ 12 ♔c1 ♖b8 13 ♕xa7 ♖d8 hasn't been recommended for White on the basis of M.Stean-E.Geller, Moscow 1975 in which White forced a draw with 14 ♕b7 ♘xa1 15 ♕c6+ ♖d7 16 ♕c6+. However, Finkel's 14 ♖d1 ♕g6 15 ♘h4 ♕e4 16 ♘c3! ♕xh4 17 ♔xc2 ♕xc4 18 b3 ♕g4 19 a4! opens the queenside and leaves White with a strong initiative.

Another move order option for White is to begin with 6 0-0, but then 6...g6!? 7 d4 cxd4 8 ♘xd4 ♗g7 causes a few problems; especially with 9 ♘e2 ♘e5!? and 9 ♗e3 ♘f6 10 f3 ♖c8!?.

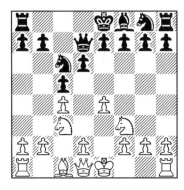

6...♘f6

The main line, but Black can also try to avoid a Maróczy position, or at least a certain version of it, with 6...g6 7 d4 ♗g7!?. This is Kasparov's invention which enjoyed a burst of popularity at the end of the last century, but is now a fairly infrequent visitor to the tournament hall. Black hopes to force White into a ♗e3 set-up after 8 ♗e3 cxd4 9 ♘xd4, but White can, and probably should, prefer to head for a Nimzo structure: 8 d5! ♗xc3+ 9 bxc3 ♘a5 10 ♘d2! e5 11 0-0 ♘f6!? 12 f4 exf4 13 ♖xf4 ♘h5 14 ♖f1 0-0 15 e5! (refusing to allow Black to blockade the position and now both white minor pieces have promising futures) 15...dxe5 16 ♘e4 f5 17 ♘xc5 ♕d6 18 ♘e6 and White enjoyed the advantage in S.Rublevsky-G.Vescovi, Poikovsky 2002.
6...♘e5!? was also quite fashionable in the late-nineties, but is now rarely seen, largely due to the aggressive 7 d4 ♘xf3+ 8 gxf3 cxd4 9 ♕xd4 when White's lead in development outweighs his split kingside. J.Shaw-C.Ward, British Ch., Scarborough 2001 continued 9...e6 10 ♗e3 ♘e7 11 0-0-0 ♘c6 12 ♕d2 ♘e5 13 ♕e2 ♕c6 14 b3 ♗e7 15 ♖hg1 when White was better and gained a strong attack

after 15...0-0?! 16 f4 ♘d7 17 f5 ♗f6 18 ♗d4!.

7 0-0

This avoids 7 d4 cxd4 8 ♘xd4 ♕g4 as we discuss in Oral-Krush (Game 34). However, 7 0-0 ♘e5!? currently appears to be a better way of avoiding a standard Maróczy than 8...♕g4. 7 d4 is also a good move order as after 7...cxd4 8 ♘xd4 g6 White can aim to avoid the 9 0-0 ♗g7 10 ♘de2 ♕e6 of Game 36 with 9 f3!? (9 ♘de2 ♕g4!? is a little annoying for him), although then Black can try 9...♘xd4!? 10 ♕xd4 ♗g7 along Gurgenidze Accelerated Dragon lines.

7...g6

Fianchettoing is by far Black's main response, although he can instead prefer to reach a Hedgehog-type position with 7...e6 8 d4 cxd4 9 ♘xd4 ♗e7 as we discuss in Game 33, although doing so here is much less common than with the knight on d7. Instead, 7...♘e5!? appears to be a superior version of 6...♘e5 when practice has shown that 8 ♘xe5 dxe5 9 d3 e6 10 f4 ♗d6 11 f5 0-0-0! is fine for Black. White can try 8 d3, but then 8...e6 (8...♘xf3+ 9 ♕xf3 g6 was also considered quite solid, but then 10 ♕e2! ♗g7 11 f4 0-0 12 h3 ♘e8 13 f5 gave White the kingside initiative, while Black lacked counterplay, in D.Gormally-A.Muir, British Ch., Scarborough 2004) 9 ♘e1!? (preparing f4 and this is very similar to Benjamin's 7 c4 in Game 25) 9...♗e7 10 f4 ♘c6 11 ♘f3 ♕c7 12 h3 a6 13

♗e3 0-0 14 a4 ♖ad8! gave Black sufficient counterplay with a timely ...d5 in G.Kasparov-V.Akopian, internet blitz 1998.

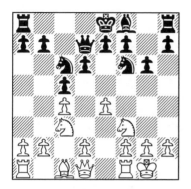

8 d4 cxd4 9 ♘xd4 ♗g7 10 ♘de2

Avoiding the threat of 10...♘xe4! and one should be aware that 10 ♗e3 is no longer possible here due to 10...♘g4, and so those looking for a ♗e3 set-up should prefer to begin with 6 d4 or with 6 ♘c3 ♘f6 7 d4.

10...0-0

10...♕e6!? is a fascinating alternative and is analysed in Game 36, although if allowing this unbalancing choice isn't White's preferred cup of tea then he can begin with 7 d4.

11 f3

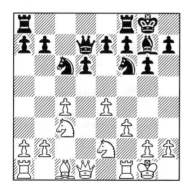

This was once the main line after 5 c4 and is still an important position; see Games 37 and 38. The ♘de2 approach has posed some problems for Black, but recently he has solved

them with a new move order of his own: 5...♘f6 6 ♘c3 g6 7 d4 cxd4 8 ♘xd4 ♗g7 9 0-0 0-0. After 10 f3, 10...♘c6 would return play to normal lines, but Black has delayed ...♘c6 for a reason and Ivanchuk's 10...♖fc8 11 b3 d5! currently looks like a clean equaliser. This is analysed in Game 39, while it's worth noting that White needs something against this move order; it's certainly put Rublevsky off 5 c4 for the time being.

Game 33
S.Rublevsky-A.Kalinin
Aeroflot Open, Moscow 2002

1 e4 c5 2 ♘f3 d6 3 ♗b5+ ♗d7 4 ♗xd7+ ♕xd7 5 c4 ♘f6

5...♘c6 6 ♘c3 ♘f6 transposes, while Black can reach a Hedgehog-type structure against all of White's move order options, including 5...♘c6 6 0-0 ♘f6 7 ♘c3 e6 when, with the black knight on c6 and not d7, White doesn't have a promising alternative to 8 d4.

6 ♘c3 ♘c6 7 0-0 e6 8 d4 cxd4 9 ♘xd4 ♗e7 10 ♗e3

Aggressive, fairly promising and the choice of Mr Bb5, although White can often also opt to fianchetto.

10...0-0 11 ♕e2

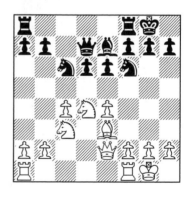

11...♖fe8

Flexible, although the potential X-ray down the e-file is never a problem for

Rublevsky, who'd previously faced a different set-up in the shape of 11...♖fd8 12 ♖ad1 ♖ac8. However, after 13 f4 Black was never able to effectively break with ...d5 in S.Rublevsky-S.Klimov, Russian Ch., Krasnoyarsk 2003, and 13...♕c7 14 b3 a6 15 ♔h1 ♘d7 16 ♘xc6 ♕xc6 17 ♗d4! prepared to meet 17...♗f6 with 18 e5!, while after 17...♕c7 18 ♖d3! ♕a5 19 ♖h3 White enjoyed good attacking chances.

Probably the best way for Black to counter White's aggressive aims is to bring his queen to a5, and to do so somewhat faster than Klimov managed. Lugovoi has done fairly well with 11...a6!? 12 ♖ad1 ♖fc8 13 b3 ♕c7 14 f4 ♕a5! when the threat to the c3-knight isn't so easy for White to meet without disrupting his set-up, although 15 ♘xc6 ♖xc6 16 ♗d4!? ♗d8!? (or 16...♘d7 17 ♖d3! preparing to attack and keeping ♘d5 in reserve) 17 e5 gave White some pressure in V.Yandemirov-A.Lugovoi, Moscow 2004. However, Black then defended well with 17...♘e8! 18 ♔h1 ♗b6! 19 ♗xb6 ♕xb6 20 ♘e4 ♕c7 when he remained very solid and White struggled to find anything against the equalising plan of ...♕e7 and ...f5.

12 ♖ad1 ♖ad8 13 f4! ♕c7 14 ♔h1 a6

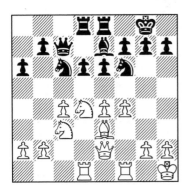

15 ♘xc6! ♕xc6

Rublevsky has cleverly exploited the absence of a rook on c8 to decoy the black queen before she reaches a5. Kalinin probably would have preferred to recapture with 15...bxc6 in an ideal world, but here White has 16 c5! d5 17 e5 ♘d7 18 b4 to retain the advantage.

16 ♗d4 ♖c8 17 b3 ♗d8?

The white bishop is well placed on d4, but now, without the option of a ...♘e8 retreat, Black lacks the time to remove the bishop with ...♗b6 and so he should have continued to solidly defend with 17...♘d7.

18 e5! dxe5 19 fxe5 ♘d7 20 ♘e4 ♗e7 21 ♖d3

Swinging the rook into the attack, while Black is rather vulnerable on f7 and h7, and Rublevsky finishes him off in some style:

21...♘c5 22 ♗xc5 ♗xc5 23 ♘g5 ♖c7 24 ♕h5 h6

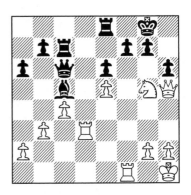

25 ♖xf7!! hxg5 26 ♖xc7 ♖f8 27 ♖xg7+! ♔xg7 28 ♕xg5+ ♔f7 29 ♕f6+ 1-0

Game 34
T.Oral-I.Krush
Montreal 2001

1 e4 c5 2 ♘f3 d6 3 ♗b5+ ♗d7 4 ♗xd7+ ♕xd7 5 c4 ♘c6 6 ♘c3 ♘f6 7 d4 cxd4 8 ♘xd4 ♕g4!?

Black wants to avoid the main lines and hopes for an easy game with an early queen exchange. However, White's critical response quickly leads to a rather sharp position and so 8...♕g4 has appealed to the likes of Sutovsky.

9 ♕xg4 ♘xg4 10 ♘xc6!? bxc6 11 ♗f4!

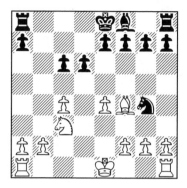

White intends to use his superior development to follow up his last by weakening the black structure with e5.

11...♖b8

Sutovsky's choice, although this doesn't distract White too much as he is fairly happy to go long to help exploit his superior development. Black shouldn't though prevent e5 with 11...e5 as then 12 ♗g3, intending h3 and c5!, favours White, but he does have some other options:

a) 11...g6?! prepares to exchange the bishops, but is quite slow when 12 h3 ♗h6 13 ♗xh6 ♘xh6 14 c5! f5!? 15 0-0-0 0-0-0 16 ♖he1 f4 17 cxd6 exd6 was the course of I.Glek-T.Wippermann, Bad Zwesten 2001. The black structure is already vulnerable here and so White should increase the pressure with Glek's suggestion of 18 ♘e2! ♖hf8 19 ♘d4 ♖f7 20 ♖e2! when the threat of 21 ♖c2 leaves White clearly on top.

b) The radical 11...g5!? is Black's best alternative, although 12 ♗xg5 ♘e5 (hitting c4 whereas 12...♗g7 isn't so good due to 13 ♔e2! ♗xc3 14 bxc3 when White should meet 14...♘e5 with 15 c5! and 14...♖g8 with 15 f4! as Goldin has analysed) 13 b3 ♖g8 14 ♗h4! appears to keep the upper hand as the rook would be trapped should it ever grab on g2. Black retains some compensation with 14...♖g4! 15 ♗g3 ♗g7 16 ♔d2 ♘g6 which

has led to a couple of early draws, but 17 ♖ae1! h5 18 h3 ♖g5 19 h4! looks good for White as 19...♖g4 20 ♘d1! ♗f6 (or 20...♘e5 21 ♘e3 ♖g6 22 ♘f5 and Black has lost the initiative) 21 ♔d3 ♗xh4 22 ♘e3 trapped the rook to win the exchange in E.Miroshnichenko-A.Truskavetsky, Alushta 2001.

12 h3!?

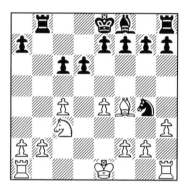

12...♘f6?!

This doesn't work out well and so Black needs to improve here. However, 12...g5 isn't fully convincing due to 13 hxg4! gxf4 14 0-0-0 ♗g7 15 ♔c2 when White had neutralised any pressure down the diagonal and could begin to exploit his superior structure after 15...♗e5 16 ♖h5! in A.Frois-D.Fernando, Porto 2001. 12...♘e5!? 13 ♗xe5 dxe5 is less clear though and is certainly critical. The doubled e-pawns give Black control over d4, while it's not easy for White to make progress on the queenside. Kaufman suggests 14 ♘a4!? e6 15 ♔e2 when the bishop can't enter the game, while after 15...h5 the white king is well placed to defend the kingside. White is probably slightly better here, although advancing on the queenside remains tough and pushing the b-pawn will first require a well arranged c5.

13 0-0-0 ♘d7 14 ♖he1 g6 15 e5!

Levering open the position to spoil the black structure, whilst exploiting the b8-rook's position as now White doesn't have to recap-

ture with the bishop.
15...dxe5 16 ♖xe5!

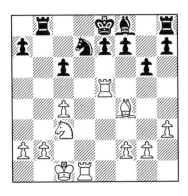

16...♗g7 17 ♖a5 ♖b7

Surprisingly the usually well-prepared Van Wely had already fallen for this; he preferred the more challenging 17...♗xc3!? 18 bxc3 ♖b7, although 19 ♗e3 c5 20 ♖b5! ♖b6 21 a4! a6 22 ♖xb6 ♘xb6 23 ♔c2 ♘xc4 24 ♗xc5 still left White much better due to his passed c-pawn and bishop in D.Reinderman-L.Van Wely, Dutch Ch., Rotterdam 2000.

18 ♘a4 0-0 19 b3 f5?!

White enjoyed a strong grip and pressure in any case, but Black doesn't have time for this. Oral now finished crisply:

20 ♗e3 ♖a8 21 ♖a6 ♖c7 22 ♖xd7! ♖xd7 23 ♘b6 axb6 24 ♖xa8+ ♔f7 25 ♗xb6 ♗h6+ 26 ♔c2 1-0

Game 35
I.Morovic Fernandez-I.Stohl
Croatian Team Ch. 2001

---

1 e4 c5 2 ♘f3 d6 3 ♗b5+ ♗d7 4 ♗xd7+ ♕xd7 5 c4 ♘c6 6 ♘c3 g6

If White wishes to employ a ♗e3 set-up then he should meet 6...♘f6 7 d4 cxd4 8 ♘xd4 g6 with 9 f3 and not with 9 0-0 ♗g7 when 10 ♗e3 runs into 10...♘g4, while 10 f3? ♘xe4! is even worse for White.

7 d4 cxd4 8 ♘xd4 ♗g7 9 ♗e3 ♘f6 10 f3 0-0 11 0-0 a6!

Black essentially has two main plans in these Maróczy positions. He can play dynamically in the centre with ...e6, usually aiming to break with ...d5, or he can play the position along Accelerated Dragon lines, preparing ...b5 and usually intending ...♕d7-d8-a5. 11...a6! is quite clever and is a main reason why White began to adopt a set-up with ♘de2 instead of ♗e3. If he counters with 12 a4 then Black will play in the centre with 12...e6, but against other moves Black gains good play on the queenside.

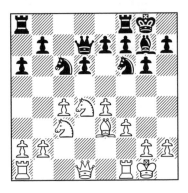

12 ♖c1

Morovic Fernandez realises that 12 a4 e6 would be fine for Black, but now Stohl gets in ...b5. Black should likewise meet 12 ♕d2 with 12...b5 13 ♘xc6 ♕xc6 14 cxb5 axb5 as Stohl has also done and 15 ♖ac1 ♕b7 16 b3 ♖fc8 left him with a very comfortable position, having broken the bind, in D.Pavasovic-I.Stohl, Portoroz 1999.

12 a4 does though remain the main move when Black must play dynamically after 12...e6!?. A good example unsurprisingly being D.Sadvakasov-G.Kasparov, Astana 2001: 13 ♖c1 (instead 13 ♕d2? doesn't pay sufficient attention to the c-pawn and after 13...♘a5! 14 ♕d3 ♕c7 15 b3 e5! 16 ♘c2 ♘xb3 a pawn had dropped off in I.Buljovcic-D.Popovic, Subotica 2001) 13...♘e5 14 ♕e2! (continuing to find the most challenging moves, while Kasparov later faced 14 b3 when 14...d5! 15

cxd5 exd5 16 ♘xd5 ♘xd5 17 exd5 ♖fe8! 18 ♗f2 ♕xd5 fully equalised in V.Akopian-G.Kasparov, Bled Olympiad 2002) 14...♖fc8! (these positions can be rather tricky to handle, but this was the right rook so that fxg7 won't come with tempo; Kasparov giving the variation 14...♖ac8?! 15 b3 d5 16 f4! ♘eg4 17 e5 ♘xe3 18 exf6! ♘xf1 19 fxg7 ♖fd8 20 cxd5 which he assesses as being clearly better for White) 15 b3 d5!

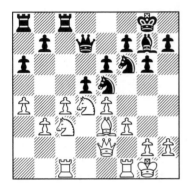

16 cxd5 (here 16 f4 wasn't so promising and then 16...♘eg4 prepares to gain good dark-square compensation after 17 cxd5 with 17...♘xe3! 18 ♕xe3 ♘g4 19 ♕d3 e5, while 17 e5?! ♘xe3 18 exf6 ♘xf1 19 fxg7 dxc4 leaves White vulnerable on d4 and b3 as well as down the c-file) 16...exd5 17 f4 ♖xc3!? 18 ♖xc3 ♘xe4 19 ♖c2 ♘g4 20 ♖fc1 h5! 21 ♖c7 ♕d6 22 ♘f3 ♗f6 and the strong e4-knight gave Black good compensation for the exchange. White later attempted to improve with 21 h3!? in C.Lupulescu-D.Stoica, Balatonlelle 2001, but here Black should consider 21...♘g3!? 22 ♕f3 ♘xe3 23 ♕xe3 ♖e8! 24 ♕xg3 ♗xd4+ 25 ♔h1 ♕f5 (Nisipeanu and Stoica) with pretty reasonable activity.

12...♘xd4! 13 ♗xd4 b5 14 ♘d5

Allowing further simplification, although after 14 cxb5 axb5 15 a3 ♕b7 Black has a fine position and can look to advance on the queenside, while White rather lacks a good plan of his own.

14...♘xd5 15 cxd5

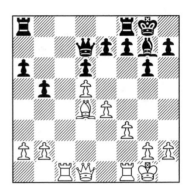

15...♗h6!

The key follow-up to 12...♘xd4 as Black mustn't rush to exchange pieces for 15...♗xd4+ 16 ♕xd4 ♖fc8 17 ♕b6! would be rather unpleasant for him.

16 ♖c2 ♖fc8 ½-½

Here the game ended. Had White aimed to keep the c-file with 16...♖fc8 17 ♖ff2 then Stohl had prepared further liquidation with the sequence 17...e5! (exploiting Black's useful control over e3) 18 dxe6 ♕xe6 19 b3 d5! as then 20 e5?! ♗f4 leaves the e5-pawn a little weak.

Game 36
A.Alavkin-S.Voitsekhovsky
Voronezh Open 2004

---

1 e4 c5 2 ♘f3 d6 3 ♗b5+ ♗d7 4 ♗xd7+ ♕xd7 5 c4 ♘f6 6 ♘c3 ♘c6 7 d4 cxd4 8 ♘xd4 g6 9 0-0 ♗g7 10 ♘de2 ♕e6!?

A fascinating move which first appeared in the famous Kasparov versus the World game, and which is very modern and dynamic. Black breaks up the white bind and even wins both central pawns at the cost of the exchange. If White doesn't like the resulting complex positions he can though avoid this option with 9 f3 ♗g7 10 ♘de2 0-0 and only then 11 0-0, reaching the subject of our next illustrative game.

11 ♘d5!

White should accept the challenge as the only alternative is 11 ♕b3 when 11...0-0! 12 ♘f4 ♕c8 is fine for Black as the queen is not well placed on b3 and 13 ♘fd5 e6 14 ♘xf6+ ♗xf6 15 ♗h6 ♖d8 16 ♖ac1 ♘e5 left White with nothing better in B.Damljanovic-I.Stohl, European Team Ch., Batumi 1999 than to retreat with 17 ♕d1!, although then 17...a6 18 b3 ♕c6 (Stohl) doesn't promise him anything.

11...♕xe4! 12 ♘c7+ ♔d7 13 ♘xa8 ♕xc4

14 ♘b6+

Spoiling the black structure, but now Black does gain a semi-open a-file for his rook. Instead 14 ♘c3!? deserves attention when 14...♖xa8 15 ♖e1 ♖c8 (15...♖d8!? preparing to push the d-pawn, such as with 16 h3 h6! 17 ♗e3 ♔e8 18 ♖c1 d5, is a more active try) 16 h3 h6 17 ♗e3 left Black struggling to activate

his pieces in R.Antonio-M.Rytshagov, Istanbul Olympiad 2000 and then the slow 17...♔e8 18 ♖c1 ♔f8 19 ♕d2 ♕h4 20 ♘b5! a6 21 ♘d4 favoured White.

14...axb6 15 ♘c3

15...♖a8

This position has now been tested several times and Black doesn't have to rush to bring his rook to the a-file. Instead 15...b5!? makes good use of the b-pawns, although then 16 ♗e3 ♖a8?! (Black doesn't get anywhere on the queenside after this and so he should prefer 16...♖d8! when 17 ♖c1 b4 18 ♘a4 ♕b5 19 a3 ♔e8 20 axb4 ♕xb4 21 ♗d2 ♕d4 22 ♗c3 ♕xd1 23 ♖fxd1 e5 saw the strong black centre supply full compensation in V.Baklan-M.Pavlov, Alushta 2002) 17 ♖c1 ♔e8 18 b3 ♕g4 19 f3 ♕h5 20 a4! saw White, having neutralised Black's play, start to press forwards on the queenside in S.Rublevsky-B.Vuckovic, Herceg Novi 2000.

As Black needs to activate his minor pieces, 15...e6!? deserves attention and may well be best. 16 ♗e3 ♘d5! 17 ♘xd5 ♕xd5 18 ♕xd5 exd5 19 ♗xb6 appears strong, but allows Black to reveal his idea; 19...♗xb2 20 ♖ab1 ♗c3! 21 ♗e3 ♔c7 22 ♖fd1 d4 23 ♗d2 ♖a8 and the d-pawn is awkward for White who offered a draw after 24 ♖b3 ♖xa2 25 ♗xc3 dxc3 26 ♖xc3 in M.Turov-E.Andreev, Tula 2001, as the knight and two pawns fully compensate here for the exchange.

16 ♗e3!?

Hoping to encourage Black to advance his b-pawn, but clamping down on the queenside as Kasparov did with 16 a4 is more challenging. Then Stohl's logical suggestion of 16...♘b4!? (intending 17...♘fd5) 17 ♕f3 ♕c6! really deserves a test. Instead the World voted for 16...♘e4 when 17 ♘xe4 ♕xe4 18 ♕b3! f5 19 ♗g5 ♕b4 20 ♕f7 left White with slightly the better chances, albeit in a very complicated position, in G.Kasparov-the World, Internet correspondence 1999.

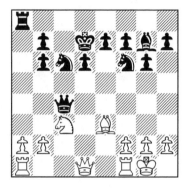

16...♖a6!

Wisely covering b6 and keeping the b- and d-pawns in reserve as 16...b5?! transposes to 15...b5!? 16 ♗e3 ♖a8?!, while 16...d5?! is premature in view of 17 ♖c1! d4 18 ♘e2 and Black loses one of his centre pawns.

17 ♖c1 ♔e8 18 ♕d2 ♘e4!

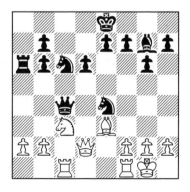

Exchanging knights to open up Black's strong bishop and Alavkin, partly hindered by the pressure against a2, never got anywhere against the solid black position:

19 ♘xe4 ♕xe4 20 b3 b5 21 ♖fe1 ♕f5 22 ♗g5 ♗f6! 23 h4 ♗xg5 24 hxg5 ♔f8 25 ♖c3 ♘e5 26 f3 ½-½

Game 37
S.Rublevsky-Ki.Georgiev
Poikovsky 2001

1 e4 c5 2 ♘f3 d6 3 ♗b5+ ♗d7 4 ♗xd7+ ♕xd7 5 c4 ♘f6 6 ♘c3 ♘c6 7 0-0 g6 8 d4 cxd4 9 ♘xd4 ♗g7 10 ♘de2 0-0 11 f3

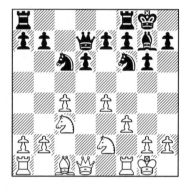

Bolstering e4 and facilitating ♗g5 as an immediate 11 ♗g5?! runs into 11...♕e6. Black now has two main plans to avoid being squashed: to aim for queenside counterplay with ...a6 and ...b5, usually involving improving his queen with ...♕d8-a5, as we'll see Georgiev do, or to play dynamically in the centre with an ...e6 approach, as we'll analyse in the next illustrative game.

11...♕d8

Preparing to bring the queen into play via a5, although if Black isn't after an ...e6 set-up, then he often begins with 11...♖fc8. The rook may though be better placed elsewhere and so it appears more flexible to begin with 11...♕d8 or with 11...a6!? 12 a4 ♕d8. Indeed the inclusion of ...a6 and a4 is quite useful for

Black who can aim to target b3 and to exploit the b4-square, while the game especially here takes on a manoeuvring feel:

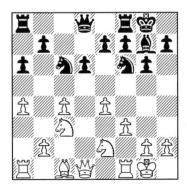

a) 13 ♗e3 is the main response when 13...♕a5 14 ♔h1 (a fairly useful prophylactic move, although White has tried a number of others without proving an advantage, while 14 ♘d5!? should probably be met by 14...♘d7 when Rogozenko has shown that the ambitious 15 b4?! can be rebuffed with 15...♕d8! 16 ♖b1 e6 17 ♘df4 a5!, gaining control over b4 and c5 and meeting 18 b5 with 18...♘ce5) 14...♖ab8 (supporting a later ...b5 and still allowing Black to rearrange his major pieces in Accelerated Dragon style with ...♖fc8, ...♕d8 and ...♕f8) 15 ♖b1! ♘d7! 16 ♕d2 ♔h8!? (Black has an ambitious idea in mind, although 16...♖fc8 was also quite playable when 17 b3 ♕d8 18 ♖fd1 ♕f8 leaves Black very solid, having shored up his king's position and it's not easy for White to advance here with f4 always met by ...f5!) 17 b3 f5 was the ambitious course of D.Batsanin-E.Najer, Russian Team Ch. 2002. White should now have gone in for 18 exf5 when 18...gxf5 leads to a rather unclear position, but Black should avoid 18...♖xf5 when White changes course with 19 ♘d4! and if then 19...♘xd4 20 ♗xd4 ♗xd4 21 ♕xd4+ ♕e5 he will begin to pressurise e7 after 22 ♕d2!.

b) Rublevsky has preferred to remain flexible with 13 ♔h1!? when 13...♘d7 (with White

angling for the sharp b4, there may be no need for this and 13...♕a5 14 ♖b1!? ♖ac8 15 ♗e3 ♖fd8 16 ♕d2 ♕b4! 17 b3 e6! 18 ♗g5 ♖d7 was very solid for Black and left White struggling for a plan in E.Miroshnichenko-L.Van Wely, Panormo [rapid] 2002) 14 ♖b1!? ♕a5 15 ♗d2!? e6 16 ♗e1 ♕c7 17 b3 saw Black decide that he could safely advance with 17...f5! in K.Kiik-A.Huzman, Rethymnon 2003 and 18 exf5 gxf5 19 ♘f4 ♖ae8 20 ♘h5 ♗h8 21 ♘e2 ♘f6 left him with a pretty comfortable position.

12 ♔h1

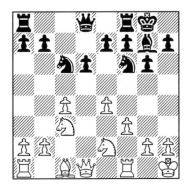

12...♖c8!?

Black usually prefers 12...a6 here, transposing after 13 a4 to positions we considered above. However, Georgiev is in no hurry; his king's rook will prophylactically cover e8, thereby helping to take the sting out of any ♘d5, ...♘xd5, exd5 exchange, while this also usefully avoids dropping the e-pawn to a ♘d5 trick (with queens on d2 and a5) should the c6-knight move.

13 ♗g5 a6 14 a4 ♖e8 15 ♖b1 ♕a5 16 ♗h4

The bishop is a little misplaced here and so White should consider 16 ♕d2, although then 16...♕b4 17 b3 ♘d7! is thematic and reaches a fairly reasonable position for Black.

16...♘e5!

Opening the c8-rook's path and the knight will cover c5, e5 and f6 from d7, making it very difficult for White to advance.

17 b3 ♘ed7 18 ♕d2 ♕h5 19 ♗g5 h6 20 ♗e3 ♔h7 ½-½

Slightly prematurely the players ceased work here. The position is though roughly level and Rublevsky obviously didn't want to risk a double-edged f4 advance, while 21 ♘f4 ♕a5 would still have left White struggling for a good plan.

Game 38
E.Miroshnichenko-S.Atalik
Bled Open 2000

---

1 e4 c5 2 ♘f3 d6 3 ♗b5+ ♗d7 4 ♗xd7+ ♕xd7 5 c4 ♘c6 6 ♘c3 ♘f6 7 d4 cxd4 8 ♘xd4 g6 9 0-0 ♗g7 10 ♘de2 0-0 11 f3

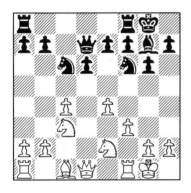

11...♖fd8

This is fairly rare, but Atalik wants to bolster his d-pawn before advancing it after ...e6. However, Black often begins with ...e6, although he can choose whether or not to first flick in 11...a6. Then 12 a4 e6 13 ♗g5 gives Black a choice:

a) 13... ♕c7 has received a number of outings, and from c7 the queen is well placed; avoiding any problems down the d-file, still supporting the d6-pawn and she is able to be activated via a5. However, 14 b3 ♘d7 15 ♔h1! (a useful prophylactic move to avoid any annoying ...♕b6 problems) 15...♘c5 16 ♖b1 ♖fe8 17 ♗h4! ♘b4 (a standard plan to

invade b3; making use of ...e6 and having both knights on the queenside) 18 ♕d2 ♘cd3 19 ♘a2! ♘xa2 20 ♕xd3 ♘b4 21 ♕d2 ♘c6 22 ♖fd1 ♗f8 23 ♗f6 consolidated White's grip on the position in S.Rublevsky-R.Leitao, Istanbul Olympiad 2000.

b) 13...h6 14 ♗h4 ♕c7 15 ♔h1 ♘d7 16 ♖b1 is similar and was seen in J.Ehlvest-S.Atalik, European Ch., Ohrid 2001. Atalik opted for 16...♖fe8, but he later preferred 16...♖ae8!?; his notable idea being to meet 17 f4 with 17...f5! when Black has good central control after 18 b3 ♘c5 19 exf5 gxf5 and this concept deserves more outings, although 16 b3!? remains critical.

Black should be aware that he does usually need a rook on d8 if he is to achieve ...d5, with one premature example of that break being the 11...♖ac8 12 b3 a6 13 a4 e6 14 ♗g5 h6 15 ♗h4 d5? of R.Palliser-J.Lappage, Oxford 2003 when simplest was 16 exd5 exd5 17 ♗xf6! ♗xf6 18 ♘xd5 ♕d6 19 ♘xf6+ ♕xf6 20 ♕d2 ♖fe8 21 ♖ae1 with a clear extra pawn.

12 ♗g5

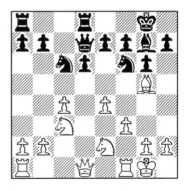

12...h6

Continuing to play dynamically as Black may wish to expand on the kingside after 13 ♗h4 with a timely ...g5. Here though he should most certainly avoid 12...a6? which badly underestimates the power of the g5-bishop and then 13 ♗xf6! ♗xf6 14 ♘d5!

wrecked the black structure on f6, as White was also threatening to win an exchange with ♘b6, in G.Vescovi-L.Coelho, Sao Paulo Zonal 2001.

13 ♗e3 e6 14 ♕d2

White later attempted to improve here with 14 ♕c1!? which may well be why Atalik switched to 11...a6 12 a4 e6. Then 14...♔h7 (14...d5? 15 cxd5 exd5 16 ♗xh6 now doesn't offer Black compensation as the white queen isn't attacked after 16...dxe4 when 17 ♗xg7 ♔xg7 18 fxe4 ♕d2 19 ♖d1 maintains control of d2) 15 ♖d1 ♕e7 16 ♖b1 ♖ac8 17 ♕d2 ♖d7! wasn't though particularly bad for Black, who intended to double and then to play ...d5, in D.Sadvakasov-N.Sedlak, Subotica 2000.

14...d5! 15 cxd5 exd5 16 ♗xh6 ½-½

The players shook hands after this, but Atalik's idea was to meet 16 ♗xh6 with 16...dxe4 17 ♕xd7 ♖xd7 18 ♗xg7 ♔xg7 19 fxe4 ♖d2! when 20 b3 ♘xe4 21 ♘xe4 ♖xe2 regains the pawn and 22 ♘d6 ♗e7 (Atalik) leaves White with nothing.

Game 39
S.Rublevsky-A.Grischuk
Poikovsky 2004

---

1 e4 c5 2 ♘f3 d6 3 ♗b5+ ♗d7 4 ♗xd7+ ♕xd7 5 c4 ♘f6 6 ♘c3 g6

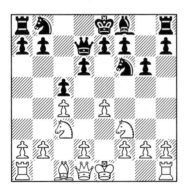

7 0-0

When confronted with his own important

idea, Ivanchuk preferred 7 d4 cxd4 8 ♘xd4 ♗g7 9 f3 0-0 so that he'd didn't have to castle, but could opt for 10 ♗e3. Forcing White into a ♗e3 set-up, rather than a ♘de2 one, can though be considered a success for Black who has usually now simply gone 10...♘c6, but 10...♖c8!? remains playable. 11 b3 a6 then threatens 12...b5, but after 12 ♕d2 ♘c6 13 0-0 Black doesn't appear to have to transpose to normal lines, but can equalise with 13...♘xd4! 14 ♗xd4 b5 15 cxb5 axb5 16 ♖ac1 ♖c6 17 ♗e3 ♕b7 as he did in S.Vokarev-A.Motylev, Russian Team Ch. 2005.

7...♗g7 8 d4

The only real alternative is 8 e5!?, although then 8...dxe5 9 ♘xe5 ♕c8 should be fairly comfortable for Black and White is in danger of being left with a backward d-pawn. R. Rabiega-A.Kosten, Austrian Team Ch. 2004 continued 10 ♕a4+ ♘bd7 11 ♖e1 0-0! 12 ♘f3 e6 13 d3 ♕c7 14 ♗g5 ♘g4!, intending 15...♘ge5, and Black was very comfortable.

8...cxd4 9 ♘xd4 0-0 10 f3 ♖c8 11 b3 d5!

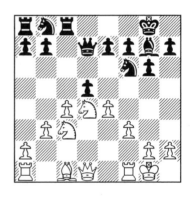

12 exd5

By far White's main response, whereas the aggressive 12 e5 ♘e8 13 ♘xd5 e6 14 ♘c3 ♗xe5 risks more than it gains for White. However, with 15 ♘ce2 (and not 15 ♘de2? b5!) 15...♖d8 16 ♗b2 ♘c6 17 ♘xc6 ♕xc6 (G.Kuba-W.Wittmann, Austrian Team Ch. 2004) 18 ♕c2 White should be able to ensure equality.

Curiously considering the strong grand-masters who've opted for 12 e5, 12 ♘xd5!? hasn't yet been tried in practice. Then 12...♘xd5 13 e6 exd5 can be met by 14 f4! exd5 15 e5 with an edge, and so Black has to go in for 12...e6! 13 ♘xf6+ ♗xf6 14 ♗e3 ♖d8 when 15 ♘e2 ♛e7! (gaining a useful tempo) 16 ♛e1 ♗xa1 17 ♛xa1 gives White some compensation for the exchange due to his dark-square play, although Black can probably defend well enough with 17...♘c6 and 18...f6.

12...♘xd5 13 ♘xd5 e6

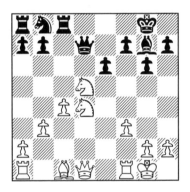

14 ♗h6!

Exploiting the temporary advantage of the extra knight on d5 to swap off the potentially strong fianchettoed bishop. Instead, as we saw in the Introduction, 14 ♗e3 exd5 15 cxd5 ♘a6 gave Black full equality in A.Delchev-

V.Ivanchuk, European Ch., Silivri 2003. However, if Black is determined to only cede the draw if White plays accurately then he should probably prefer 15...♛xd5!? when 16 ♛d2 ♘c6 17 ♖ad1 ♘xd4 18 ♗xd4 ♖d8 19 ♗e3 ♛xd2 20 ♖xd2 ♖xd2 21 ♗xd2 ♗d4+ 22 ♔h1 f5 actually gave Black the edge, as his king centralised faster than White's, in R.Lendwai-A.Czebe, Oberwart 2004, although he eventually had to cease his winning attempts on move 122 (!) in the face of solid and accurate defence.

14...exd5 15 ♗xg7 ♔xg7 ½-½

Here a draw was agreed and Rublevsky hasn't repeated 5 c4 since. However, after 15...♔xg7 Black could certainly make White find 16 ♘b5! before shaking hands as 16 cxd5?! ♛xd5 17 ♘e2 ♛e5 18 ♛d4?! ♘c6 19 ♛xe5+ ♘xe5 gives Black a small, but definite edge and then 20 ♖ac1 b6!? 21 ♖fd1?! ♖xc1! 22 ♖xc1 ♖d8 23 ♘c3 ♖d2 24 ♖e1 ♘d3 25 ♖e2 ♖xe2 26 ♘xe2 ♔f6! gave Black a big edge in the ending, which he went on to convert, due to his superior king in V.Yandemirov-E.Najer, Russian Team Ch. 2004.

After 16 ♘b5 White shouldn't though have any problems and 16...dxc4! 17 ♘d6 ♖d8 18 ♘xb7!? ♛xd1 19 ♖fxd1 ♖xd1+ 20 ♖xd1 cxb3 21 axb3 ♘c6 22 ♖d7 a5! 23 ♖d6 ♖c8 was agreed drawn in C.Lupulescu-A.Colovic, Subotica 2003.

Summary

Ivanchuk's 11...d5 is causing White real problems at the moment. The main question currently is whether White can avoid it and reach a ♗e3 set-up instead. If so then the ♗e3 systems could be set for a revival. Black doesn't though have to follow Ivanchuk's lead against the ♘de2 set-up and in recent years he has begun, after a slow start, to get his act together, especially by employing a quick ...e6.

Move order issues have dominated this chapter. As we saw at the beginning of it, Black has a number of ways to avoid the main lines, although 8...♕g4 no longer appears as promising as it once did. For White, it appears simplest to meet 5...♘c6 with 6 d4, while he also needs to consider how he intends to meet, or even avoid, the intriguing 10...♕e6 approach.

1 e4 c5 2 ♘f3 d6 3 ♗b5+ ♗d7 4 ♗xd7+ ♕xd7 5 c4 *(D)*
5...♘f6 6 ♘c3 g6

      6...♘c6 7 d4 cxd4 8 ♘xd4

         8...e6 – *Game 33*

         8...♕g4 – *Game 34*

         8...g6

            9 ♗e3 – *Game 35*

            9 0-0 ♗g7 10 ♘de2 *(D)*

               10...♕e6 – *Game 36*

               10...0-0 11 f3

                   11...♕d8 – *Game 37*

                   11...♖fd8 – *Game 38*

7 0-0 ♗g7 8 d4 cxd4 9 ♘xd4 0-0 10 f3 ♖c8 11 b3 d5 *(D)* – *Game 39*

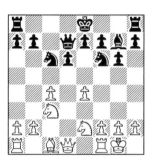
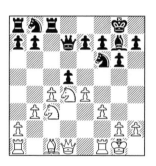

     5 c4   *10 ♘de2*   *11...d5*

CHAPTER SIX

Rare Third Moves for Black

1 e4 c5 2 ♘f3 ♘c6 3 ♗b5

Against the Rossolimo, Black has a tried a whole host of alternatives to the fashionable 3...♘f6!? and the main lines of 3...e6 and 3...g6. However, with the exception of 3...d6 which is another route into Chapter One, they aren't especially promising and shouldn't really be used as more than surprise weapons; and several not even as that!

a) 3...e5 is another central pawn move which has been a little neglected in the past, but which allows White some dangerous options as we'll see in Game 40.

b) Black doesn't have to allow White the option of doubling his pawns on c6, but after 3...♕c7 White can gain a promising initiative and a favourable Open Sicilian position with an exchange on c6, meeting ...♕xc6 with d4 as he does in Game 41.

c) Very similar, albeit a little more popular, is 3...♕b6 when again active play is White's best course as we'll see in Game 42.

d) Black can also try to prevent 4 ♗xc6 by moving his knight, but 3...♘d4?! 4 ♘xd4 cxd4 doesn't impress in the absence of a white knight on c3. I'm not a big fan of statistics in chess, but here they are very telling; Black has scored just a miserable 20% from this position on my databases. 5 c3 then prepares to

take over the centre, although 5 c4 and 5 0-0 are both also promising. The latter delays c3, hoping for 5...g6 6 c3, while intending to meet 5...e5 with 6 d3 and f4, although Black might consider 5...♕b6!? when 6 ♗a4 e6 7 d3 ♘e7 8 ♘d2 ♘c6 9 f4! restricted White to just a pleasant edge in A.Rawlinson-A.Lopez, Cork 2005. After 5 c3,

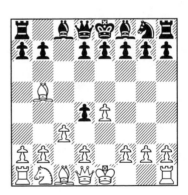

Black doesn't want to just concede the centre with 5...dxc3 6 ♘xc3, but 5...a6 (or 5...♕b6 6 ♕e2! e6 7 0-0 ♘e7 8 cxd4 a6 9 ♗a4 ♕xd4 10 ♘c3 b5 11 ♗b3 ♘c6 12 d3 ♗c5?! and White exploited the misplaced black queen with 13 ♘d5!, intending a strong 14 ♗e3 in A.Bezgodov-A.Kazmin, Smolensky 1992) 6 ♗a4 b5 7 ♗c2 ♕b6 8 0-0 e6 9 cxd4

♕xd4 10 d3 ♗b7 11 ♘c3 ♖c8 12 ♗e3 ♕b4 13 ♗b3 ♘e7 14 d4 saw White simply develop and then fully take over the centre with careful play in M.Palac-H.Colpa, Omis 2004.

e) A superior and more popular course of action for Black is the modern 3...♘a5!? which even received the attention of a *New in Chess Magazine SOS* article in 2004. However, this hasn't yet fully caught on as White doesn't have to go along with Black's hopes of reaching an Open Sicilian position. Instead he can opt for a c3 set-up as we'll see in Game 43.

f) Black can also attack the bishop and 3...a6?! could be seen as a critical test of 3 ♗b5, but White is actually quite happy to exchange with 4 ♗xc6. After 4...bxc6, White is effectively a tempo up on Games 1-3 of Chapter One, while 4...dxc6 5 d3 g6 likewise gives him an improved version of Chapter Nine. Instead 5...♕c7 prepares to gain some central control with ...e5, but 6 ♗e3 e5 7 ♘bd2 f6 8 a4!

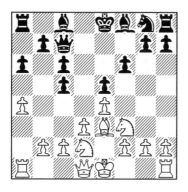

8...♗g4?! (although even 8...a5 9 ♘c4 is promising for White; he is well coordinated, still has a clamp on the black queenside and will increase the pressure by bringing his queen to c3 and/or by breaking with f4) 9 a5 0-0-0 10 ♘c4 h5 11 h3 ♗e6 12 ♘fd2 was good for White in E.Kengis-M.Thaler, Bern 1992, and especially after the continuation 12...♕f7? 13 f4!.

Game 40
V.Baklan-G.Grosselohmann
Werther Schloss Open 2004

1 e4 c5 2 ♘f3 ♘c6 3 ♗b5 e5

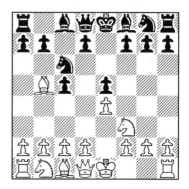

It usually takes Black some time to prepare this central advance, but playing it so early isn't exactly promising for him. White can quickly open the centre with c3 and d4, while it's not so easy for Black to develop quickly and he is somewhat hindered by gaining ...c5 so early in this Lopez position.

4 0-0

White should delay the fairly common 4 ♗xc6 dxc6 to await a favourable moment for the exchange, such as after 4 0-0 ♗e7?!. After the immediate exchange, 5 ♘xe5 ♕d4 regains the pawn, while 5 d3 f6! gives Black a reasonable version of the Ruy Exchange. He already has a clamp on d4 and that should be enough to ensure him of roughly equal chances, while 6 h3 ♘e7 7 ♗e3 ♘g6 8 ♕d2 ♗e7 9 ♘c3 ♘f8! 10 ♘e2 ♘e6 was fine for Black in S.Maze-K.Shirazi, Sautron 2004.

4...♘ge7 5 c3!

Black's last was necessary to cover c6 and thus also e5, whereas 4...d6 5 c3 ♗e7 6 d4 leaves Black wishing he hadn't played ...c5 so early in this unique version of the Spanish. In the game Grosselohmann now hopes to meet the threat of d4-d5 by liquidating on d4, but this can be countered with a promising gambit. Another fiendish idea for White after 4...♘ge7 is 5 ♗c4!?, switching direction and hoping for 5...g6? 6 ♘g5! (Emms), although 5...♘g6 is playable for Black.

5...g6

Black can also expand in Lopez style with 5...a6 6 ♗a4 b5, although here he has already had to compromise his position with ...♘ge7 to support c6 and e5. After 7 ♗b3 d6 8 a4! ♗b7 9 d4 White enjoys a superior form of the Ruy with Black rather missing a knight on f6 to compete for d5 with and to put pressure on e4.

6 d4 cxd4 7 cxd4 exd4

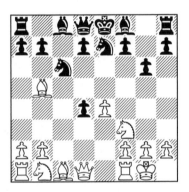

8 ♗f4!

A dangerous gambit to exploit the weakness of d6, whereas 8 ♘xd4 ♗g7 9 ♗e3 0-0 10 ♘c3 d5! 11 ♗xc6 bxc6 12 exd5 ♘xd5! was a fairly promising pawn sacrifice for Black in A.Kovalev-S.Zavgorodniy, Alushta 2003.

8...♗g7 9 ♗d6

Establishing a firm bind on the position in return for the pawn, while it should be noted that this position often arises, as indeed Baklan-Grosselohmann actually did, via 3...g6 4 0-0 ♗g7 5 c3 e5 6 d4 cxd4 7 cxd4 exd4 8 ♗f4 ♘ge7 9 ♗d6.

9...0-0 10 ♘a3!?

10 ♘bd2 also offers White good compensation and has been the main move, but Baklan wants to have the option of leaping

into b5 and then c7. After 10 ♘bd2, critical is still 10...a6 (10...h6 11 ♘b3 a6 12 ♗c4 b5 13 ♗d5 ♖e8 14 ♖e1 a5 15 ♖c1 ♖a6 16 ♘c5 left Black stuck in a strong bind in T.Oral-A.Jakubiec, 2nd Bundesliga 2000) 11 ♗c4 b5 12 ♗d5 ♗b7 13 ♘b3 ♘xd5! 14 ♗xf8 ♕xf8 15 exd5 ♘b4 when the unopposed bishops gave Black compensation for the exchange in A.Dreev-S.Lputian, Simferopol 1988.

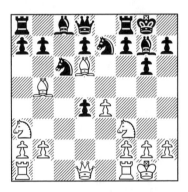

10...♖e8?

Too slow, while this also weakens f7. Instead Black must chase the bishop with 10...a6 11 ♗c4 (11 ♗d3!? may be stronger as 11...b5 12 ♘c2 ♗b7 13 a4 leaves b5 and d4 both looking rather vulnerable) 11...b5 when 12 ♗b3 has scored well for White in practice, but 12...♘a5! (removing the dangerous prelate, whereas 12...♗b7 13 ♖c1 ♖c8 14 ♕d2 h6?! 15 h4! ♔h7 16 h5 left Black under serious kingside pressure in M.Dzhumaev-E.Jorge Bort, Linares 2000) 13 ♖c1 ♘xb3 14 ♕xb3 ♗b7 15 ♖fe1 ♖e8 left White unable to find anything better than to force a draw with 16 ♗c7 ♕c8 17 ♗d6 in S.B.Hansen-H.Teske, Bundesliga 2002, while improvements after 12...♘a5 aren't so easy to find.

11 ♗c4! a6?

Failing to spot the threat, although after both 11...♘a5 12 ♘b5 ♘ec6 13 ♗d5 and 11...♕b6 12 ♘b5 ♘a5 13 ♗d3 Black would have been unable to prevent the loss of an exchange.

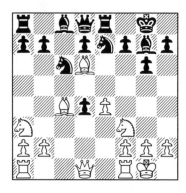

12 &xf7+! &xf7 13 ₩b3+ &f6

13...&d5 14 ₩xd5+ &e6 15 &g5+ would have been crushing, but now Black is mated.

14 e5+ &f5 15 ₩f7+ &g4 16 h3+ 1-0

Game 41
E.Rozentalis-B.Kristensen
Copenhagen 1988

---

1 e4 c5 2 &f3 &c6 3 &b5 ₩c7 4 0-0

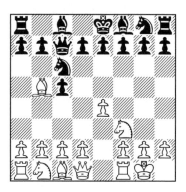

4...&f6

Sensibly developing and, while the queen does cover c6, 4...a6 costs Black more time than he can afford. Then 5 &xc6 ₩xc6 (or 5...dxc6 when play is very similar to Kengis-Thaler – see 3...a6?! above – and 6 a4! &f6 7 d3 a5 8 &bd2 g6 9 b3! &g7 10 &b2 0-0 11 &e5 ₩d8 12 &c4 gave White a clear edge in M.Adams-S.Zhigalko, Rethymnon 2003) 6 d4

cxd4 7 &xd4 sees White quickly gain a large lead in development. After 7...₩c7 8 &c3 e6 9 &e1! d6 10 &g5 sacrifices on d5 are in the air to exploit that and we've reached a position which can also arise from 3...₩b6; which just reminds one how closely related the two queen moves are.

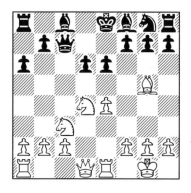

Now Avrukh has tried 10...&e7!? (10...&f6 11 ₩d2 transposes, but also gives White another dangerous option in 11 &xf6!? gxf6 12 ₩h5, intending 12...&c5 13 &f5!), hoping for 11 &xe7?! &xe7 12 ₩h5 &c5!, but instead 11 ₩d2! &f6 12 &f5! is rather dangerous for Black despite his extra material. Then 12...exf5 13 exf5 0-0! 14 &xe7! ₩xe7 15 &e1 ₩d7!? (15...&e6 16 &d5 ₩d8 17 &xf6 gxf6 18 ₩h6! &h8 19 fxe6 fxe6 20 &xe6 saw White, after some inspiring play, regain most of his material and still be left with good attacking chances in A.Ardeleanu-D.Bondoc, Romania 1994) 16 &xf6 ₩xf5! 17 &d5 &h8 18 &e7 &e6 was suggested by Ardeleanu as the best way for Black to keep his king safe, although 19 &b6! retains a clear advantage.

Another possible move order is 4...e6 when White should probably play as in our main game with 5 &c3 &f6 6 &e1, whereas 5 &e1 &ge7 6 c3!? a6! 7 &a4 b5 has been acceptable for Black in practice, but should obviously be compared to Chapter Eight.

5 &e1!

The best move order as 5 &c3 &d4! (effective now the knight is on c3) transposes to a critical position of the next chapter and there is no reason to allow that when 5 ♖e1 gives White good attacking chances.

5...e6 6 ♘c3

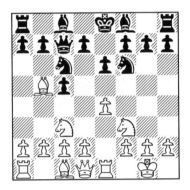

6...a6?!

This doesn't work here as ♖e1 didn't just support ♘d5 ideas, but also e5. However, 6...d6 is hardly a great position for Black when Nunn's suggestion of 7 ♗xc6+!? ♛xc6 8 d4 cxd4 9 ♘xd4 ♛d7 10 ♛f3 looks like the simplest way to a white advantage. In practice White has tended to opt for the sharper 7 d4 cxd4 8 ♘d5! and then 8...♛d8 9 ♘xd4 ♗d7 10 ♗g5! leaves Black under severe pressure and this is not a recommended way of playing for him! 10...♗e7 11 ♘xe7 clearly favours White and so Black has to leave the pin with 10...♖c8!? as 10...exd5? loses to in style to 11 ♗xc6! (the flashy method whereas 11 ♘xc6 easily does the job after 11...♗xc6 12 exd5+ ♔d7 13 dxc6+ bxc6 14 ♛f3!) 11...bxc6 12 exd5+ ♗e7 13 ♗xf6 gxf6 14 dxc6 ♗c8 15 ♛f3! ♖b8 16 ♖e3 ♖xb2 17 ♖ae1 ♗e6 18 ♖xe6! fxe6 19 ♛h5+ and 1-0 in E.Rozentalis-E.Slekys, USSR 1988.

Relatively best is 6...♘g4!?, although 7 ♗xc6! bxc6 can just be met by Kaufman's 8 d3 with an edge, whereas 8 e5!? f6 9 d4! cxd4 10 ♛xd4 ♘xe5 11 ♘xe5 fxe5 12 ♖xe5 wasn't fully clear, but did soon supply a dangerous initiative in A.Shirov-L.Van Wely, Bundesliga

2003 (which had begun 3...♘f6 4 ♘c3 ♛c7 5 0-0 e6 6 ♖e1).

7 ♗xc6 ♛xc6 8 d4 cxd4 9 ♘xd4 ♛c4

The best try as the queen must try to stay in touch with d5.

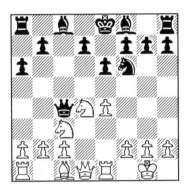

10 e5! ♘d5 11 ♘e4 f5?

Now Black is routed and he does better with the 11...b5 12 b3 ♛c7 of A.Vydeslaver-M.Ravia, Tel Aviv 2003. 13 ♘f5!? ♛xe5 14 ♘ed6+ ♗xd6 15 ♖xe5 ♗xe5 16 ♘d4 was then enough to win the black queen, although Black was able to put up a lot of resistance and so White should consider 13 ♗g5!? or 13 ♗b2, intending 14 ♘d6+.

12 b3 ♛b4 13 a3 ♛a5 14 ♘xf5!

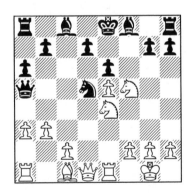

Opening the e-file after which the vulnerable black monarch won't have long to live due to his lack of piece and pawn cover.

14...exf5 15 ♘d6+ ♗xd6 16 exd6+ ♔f7

Rozentalis now regains his piece without losing his huge attack, which he does finish off in some style, while after 16...♔d8 White mates with 17 ♗g5+ ♘f6 18 ♕e2.

17 ♖e5 ♕c3 18 ♕xd5+ ♔g6 19 h4! h6 20 ♖xf5! ♕xc2 21 ♕f7+ ♔h7 22 ♗xh6 1-0

> ### Game 42
> ## I.Glek-O.Heinzel
> *Bad Zwesten Open 2002*

1 e4 c5 2 ♘f3 ♘c6 3 ♗b5 ♕b6 4 ♘c3

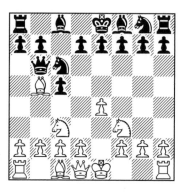

4...e6

Wisely covering d5, while 4...a6 5 ♗xc6 ♕xc6 6 d4 leaves the black queen and b6 both rather vulnerable after 6...cxd4 7 ♘xd4, and 4...♘d4? is too ambitious here due to 5 ♘xd4 cxd4 6 ♘d5! ♕d8 (hoping to trap one of the advanced minor pieces, but there is a tactical flaw) 7 ♕h5! when Black has to try the grim 7...♘f6 8 ♘xf6+ gxf6 as 7...a6? 8 ♕e5! f6 9 ♘c7+ ♔f7 10 ♕d5+ forced resignation in I.Smirin-Y.Afek, Israel 1992.

5 ♗xc6!

A timely exchange which either leaves White positionally better after 5...bxc6 or still able to gain a strong initiative after 5...♕xc6. Instead 5 0-0 shouldn't be met by 5...a6?!, but by 5...♘ge7!. This is quite solid for Black and White has struggled to show an advantage after 6 ♖e1 a6 7 ♗f1 ♘g6! when Black con-

trols e5 and hopes to enjoy good play on the dark squares along Taimanov Sicilian lines. White has thus tried to change the structure with 8 b3 ♗e7 9 ♗b2 0-0 10 ♘e2!? which frees up the c-pawn, but 10...d5! 11 e5?! d4! 12 ♘g3 ♕c7 13 ♕e2 ♘b4! blunted the b2-bishop and favoured Black in Zhang Zhong-Bu Xiangzhi, Tianjing 2003.

5...♕xc6 6 d4

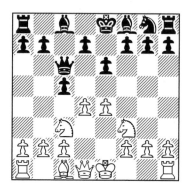

6...b5?!

Heinzel's wish not to further open the position is understandable, but this gives Glek targets on the queenside. Instead 6...cxd4 7 ♘xd4 ♕c7 8 0-0 is the usual choice when Black could really do with covering b5 with 8...a6. That does though vindicate White's decision to exchange on c6 without waiting for ...a6, and 9 ♖e1 d6 10 ♗g5 transposes back to the critical note to Black's fourth move in Rozentalis-Kristensen. Instead 8...♘f6 9 ♖e1 d6 tries to omit ...a6, but then 10 ♗g5 remains promising as is simply 10 ♘db5! ♕d8 11 ♗f4 e5 12 ♗g5 a6 13 ♘a3 b5 14 ♘d5 with a pretty favourable Sveshnikov for White.

7 d5! ♕b7 8 0-0 b4 9 ♘a4

White doesn't mind having his knight on the rim here as he can undermine the black queenside with a3.

9...d6 10 c4 e5 11 ♖e1 ♗g4?! 12 h3 ♗xf3 13 ♕xf3

The position might be blocked, but it is

quite favourable for White, largely because of his extra space which, along with his better development, grants him promising options on both flanks.

13...g6 14 a3!

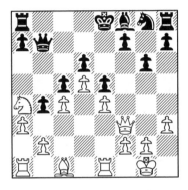

14...b3

White now simply rounds the pawn up as Black doesn't want, with an exchange on a3, to create pressure down the a-file as well as a b4-break, while 14...a5 15 ♗e3 is also quite unpleasant for him. Indeed after 15...♗g7 White can open the position with 16 axb4 axb4 17 ♗xc5! dxc5 18 ♘xc5 ♖xa1 19 ♖xa1, netting a strong initiative and two very dangerous connected passed pawns for the piece deficit.

15 ♘c3 ♕d7 16 ♘b1! ♖b8 17 ♘d2 ♗h6 18 ♘xb3 ♕a4 19 ♘d2 ♗xd2 20 ♗xd2 ♖b3

Glek ruthlessly exploits his superior pieces after this to hunt after both the black king and queen. However, 20...♖xb2 21 ♖eb1! ♖b6 (21...♖xd2? 22 ♖b8+ ♔e7 23 ♖b7+ is immediately decisive) 22 ♕g4 would also have left White, who intends to meet 22...♕d7 with 23 ♗a5!, with an excellent position.

21 ♕g4 ♕d7 22 ♕d1 ♖xb2 23 ♖b1 ♕b7 24 ♖xb2 ♕xb2 25 ♖e3! ♔f8 26 ♖b3 ♕d4?

26...♕a2 27 f4 would have been crushing, but now the queen is trapped.

27 ♕c2 ♕a1+ 28 ♔h2 ♔g7 29 ♗c3 1-0

Game 43
R.Rabiega-F.Hegeler
2nd Bundesliga 1999

1 e4 c5 2 ♘f3 ♘c6 3 ♗b5 ♘a5!?

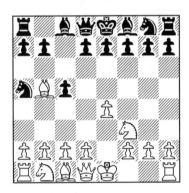

4 c3

White most certainly isn't committed to a c3 set-up and those with some experience of the Open Sicilian may well prefer 4 d4 a6 5 ♗e2 cxd4 6 ♘xd4. In the Taimanov the c6-knight does though sometimes go to a5 and White hasn't yet found a way to exploit its position after 6...♕c7! 7 0-0 e6. The aggressive path is 8 f4!? b5! (best as 8...♗c5?! misplaces the bishop and 9 ♔h1 b5 10 c3! ♘e7 11 b4 ♗xd4 12 ♕xd4 left Black under pressure on the dark squares in D.Pikula-N.Nikolic, Kragujevac 2000) 9 ♔h1 ♗b7 10 ♗f3, although then 10...♘f6! 11 e5 ♘d5 12 a4 b4 13 ♕e2 ♗c5 gave Black good counterplay in P.Hertel-V.Dambrauskas, Cuxhaven 2000.

4...a6

Even if Black intends ...♘f6, he has tended to flick this in so that the bishop can't later retreat to d3 as it did after 4...♘f6 5 e5 ♘d5 6 d4 cxd4 7 cxd4 e6 8 0-0 a6 9 ♗d3 in V.Nevednichy-M.Quinn, Bled Olympiad 2002. Black must be very careful in these c3 Sicilian positions not to allow his knight to remain out of play on a5, while after 9...b5 10

♘g5! ♗e7 11 ♕h5 ♗xg5 12 ♗xg5 ♕b6 13 ♗e3 d6?! 14 ♘c3 ♘xc3 15 bxc3 ♕c6 16 ♕g5! g6 17 ♕f6 he was in a huge mess on the dark squares.

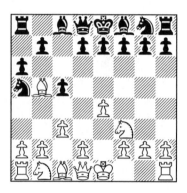

5 ♗a4

Now ...b5 will come with tempo, although the bishop does get to retreat on to the b1–h7 diagonal and White can hope to undermine on the queenside with a4. However, 5 ♗e2!? is a serious alternative and has been endorsed by Kaufman. After 5...♘f6! 6 e5 ♘d5 7 d4 cxd4 8 0-0 e6 both recaptures are possible, but 9 cxd4 ♗e7 10 ♘c3! ♘xc3 (Bosch prefers 10...0-0, intending 11 ♗d3 d6 12 ♕c2 g6, although after 13 ♗h6 ♖e8 14 exd6! ♕xd6 15 ♘e4 White has quite a pleasant IQP position) 11 bxc3 0-0 12 ♗d3 d6 13 ♖e1 appears to be a slightly improved c3 Sicilian line for White, as Black would like to have had his queen's bishop on the h1–a8 diagonal by this point.

5...b5!?

This increases Black's options compared with 5...e6 when 6 0-0 b5 7 ♗c2 ♗b7 8 d4 cxd4 9 cxd4 ♗e7 10 d5! (10 ♕e2 is also good, but Marzolo wants to use his extra space to challenge Black and to leave the black queenside pieces rather offside) 10...♕c7 11 ♘c3 ♖c8 12 ♗d3! ♘f6 13 ♗g5 b4 14 ♘e2 exd5 15 e5 ♘e4 16 ♗xe7 ♔xe7 17 ♘g3 and White enjoyed excellent compensation in C.Marzolo-T.Coste, St Chely d'Aubrac 2003.

6 ♗c2

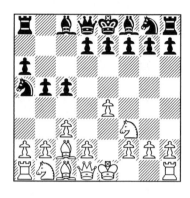

6...d5?!

This doesn't work out well as White is far from forced to capture, but Black hasn't done too well here in any case with 6...e6 transposing to the last note, while 6...d6 7 0-0 e6 8 d4 ♗b7 9 ♖e1 ♗e7 10 ♘bd2 ♕c7 11 ♘f1! ♘f6 12 ♘g3 saw White maintain his strong centre, and prepare to attack should Black go short, in J.Boudre-E.Mensch, French Team Ch. 2000.

7 ♕e2

Now Black could try 7...d4!?, although then White has 8 e5!, aiming to target Black down the weakened h1–a8 diagonal. 7 d4!? is likewise strong when 7...dxe4 8 ♗xe4 ♗b7 9 ♗xb7 ♘xb7 10 0-0 ♘f6 11 ♕e2 actually just transposes back to the game.

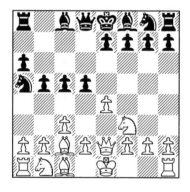

7...dxe4 8 ♗xe4 ♗b7 9 ♗xb7 ♘xb7 10 0-0 ♘f6 11 d4 e6 12 ♖d1 c4?!

Trying to close the position, but this actually just helps White to open lines on the queenside and against the black monarch even faster.

13 b3! ♕d5 14 a4! ♖c8 15 axb5 axb5 16 bxc4 bxc4

16...♕xc4 17 ♕xc4 ♖xc4 18 ♖a8+ ♘d8 19 ♘e5 was also very promising for White and would have netted at least the b5-pawn, but Hegeler is never now quite able to complete his development and to fully cover c4.

17 ♘e5 ♗d6 18 ♘d2 ♘a5 19 ♖xa5! ♕xa5 20 ♘dxc4 ♕a6?

21 ♘xd6+?!

20...♕c7 should have been preferred when

21 ♘xd6+ ♕xd6 transposes to the game as here Rabiega missed the immediately decisive 21 ♘xf7! when 21...♔xf7 22 ♘e5+ collects the black queen.

21...♕xd6 22 ♕b5+ ♔e7?

Clearly shocked by the exchange sacrifice, Hegeler continues to overlook the tactics. He could have put up much more resistance with 22...♘d7 23 ♗a3 ♕c7, although clearly this is still excellent for White, such as with 24 ♖e1 when the black monarch is stranded in the centre and Black is effectively playing a rook down.

23 ♗a3! ♕xa3 24 ♕b7+ 1-0

Without waiting for 24...♔d8 25 d5!.

Summary

Many of the lines in this chapter have been used as surprise weapons and I was hoping to be able to recommend a few to creative readers. However, the relatively common 3...♕b6 and 3...♕c7 just appear too risky, so long as White understands that he can reach a very dangerous attacking position with a timely exchange on c6 followed by breaking with d4.

3...♘a5 can though still be used by those seeking to leave the beaten-track, and Black has been scoring reasonably well if White breaks with d4. However, 4 c3 appears fairly promising for White whether he opts for 4...a6 5 ♗e2 or for 5 ♗a4. The only other option which deserves a few more tests is 3...e5 which theory has been a little unkind to, although White does have a fairly dangerous gambit in reply.

1 e4 c5 2 ♘f3 ♘c6 3 ♗b5 *(D)*
3...♘a5

> 3...e5 *(D)* – *Game 40*
> 3...♕c7 – *Game 41*
> 3...♕b6 – *Game 42*

4 c3 *(D)* – *Game 43*

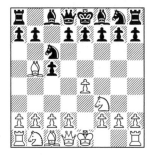

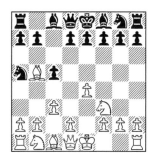

3 ♗b5	*3...e5*	*4 c3*

CHAPTER SEVEN

3...♞f6: The Fashionable Line

1 e4 c5 2 ♞f3 ♞c6 3 ♗b5 ♞f6!?

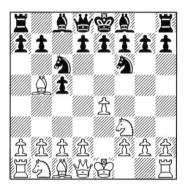

Five years ago this was just another sideline against the Rossolimo, albeit quite a fighting choice. It is now though rather fashionable; at least partly because White's main response is 4 ♞c3 and this position can also arise via 3 ♞c3 ♞f6 4 ♗b5. Thus by employing 3...♞f6 many Black players aim to kill two birds with one stone. It must though be pointed out that having some experience of the 3...g6 variation is rather useful for Black should White avoid 4 ♞c3 against 3...♞f6. Many grandmasters have that and so this modern defence, which combines a degree of solidity with some dynamism, has appealed to Vladimir Kramnik, Joel Lautier and Loek van Wely, as well as to

the young talents Pavel Eljanov and Merab Gagunashvili, while it was also recently employed by Vishy Anand.

4 ♞c3

The main move, but this is far from forced and those who face 3...♞f6 via the Rossolimo, as opposed to after 3 ♞c3, may well prefer one of the alternatives. Naturally if 4 e5 worked then 3...♞f6 wouldn't be a good move, but it is hard for White to exploit the knight's early arrival on d5 with 4...♞d5!, while after 5 0-0 g6 play usually transposes to Game 76 of Chapter Ten. White can also begin with 5 ♞c3, but then 5...♞c7 6 ♗xc6 dxc6 7 d3 g6 8 0-0 ♗g7 9 ♖e1 0-0 10 ♞e4 ♞e6 11 ♗e3 b6 transposes to an important 3...g6 line, which we also witnessed in the Introduction in Benjamin-Ni Hua.

After 4 e5 ♞d5 5 0-0, also possible though is 5...♞c7 6 ♗xc6 dxc6 7 h3 when 7...g6 is the usual course, but Black can prefer to play in a more independent vein with 7...♗f5!?. This has held up fairly well in practice with S.Movsesian-V.Chuchelov, Bundesliga 2005 continuing 8 d3 h6 9 ♞bd2 e6 10 ♕e2 ♞b5 11 ♞e4 ♞d4 12 ♞xd4 ♕xd4! (12...cxd4 would iron out Black's structure, but leave it a little rigid; this correct recapture allows him to generate some pressure) 13 ♞g3 ♗g6 14 ♔h2 h5! 15 f4 h4 16 ♘h1 c4! with a good game for Black.

Those happy to meet 3...g6 with the 4 ♗xc6 of Chapter Nine, should probably opt for 3...♘f6 4 ♗xc6 dxc6 5 d3 when Black usually goes 5...g6, transposing, although he can also prefer an independent path as we'll see in Game 44. Another white approach is the flexible 4 ♕e2 when we'll examine two sharp lines after 4...g6 in Game 45.

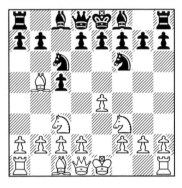

4...♕c7!

It is this move which has done much to greatly increase the popularity of 3...♘f6 after both 3 ♗b5 and 3 ♘c3. The queen doesn't really want to recapture on c6, but does control the key e5-square from c7. Black will often aim to gain a central clamp with ...♘d4 and ...e5, aiming to leave White struggling for a plan, although he can also be more ambitious with ideas of ...♘d4 and ...♘g4.

Black should avoid 4...d6?! 5 e5 ♘g4!? 6 0-0! ♘gxe5 7 ♘xe5 dxe5 8 ♗xc6+ bxc6 9 ♕h5 ♕c7 10 ♖e1 e6 11 d3 which was quite favourable for White in Z.Medvegy-A.Lopez, EU Ch., Cork 2005. Likewise the old main line of 4...♘d4? is best avoided due to the direct and strong 5 e5 ♘xb5 6 ♘xb5 ♘d5 7 ♘g5! as Graf demonstrates in Game 46. However, Kramnik has employed both 4...g6 (Game 47) and 4...e5 (Game 48); the former encourages the white e-pawn to advance and is a little risky, and while White can gain an edge against the latter, Black does obtain reasonable drawing chances.

5 0-0 ♘d4

Black's main move which thematically exploits the weakened d4-square. Instead he should probably avoid 5...e6 6 ♖e1 which actually transposes back to Game 41, and Rozentalis-Kristensen certainly revealed this to be a fairly promising position for White. However, 5...a6!? may not be so bad due to 6 ♗xc6 dxc6 7 e5 (previously praised, but White may have to prefer 7 h3 e5! 8 d3, although then 8...♗d6 leaves Black very solid and probably not worse) 7...♘d5 8 ♘e4 ♗g4!; a strong novelty and pawn sacrifice. After 9 ♘xc5 e6 10 ♘d3 ♖d8 Black enjoys a bind on the position as well as the initiative and 11 b3 c5 12 ♗b2 b5! 13 c4 ♘b6 14 ♘de1 ♕c6 gave him good compensation in D.Lima-V.Zvjaginsev, Tripoli 2004.

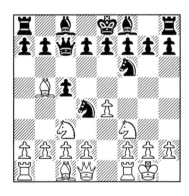

6 ♖e1

The main move, supporting e4 and keeping ♘d5 and e5 ideas in reserve. However, White can also be more aggressive with 6 ♘xd4 cxd4 7 ♘d5 ♘xd5 8 exd5, intending 8...♕c5 9 c4 and to sacrifice a couple of pawns for the initiative as we'll see in Game 49.

6...a6

Putting the question to the bishop, before deciding (unless White opts for 7 e5) how best to develop. Instead Black should avoid 6...♘xb5?! 7 ♘xb5 ♕b6 8 c4 d6 9 d4 cxd4 10 e5! which led to a promising white initiative in Kr.Georgiev-M.Godard, Agneaux 1998. However, 6...e5 is playable, although 7 ♗c4! d6 8 d3 (meeting 8...♗g4 with 9 ♘b5) 8...♗e7 9 ♘d2! ♗g4 10 f3 ♗e6 11 ♘f1 ♘d7 12 ♘d5 ♗xd5 13 ♗xd5 ♘f6 14 ♘e3 saw White successfully gain control over d5 in A.Volokitin-M.Gagunashvili, Batumi 2003.

7 ♗f1

Retreating the bishop from danger like this has been White's most popular choice so far, but he can also opt for 7 ♗c4 or for the aggressive 7 e5!?; both of which we'll examine in a battle between two Ukrainian stars in Game 50.

7...e5

Completing his central bind and Black is very solid here as we'll see in Game 51, in which we also examine 7...♘g4!?.

Game 44
S.Rublevsky-M.Gagunashvili
European Club Cup, Rethymnon 2003

---

1 e4 c5 2 ♘f3 ♘c6 3 ♗b5 ♘f6 4 ♗xc6 dxc6

The alternative recapture isn't advisable with the knight already on f6 as White can play against it to gain a pleasant edge. Indeed after 4...bxc6?! 5 e5 ♘d5 6 0-0 g6 7 c4! ♘c7 8 d4 (ironing out the black pawns, but developing rapidly is of much more importance)

8...cxd4 9 ♕xd4 ♗g7 10 ♕h4! the black kingside was rather vulnerable in G.Vescovi-G.Milos, Sao Paulo 2002 and 10...♗a6 11 ♘c3 ♘e6 12 ♖e1! ♕c7 13 ♗d2 f6 14 ♗h6 saw White retain a large advantage.

5 d3

5...♗g4

Black hopes to free his position by exchanging off the light-square bishop, but this isn't enough to equalise as White can make good use of his queen quickly finding herself in an active role. Here Black's best is probably just 5...g6 when 6 h3 ♗g7 7 ♘c3 ♘d7 8 ♗e3 e5 is one route into the main line of Chapter Nine. Those seeking an independent path can though consider Lautier's 5...♘d7!? when 6 e5!? ♘b6 7 ♘bd2 ♗f5 8 0-0 e6 9 b3 ♗e7 10 ♗b2 0-0 11 ♖e1 a5! 12 a4 ♘d5 saw Black's sensible development leave him very solid in V.Bologan-J.Lautier, Poikovsky 2003, although White's kingside prospects still shaded it for him after 13 ♘e4 ♕c7 14 ♘fd2 b5 15 ♘g3 ♗g6 16 ♕g4!, intending to launch the h-pawn.

6 h3!

White is happy to recapture with the queen, while after 6 ♘bd2 ♘d7 7 h3 Black doesn't have to exchange on f3 and 7...♗h5 8 g4 ♗g6 9 ♘c4 f6! 10 0-0 e5 11 ♘e3 ♕c7 12 a3 (angling for a b4-break to gain a useful queenside initiative as we'll often see White doing in Chapters Nine and Ten, but here

Black can prevent it) 12...a5 13 a4 ♗f7 14 ♕e2 g5 15 ♘f5 h5! gave Black, who was very solid, some counterplay and the position was roughly level in E.Alekseev-P.Eljanov, Biel 2004.

6...♗xf3

The talented Gagunashvili presumably didn't like the idea of retreating here when White can even be quite aggressive with 6...♗h5 7 g4 ♗g6 8 e5!, intending 8...♘d5 9 e6 fxe6 10 ♘e5 when it's well worth a pawn to smash up the black structure.

7 ♕xf3

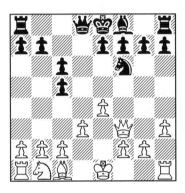

7...e5

Gagunashvili later discovered that Black has left it too late to gain a favourable version of Chapter Nine due to 7...g6 8 ♗d2! when White neutralises the long diagonal and was left slightly for choice after 8...♗g7 9 ♗c3 0-0 10 ♘d2 ♘e8 11 ♗xg7 ♘xg7 12 ♕e3 in L.Nisipeanu-M.Gagunashvili, Saint Vincent 2004.

8 ♘d2 ♘d7 9 ♕g3!

Now Black is unable to easily castle and equalise. The knight is coming to c4 to put pressure on e5, as well as the d6-square, while the queen targets e5 and g7 as well as supporting the ideal f4-break. Indeed White is on the verge of enjoying a very promising set-up and again Black must play radically to challenge him.

9...♕f6!? 10 ♘c4 ♗e7 11 f4 exf4 12

♗xf4 0-0

Black later deviated with 12...♕g6, but White isn't adverse to a queen exchange, although he must be careful not to cede control over e5. Thus after 13 0-0 0-0 14 ♕xg6 hxg6, 15 ♖ae1!? to support an e5-advance deserves serious consideration, whereas 15 ♘a5 ♗f6! 16 ♘xb7 ♗xb2 17 ♖ab1 ♗d4+ 18 ♔h1 c4! 19 dxc4 ♗e5! 20 ♗xe5 ♘xe5 21 ♘d6 ♖fb8 gave Black a strong knight and sufficient counterplay in T.Nedev-L.McShane, Calvia Olympiad 2004.

13 0-0 b6 14 ♘e3!

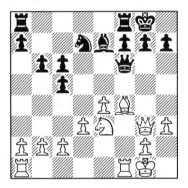

Black last was a little slow and so Rublevsky prepares to crank up the pressure by installing a strong knight on f5, while now 14...♕xb2?! 15 ♘f5 ♗f6 16 ♖ab1 ♕c3 17 ♖b3! (Rublevsky) would have left Black in serious trouble on the kingside.

14...♕g6 15 ♘f5 ♗f6 16 ♕f3!

Keeping the queens on but now the black one is rather sidelined, and so White prepares to take over the centre.

16...♖fe8 17 c3! ♖ad8 18 ♖ad1 ♘e5?!

Before this Black was at least fairly solid, whereas now White gets to advance with tempo and it wasn't long before Rublevsky exploited the d4 advance to launch a decisive rook lift:

19 ♕e2 ♗g5?! 20 d4 cxd4 21 cxd4 ♘d7 22 ♗xg5 ♕xg5 23 ♖d3! ♘f6 24 ♖g3 ♖xe4 25 ♕f2 1-0

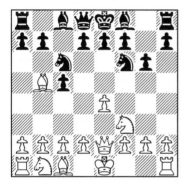

Game 45
M.Adams-D.Komarov
French Team Ch. 2003

1 e4 c5 2 ♘f3 ♘c6 3 ♗b5 ♘f6 4 ♕e2 g6

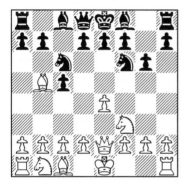

5 e5

Just because White supported his e-pawn on the last turn doesn't mean that it can't still advance and Adams has a greedy idea in mind. Instead 5 0-0 ♗g7 6 c3 is also seen, but this position arises more often via 3...g6 4 0-0 ♗g7 5 c3 ♘f6 6 ♕e2 and we'll deal with it in Chapter Ten (see Game 77).

Instead 5 ♘c3 ♗g7 6 e5 keeps play in independent channels and is fairly dangerous for Black. After 6...♘g4 7 ♗xc6 dxc6 8 h3 ♘h6 9 g4! (restricting the knight, whereas 9 ♘e4 b6 10 d3 ♘f5 11 ♗g5 ♘d4 12 ♘xd4 ♕xd4 13 ♘f6+ ♔f8 14 c3 ♕d8 was fine for Black, as White now had to retreat when he hadn't sufficiently damaged the solid black position, in V.Tseshkovsky-I.Nataf, Herceg Novi 2005) 9...0-0 10 d3 we reach a sharp position in which Pedersen liked White, although he only considered 10...f5 which gives White promising kingside play. Instead 10...f6! 11 ♗f4?! (this was a Dvoretsky recommendation, but it allows a tactic although Black is fine in any case) 11...♘xg4! (a strong combination, although 11...♘f7 12 0-0-0 fxe5 13 ♗g3 ♗e6 14 ♘xe5 ♗d5 sufficed for an im-

pressively easy draw for Black in A.Karpov-M.Chiburdanidze, Bilbao 1987) 12 hxg4 fxe5 regains the piece with a large advantage, and the desperate 13 ♗xe5?! ♗xg4 14 ♖xh7 ♗xe5 15 ♖h6 ♗g7 16 ♖xg6 ♗xf3 17 ♕e6+ ♔f7 was badly insufficient for White in J.Cubas-T.Nedev, Calvia Olympiad 2004.

5...♘d5

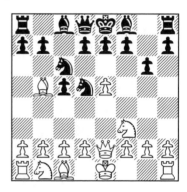

6 ♕c4

The logical follow-up to White's previous play, although 6 0-0 is also possible when 6...♘c7 7 ♗xc6 dxc6 8 h3 ♗g7 9 d3 0-0 10 ♘bd2 ♘e6!, importantly supporting c5, while also covering d4 and g5, gave Black a reasonable 3...g6 system in A.Minasian-M.Gagunashvili, Dubai 2003.

6...♘c7

This gives Black reasonable compensation for the pawn and it's noticeable that Adams later switched to 4 ♘c3. Another promising idea for Black is Hausrath's 6...♘cb4!? when 7 ♕xc5? loses to 7...b6 8 ♕c4 a6. Instead 7 a3 (or 7 ♕b3 a6 8 ♗c4 e6! when 9 ♘c3 is well met by 9...b5 10 ♗xd5 exd5 11 ♘xd5 c4) 7...a6 8 ♗a4 b5! 9 ♕e4 bxa4 10 axb4 ♘xb4 11 0-0 ♖b8 left Black actively placed and not even a pawn in arrears in J.Jens-D.Hausrath, Belgian Team Ch. 2003. After 12 e6?! f6! 13 exd7+ ♗xd7 14 ♘a3 ♗c6 15 ♕e3 ♕d5 16 ♖e1 e5 Black was already for choice and so 6...♘cb4!? is another good reason to avoid pawn grabbing after 4 ♕e2.

7 ♕xc5

Now Black nets the bishop-pair as compensation and is able to open the position to assist it, but after 7 ♗xc6!? dxc6 8 ♕xc5, 8...♗g4! (Komarov) is awkward, although critical is 9 ♕e3! ♘d5 10 ♕b3 ♘f4 11 0-0 ♕b6! when Black retains sufficient pressure for the pawn.

7...♘xb5 8 ♕xb5 d6! 9 exd6 ♕xd6

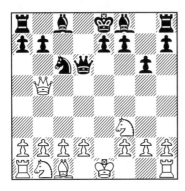

10 0-0!

Wisely giving getting castled the priority, even at the cost of a damaged kingside, rather than try to get in d4 with 10 c3 when 10...♗g4! 11 ♕xb7 ♕e6+ 12 ♔d1 ♖b8 13 ♕a6 ♕d5 (Komarov) leaves White pretty weak on the light squares.

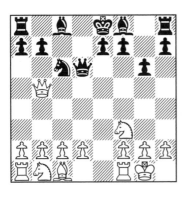

10...♗g7 11 c3 ♗g4! 12 d4 ♗xf3 13 gxf3 0-0 14 ♘d2 ♖fd8 15 ♘e4 ♕c7 16 ♔g2

The damage to the white kingside supplies reasonable play for the pawn, although Komarov's notes suggest that the accurate 16 ♕g5! e5 17 ♕g3 would have retained an edge, although this doesn't seem so clear after 17...f5!? 18 ♘c5 ♕f7!.

16...h6 17 ♗e3 e6 18 ♕e2 b6 19 ♖ad1 ♘e7

Black is now very solid and Komarov was to make it pretty much impossible for Adams to put his extra pawn to any effective use:

20 ♘g3 ♖ac8 21 ♖fe1 ♕c6 22 ♗c1 ♖d5 23 ♕e4 ♕c4 24 a3 ♘f5! 25 ♘xf5 ♖xf5 26 d5! exd5 27 ♕xc4 dxc4 28 ♖e7 a5 29 a4 ♗f8 30 ♖b7 ♗c5 31 ♗e3! ♖c6 32 ♖d8+ ♔g7 33 ♖bb8 ♖e6 34 ♗d4+ ♗xd4 35 ♖xd4 ♖c6 36 ♖b7 g5 37 ♖e4 ♖cf6 ½-½

Game 46
A.Graf-E.Gisbrecht
German Ch., Saarbruecken 2002

1 e4 c5 2 ♘f3 ♘f6 3 ♘c3 ♘c6 4 ♗b5 ♘d4? 5 e5! ♘xb5 6 ♘xb5 ♘d5 7 ♘g5!

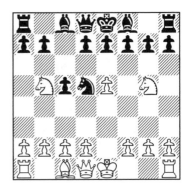

The older 7 0-0 and 7 c4 are also fairly dangerous, but it is this idea of Igor Zaitsev's which has really made 4...♘d4 appear mistaken. Black must meet the huge threat of 8 ♕f3, but he may well not have a satisfactory defence.

7...h6?!

Trying to drive the knight away or to exchange knights after 8 ♕f3, but White has a strong response. However, weakening d6 is just as bad and 7...e6?! 8 ♘e4 f6 9 0-0 ♗e7 10 ♘bd6+ ♔f8 11 c4! ♘f4 12 d4 ♘g6 13 exf6 gxf6 14 ♗h6+ ♔g8 15 dxc5 was already almost a decisive advantage in B.Macieja-R.Tomczak, Polish Ch., Warsaw 2002. Instead 7...f5 8 0-0 a6 9 ♘c3 simply leaves White solidly better, while after 7...f6 8 ♕f3 the black position remains rather critical:

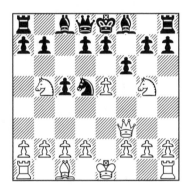

a) 8...♘b4?! (intriguing, but objectively this falls short) 9 exf6 exf6 10 c3! ♘c6 was seen in T.Sammalvuo-Se.Ivanov, Joensuu 2002 when White got too carried away with 11 ♕d5, whereas simply 11 ♕h5+ g6 12 ♕e2+ ♘e5 (or 12...♕e7 13 ♘d6+ ♔d8 14 ♘gf7+ ♔c7 15 ♘e8+ ♔b6 16 ♕xe7 ♗xe7 17 ♘xh8 which is also very good for White) 13 f4 would have won material.

b) 8...fxg5 9 ♕xd5 e6 10 ♕f3 clarifies the situation, but only to show that Black had a poor structure and an unhappy king in N.Mitkov-M.Bueno Abalo, Mondariz 1999.

c) 8...♘c7 9 exf6 exf6 10 ♕e4+ sees White putting his superior development to good use when Black does well to reach move 20; e.g., 10...♘e6 11 ♘xh7! d5?! 12 ♕g6+ ♔e7 13 0-0 a6 14 ♘c3 ♘f4 15 ♖e1+ ♔d6 16 ♕g3 and Black gave up, as 16...g5 is met by 17 ♘xf8 and 18 d4, and 16...♖xh7 by 17 ♘xd5!, in A.Naumann-A.Mallahi, Yerevan 1999.

8 ♘xf7! ♔xf7 9 ♕f3+

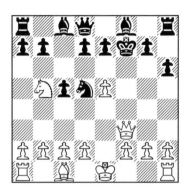

9...♘f6

Desperately trying to return material as unsurprisingly the black king cannot survive after 9...♔e6? 10 c4. A.Collinson-M.Turner, England 1990 continued 10...♘b6 11 d4! d5 12 dxc5 dxc4 (12...♘xc4 13 ♘d4+ ♔d7 14 e6+ ♔c7 15 ♗f4+ also wins) 13 cxb6 (good enough, but 13 ♗e3! is even better as 13...♘d5 14 0-0-0 gives White his killer d4-check after all and wins on the spot) 13...♕xb6 14 ♘c3 ♕c6 15 ♘e4 g6?! 16 ♗e3 ♔d7 17 e6+! ♔xe6 18 ♖d1 and Black was routed.

10 exf6 exf6

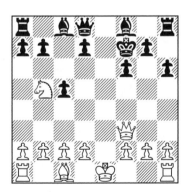

11 ♕d5+!

Stopping Black from gaining a reasonable position with 11...d5 and now Graf quickly sets about making good use of his much safer king and his control over d5.

11...♗g6 12 0-0 ♕b6 13 ♕d3+ ♔f7 14 ♖e1 ♕c6 15 ♘c3! c4 16 ♕e4 ♗c5?

16...♕xe4 17 ♖xe4 would have netted a clear pawn, but Black could then develop and Gisbrecht had to try that. Now after 17 ♕xc4+ ♔g6 18 d4 ♗b6 19 ♕d3+ ♔f7 20 d5 the queens stay on and Black can't develop; unsurprisingly he thus decides not to continue.

17 ♕xc4+ 1-0

Game 47
B.Macieja-T.Nedev
European Ch., Silivri 2003

---

1 e4 c5 2 ♘f3 ♘c6 3 ♘c3 ♘f6 4 ♗b5 g6

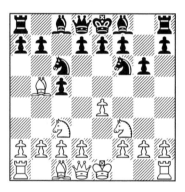

5 h3!?

Stopping the knight from going to g4, but this is a little slow and allows Black to prevent 6 e5. Instead White can immediately go on the offensive with 5 ♕e2 ♗g7 6 e5 (transposing to the note to White's fifth in Adams-Komarov) or with the direct 5 e5 ♘g4 6 ♗xc6 dxc6 7 h3. After 7...♘h6 8 g4! f5! (Black mustn't let the knight be forcefully hit by 9 ♕d2) 9 g5 ♘f7 10 d3 ♗e6 (10...♗g7 should probably be met by 11 ♕e2!? so that White can transpose with 11...♗e6 12 h4) 11 ♕e2! ♗g7 12 h4! ♗d5 13 ♘xd5! (an important follow-up to White's novelty on the last turn and now 13...cxd5?! 14 e6 ♘d6 15 h5

gives White a promising initiative) 13...♕xd5 14 c4 ♕e6 15 ♗f4 h6 16 0-0-0 White's forceful and very accurate play gave him the edge in A.Khalifman-J.Lautier, Wijk aan Zee 2002.

5...♗g7

This rather risky idea was later used by Kramnik, although few players would probably enjoy having their kingside pieces fairly badly restricted. A more promising option here could well be to play akin to the main lines with 5...♕c7!? when 6 0-0 ♗g7 7 ♖e1 e5! 8 ♗c4 0-0 9 d3 d6 leaves Black very solid and with a good version of the 3...g6 variation. After 10 ♘d2 ♗e6 11 ♘f1! (White's only idea is to head for d5, but Black can cover that square) 11...h6 12 ♘e3 ♖ad8 13 ♗d2 (or 13 ♘cd5 ♗xd5! when White doesn't want a useless pawn on d5, but 14 ♗xd5 ♘e7 is fine for Black) 13...♘e7! 14 ♕e2 ♕c8 White couldn't establish a piece on d5 in L.Fressinet-J.Lautier, Paris (rapid) 2001, but not doing so allowed Black to fully equalise with 15 a4 d5!.

Black can also try 5...♘d4 as Nedev had previously done, when he hopes that ...g6 is more useful than h3, especially as Black doesn't intend to meet 6 e5 ♘xb5 7 ♘xb5 with ...♘g4 in any case. Here 7...♘d5

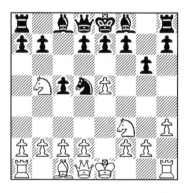

8 ♘g5 isn't as promising as in Graf-Gisbrecht, while Black has tested this line against a few 2700 strength players and he obtained a reasonable position after 8 0-0 (instead the older 8 ♕e2!? still looks rather

critical when 8...♘f4? doesn't convince due to 9 ♕c4 ♘xg2+ 10 ♔f1 a6 11 ♘c3, winning a piece, while 8...♘c7 9 d4! ♘xb5 10 ♕xb5 cxd4 11 ♗g5!, whilst not fully clear, did give White an attractive attacking position in V.Egin-V.Tukmakov, USSR Team Ch. 1979) 8...a6! (8...♘c7 9 ♘xc7+ ♕xc7 10 d4! cxd4 11 ♕xd4 again left Black vulnerable on the kingside in J.Lautier-I.Nataf, Mondariz Balneario Zonal 2000.) 9 c4! ♘f4! 10 ♘c3 ♘e6 11 d4 cxd4 12 ♘xd4 ♗g7 when the knight performed an excellent job of keeping White at bay in P.Svidler-T.Nedev, Neum 2000.

6 e5! ♘g8 7 ♗xc6 dxc6

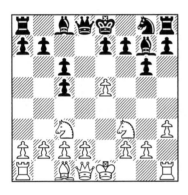

8 d3!

White shouldn't rush to castle short as that reduces his kingside options. P.Svidler-V.Kramnik, Dortmund 2004 witnessed 8 0-0 ♘h6 9 ♘e4 b6 10 d4 ♘f5!? 11 dxc5 ♗a6 when the black minor pieces were well placed and that, along with the lack of outposts for the white knights, supplied reasonable compensation for the pawn. However, White now had to exchange the queens as 12 ♖e1? ♕xd1 13 ♖xd1 ♗e2! 14 ♖e1?! ♗xf3 15 gxf3 ♘d4 crippled his structure and already left Black much better.

8...♘h6

One must presume that Kramnik has an improvement ready after 8 d3, but that is probably not 8...f6 when 9 ♗f4 fxe5 10 ♗xe5 ♘f6 11 ♕d2 0-0 12 0-0 ♗f5 13 ♖ae1 c4 14

d4 b5 15 ♗e2! simply prepared to double on the e-file, retaining a pleasant edge in J.Ryan-J.Markos, EU Ch., Cork 2005.

9 ♗e3!

Forcing Black to cover c5 and thereby gaining a useful move before advancing on the kingside in a bid to restrict the knight.

9...b6 10 g4 f5 11 exf6! exf6 12 ♕e2 ♕e7!

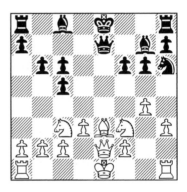

13 d4

This turns out well, but may not be best. Instead 13 0-0-0!? is just as critical when Black doesn't want to castle and so should try 13...f5 14 g5 ♘f7 (threatening to win a piece with 15...♗xc3 16 bxc3 f4) 15 ♖he1 0-0 (necessary to avoid 16 ♗xc5!) 16 d4 ♗e6!?, refusing to open up the centre for the white pieces and encouraging White to open the long diagonal and b-file with an exchange on c5. This isn't clear, but appears acceptable, if still risky, for Black and may well be what Kramnik intended.

13...cxd4?

Now White gains a strong initiative which he never relinquishes. Black had to instead get his g7-prelate into play with 13...f5! when 14 g5 ♘f7 15 dxc5 ♗xc3+ 16 bxc3 0-0 (Postny), intending 17 cxb6 ♖e8!, appears to be quite a promising pawn sacrifice after which White could easily be left overextended and with a homeless king.

14 ♘xd4 ♗b7 15 0-0-0 ♘f7 16 ♖he1 0-0

17 ♕c4 b5 18 ♕f1 ♘e5 19 f4 ♘c4 20 ♗g1 ♕f7 21 b3 ♘b6 22 ♘e6!

Macieja has cleverly delayed advancing his knight until the optimum moment. Now 22...f5 23 ♘xg7 ♕xg7 24 ♗d4+ would have begun a decisive kingside attack, but Nedev doesn't last long with a knight entrenched on e6.

22...♖fe8 23 f5 ♗f8 24 ♗c5 ♘d7 25 ♗xf8 ♘xf8 26 ♘e4 ♘xe6 27 ♘d6! 1-0

Game 48
M.Carlsen-J.Chakkravarthy
Dubai Open 2004

---

1 e4 c5 2 ♘f3 ♘c6 3 ♘c3 ♘f6 4 ♗b5 e5 5 ♗xc6

White's only hope for an advantage lies with this and his active follow-up as otherwise he struggles to do anything effective due to Black's control of d4.

5...dxc6 6 ♘xe5! ♘xe4

Essential to regain the pawn as Black will win back his piece, but this comes at the cost of falling behind in development.

7 ♘xe4 ♕d4

8 0-0

Vacating e1 for a rook, although 8 d3!? ♕xe5 9 f4! appears to be enough for an edge. 9...♕d5 is then the most natural square for the queen, when Glek has analysed 10 ♕e2 ♗e6!? (10...♗e7?! 11 c4! ♕d8 12 0-0 0-0 13

f5! ♖e8 14 ♗e3 ♗f6 15 ♖ad1 ♗d4 16 ♔h1 ♖e5 17 g4 continued to prevent the light-square bishop from joining in the game in I.Glek-V.Kupreichik, 2nd Bundesliga 2000) 11 c4! (again White must play actively as Black is very solid and may still enjoy the bishop-pair if he's allowed to castle) 11...♕f5 12 ♘g3 ♕g4 13 ♕xg4 ♗xg4 14 h3 ♗d7 15 f5 ♗e7 16 0-0 ♗f6 17 ♘e4 when the absence of queens means that Black's problems aren't as great as Kupreichik's were, but the white e4-knight remains somewhat superior to the black light-square bishop.

On the other hand 8 ♕e2 appears to be fine for Black after 8...♕xe5 9 d4!? cxd4 10 f4 due to 10...♕a5+! 11 ♗d2 ♗b4 when the temporary complications are acceptable for him. Thus White has also tried 9 f4, but the brave 9...♕xf4! 10 d4 (10 ♘f6+ ♔d8 11 ♕e8+ ♔c7 12 ♕xf7+ ♔d8! leaves White with nothing better than a repetition, but not 12...♔b8?? 13 ♘d7+!) 10...♕h4+ 11 g3 ♕e7 appears to be fully playable for Black, at least so long as he's happy with a draw. 12 dxc5 is met by 12...♕e6, while 12 0-0!? f5! 13 ♘d6+ ♔d7 14 ♕xe7+ ♗xe7 15 dxc5 ♗xd6! 16 ♖d1 ♔e8 17 cxd6 ♗e6 18 ♗g5 ♔d7 saw Black fully blockade the d6-pawn after which he could begin to advance on the kingside in V.Anand-V.Kramnik, Monaco (rapid) 2003.

8...♕xe5

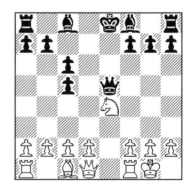

9 d4!?

Very aggressive, while White has done well in practice with 9 d3 ♗e7 10 ♗d2 0-0 11 ♗c3, but largely because Black hasn't neutralised the kingside pressure with 11...♕d5! (11...♕f5?! 12 ♕e2 ♕g6 13 f4! ♗d7 14 ♕f2 ♕f5 15 ♖ae1 ♖fe8 16 ♘g3 ♕d5 17 ♖e5! instructively began a strong kingside attack in M.Rytshagov-A.Ziegler, Gothenburg 1999) 12 ♕f3 ♗f5 13 ♕g3 ♗g6, intending 14 f4 f6 (Smirin).

9...cxd4?!

Now both members of the royal family remain in danger down the e-file and 9...♕xd4! would have been the critical test of Carlsen's idea. His notes simply mention that this is too risky for Black in view of 10 ♕e2, but that doesn't seem at all clear after 10...♗e6!. Then 11 ♘g5 is met by 11...♕c4, while 11 ♖d1 ♕e5 12 f4 ♕f5 13 ♘g5 ♗e7! is also at least fine for Black. In a previous game White had thus preferred 10 ♕f3 ♗e7 11 ♗g5, but then 11...f6! 12 ♖ad1 ♕xb2 13 ♘d6+ ♗xd6 14 ♖fe1+ ♔f7 15 ♖xd6 ♖f8! 16 c3 ♔g8 saw Black get his king to safety and 17 ♗xf6!? certainly didn't give White any more than a draw in R.Ovetchkin-D.Kokarev, Voronezh 2003.

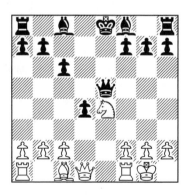

10 ♖e1 ♗e6

This runs into a strong idea and so the alternative way of blocking the e-file should have been preferred when 10...♗e7 11 ♗g5 0-0! 12 ♗xe7! ♕xe7 13 ♕xd4 leaves the better centralised White with the edge, but that is probably preferable to 12 ♘f6+ ♗xf6 13 ♖xe5 ♗xe5 when Black enjoyed good compensation for the queen in V.Jansa-R.Tomczak, Bundesliga 1991.

11 ♗g5!

Now Black can't castle long, but 12 ♘f6+ isn't such an easy threat to deal with and after 11...♕d5, 12 ♗f6! (Carlsen) keeps up the strong pressure.

11...♗e7

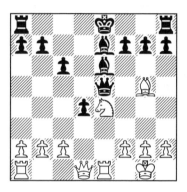

12 f4!

Spurning the queen to continue targeting the unhappy black monarch down the e-file.

12...♕d5 13 ♗xe7 ♔xe7 14 f5 ♕xf5 15 ♕xd4!

White's aggressive play has left him with a strong attack and he will now at least regain his pawn on b7, whilst keeping up the pressure. However, aided by some generous defence, Carlsen was instead able to return to his favourite theme of pressure down the e-file to quickly finish Black off.

15...♕d5? 16 ♕b4+ c5 17 ♘xc5 a5 18 ♕a3 ♕d4+ 19 ♔h1 ♕b4 20 ♕e3! 1-0

Game 49
M.Ulibin-B.Avrukh
Biel 2003

---

1 e4 c5 2 ♘f3 ♘c6 3 ♘c3 ♘f6 4 ♗b5 ♕c7 5 0-0 ♘d4 6 ♘xd4 cxd4 7 ♘d5

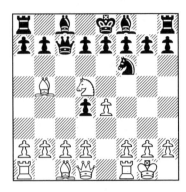

Several commentators have enjoyed pointing out that this variation is effectively a reversed English Four Knights, but with an extra tempo for White. If one does indeed view the position as that then this is one of two ambitious tries (the other being 6 ♖e1 a6 7 e5!? – the subject of Game 50) to put the extra move to immediate and active use.

7...♘xd5 8 exd5

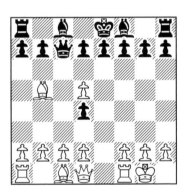

8...♕c5

Black can also play more solidly with 8...a6 9 ♗a4 g6 10 d3 and now the solid 10...h6!? 11 ♖e1 ♗g7 12 ♕e2 ♗f6, intending ..♔f8-g7 deserves testing. Greenfeld suggested this plan without the inclusion of ...a6 and ♗a4, and if this is the correct path for Black then he should probably delay ...a6, keeping ...♕c5 as an option and helping to slow down any queenside play from White. The need to find

an improvement like 10...h6!? can be seen from the 10...b5?! (or 10...♗g7 11 ♗g5! b5 12 ♗b3 e6 13 ♕d2 h6 14 ♗h4! with an edge) 11 ♗b3 ♗g7? 12 d6! of J. Benjamin-H.Nakamura, New York (blitz) 2004 when 12...♕xd6 loses to 13 ♕f3, but otherwise simply 13 dxe7 is strong.

9 c4!

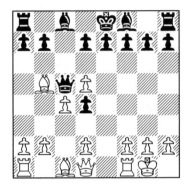

This idea of Anand's reinvigorated 6 ♘xd4 as otherwise White is simply struggling for sufficient compensation after Black's slightly greedy last.

9...a6

Anand was rewarded for his novelty with the inaccurate 9...dxc3? 10 ♕b3! (exploiting the fact that the bishop doesn't have to retreat to a4) 10...a6 11 ♗e2 in V.Anand-P.Leko, Linares 2003. Leko, who was somewhat behind in development, now tried to keep lines closed with 11...c2, but after 12 d4! ♕d6 Anand points out that he should have played 13 g3! when an immediate 13...g6 loses to 14 ♗f4 ♕f6 15 ♗e5, and a delayed 13...♕f6 14 ♕xc2 g6 to 15 ♗f4 d6 16 ♗xa6!. Thus Black would have had to grovel with 13...e6, but after 14 ♗f3 White retains a large advantage.

10 b4 ♕xb4 11 ♗a4 b5!

White is happy to sacrifice to open lines, but this dynamic response sees Black return the pawn to gain time to develop. Instead nobody has yet dared to venture the very greedy 11...♕xc4 when 12 ♗b3 ♕d3 13 ♗b2

(Greenfeld) activates the white dark-square bishop and offers excellent compensation. However, Black has also tried an immediate 11...g6 when 12 ♗b3!? (the older 12 d3 b5 13 ♗b3 ♗g7 14 a4! may be objectively stronger and is also hard for Black to defend against; 14...bxc4 15 ♗xc4 ♕b7 16 ♖e1 d6 17 ♗g5 forces the ugly and weakening 17...f6 when 18 ♖b1 ♕c7 19 ♗d2 ♔f7 20 a5!, preparing to increase the queenside pressure, favoured White in J.Gdanski-M.Dziuba, Dzwirzyno 2004)

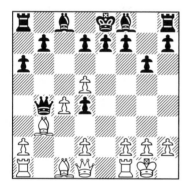

12...♗g7 13 a4 d6 14 ♗a3 ♕a5 15 ♖e1 ♕d8 16 c5! is a new and critical idea, introduced in P.Svidler-L.Van Wely, Monaco (rapid) 2005. After 16...0-0 17 ♖c1 the sharp position was tough for both sides to play at a fast time limit, but Black was certainly under some pressure. Svidler was no doubt happy to see the position opening with 17...dxc5 18 ♗xc5 when 18...♖e8 19 a5!? ♗f5 20 ♕f3 maintained dangerous compensation; g4 and d6 being but one idea. After 20...♕xa5 21 ♗xe7 ♕xd2? 22 d6 ♗f8, 23 g4? wasn't sufficient, but 23 ♖cd1 ♕a5 24 g4 ♗e6 25 ♖xe6! fxe6 26 ♗xe6+ ♔h8 27 ♗f6+ ♗g7 28 ♗xg7+ ♔xg7 29 ♕f7+ ♔h6 30 h4 would have finished the job nicely. However, the alternative move 21...♗h6! would have improved, but Svidler's concept certainly deserves further exploration.

12 cxb5

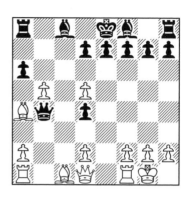

12...g6!?

Allowing the pawn to advance to b6, but Avrukh has things covered. Once again Black has a more solid alternative which also appears quite playable and 12...axb5 13 ♗b3 g6 14 d3 ♗g7 15 ♗d2!? ♕d6 16 ♕e1 may give White compensation, but 16...♕f6! (or even 16...♕e5 17 ♕c1 0-0 18 ♖e1 ♕d6! 19 ♗f4 ♕b4 when it's not clear that White has anything better than repeating with 20 ♗d2 with the black queen threatening to invade on c3) 17 ♗b4 d6 18 a4 0-0! 19 axb5 ♖b8 20 ♗c4 ♗d7 21 ♖a5 ♖b7, whilst not completely clear, did leave the b5-pawn more of a weakness than a strength in D.Frolov-A.Shariyazdanov, Tomsk 2004.

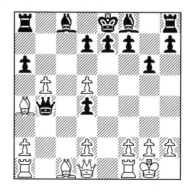

13 b6! ♗g7!

The b-pawn must be allowed to live as 13...♕xb6? 14 ♗a3 ♗g7 15 ♖e1 ♗f6 16 ♖b1 prepares a decisive breakthrough on e7, but Avrukh is able to blockade it and to begin to target d5.

14 d3 0-0 15 ♗g5 ♗b7 16 ♖e1

16 ♖b1 ♕d6 17 ♕g4!? also appears dangerous, but after 17...e6! 18 dxe6 dxe6 19 ♖fc1 ♖fc8 the b-pawn isn't going anywhere and Black can begin to mobile his central pawns with ...f5 and ...e5. This could also have arisen in the game after 17...dxe6 18 ♖b1 ♕d6 19 ♕g4 ♖fc8 and Avrukh feels it's dynamically balanced. Black shouldn't be worse, but the b6-pawn must be watched and it was now a shame that the Sofia draw rules didn't apply at Biel.

16...e6 17 dxe6 ½-½

Game 50
A.Volokitin-P.Eljanov
Ukrainian Team Ch. 2002

**1 e4 c5 2 ♘f3 ♘c6 3 ♘c3 ♘f6 4 ♗b5
♕c7 5 0-0 ♘d4 6 ♖e1 a6**

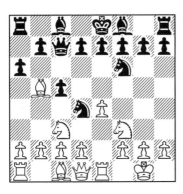

7 e5!?

Critical, as White allows his structure to be damaged in return for rapid development and pressure down the e-file. Kasparov did prefer 7 ♗c4 against Leko at the 2003 Linares, but Eljanov's 7...♘g4! (7...d6 8 ♘d5 ♘xd5 9 exd5 g6 10 ♘xd4 cxd4 11 d3 h6!, wisely preventing 12 ♗g5, was very solid for Black after 12 b4 ♗g7 13 ♕e2 ♗f6 14 ♕f3 ♔f8 although

White retained a nominal edge in Kasparov-Leko, but Van Wely has subsequently defended this line with relative ease) looks like a strong riposte when White has struggled to prove any advantage at all and he has thus far been loathe to weaken his kingside with g3, without his bishop's being back on f1:

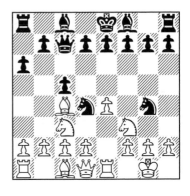

a) 8 ♗xf7+?! and now simplest is 8...♔d8!? 9 g3 ♘xf3+ 10 ♕xf3 ♘e5 11 ♕f4 g5! 12 ♕f5 d6 13 ♗e6 ♗xe6 14 ♕xe6 ♘f3+ which netted the exchange in L.Eriksson-M.Pavlovic, Dos Hermanas (online blitz) 2004.

b) 8 e5!? ♘xf3+ 9 ♕xf3 ♘xe5 10 ♕f4 is another aggressive try, but 10...f6! 11 ♘d5 ♕c6 12 ♖xe5 fxe5 13 ♕xe5 d6 14 ♕h5+ g6 15 ♕f3 ♗g7! left White starting to struggle for compensation in Y.Balashov-P.Eljanov, Moscow 2004.

c) 8 d3!? is a combative, but not fully sufficient, response when 8...♘xf3+ 9 ♕xf3 ♕xh2+ 10 ♔f1 ♘e5 11 ♗xf7+ ♘xf7 12 ♗f4, intended 12...♕h4 13 ♘d5 d6 14 ♗g3! in E.Moradiabadi-P.Eljanov, Dubai 2004, but Postny's 12...♘e5! 13 ♗xh2 ♘xf3 14 gxf3 e6 would have given Black a pleasant endgame advantage.

7...♘xb5 8 exf6 ♘xc3

Black doesn't have to let the c1-bishop into the game, but the materialistic 8...gxf6 9 ♘d5! ♕c6 10 c4! ♘c7 11 ♘xc7+ ♕xc7 12 d4 gives White a strong initiative for the pawn and 12...e6 13 b3! d6 14 ♗b2 ♗g7 15 dxc5 dxc5 16 ♘g5 e5 17 ♘e4 saw Black starting to suffer in I.Khairullin-S.Zhigalko, Kirishi 2005.

9 fxg7 ♗xg7 10 dxc3 d6

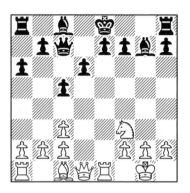

11 ♘g5!?

Continuing aggressively, while advancing the queen, again hoping to target the black kingside, also isn't too problematic for Black. Indeed 11 ♕d5 h6! (preventing 12 ♘g5 and preparing to meet 12 ♘h4 with 12...♗f6 13 ♕h5 ♗xh4! 14 ♕xh4 ♗e6) 12 ♕h5 e5! 13 ♘h4 can now be met by simply 13...♗e6 and 14 f4 0-0-0 15 ♗e3 ♖dg8 16 ♖ad1 ♗f8 was roughly equal in T.Nedev-S.Atalik, Kansas 2003, while 11 ♕d3 h6 12 ♗f4 e5 13 ♗g3 ♗e6 14 ♘h4 c4! 15 ♕f3 ♕d7 16 h3 0-0-0 was very comfortable for Black in M.Adams-V.Anand, Bundesliga 2005.

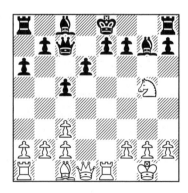

11...h6?!

Now Volokitin gets to demonstrate his tal-

ent with some fine sacrifices and Eljanov was later to improve with 11...♗f5! when 12 f4 (preventing ...e5, while 12 a4 ♕c6 13 ♕e2 ♗f6 14 ♘e4 ♗xe4 15 ♕xe4 ♕xe4 16 ♖xe4 d5 gave Black a very easy draw in V.Anand-V.Kramnik, Linares 2003) 12...♕d7 13 h3 h6! 14 ♘e4 0-0-0 (now Black has avoided any pressure down the e-file) 15 ♕f3 ♖hg8 16 ♗e3 ♗xe4 17 ♕xe4 ♗f6 18 f5 h5! was fine for him in T.Nedev-P.Eljanov, Bled Olympiad 2002. Volokitin has instead suggested 12 ♕f3!? ♗g6 13 h4 which he optimistically assessed as clearly favouring White, but, as well as Greenfeld's 13...♕c6!?, Black appears to be fine after 13...h5 14 ♕g3 ♕d7!, avoiding 15 ♘e6 and 15 a3 ♗f6 16 ♘e4 ♗xe4 17 ♖xe4 0-0-0 18 ♗g5 ♖dg8! 19 ♕e3 ♗xg5 20 hxg5 e6 didn't see White getting anywhere in L.Mkrtchian-T.Sterliagova, Sochi 2004.

12 ♗f4!

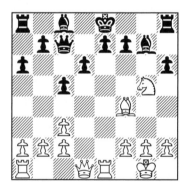

12...0-0

Rushing towards relative safety and avoiding 12...e5? 13 ♘e4 exf4? 14 ♘xd6+ ♔f8 15 ♖e8 mate and 12...hxg5? 13 ♗xd6 ♕d7 14 ♖xe7+ ♕xe7 15 ♗xe7 ♔xe7 16 ♕d5 when Black can't coordinate his extra pieces in time to deal with the extra queen.

13 ♘e4 f5?!

Rather provocative, but after 13...♗f5 14 ♕h5 ♗g6 15 ♕h4 Black doesn't actually have sufficient time to fully ease the kingside pressure. Then 15...h5 (or 15...f5?! 16 ♘d2! ♗f6

17 ♕g3 ♔g7 18 ♖e6 ♖h8 19 ♖ae1 b5 20 ♘f3 and White was all set to break through in B.Savchenko-R.Farakhov, Essentuki 2003) 16 ♖ad1 ♖ae8 17 ♗g5! f6 18 ♗c1 ♕c8 19 h3 ♖f7 20 ♖d3! began to increase the pressure, and favoured White, in L.Yurtaev-V.Ivanchuk, Frunze 1988.

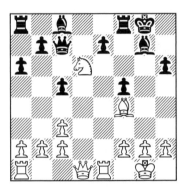

14 ♘xd6! exd6 15 ♗xd6 ♕f7 16 ♗xf8?!

The rooks do operate on good open files, but the bishop-pair is able to cover several key squares after this and so White should have preferred 16 ♖e7! ♕g6 (16...♕c4?! 17 ♖xg7+! ♔xg7 18 ♗xf8+ ♔xf8 19 ♕d8+ ♔g7 20 ♖e1 gives White a decisive attack) 17 ♕d5+ ♔h7 18 ♗e5 ♖g8 19 ♖e1 (Volokitin) with a very strong attack, while Black can't complete his development.

16...♗xf8 17 ♕d8 b5 18 ♖ad1 ♗b7 19 ♕b6! ♕g7 20 ♕e6+ ♔h8 21 g3

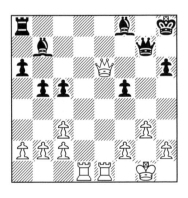

21...♗e4!

Sensibly blocking the e-file, although the exposed black king now allows White to pick off a pawn.

22 ♖d7 ♕g8 23 ♕e5+ ♗g7 24 ♕xc5 ♖e8 25 ♕d6 ♖e6 26 ♕c7 ♖c6 27 ♕d8 ♕xd8 28 ♖xd8+ ♔h7

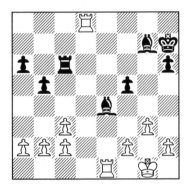

29 ♖d7?!

Trying to prevent any counterplay is far from easy in this complex position, but after this Eljanov was able to unravel when the rooks contained the bishops, but could do no more. The last chance for the advantage was, as Volokitin later observed, 29 ♖ed1!? ♗e5 30 ♔f1 ♔g6 31 f4!, retaining some winning chances.

29...♔g6! 30 ♖ed1 ♗e5 31 ♖1d2 h5! 32 ♖e7 ♔f6 33 ♖h7 ♔g6 34 ♖e7 ♗g7 35 ♖ed7 ♗f8 36 ♖d8 ½-½

Game 51
T.Oral-A.Kovalev
Czech Team Ch. 2002

---

1 e4 c5 2 ♘f3 ♘c6 3 ♗b5 ♘f6 4 ♘c3 ♕c7 5 0-0 ♘d4 6 ♖e1 a6 7 ♗f1

Continuing the theme of a reversed English Four Knights as White retreats his bishop out of harm's way and prepares to meet 7...d6 with 8 ♘d5! ♘xd5 9 exd5, intending 10 c3 or 9...♗g4 10 ♗e2 ♘xe2+ 11 ♕xe2 with useful pressure down the e-file.

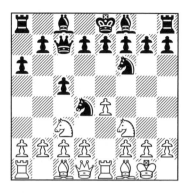

7...e5

Still the main line, although in the past couple of years Bauer's idea of 7...♘g4!? has been growing in popularity. After 8 g3 (more aggressive is Greenfeld's suggestion of 8 e5!? ♘xf3+ 9 ♕xf3 ♘xe5 10 ♕e4 which could certainly do with a test, and there is a surprising amount of compensation, such as after 10...d6 11 d4 cxd4 12 ♘d5 ♕c6 13 ♕xd4 ♗f5 14 f4 ♘g4 15 ♗d2 e6 16 c4 or with 12...♕d8 13 ♕xd4 e6 14 f4 ♘c6 15 ♕c3) 8...♘xf3+ 9 ♕xf3 ♘e5 Black is very solid, enjoys good control over d4 and has challenged White to find a good way to make some constructive use of the kingside fianchetto.

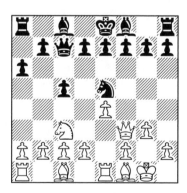

E.Sutovsky-L.McShane, Malmö 2003 continued 10 ♕d1 (instead 10 ♕e3!? e6 11 ♗g2 d6 12 ♘e2 ♗e7 13 f4 ♘c6 14 c3, preparing

d4, merits attention when 14...c4!? 15 d4 cxd3 16 ♕xd3 0-0 17 ♗e3 b5 18 a4! gave White a small edge in the resulting Open Sicilian position in H.Elwert-J.Van Oosterom, correspondence 2004) 10...e6 11 f4 ♘c6 when White doesn't really have a good version of the Closed Sicilian. Black may not be able to fianchetto, but White is badly missing his king's knight to fight for control of d4 with and after 12 d3 ♗e7 13 ♗g2 0-0 14 ♗e3 b5 Black is solid and developing counterplay. Sutovsky thus tried 12 e5!?, but then 12...d5 13 exd6 ♗xd6 14 ♘d5 ♕d8 15 ♗g2 0-0 16 ♘e3 ♕d7 17 ♕f3 ♖b8 18 ♘c4 ♗c7 and ...♘d4 was very comfortable for Black.

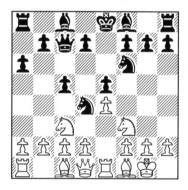

8 ♗c4

Moving the bishop again now that Black has weakened the a2-g8 diagonal, but such a slow approach is unsurprisingly not especially challenging, especially given that ...e5 is a key part of Black's plans after 4...♕c7. White does though have alternatives; two of which deserve further attention:

a) 8 ♘d5!? ♘xd5 9 exd5 d6 10 c3 ♘xf3+ 11 ♕xf3 ♗e7 12 d4! logically tries to exploit White's superior development, when 12...0-0 13 ♕g3! (13 dxe5 dxe5 14 ♕g3 ♗d6! 15 c4 f5 16 ♗d2 ♖f6 17 ♕a3 a5 favoured Black due to his kingside prospects in A.Sokolov-J.Lautier, French Ch., Aix les Bains 2003) – another suggestion from Greenfeld's detailed *New in Chess* survey on 4...♕c7 – is critical.

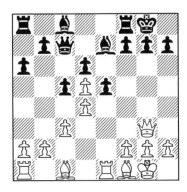

Now 13...cxd4 14 cxd4 exd4!? (14...♗f6 15 dxe5 ♗xe5 16 ♗f4 f6 17 ♗d3 gives White a pleasant edge, while 14...♕a5 15 ♗h6 ♗f6 16 dxe5 dxe5 17 ♗c4 ♗d7 is very solid for Black, although the passed d-pawn should grant White a small advantage after 18 ♗g5!) 15 ♗d3! (Greenfeld) looks to play on the kingside, but 15...♕d8! intends ...♗d7 and to meet ♗h6 with ...♗f6, while Black is fairly happy to return the d4-pawn in return for some exchanges and activity. White might thus try 16 ♗d2 ♗d7 17 ♗b4, but then 17...♖e8! 18 ♗xd6 ♗xd6 19 ♕xd6 ♗b5! appears to fizzle out to a draw.

b) 8 h3 d6

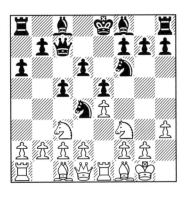

9 ♘h2?! (trying to weaken Black's control over d5, but Illescas was well enough developed here not to be too inconvenienced) 9...♗e7 10 a4 ♗e6 11 ♘g4!? was

V.Gashimov-M.Illescas Cordoba, Calvia Olympiad 2004 when 11...♘xg4 12 hxg4 ♕d7 13 ♘d5! ♗xg4! 14 f3 ♗e6 15 c3 ♘c6 16 ♘b6 ♕d8 17 ♘xa8 ♗h4! led to a great scrap, but a simpler way to a favourable position for Black was Notkin's 11...♘xe4! 12 ♘xe4 f5 when Black gains a very strong centre and good attacking chances.

c) 8 d3!? blocks in the light-square prelate, but is not without venom and 8...d6!? (8...♗e7 is less accurate in view of 9 ♗g5 d6 10 ♗xf6! ♗xf6 11 ♘d5 ♕d8 12 c3 ♘xf3+ 13 ♕xf3 ♗g5 14 d4! with an edge in S.Belkhodja-D.Hausrath, 2nd Bundesliga 2003) 9 ♗g5! ♗e6!? may not suffice for equality due to 10 ♗xf6 gxf6 11 ♘d5! ♗xd5 12 exd5 f5! 13 ♘xd4 cxd4 14 ♕h5! with good play on the light squares, especially after 14...♕d7 15 g3.

8...d6

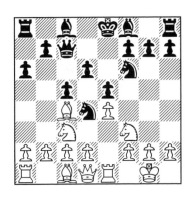

9 h3

Wisely preventing 9...♗g4, while 9 ♘g5?! h6! works for Black. Still he must be precise with 10 ♘xf7!? ♖h7 11 ♘d5 ♘xd5! 12 c3! (L.Dominguez-T.Radjabov, Tripoli 2004) 12...♘b6! when neither 13 ♘xe5 dxe5 14 ♕h5+ ♔d8 nor 13 ♕h5 ♘f3+!, intending 14 gxf3 g6, offers White objectively anywhere near enough compensation.

9...♗e6 10 d3 b5!

Having prevented White from occupying d5, Kovalev now forces the exchange of the white light-square bishop and quickly gains a fairly promising set-up.

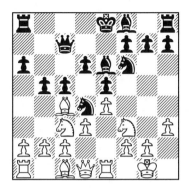

11 ♗xe6 fxe6 12 a4

White later tried 12 ♘xd4, but 12...exd4!? 13 ♘e2 ♕f7 14 f4 ♗e7 15 f5 exf5! 16 exf5 ♘d5 17 ♘f4 ♘xf4 18 ♗xf4 0-0 was fine for Black at this point in S.Movsesian-A.Volokitin, Sarajevo 2005.

12...b4! 13 ♘xd4 cxd4 14 ♘a2 a5 15 c3!

White must try to activate his knight and to prevent Black from doubling against c2, although it does already slightly feel like White is the side trying to equalise.

15...bxc3 16 bxc3 ♗e7 17 cxd4 exd4 18 ♗g5 0-0 19 ♘c1?

Missing a tactic, whereas 19 ♕b3 would have been much less clear, although after

19...♕d7 the a2-knight is still a little offside.

19...♘xe4! 20 ♗xe7 ♘xf2 21 ♕b3 ♕xe7 22 ♖a2?

Overlooking a strong intermezzo; White had to take on e6 and then try to defend after 22 ♕xe6+ ♕xe6 23 ♖xe6 d5 24 ♖e2 ♘d1! or with the slightly more risky 22 ♖xe6!? ♘xh3+! 23 ♔h2! ♕f7 24 ♖xd6.

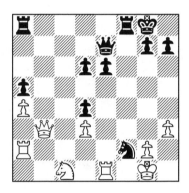

22...♖ab8! 23 ♕c4

23 ♕xe6+ ♕xe6 24 ♖xe6 ♖b1 25 ♖e1 ♘xh3+! 26 gxh3 ♖c8 (Vlassov) would have given Black a winning ending, but it's not long now before Kovalev makes good use of his advanced knight to create a winning attack.

23...♖bc8! 24 ♕b3 ♖c3 25 ♕b5 ♕h4 26 ♖ae2 ♘xh3+! 27 gxh3 ♕g3+ 0-1

Summary

There are no signs of recent interest in this starting to wane, while 3...♘f6 should appeal to those seeking to avoid the more standard positions arising after 3...e6 and 3...g6. Club players keen to follow fashion should though make sure that they are happy with the transpositions to 3...g6 systems after 4 e5 and 4 ♗xc6.

4 ♕e2 doesn't appear too promising, but Rublevsky's 4 ♗xc6 remains a perfectly viable alternative for White to 4 ♘c3. After 4 ♘c3, Black must avoid 4...♘d4, while 4...g6 leads to some rather complex positions and critical then is Khalifman's 5 e5, as 5 h3 should probably be met by just 5...♕c7 and not by 5...♗g7. Kramnik's other choice of 4...e5 appears to be fine for Black if one copies Carlsen's aggressive play, but following Glek's path instead looks like the route to an edge for White.

4 ♘c3 ♕c7 is a strong move and gives Black a dynamic and interesting position. 5 0-0 ♘d4 6 ♘xd4 cxd4 7 ♘d5 is still dangerous, but Black appears to be objectively fine due to Avrukh's 11...b5. Instead after 6 ♖e1 a6, Black appears to have worked out promising defences to 7 ♗c4 and 7 e5 (7...♘g4 and 11...♗f5 respectively), and so future attention may well focus more on 7 ♗f1. Then 7...♘g4!? is quite critical, while after 7...e5 White should seriously explore both 8 ♘d5 and simply 8 d3.

1 e4 c5 2 ♘f3 ♘c6 3 ♗b5 ♘f6 *(D)*
4 ♘c3

       4 ♗xc6 – *Game 44*
       4 ♕e2 – *Game 45*

4...♕c7

       4...♘d4 – *Game 46*
       4...g6 – *Game 47*
       4...e5 – *Game 48*

5 0-0 ♘d4 *(D)* **6 ♖e1**

       6 ♘xd4 – *Game 49*

6...a6 *(D)*

       7 e5 – *Game 50*
       7 ♗f1 – *Game 51*

3...♘f6

5...♘d4

6...a6

CHAPTER EIGHT

3...e6: Creative and Dynamic

1 e4 c5 2 ♘f3 ♘c6 3 ♗b5 e6

This is a fairly deep and complex response to the Rossolimo. Black gives himself the option of breaking with ...d5, but more importantly prepares to cover his c6-knight with ...♘ge7. However, doing so is a little slow and White can aim to exploit that with an exchange on c6, by quickly opening the centre with d4 or by aiming to build a strong centre with c3 and d4. Those three main plans all have their own subtleties and thus it requires some skill to handle the black side of 3...e6, although doing so can be a rewarding experience as Michal Krasenkow, Joel Lautier, Alexander Moiseenko, Ruslan Sherbakov and Evgeny Sveshnikov, as well as Garry Kasparov (when preferring the Sveshnikov to the Najdorf of late) have shown.

4 0-0

White's main response, although there has been a fair amount of interest of late in 4 ♗xc6. After 4...bxc6, the White position appears to be easier to play; he will aim to advance with f4 and/or e5 and thus cramp Black, while White wants to provoke ...d5, thereby allowing him to fix the black centre and to begin to target the doubled c-pawns. However, it's not so easy for White as he must aim not to allow Black to slowly and carefully advance in the centre, usually after a well-timed and supported ...e5. That advance enables Black to activate his light-squared bishop and bringing that piece into play is often crucial as to whether his opening stands or fails.

The positions arising after 4 ♗xc6 bxc6 aren't especially easy for either side to handle, although there are a number of general motifs, while Jonathan Rowson, in an excellent *New in Chess Yearbook* survey, succinctly explained the main error which both sides can commit, namely drifting. It's all too easy to ignore the opponent's intentions just for a move, when suddenly White has forced the ugly ...d5 or Black has gained a strong centre with ...e5 and White lacks any play. Move order issues and transpositions are also important after the exchange on c6 and we will consider White's three choices in descending order of popularity: 5 d3 first with the main response of 5...♘e7 being examined in Game 52 and Black's alternatives to that in Game 53; 5 0-0 is the subject of Game 54; and 5 b3 that of Game 55.

Black must though avoid 4...dxc6?! when his position lacks dynamism and 5 d3 ♘e7 6 h4 h5 7 e5! (having weakened the black kingside White clamps down in the centre and makes ...f6 much less likely to succeed) 7...♘g6 8 ♘c3 ♗e7 9 ♕e2 ♕c7 10 ♕e4 already left White clearly better in L.Psakhis-N.Stanec, Pula Zonal 2000.

One dangerous plan for White against 3...e6 is to exploit Black's slow development by seizing a quick initiative with an exchange on c6 and, after ...♘xc6, a quick d4. He should probably castle first though if he wants to employ that rather than opt for an immediate 4 ♘c3. Now 4...♘e7 5 0-0 transposes to our next note, but Black should probably seize the chance to immediately occupy the hole with 4...♘d4. This is the Anderssen variation and is quite an important position for it also frequently arises via 2 ♘f3 e6 3 ♘c3 ♘c6 4 ♗b5 ♘d4 and 2 ♘c3 ♘c6 3 ♗b5 ♘d4 4 ♘f3 e6.

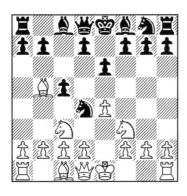

Here 5 ♘xd4?! cxd4 6 ♘e2 doesn't con-

vince after 6...♕g5!, while 5 0-0 a6 6 ♗d3 ♘e7 transposes after 7 ♘xd4 cxd4 8 ♘e2 to the note to White's fifth move below. That is quite comfortable for Black, but Scheveningen and Taimanov exponents can prefer 6...♘c6!? when 7 ♗e2! d6 8 d4 cxd4 9 ♘xd4 leads to the former and 7...♘ge7 8 d4 cxd4 9 ♘xd4 to the latter, although 7...g5!? may also be possible. Instead 7 ♖e1 isn't an especially effective move as Black appears to be fine even if he allows ♗f1 and d4, but 7...g5! leaves White slightly struggling for a plan and after 8 g3 d6 9 b3 ♗g7 10 ♗b2 h6 11 ♗f1 ♘ge7 Black's extra kingside space was fairly useful in G.Souleidis-H.Bousios, Halkidiki 2002.

4...♘ge7

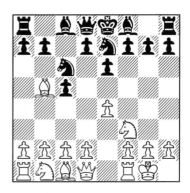

5 c3

Once again 5 ♘c3 is possible when 5...a6 6 ♗xc6 ♘xc6 7 d4 cxd4 8 ♘xd4 and 9 ♖e1 will lead to Games 59 and 60. However, again 5...♘d4 6 ♘xd4 cxd4 is a little awkward for White, although he does now have the option of 7 ♘e2 a6 8 ♗a4!? (8 ♗d3 is often met by 8...♘c6 9 c3 ♗c5, but 8...d5 remains an efficient equaliser and, for example, 9 exd5 ♘xd5! 10 c3 dxc3 11 dxc3 ♕c7 12 ♗e4 ♘f6 13 ♗f3 ♗d6 14 h3 0-0 15 c4?! ♘d7! and 16...♘e5 gave Black a good game in M.Thesing-Cu.Hansen, Bundesliga 2000) 8...♘c6 9 d3. However, even this is fairly comfortable for Black and 9...♗c5 10 ♗xc6 dxc6 11 ♘g3 ♗d6! 12 f4 f5!? 13 exf5 exf5 14 ♖e1+ ♔f7 15 c3 ♕b6 gave Black a good game in D.Tyomkin-I.Nataf, Montreal 2004.

White can also improve his queen's bishop with 5 b3 when the pressure against g7 can be awkward. This approach, which we'll consider in Games 56 and 57, is slowly growing in popularity and was Kaufman's suggestion against 3...e6.

Another important, if not especially fashionable, alternative to 5 c3 is Glek's preferred 5 ♖e1 when we'll deal with 5...♘d4 and 5...a6 6 ♗e2 in Game 58. That is quite a quiet approach, but 6 ♗xc6 ♘xc6 7 d4 cxd4 8 ♘xd4 certainly isn't when Black must be careful as he is behind in development. The recommended course is 8...♕c7, intending 9 ♘c3 ♗d6, which we'll see in Game 59, with the other main set-up with 8...d6 being the subject of Game 60.

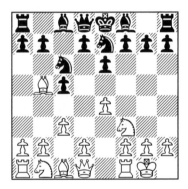

5...a6

Standard and popular, but not forced, whilst Rublevsky's success in the main line might well soon see 5...d5 start to gain ground in the popularity stakes; see Game 61 for details of this central advance.

6 ♗a4

The main line, but White can also retreat with 6 ♗e2!? when play has similarities with both 5 ♖e1 a6 6 ♗f1 and the c3 Sicilian after 6...d5 7 exd5 ♘xd5, although those with some experience of the French Tarrasch as Black

might prefer 7...exd5!? and then 8 d4 c4 or even 8...cxd4. After the usual recapture with the knight, White will often be left with a three v two queenside majority, but recent results have confirmed that here that shouldn't overly trouble Black. 8 d4 cxd4 9 ♘xd4 ♗d7 10 ♗f3!, immediately improving the bishop, is the best try for an advantage and after 10...♘xd4 11 ♕xd4 ♗c6 12 ♘d2, 12...♘e7 13 ♕g4! is a little awkward for Black and so he should go 12...♕c7 13 ♘c4 b5! or 12...♖c8 13 ♘c4 b5 14 ♘e5 ♗b7 15 c4 bxc4 16 ♘xc4 ♖c7 17 ♖d1 ♕f6! 18 ♕xf6 gxf6 19 b3 ♗c5 20 ♗d2 ♔e7 when the strong d5-knight kept the white forces at bay and the position was roughly equal in V.Zvjaginsev-B.Macieja, Panormo 2001.

6...b5

Rublevsky has also faced 6...c4!? which ambitiously clamps down on d3 to prevent White from gaining his ideal centre, but is rather double-edged as Game 62 reveals.

7 ♗c2

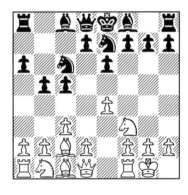

The white bishop has undertaken a Lopezesque manoeuvre and Black must always watch out for later kingside pressure. Now 7...c4 will transpose into Game 62, but 7...b5 remains the main response. This used to be consider a little ambitious but fine for Black after 8 a4 ♘g6 or 8 d4 cxd4 9 cxd4 ♘b4!. However, White has realised that he can keep those two breaks in reserve and so he usually now prefers either 8 ♖e1 (Game 63) or the choice of Adams and Rublevsky, 8 ♕e2 (see Game 64).

Game 52
V.Malakhov-T.Nedev
European Club Cup, Rethymnon 2003

---

1 e4 c5 2 ♘f3 ♘c6 3 ♗b5 e6 4 ♗xc6 bxc6 5 d3 ♘e7

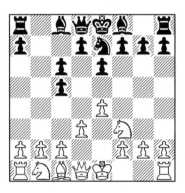

6 ♕e2

This flexible move (a fairly recent development) keeps White's options fully open and waits to see how Black intends to play in the centre. Instead 6 0-0 transposes to Game 54, while White has tried a number of other approaches:

a) 6 ♘g5 is the direct approach, but White usually prefers to delay this these days. After 6...♘g6?! 7 f4! White gains some useful space on the kingside as well as control over e5 and so Black tends to prefer 6...h6 (or 6...f6 7 ♘h3 and, now that the white knight is a little misplaced and e5 not possible in reply, 7...d5!? is playable when 8 ♘c3 ♘g6 9 ♕h5 ♗d6 should probably still be met by 10 f4, as 10 ♘f4 ♗xf4 11 ♗xf4 0-0 12 ♗d2 f5! saw Black mobilising his central pawns to gain sufficient counterplay in M.Adams-A.Vaisser, French League 2001) 7 ♘h3 g6 with a standard anti Closed Sicilian set-up. Black intends ...♗g7, ...e5 and then usually ...f5 or sometimes ...d5,

while 8 ♗d2!? ♗g7 9 ♗c3 e5 10 f4 d5! 11 ♘f2 ♕b6 gave him good counterplay in J.Rowson-S.Ansell, British Ch., Scarborough 2001.

b) 6 h4!? is typically modern chess as White aims to prevent Black from settling his knight on g6 and from fianchettoing.

It is probably best met by 6...h5 7 ♕e2 (7 e5!? is the cramping move White would like to play, but after 7...♘g6 8 ♘bd2 f6! 9 ♘c4 ♘xe5 10 ♘fxe5 fxe5 11 ♘xe5 ♕f6 12 ♕e2 d6! Black regains control over e5 and should be fine) 7...f6!, fighting for control of the all-important e5-square. White must prevent ...e5 with 8 e5!, but practice has shown that Black isn't worse, although the position remains complex, after 8...fxe5 9 ♕xe5 ♘f5 10 ♗g5 ♗e7 11 ♘c3 d6 or 9 ♘xe5 d6 10 ♘c4 ♘f5! 11 ♗g5 ♗e7 12 ♗xe7 ♕xe7 13 ♘c3 e5 when the c8-bishop could come to e6 and the f5-knight was well-placed, leaving Black already slightly for preference, in Y.Shabanov-S.Arkhipov, Smolensk 2000.

c) 6 ♘h4!? is another way of freeing the f-pawn's path and has been tested by Luke McShane. However, after 6...♘g6 (best, whereas 6...g6 7 ♕e2 ♗g7 8 0-0 0-0 9 f4 d6 10 ♘f3 f5?! 11 e5! d5 12 c4! gave White an ideal set-up and fixed the c5-weakness in L.Webb-M.Mitchell, British Ch., Edinburgh 2003) 7 ♘xg6 hxg6 he discovered that 8 e5 c4! was awkward and so later preferred 8 0-0 e5 9 f4, but then 9...d6! 10 fxe5 dxe5 left Black rather active in L.McShane-I.Nataf, Esbjerg 2001 when 11 ♕e1 was met by 11...c4, while 11 ♘d2?! c4! 12 ♘xc4 ♕h4 13 h3 ♗xh3 would have regained the pawn with advantage.

6...♕c7

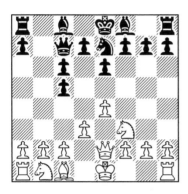

7 ♘h4!?

Opening the f-pawn's path and this currently appears the most promising course as a couple of Anand games have revealed. R.Ponomariov-V.Anand, Linares 2003 saw 7 ♘g5 h6! (again wisely not letting the knight retreat to f3 after f4) 8 ♘h3 g6 9 f4 ♗g7 10 c4 e5 11 ♘c3 d5! 12 0-0 0-0 with sufficient counterplay. Now that White has played f4 it can be more difficult for him to maintain central control, while here Anand was ready to exploit the slightly offside knight with 13...♗xh3 14 gxf3 and then 14...f5. The earlier game V.Anand-A.Grischuk, Wijk aan Zee 2003 had instead seen 7 ♘c3 ♘g6 8 ♘g5 e5! 9 ♕h5 d6 10 0-0 h6 11 ♘h3 ♗e7 12 ♔h1 ♗f6 when Black was very solid and ready to meet 13 f4?! with exchanges on h3 and f4. Without that though White lacked a good plan and so Anand went 13 ♘g1 which he accompanied with an early draw offer.

7...h6

Weakening the kingside like this is a little double-edged, but one can understand Black's desire to avoid 7...♘g6 8 ♘xg6 hxg6 9 e5!

when the central clamp will force him to further weaken his structure. However, 7...h6 does at least prepare to meet 8 f4 with the strong 8...g5! and so Malakhov first prepares the advance.

8 g3 g6 9 f4 ♗g7 10 ♘f3 0-0 11 ♘bd2

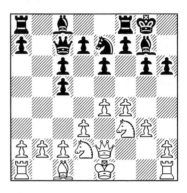

11...f6

White has a harmonious position and so Black needs counterplay and to activate his light-square bishop. Placing it on a6 as Nedev does is not so bad, but does require an energetic follow-up. Perhaps he should thus have first inserted 11...d5!? 12 0-0 and then gone for 12...♗a6, intending 13 c4 ♖ab8! 14 ♘b3 dxc4 15 dxc4 ♖b4.

12 e5! fxe5 13 fxe5 g5! 14 ♕e4! ♘f5 15 0-0 ♗a6

Sensibly avoiding the greedy 15...g4? 16 ♕xg4 ♘e3 due to 17 ♕g6 ♘xf1 18 ♘e4 (Notkin) with a huge attack.

16 ♘b3 ♘d4?

Badly underestimating the weakness of his kingside, whilst it was essential to keep the knight on f5 and to continue with Notkin's suggestion of 16...d5! 17 exd6 ♕xd6. That does leave the black structure badly crippled, but he is pretty active here with a great g7-bishop, a strong f5-knight and ideas of ...c4 and ...♘xg3. 18 ♔g2 might retain control, but this is far from the stable advantage White sought with 4 ♗xc6.

17 ♘bxd4 cxd4

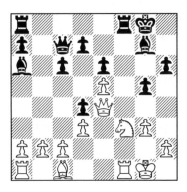

18 ♗xg5! ♖xf3

The weakness of the black kingside is fatal even after this, but 18...hxg5 19 ♘xg5 ♖f5 20 ♖xf5 exf5 21 ♕xf5 ♕xe5 22 ♕f7+ ♔h8 23 ♕g6 would also have been decisive.

19 ♕xf3 hxg5 20 ♕f7+ ♔h8 21 ♖ae1! ♖f8 22 ♕h5+ ♔g8 23 ♖xf8+ ♔xf8 24 ♕xg5 d6 25 ♖f1+ ♔g8 26 ♕g6 dxe5 27 ♕xe6+ ♔h8 28 ♖f5 1-0

Game 53
M.Adams-M.Krasenkow
Istanbul Olympiad 2000

---

1 e4 c5 2 ♘f3 ♘c6 3 ♗b5 e6 4 ♗xc6 bxc6 5 d3

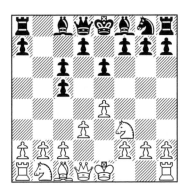

5...d6!?

Krasenkow is a 3...e6 expert and so we must take this relatively rare move seriously,

even though playing ...d6 is often considered suspect due to an e5-break or to c3 and d4. As well as the 5...♘e7 of Game 52, Black has also tried a number of other set-ups:

a) 5...♕c7 gives White a choice:

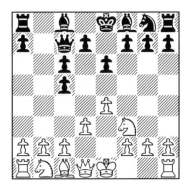

a1) 6 e5!? is the interesting option, thematically trying to clamp down on the black position and forcing Black to further weaken his structure by advancing his f-pawn. Black must challenge with 6...f6! when 7 ♕e2 fxe5 8 ♘xe5 does on the one hand see the black knight being developed actively to f6, but Black's inability to challenge with 7...♘g6 has meant that he must now find another way to deal with the strong e5-steed. Then 8...♘f6 9 0-0 ♗e7 10 f4! (clamping down on e5) 10...0-0 11 ♘d2 (heading for f3 and White intends to restrain the black centre with knights on c4 and f3) 11...d6 12 ♘ec4 ♗d7 13 b3 appears to give White an edge and after 13...♘d5 14 ♘e4 ♖f7 15 g3 a5 16 a3!? a4 17 bxa4 ♘b6 18 ♘xb6 ♕xb6 19 c4! he had continued to restrain Black's counterplay and retained the advantage, although Black was still very solid, in F.Volkmann-A.Moiseenko, European Team Ch., Plovdiv 2003.

a2) White does, however, usually prefer the standard 6 0-0 ♘e7 7 ♘g5 with similar aims to those considered in Malakhov-Nedev. A promising defence is then 7...f6!? 8 ♘h3 d6 (and not 8...d5? 9 f4 ♘g6 10 ♕h5! ♕f7 11 c4 ♗d6 12 ♘c3 0-0 13 b3! ♗d7 14 ♗a3 which soon won the c5-pawn in S.Kindermann-K.Van der Weide, Bad Wiessee 2002) 9 f4 g6 10 c4 ♗g7 11 ♘c3 0-0

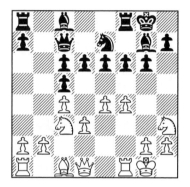

12 ♔h1 ♗d7 when the early absence of a weakening ...h6 makes it hard for White to get anywhere on the kingside. Furthermore, the knight can be slightly misplaced on h3 and 13 ♗e3 e5 14 fxe5 fxe5 15 ♘f2 h6 16 ♕d2 ♔h7 17 ♘e2 a5 18 ♘g3 ♗e6 19 ♖ae1 ♘g8 left Black very solid and play was about equal in M.Chandler-P.Wells, British League 2003.

b) Black should though avoid the surprisingly common 5...d5?! when it's very easy for his centre to become static, while White enjoys the clear cut plan of blockading it and then targeting c5 or advancing on the kingside. Some Rossolimo experts have here been employing an immediate 6 c4!? ♘f6 7 ♘c3 ♗e7 8 0-0 0-0 9 b3 ♕c7 10 e5 ♘d7 11 ♗f4

with the standard edge in H.Hamdouchi-J.Montell Lorenzo, Salou 2000. Black must now avoid making his position worse with a premature ...f6 and here 11...f6?! 12 exf6 ♕xf4 13 fxe7 ♖e8 14 ♖e1 ♕f6 15 ♖c1 ♖xe7 16 ♘a4 simply made it even easier for White to start exploited the crippled black structure.

c) Better is 5...f6, although this does leave Black vulnerable to an early ♘h4, such as with 6 0-0 ♘e7 7 ♘h4! when 7...g6 8 f4 d6 9 ♘f3! ♗g7 sees Black apparently heading for a standard set-up. White could allow that and just play 10 c4 (with his knight being better on f3 than h3), but also promising is Nevednichy's 10 e5!?, immediately further breaking up the black structure and avoiding 10...e5.

6 e5

Now Black must either accept isolated doubled c-pawns or play an advance he'd rather not with ...d5. Instead 6 0-0 e5 7 c3 has been criticised, presumably because White has played d3 and so d4 will lose a tempo. However, this may not be such a bad choice, because the black e-pawn has moved twice and after 7...♘f6 8 d4 play has transposed to the note to Black's sixth in Game 1. Here Black has often preferred 7...♘e7, but 8 d4! cxd4 9 cxd4 ♘g6?! (9...exd4 10 ♘xd4 ♗d7 improves, although White retains an edge with 11 b3) 10 dxe5 dxe5 11 ♕c2 ♕c7 12 ♗e3 ♗d6 13 ♖c1 began to exploit the weaknesses of c6 and c5 in L.Yudasin-J.Bonin, New York 2001.

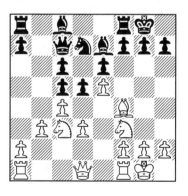

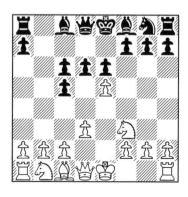

**6...dxe5 7 ♘xe5 ♕d5! 8 ♘f3 c4 9 ♘c3
♗b4 10 ♗d2 ♗xc3 11 ♗xc3 ♘e7!**

Black may have conceded the bishop-pair,
but he is solid and has good play on the light
squares. The knight will stand well on f5 and
with this Krasenkow improves over the earlier
11...♘f6 12 dxc4 ♕xc4 of A.Ardeleanu-
C.Nanu, Calimanesti 1999 when Smirin's 13
♘d2! ♕d5 14 0-0 keeps the queens on, prepares to exchange on f6 and gains the advantage.

12 dxc4 ♕xc4

13 ♘d2

13 ♕d4 ♕xd4 14 ♗xd4 ♗a6 would have
been fine for Black, but Adams fails to prove
any advantage with the queens on.

**13...♕d5 14 ♕g4 ♘f5 15 b3 h5 16 ♕f4
f6! 17 0-0-0 e5 18 ♕b4 c5 19 ♕b5+
♗d7 20 ♕a5 0-0 21 ♘c4 ½-½**

Here a draw was agreed; definitely a success for Krasenkow's 5...d6!? concept, although Rowson feels that Black should have
played on. Indeed his 21...♘d4 leaves Black a
touch better, although the white position remains rather solid.

> ### Game 54
> ## L.Galego-M.Krasenkow
> *European Team Ch., Leon 2001*

**1 e4 c5 2 ♘f3 ♘c6 3 ♗b5 e6 4 ♗xc6
bxc6 5 0-0**

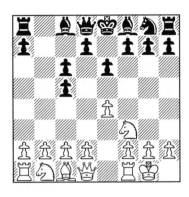

5...♘e7

Once again Black's main defence is to
bring his knight to g6 to cover the kingside
and especially e5. Instead we considered 5...f6
6 d3 via 5 d3 f6 6 0-0 in Adams-Krasenkow,
while 5...f6 6 b3 will be seen in the note to
Black's fifth in Game 55. After castling,
5...d6?! is though much less effective due to 6
c3 or to 6 e5! which now pretty much forces
6...d5, with 6...dxe5 7 ♘xe5 ♕d5 ineffective
with g2 securely defended.

6 d3 ♘g6

Once more 6...f6 7 ♘h4! is a little awkward
for Black when 7...♘g6?? 8 ♕h5 wins on the
spot, while 7...g6 8 f4 ♗g7 9 ♘f3 ♕c7 10
♕e1 leaves White with more space and the
slightly more favourable set-up.

7 ♘g5

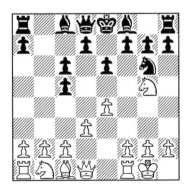

7...e5!

Clamping down on f4, but Black has also tested some other ideas on a number of occasions:

a) 7...♗e7

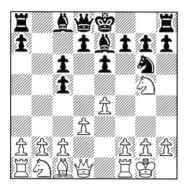

8 ♕h5! d6 (or 8...♗xg5 9 ♗xg5 ♕b6 when practice has shown 10 ♘d2! to be a promising gambit, leaving Black rather vulnerable on the dark squares) 9 f4! ♗xg5 10 fxg5 e5 11 ♗e3 ♗e6 12 ♘d2 ♕d7?! (12...0-0 and a quick ...f6 is a better way to minimise White's edge) 13 h3 (remaining alert!) 13...0-0 14 ♖f2 ♔h8 15 b3 ♕e7 16 ♘f1 a5 17 ♘g3 and White gained a very strong kingside attack in E.Rozentalis-S.B.Hansen, Bundesliga 2001.

b) 7...h6!? 8 ♘h3 d5 advances in the centre once again only because the white knight is sidelined and 9 e5 impossible in reply. After 9 ♘f4 ♘xf4 10 ♗xf4 ♕f6! 11 ♕c1 g5! 12 ♗g3 ♖g8 13 ♘c3 h5 White was under some pressure on the kingside in D.Sadvakasov-L.Van Wely, Amsterdam 2002. He thus countered with 14 f4, but 14...gxf4 15 ♕xf4 ♕xf4 16 ♗xf4 ♗a6 17 ♖ae1 d4! and 18...c4 saw Black successfully activate his light-square bishop with a pretty reasonable position.

c) 7...f6?! is now too slow an approach and 8 ♘h3 ♗e7 9 f4 0-0 10 ♘d2 d6 11 b3 a5 12 a4 f5 13 ♗b2 ♗f6 14 ♗xf6 ♕xf6 15 ♕h5 left Black quite solid, but White better and with the easier position to improve in G.Seul-L.Van Wely, Antwerp 1999.

8 ♕h5

As Black appears to have prevented f4, White carries out his other idea behind 7 ♘g5. However, it is surprising that Cherniaev's ambitious idea of still going 8 f4!?

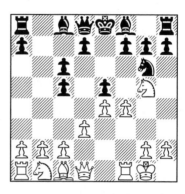

hasn't yet been tested, especially as White has struggled of late after 8 ♘g5. Here 8...exf4 9 ♕h5 ♕f6!? might be playable, but is a little risky, although too is 8...♘xf4 in view of 9 ♘xf7!? (not essential, although 9 ♗xf4 exf4 10 ♘h3 ♖b8! is annoying for White as 11 b3 ♗d6 weakens his dark squares and indirectly defends f4) 9...♘xf7 10 g3. The greedy 10...♕g5 then doesn't convince, but might have to be tried if Black is desperate to win as 10...♔g8 isn't fully desirable, while 10...g5 11 gxf4 exf4 12 ♕h5+ ♔g7 13 ♗xf4! gxf4 14 ♕g4+ (and not 14 ♖xf4? ♖g8!) 14...♔h6 15 ♕h3+ is a perpetual.

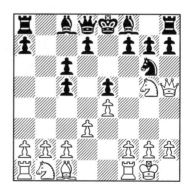

8...♕e7

As 8...h6? runs into 9 ♘xf7! ♔xf7 10 f4, Black must prepare that push, although he can also do so with 8...♕f6!? which leads to a rather unclear position after 9 g3!? (the active try whereas 9 ♘c3 d6 10 ♘xh7? ♕d8 11 g3 has been refuted by Mark Tseitlin's 11...♕d7!, intending 12 ♘xf8 ♔xf8 13 ♕g5 f6! and 14...♕h3, while 10 ♘e2 h6 11 ♘h3 ♘h4 prevented 12 f4? due to 12...g6! and led to a fairly attractive repetition with 12 ♘g5 ♘g6 13 ♘h3 ♘h4 in A.Sokolov-J.Lautier, French Ch., Val d'Isere 2002) 9...h6 10 ♘h3 d5!? 11 f4 c4, which deserves a test. However, the slightly less interesting 10...d6 11 ♔g2 ♗e7! (wisely developing as there isn't anything for Black on the kingside) 12 f4 exf4 13 ♘xf4 ♘xf4+ 14 ♖xf4 ♕e6 was also fine for Black in P.Jaracz-I.Nataf, European Ch., Ohrid 2001.

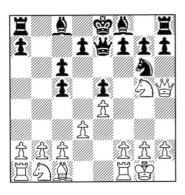

9 ♘h3?!

Drifting and White clearly didn't appreciate the need to act with this and his next move. He had to avoid losing material with 9 f4? exf4 10 ♗xf4 ♘xf4 11 ♖xf4 g6 12 ♕g4 d6 13 ♕h4 h6, but the knight didn't have to retreat so compliantly. Instead 9 ♘a3 waits for 9...h6 when 10 ♘h3 threatens 11 f4. However, Black should be fine after 9...d6 10 ♘c4 h6 11 ♘h3 ♗e6 or after 10...d5!? when 11 ♘a5 ♕c7 sidelined the knight, which wants to be on a4 and not on a5, in S.Berry-A.Harley, British League 2002 and 12 ♗d2 h6 13 ♘f3?! ♗d6 14 c4 dxe4 15 dxe4 ♘f4! grabbed the initia-

tive as the white queen was left a little low on squares.

9 ♘a3 may not be the best way to handle the knight, but Krasenkow had earlier shown that 9 ♘c3 also isn't a problem for Black with 9...d6 10 a3 h6 11 ♘h3 ♘h4 (preparing kingside counterplay, while the c8-bishop is already quite useful) 12 f4 g6 13 ♕e2 ♗xh3 14 gxh3 ♗g7 15 ♔h1 f5!? 16 exf5 ♘xf5! 17 fxe5 ♗xe5 being roughly level in Peng Xiaomin-M.Krasenkow, Shanghai 2001.

9...d6 10 ♗g5?! ♕b7! 11 b3 ♗d7

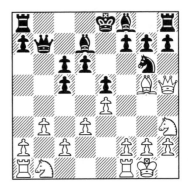

Black is handling his pieces well and has successfully solved the problem of the light-square bishop. 12...♕c8 is now a large threat and already Black is slightly for choice with White unable to play f4 and with the white pieces not well coordinated.

12 f3 h6 13 ♗e3 ♕c8 14 ♘d2 d5!

Thematically taking over the centre and leaving White starting to struggle for effective moves.

15 ♖ae1 ♗e7?!

Krasenkow later preferred to cash in with 15...♗xh3 16 ♕xh3 ♕xh3 17 gxh3 ♗e7 when the weakness of the white kingside is more important than that of c5, while ...0-0 and ...f5 is on the cards. Galego now gets back into the game to an extent, although he is soon outplayed once more and is undone on the kingside:

16 g4! d4 17 ♗f2 ♕c7 18 ♗g3 ♗e6 19

f4?! exf4 20 ♘xf4 ♘xf4 21 ♗xf4

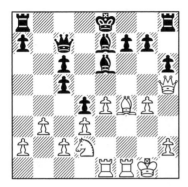

21...♕d7! 22 ♕e5 ♗xg4 23 ♕xg7 0-0-0 24 ♕e5 ♔b7 25 ♗g3 f6 26 ♕f4 ♗h3 27 ♖f2 ♖dg8 28 ♔h1 h5 29 ♘f3 h4! 30 ♘xh4 ♖g4 31 ♕f3 ♖gxh4 32 ♗xh4 ♖xh4 33 ♖g1 ♖h7 34 ♕g3 ♗e6 35 ♕g6 ♗d8 36 ♖g3?! f5! 37 ♔g1 ♗h4 38 exf5 ♗xg3 0-1

Game 55
E.Sutovsky-H.Nakamura
Pamplona 2003

---

1 e4 c5 2 ♘f3 ♘c6 3 ♗b5 e6 4 ♗xc6 bxc6 5 b3

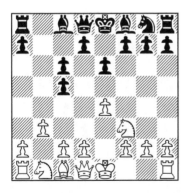

5...d5!?

Provocative, but positionally very committal and Black should objectively prefer one of his many alternatives:

a) 5...f6 6 0-0 (usual, although White has experimented of late with the alternatives and 6 ♘h4!? g6 7 f4 deserves a test, whereas White was effectively neutralised by 7 ♗b2 ♗g7 8 f4 ♘e7 9 0-0 0-0 10 d3 d6 11 ♘d2 e5!, blunting the b2-bishop, in M.Adams-T.Radjabov, Tripoli 2004) 6...♘e7 7 ♗b2 ♘g6 reaches an important position which also arises via 5 b3 ♘e7 and from a 5 0-0 move order. Here the sharp 8 d4 hasn't fully convinced, while 8 e5 ♗e7 leads to a further split:

a1) 9 d3 ♕c7 10 ♖e1 0-0 11 ♘bd2 fxe5 12 ♘xe5 ♘h8!, preparing ...d6 and ...e5, was a highly instructive idea in A.Bisguier-B.Gulko, Los Angeles 1991.

a2) 9 exf6 is possible, but White must meet 9...gxf6!? energetically with 10 d4! as 10 ♘c3?! e5! 11 d3 d6 12 ♘d2 f5 gave Black a mobile and unopposed centre in A.Kim-V.Mikhalevski, Moscow 2002.

a3) 9 ♘a3!? (the best try for an advantage as White is in time to meet 9...fxe5 with 10 ♘xe5 ♘xe5 11 ♗xe5 0-0 12 f4!) 9...0-0 10 ♘c4 fxe5 11 ♘fxe5 ♘xe5 should possibly be met by 12 ♗xe5!? d6 13 ♗g3, intending 13...e5 14 f4, although Black is probably not worse here with even 13...♗a6!? possible. Instead 12 ♘xe5 ♗f6 13 f4?! d6 14 ♘c4 ♗xb2 15 ♘xb2 ♗a6! 16 d3?! ♕f6! badly embarrassed White down the diagonal and against f4 in P.Brochet-S.Maze, Marseille 2001.

b) 5...♘e7 6 ♗b2 ♘g6 7 0-0 f6 is a more common route into the b3 main line which we just discussed after 5...f6.

c) 5...d6?! is again an intriguing possibility, but here it turns out that b3 is less weakening than d3 and 6 e5! dxe5 7 ♘xe5 is strong even though the black queen has a number of attractive looking squares. With aggressive play White has scored well in practice from this position:

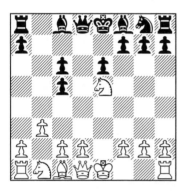

c1) 7...♕g5 8 ♘g4 f5 9 ♘e3 f4 10 ♕f3! fxe3 11 ♕xc6+ ♔d8 12 ♕xa8 exd2+ would have given White a very strong attack in B.Martinez-J.Morella, Villa Clara 2001 after Nogueiras' suggestion of 13 ♘xd2! ♕e5+ 14 ♘e4 ♕xa1 15 0-0.

c2) 7...♕d4?! 8 ♘c4! ♕xa1 9 ♘c3 ♗a6 10 0-0 ♗xc4 11 bxc4 ♗d6 12 ♕e2 ♘f6 13 ♗a3 favoured the queen over the rooks in Zhao Jun-Zhang Pengxiang, Moscow 2004.

c3) 7...♕d5!? deprives White of an effective sacrifice, but after 8 ♘f3 ♕e4+ 9 ♔f1, 9...c4 doesn't work, while otherwise the isolated doubled c-pawns should be of much more importance than the temporary slight discomfort to the white monarch.

d) 5...e5!? is the move Black would like to make work and will perhaps be seen a bit more often as after 6 ♘xe5! ♕e7 7 ♗b2 d6 8 ♘c4 (E.Shaposhnikov-D.Bocharov, Kazan 2001), Shaposhnikov observes that 8...d5! 9 ♘e5 f6 was possible as 10 ♘xc6! ♕xe4+ 11

♔f1 a5 leaves the white knight stranded, although after 12 ♘c3 ♕e6 13 ♕h5+ ♔d7 14 ♖e1 ♕xc6 15 ♘xd5 White does gain fairly dangerous attacking chances for it, but this position is by no means clear.

6 ♕e2 ♘e7 7 ♗a3!? ♘g6 8 0-0 ♕a5 9 ♗b2 ♗d6!?

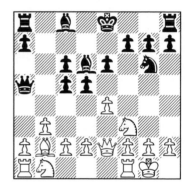

10 ♗xg7!?

As we noted in the Introduction, this does lead to a very rich position, but objectively White should probably prefer 10 e5 ♗e7 11 d3 or earlier 6 d3, with an edge in both cases.

10...♘f4 11 ♕e3 ♖g8! 12 e5 ♘xg2! 13 ♕h6! ♘e1! 14 exd6!

14 ♖xe1 ♗f8 15 ♕h5 ♖xg7+ 16 ♔h1, which is about equal, would have been a calm way out of any kingside trouble, but Sutovsky wants to keep up the complications.

14...♘xf3+ 15 ♔h1

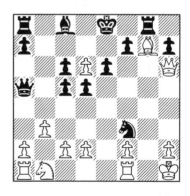

15...♗a6?!

After some very accurate play, the young American loses his way and underestimates a strong temporary piece sacrifice. Instead he should have redeployed his queen and 15...♕d8! 16 ♕xh7 ♔d7 would have led to a fascinating scrap in which White must find a way to untangle with his queen currently forced to stay on h7. Sutovsky offers 17 c4!? ♗a6! 18 ♗b2 ♔xd6 19 ♕h5! ♘d4 20 f4 f6 21 ♗xd4 cxd4 22 d3 ♕e7 23 ♘d2 which is still very unclear and in which all he knows is that the position is great fun to play!

16 d3 ♕d8 17 ♘d2! ♘xd2 18 ♖g1 ♕xd6

He must return the piece as 18...♘f3? loses to 19 ♗f6 ♖xg1+ 20 ♖xg1 with two killer threats.

19 ♕xd2 0-0-0 20 ♕h6 ♗b7?

Now White mops up the h-pawn and his bishop is vastly superior to Black's which, unfortunately for Nakamura, remains a major problem piece. Here Black had to be more active with either 20...e5!? (Bologan) or with 20...d4!? (Ftacnik), allowing the black queen to begin counterplay and which might still have been enough to maintain the balance.

21 ♗f6! ♖xg1+ 22 ♖xg1 ♖e8 23 ♕xh7 ♕f4!? 24 ♖g8! ♕xf6 25 ♖xe8+ ♔d7 26 ♖g8 ♕xf2 27 ♕h3!

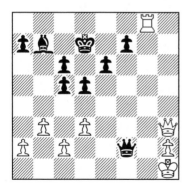

Defending his monarch and now Sutovsky coolly maintained control and correctly judged the passed pawn balance in the scram-

ble to bring home the full point:

27...c4 28 ♕g2 ♕f4 29 ♖g3 ♕c1+ 30 ♕g1 ♕xc2 31 ♕xa7 ♕d1+ 32 ♔g2 ♕e2+ 33 ♕f2 cxd3 34 ♕xe2! dxe2 35 ♔f2 d4 36 h4 c5 37 h5 ♗e4 38 ♔xe2 e5 39 h6 ♔c6 40 a4 1-0

Game 56
J.Polgar-I.Tsesarsky
Israeli Team Ch. 2000

---

1 e4 c5 2 ♘f3 ♘c6 3 ♗b5 e6 4 0-0 ♘ge7 5 b3

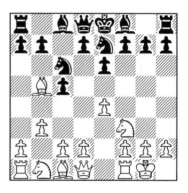

5...♘g6

The knight covers f4 and e5 from here, while it also enables Black to blunt the long diagonal without having to worry about ♘h4 in reply in reply to ...f6. However, as well as 5...a6 6 ♗xc6 ♘xc6 7 ♗b2 which we'll deal with in the next two games, Black has also tried to close down the bishop with 5...♘d4?! 6 ♘xd4 cxd4, but then 7 c3 a6 (or 7...♕b6 8 ♘a3 ♘g6 9 ♗e2 ♗e7 10 ♘b5! dxc3 11 ♘xc3 with an edge as White will regain the d4-square after 11...♕d4 12 ♗b2 0-0 13 ♕c2 – Golubev) 8 ♗d3 ♘c6 9 cxd4!? ♘xd4 (or 9...d5 10 exd5 ♕xd5 11 ♗b2 ♗e7 12 ♘a3! with the better development for White, whose his advantage grew after 12...♗f6? 13 ♘c4 ♗xd4 14 ♗e4! ♕d8 15 ♗a3 in V.Jansa-E.Sveshnikov, Gausdal 1992) 10 ♗b2 ♗c5 11 ♕h5 d6 12 e5! is fairly promising and makes

---

good use of the white bishops, while even 12...♘f5! 13 ♗xf5 exf5 14 d4 ♗a7 15 ♖d1 left White with the edge in A.Delchev-B.Macieja, European Ch., Silivri 2003.

6 ♗b2 f6!

The best way of handling the position whereas 6...d6 7 ♖e1 ♗d7 8 ♗xc6! ♗xc6 9 d4 cxd4 10 ♘xd4 leaves it difficult for Black to unravel his kingside and 10...♕g5?! 11 ♖e3 h5 12 ♘d2! ♗d7 13 ♘4f3 ♕d8 14 a4! ♕c7 15 ♘c4 also left d6 vulnerable in V.Laznicka-A.Czebe, Steinbrunn 2005.

7 ♖e1

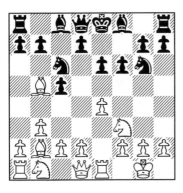

7...♕c7!?

Continuing to fight for control of e5, but an immediate 7...♗e7 is also playable when White hasn't been keen to try 8 ♗xc6 bxc6 9 e5, probably because of 9...0-0!, followed by exchanges on e5 and then ...d6 and ...e5. Instead he has preferred 8 c3, but 8...0-0 9 d4 a6 10 ♗f1 d5 is a reasonable response which has been used by Wells and Krasenkow. The IQP positions have been shown to be fine for Black and so White shouldn't hurry to exchange on d5 and c5, while 11 ♘bd2!? cxd4 12 cxd4 ♗d7 13 a3! ♗d6 14 b4, intending to exchange on d5 and then go ♘d2-b3-c5 or ♘d2-b1–c3, gave White good chances for an edge in V.Akopian-P.Wells, Lausanne 2004.

8 ♗xc6?!

Now play is similar to the 4 ♗xc6 lines and Black soon gains a strong centre. Superior is 8

c3 ♗e7 9 d4 0-0 10 ♗f1! when Black is a little cramped and 10...a6 11 g3 b5 12 h4! ♗b7 13 h5 ♘h8 14 d5 saw White increase his useful space advantage and retain the advantage in V.Akopian-A.Fominyh, Ubeda 2001.

8...bxc6

9 d3

Continuing to drift, and if even a member of the world's elite can then drifting is all too easy to do in this structure! Instead White had to challenge in the centre with 9 e5!? ♗e7 10 d4.

9...d6 10 ♘bd2 ♗e7 11 ♘c4 0-0 12 ♗c3 e5

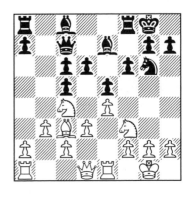

The ideal central advance and already Black is a little better with White forced to try and contain the opposition centre.

13 ♗a5 ♕b7 14 ♗d2 f5 15 ♗g5 ♗e6 16 ♘a5! ♕d7 17 ♗xe7 ♕xe7! 18 b4

Polgar has deprived Black of the bishop-pair and contains to play actively to distract Tsesarsky from the kingside whereas 18 ♘xc6? ♕c7 19 ♘g5 ♘f4! 20 g3 h6 would have trapped and won the c6-knight.

18...cxb4 19 ♘xc6 ♕b7 20 ♘a5

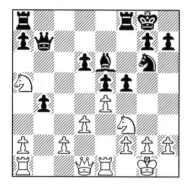

20...♕b6?!

Tsesarsky was understandably unhappy with this which squanders most of his advantage as now the knight gets to come to c4 with tempo, whereas his 20...♕c7! 21 ♘g5 ♘f4 22 ♘xe6 ♘xe6 would have prevented 23 ♘c4? due to simply 23...fxe4 and leaves White somewhat worse after 23 ♘b3 a5.

21 ♘g5! ♘f4 22 ♘xe6 ♘xe6 23 ♘c4 ♕c5 24 exf5 ♖xf5 25 ♘e3 ♖f4 26 f3 ♘d4 27 a3

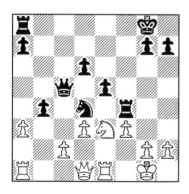

27...♘f5

White now gets to make a draw and the

last chance was 27...bxa3! 28 ♕c1 ♘f5 29 ♕xa3 ♕xa3 30 ♖xa3 ♘xe3 31 ♖xe3 a5 (Tsesarsky), retaining an edge due to the a-pawn.

28 axb4 ♖xb4 29 c3 ♖b2 30 d4 ♘xe3 31 dxc5 ♘xd1 32 ♖axd1 dxc5 33 ♖xe5 a5 34 ♖d7 a4 35 ♖ee7 a3 36 ♖xg7+ ♔h8 37 ♖xh7+ ♔g8 38 ♖hg7+ ♔h8 39 ♖h7+ ♔g8 40 ♖dg7+ ♔f8 41 ♖b7!? ♔g8! 42 ♖bg7+ ½-½

Game 57
V.Akopian-G.Kasparov
Russia v World Rapidplay, Moscow 2002

1 e4 c5 2 ♘f3 ♘c6 3 ♗b5 e6 4 0-0 ♘ge7 5 b3 a6 6 ♗xc6 ♘xc6 7 ♗b2

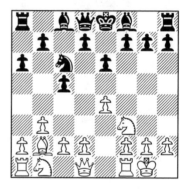

7...b5!?

Grabbing queenside space is the critical continuation and appears best, although other approaches have been tested:

a) 7...d6 is a fairly useful move and waits to see what White is up to. Now Kaufman suggests 8 c4, intending ♘a3-c2 and d4, but in practice White has usually been happy to open things up with 8 d4 cxd4 9 ♘xd4. The pressure down the long diagonal remains awkward for Black and so he often opts to bring his queen over to the kingside, but 9...♕f6 10 c4 ♗e7 11 ♕d2 ♕g6 doesn't fully convince due to 12 ♘xc6! bxc6 13 e5, breaking up the black structure when 13...d5 14 ♗a3! ♗xa3 15

♘xa3 0-0 16 ♖ac1 favoured White, due to his superior minor piece and the queenside weaknesses in A.Volzhin-M.Lanzani, Saint Vincent 2001.

b) 7...f6?! should, just like in the 4 ♗xc6 lines, be met by 8 ♘h4!, intending to launch the f-pawn such as with 8...♕e7 9 f4 b5 10 ♘a3 (preparing c4 to halt the black queenside pawns) 10...♗b7 11 c4 ♘d4 12 cxb5! ♗xe4 13 d3 ♗b7 14 ♗xd4! cxd4 15 bxa6 ♗xa6 16 ♘c4 ♕f7 17 ♖c1 when the knights were effective at preventing counterplay and the key feature of the position was the mobile white queenside pawns in V.Jansa-T.Bacherler, Passau 2000.

8 c4!?

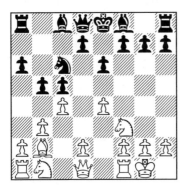

It has partly been interest in this advance, fighting for space in the centre and on the queenside, which has done much to boost the popularity of 5 b3.

8...bxc4 9 bxc4 ♖b8

Black has also harassed the bishop with 9...♕b6!?, which covers d4 as well, when 10 ♗c3 ♘d4 (best as 10...♕c7?! 11 ♘a3 d6 12 ♘c2 leaves Black struggling to blunt the diagonal; ...e5 weakens d5 too much, but ...f6 allows White to quickly open the position with d4!? or with ♘h4 and f4) 11 ♘a3! f6!? 12 ♘h4 g6 13 f4 ♕c6 14 d3 ♗b7 was seen in J.Shaw-J.Rowson, Edinburgh 2002. 15 f5?! was now revealed to be too ambitious after 15...exf5 16 exf5 0-0-0 with good counterplay

against g2 and so White should have settled for simply 15 ♘c2, retaining the advantage after 15...e6 16 fxe5 fxe5 17 ♘e3 or 15...♘xc2 16 ♕xc2 ♗g7 17 ♖ae1.

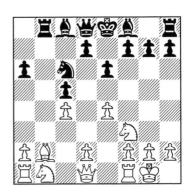

10 ♗c3 d6

Aiming to blunt the strong white bishop with ...e5, while 10...f6 is still well met by 11 ♘h4 g6 12 f4 and White was better in O.De la Riva Aguado-H.Hamdouchi, Calvia Olympiad 2004.

11 ♘a3!

With Black set to weaken the d5-square, the queen's knight heads for a promising home there.

11...e5 12 ♘c2 ♗e7 13 ♘e3 0-0 14 d3

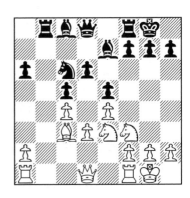

14...♕e8

Kasparov wants to prevent White from increasing the pressure with 15 ♕a4 (which would now be met by 15...♘d4), while he hopes that the queen will later come to g6. That hope is too ambitious, although trying to equalise this position isn't easy, especially at a fast time limit. Later Black unveiled the more accurate 14...♕d7!? when, with the black queen not cluttering up the back rank, ♕b8 ideas are no longer a problem. 15 ♖b1 ♖xb1 16 ♕xb1 ♗d8 17 ♘d5 ♗d8 is then similar to what actually occurred in Zhang Zhong-J.Lautier, Poikovsky 2004 where 15 ♘d2 was met by 15...♗g5! when 16 ♘d5 ♘e7 17 ♖b1 ♖xb1 18 ♕xb1 f5 left Lautier very solid. However, after an exchange on f5 White's control over d5 and e4, along with Black's problems down the b-file, saw Zhang Zhong still retain a small pull.

15 ♖b1 ♖xb1 16 ♕xb1 ♗d8 17 ♘d2 g6 18 ♘d5 f5 19 exf5 gxf5?

Too ambitious and now the alert Akopian is quick to pressurise the black central pawns. However, one can understand why Kasparov didn't want to play the essential 19...♗xf5 20 ♘e4 ♕d7 21 f3 as then he would remain passive and White could continue probing for some time, such as with ♕b3 and ♖b1, although Black should hold with accurate defence.

20 f4! ♖f7 21 ♕e1!

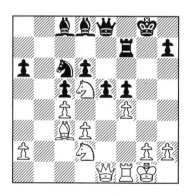

The d5-knight is colossal and prevents Black from being able to defend e5, while it's impressive as just how quickly Kasparov's position collapses.

21...♖g7 22 ♘f3 ♕g6 23 g3 ♖f7 24 fxe5 f4 25 exd6 fxg3 1-0

and with his centre gone Kasparov gave up, having seen that 26 ♕e8+ ♖f8 27 ♕xf8+! ♔xf8 28 ♘e5 is a killer.

Game 58
J.Benjamin-A.Hahn
US Ch., Seattle 2002

---

1 e4 c5 2 ♘f3 ♘c6 3 ♗b5 e6 4 0-0 ♘ge7 5 ♖e1

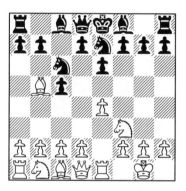

5...a6

Even though White hasn't opted for ♘c3, a fully playable, if less popular, alternative to the main line is 5...♘d4!?. After 6 ♘xd4 cxd4 it turns out that this is a vastly better version of 3...♘d4 for Black as he is able to hold d4 for long enough to complete his development, while White must now choose how far to push his c-pawn:

a) 7 c4!? looks to play on the queenside, but White is in sore need of an improvement after 7...♘g6! (previously 7...g6 8 d3 ♗g7 9 ♘d2 0-0 10 b4! d6 11 c5 b6 12 ♘c4! bxc5 13 bxc5 dxc5 14 ♗d2 had given White excellent play for his pawn in the instructive modern classic I.Glek-I.Nataf, Chalkidiki 2002) 8 d3 ♗e7 9 ♘d2 0-0 10 ♗a4 e5 (the delay in playing ...d6 has left White a little slow on the queenside, while Black is generally looking to attack on the kingside) 11 ♖b1 d6 12 b4 ♔h8

---

13 ♘f1 ♗g5! 14 ♔h1 ♗xc1 15 ♖xc1 a5! which favoured Black in F.Bellini-A.Moiseenko, Moscow 2004.

b) 7 c3 is more popular, but after 7...a6 8 ♗a4 ♘c6 Black holds d4 when 9 d3 b5 (but not 9...♗c5?! 10 ♕h5! ♗a7 11 ♗g5 ♕a5 12 ♗xc6! bxc6 13 ♘d2 when White had seized a strong initiative in C.Sandipan-E.Sveshnikov, Moscow 2002) 10 ♗b3 ♗b7 11 ♘d2 ♗e7 12 ♘f3 dxc3 13 bxc3 0-0 saw him complete his development, and be left with sufficient queenside chances, in S.Martinovic-M.Perunovic, Neum 2002.

6 ♗f1 d5! 7 exd5

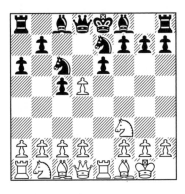

7...♕xd5

If White's new idea continues to hold up after this then more 3...e6 exponents will probably prefer the very solid 7...♘xd5. Then 8 d3 ♗e7 9 g3 has been tried on several occasions, but doesn't lead anywhere for White. However, 8 d4 can be well countered by 8...♗e7!?, not rushing to exchange on d4 and encouraging the white c-pawn forwards. After 9 c4 ♘f6 10 dxc5 ♕xd1 11 ♖xd1 ♘e4! Black avoids allowing White to actively develop as 11...♗xc5 12 ♘c3 0-0 13 ♗g5! would do. Furthermore, he is happy to exchanges pieces as then his king will be very safe on e7, from where it is well placed for the ending and to assist the advance of the extra central pawn. A.Sokolov-B.Macieja, Bundesliga 2004 continued 12 ♗e3 ♗xc3 13 ♗xc5 ♘xc5 14 ♘c3

♗d7 15 g3 ♔e7 16 ♘d4 ♖hd8 17 f4! ♗e8! 18 ♘xc6+ ♗xc6 19 ♔f2 a5 20 ♔e3 h6 21 ♖xd8 ♖xd8 22 ♖d1 ♖g8! and Black was fine as he was ready to begin kingside play with 23...g5, while the presence of rooks prevented the white king from advancing.

8 ♗d3!?

Moving the bishop again, but Benjamin's idea is to prevent ...♘f5 and, as we'll see, the black knight isn't too well placed on g6. Instead 8 ♘c3 ♕d8 has been tested on several occasions, but Black's control of d4 promises him an equal game.

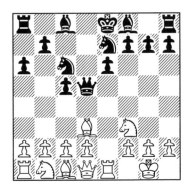

8...♘g6

The knight isn't entirely happy here and 8...g6! is probably a better way to complete Black's development. Benjamin later faced this and 9 ♗e4 ♕d6?! 10 b4! ♗g7 11 bxc5 ♕xc5 12 ♗a3 ♕a5 13 c3 ♕c7 14 d4 favoured him in J.Benjamin-A.Shabalov, Connecticut 2002. However, 9...♕d8, to lessen the impact of b4 ideas, would have been a sterner test when White can try 10 h4!?, but at some point he's got to find a way to develop that queenside.

9 ♗e4 ♕d6 10 c3! ♗e7 11 d4 0-0 12 ♗e3 cxd4 13 cxd4

This IQP position is very similar to a c3 Sicilian, in which Benjamin is also an expert, but with one important difference; the black knight is on g6, not f6, and so doesn't cover the key d5-square. Hahn should thus have opted for 13...♘b4 to cover d5 and not doing so allows Benjamin to strike.

13...♗d7?! 14 ♘c3 ♖ad8 15 ♖c1!

White has brought all his pieces into play and now intends to gain at least a useful edge with 16 d5!. Hahn prevents that, but at some cost to her position.

15...f5 16 ♗c2 f4 17 ♘e4 ♕d5 18 ♗d2 ♘b4?!

It's too late for this, although Black had to avoid 18...♘xd4? 19 ♘xd4 ♕xd4 due to 20 ♗a5, collecting an exchange down the d-file.

19 ♗b3 ♕h5

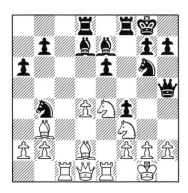

20 ♘eg5

Hitting that vulnerable e6-pawn and it's not long before Hahn's pieces are driven backwards, leaving Benjamin's to dominate the board.

20...♗xg5 21 ♗xb4 ♗e7 22 ♗xe7 ♘xe7

23 ♖c7! ♘d5 24 ♖xb7 ♗c8 25 ♖a7 ♔h8 26 ♖e5 ♕e8 27 h3 ♘f6 28 ♕e2 ♖d6 29 ♖c5! ♕g6 30 ♗c2 ♕e8 31 ♕e5 ♖b6 32 ♕c7 1-0

Game 59
I.Glek-S.Arkhipov
Russian Team Ch. 2001

---

1 e4 c5 2 ♘f3 ♘c6 3 ♗b5 e6 4 0-0 ♘ge7 5 ♖e1 a6 6 ♗xc6 ♘xc6 7 d4 cxd4 8 ♘xd4 ♕c7

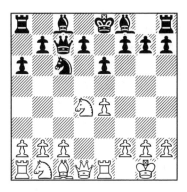

9 ♘xc6!?

Glek intends to exploit the absence of a knight on c3 by bringing his queen's knight to the more flexible d2-square. However, White might well have already inserted ♘c3 and here 9 ♘c3 brings about an important position:

a) 9...♗e7? is too risky and is often met by 10 ♘xc6 bxc6 11 e5 0-0 12 ♗f4! with which White has done well. However, even better is 10 ♘f5! when 10...exf5 (neither did 10...0-0 solve Black's problems in N.Ristic-D.Kojovic, Yugoslav Team Ch. 1999 due to the energetic 11 ♘xe7+ ♘xe7 12 ♕h5! b5 13 ♖e3! ♘g6 14 ♖h3 h6 15 ♗xh6! with a decisive attack) 11 ♘d5 ♕b8 (or 11...♕d8 12 ♗e3! d6 13 ♗b6, collecting the rook and emerging the exchange ahead) 12 ♗f4 d6 13 exf5 (Ristic) leaves White with superb compensation; 13...0-0 14 ♘xe7+ ♘xe7 15 ♗xd6 regains the piece with a huge advantage, although

13...♘e5!? is a better try, but 14 ♕h5 should still work out well for White.

b) 9...♗d6! completes Black's most reliable set-up when recent attention has focused on 10 ♘xc6 (instead 10 ♘d5!? exd5 11 exd5+ ♘e5 12 f4 is possible when after 12...0-0 13 fxe5 ♗xe5 14 ♘f3 ♗f6! 15 ♗g5! ♗xb2 16 ♖b1 ♗a3 17 ♕d3 ♗c5+ 18 ♔h1 f6! 19 ♗e3 White had sufficient compensation for the pawn, but no more than that, in A.Kornev-I.Khairullin, Russian Team Ch. 2004) 10...dxc6 11 f4!?, giving up a pawn to try and gain control over e5:

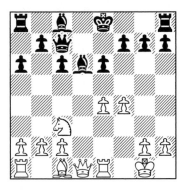

b1) 11...♗xf4 12 ♗xf4 ♕xf4 is risky, but might be playable, although White has rather dangerous practical compensation after 13 e5 0-0 14 ♕d6, especially with 14...b5?! 15 ♘e4. However, 14...b6! 15 ♖ad1 ♖a7 16 ♕xc6 returned the pawn and left Black only slightly worse after 16...♕b4! in A.Lastin-P.Kotsur, Elista 2000.

b2) 11...e5! is fairly reliable when after 12 f5 the black bishops may be a little restricted, but 12...b5 gives Black some useful space and the key question is whether White can generate enough pressure on the kingside. Thus far he hasn't found a way to with 13 ♕g4 f6 14 ♖d1 ♗c5+ 15 ♔h1 ♗b7 16 ♖d3 being repulsed by 16...♕f7! 17 ♘e2 ♖d8 which was roughly level in I.Glek-F.Nijboer, Dutch Team Ch. 2000. Glek's 16 ♕h5+!? looks like a better try as the black king must then move with

16...♕f7?? dropping a piece to 17 ♕xf7+ ♔xf7 18 ♖d7+, although 16...♔e7 17 ♖d3 g6! appears to offer Black sufficient counterplay.

9...bxc6

Now d6 becomes weak and 9...♕xc6 may appear more logical when the position resembles a Taimanov. However, after 10 ♘c3, ♘d5 ideas are again in the air and the fairly common 10...b5?! allows 11 a4! with a strong queenside initiative. Then 11...b4 12 ♘d5 ♗b7 13 ♗d2 a5 14 c3! left Black, as 14...bxc3 15 ♗xc3 would have halted his kingside development, unable to do anything but lose a pawn with 14...b3 in order to develop in I.Glek-K.Bischoff, Bad Zwesten 2002.

10 e5

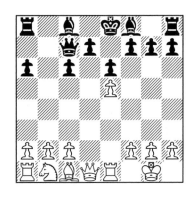

10...♗b7?!

Rightly avoiding 10...♗e7?! 11 ♕g4! 0-0? 12 ♗h6, but this is too slow as the knight has another route to d6 than going via e4. Radical measures are thus needed and so Black must advance his d-pawn now or on the next move. After 10...d5!? an exchange on d6 allows him to activate both bishops, although 11 c4!? ♖b8 12 ♘c3 ♗e7 13 ♕g4 g6 14 ♗g5! (weakening Black's dark squares) 14...h5 15 ♕f4 ♗xg5 16 ♕xg5 ♕e7 17 ♕d2 ♔f8 18 ♖e3 maintained an edge in A.Alavkin-E.Kalegin, Ufa 1999.

11 ♘d2! c5 12 ♘c4 ♗d5?

Black has drifted and 12...♗e7 13 ♕g4 ♔f8 14 ♗g5 would have been pretty bad for him, but it now turns out that he hasn't actually covered d6 after all.

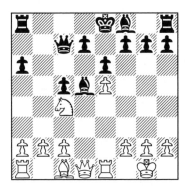

13 ♘d6+ ♗xd6 14 ♕xd5! 1-0

and the experienced grandmaster had lost a piece.

Game 60
I.Leventic-A.Fedorov
Bosnian Team Ch. 2004

---

1 e4 c5 2 ♘f3 ♘c6 3 ♗b5 e6 4 0-0 ♘ge7 5 ♖e1 a6 6 ♗xc6 ♘xc6 7 d4 cxd4 8 ♘xd4

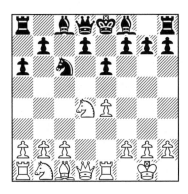

8...d6

As well as 8...♕c7, Black can also begin with 8...♗e7 when 9 ♘c3 d6 reaches our main line below, while 9...♕c7?! transposes to a rather suspect position for Black which we examined in Glek-Arkhipov.

9 ♘c3

Once again it's tempting for White to exploit his delay in playing ♘c3 with 9 ♘xc6!? bxc6 10 ♕g4 which is promising. R.Rabiega-F.Volkmann, Austrian Team Ch. 2000 continued 10...h5?! 11 ♕f3! e5 12 ♕c3 ♗d7 13 f4! f6 14 ♘d2 ♗e7 15 ♘f3 and White was much better, but even 10...e5 isn't sufficient for equality due to 11 ♕g3 g6 12 b3! as Tal has demonstrated.

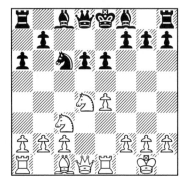

9...♗e7

Now White can target g7 and so Black has often been advised to delay completing his kingside development in favour of 9...♗d7!?. That is reasonable logic, although White retains some pressure with 10 ♘xc6! ♗xc6 11 ♖e3 ♗e7 12 ♖d3. This response has been quite rare in practice, but appears rather effective and 12...♕c7 13 ♕g4! g6 14 ♗h6 b5 15 ♖e1 gave White the initiative and ♘d5 ideas in A.Kovalev-R.Farakhov, Alushta 2004.

10 ♘xc6 bxc6 11 ♕g4 ♔f8!?

Defending g7 does require Black to make a major concession, but he can probably cope elsewhere without his rook for the time being, while it does currently support a useful ...h5 to drive back the white queen. Instead 11...g6 12 b3 gives White an edge, but Black must avoid both 11...♗f6? 12 e5! dxe5 13 ♘e4 0-0 14 ♖d1 ♕e7 15 ♗e3 and 11...0-0? 12 ♗h6 ♗f6 13 e5! dxe5 14 ♖ad1 ♕e7 15 ♘e4 and 16 ♗e3, which have been quite common ways for him to lose quickly.

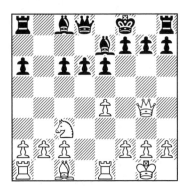

12 e5

Black doesn't mind the position closing like this as then he can develop his queenside. Thus the less popular 12 b3!? may well be more testing when it would be interesting to know what Fedorov had intended as 12...d5 (or 12...f6 13 ♗a3 e5 14 ♕g3, intending f4) 13 ♕g3! had favoured White after 13...h5 14 ♘a4!, clamping down on c5, in L.Yudasin-A.Greenfeld, Haifa 1995. Quite possibly it was Svidler's suggestion of 13...f6!? 14 e5 ♔f7 which appears to keep the white pieces at bay and retains the dynamism within the black position.

12...d5 13 ♗d2 ♖b8

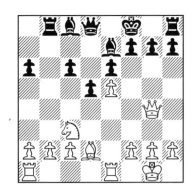

14 ♘a4

Hoping to clamp down on c5, but Fedorov is never going to allow that. However, the

black position is already the easier to play as White lacks a good plan, while Black can advance on both fronts, thereby opening avenues for his bishop and rooks.

14...c5 15 b3 h5 16 ♕e2 h4! 17 h3

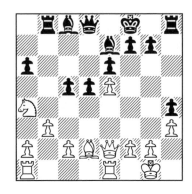

17...f5

Active and tempting, but further advances will not be so easy. Thus Black should quite possibly have preferred the calm 17...♗b7!? 18 ♖ad1 ♕c7 (Roiz), although the white position would have remained rather solid, but that is his only real asset.

18 exf6! gxf6

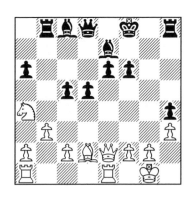

19 c4

This helps Black to advance in the centre, while 19 ♖ad1!? would also have been awkward for Fedorov who must prepare any advance very carefully, with an immediate 19...e5?! premature due to 20 c4! d4 21 f4.

19...d4 20 &f4 &b7! 21 &f3 &f7 22 &e2! d3!? 23 &d2 &d7 24 &ad1?

Fedorov has wisely avoided ...e5, which would have run into a strong sacrifice, relying instead on using his d-pawn as a decoy. This natural move is mistaken as the queen's position enables Black to hit g2 with tempo, whereas 24 &d1! &b7 25 &e3 (Roiz) would have left c5 and d3 both rather weak, whilst 25...&g8 26 f3! defends. Thus Black would have had to try 25...&c7!? 26 &xd3 &xd3 27 &xd3 &g8, but that allows a perpetual after 28 &h7+ &g7 29 &h5+.

24...&b7 25 &e3 &g8! 26 f3 e5 27 &h2 &g6 28 &xd3 &d4! 29 &xd4?

The attack was rather strong in any case, but allowing Black a mobile pawn centre most certainly doesn't help the defence.

29...cxd4 30 &e2 &g8 31 &f1 e4! 32 fxe4 &xe4 33 &d2 &xg2+ 34 &xg2 &b1+ 35 &f2 &xg2+ 36 &xg2 &e4+ 37 &f1 &b4 0-1

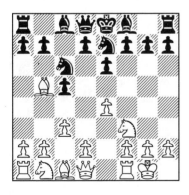

> *Game 61*
> # E.Sutovsky-I.Tsesarsky
> *Israeli Team Ch. 2001*

1 e4 c5 2 &f3 &c6 3 &b5 e6 4 0-0 &ge7 5 c3

5...d5

As we will see in Game 62, inserting 5...a6 and 6 &a4 before breaking with 6...d5 is a mistake, but this immediate advance is a playable alternative to the more popular 5...a6 6 &a4 b5 and 6...c4. White should now avoid advancing with e5 as then that pawn will be targeted and he will usually have to give up his bishop on c6, but without the light-squared bishop any kingside attack is much less effective. Thus White usually aims to quickly open the centre as we'll now see Sutovsky achieve in style.

6 exd5 &xd5

The position is very similar to a c3 Sicilian and, just like there, this is the correct recapture. Instead 6...&xd5 7 d4 cxd4 8 &xd4 &d7 9 &xc6! grants White a small, but pleasant edge.

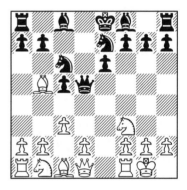

7 &e1

The main continuation with which White hopes to be able to achieve the ideal d4-d5 advance.

7...&d7

Black may well be able to improve here by immediately putting the question to the bishop with 7...a6!?. Certainly after 8 &f1 &f5! (clamping down on the d4-break as Tsesarsky tries and fails to do) 9 &a3 &d8 10 &c2 &e7 11 &e3 &h4! (leaving White with the less well-placed of his knights) 12 &xh4 &xh4 13 a3 b5 Black had no problems in S.Rublevsky-A.Pridorozhni, Russian Team Ch. 2002.

8 &a3 &f5?

Now the Black pieces really get in each other's way. Thus correct is 8...♞g6 when Sveshnikov has demonstrated that 9 ♗f1 ♗e7 10 d4 cxd4 11 ♞b5 ♖c8 12 ♞bxd4 ♞xd4 13 ♞xd4 ♕a5! is fine for Black, while 9 ♗c4 can now be met by 9...♕h5. However, even here the black pieces aren't so happy, and thus 7...a6 may well be a better way to follow-up 5...d5, as after 10 d4!

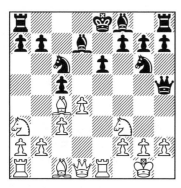

10...cxd4 (and not 10...♗e7? 11 ♗e2 ♕f5 12 dxc5! when 12...♗xc5 13 ♞b5 is strong, but 12...♖d8 13 b4 0-0 14 ♞c4 ♗c8 15 ♕b3 left White with an extra pawn and a grip on the position in P.Smirnov-D.Frolyanov, Samara 2002) 11 ♞b5 ♖c8 12 ♗e2!? (continuing to improve the white pieces with tempo and Rublevsky has shown that 12...dxc3 13 ♞g5! cxb2 14 ♗xh5 bxa1♕ 15 ♞xf7! gives White a huge attack for the rook) 12...♕d5 13 ♞fxd4 White enjoys the initiative. That grew after 13...a6?! 14 ♗f3 ♕c5 15 ♗e3! in S.Rublevsky-A.Shabalov, Elista Olympiad 1998, but after the 13...♞xd4 14 ♞xd4 ♕a5 15 a4 ♗e7 of M.Ulibin-M.Krasenkow, Swidnica (rapid) 1997, 16 ♞b5 wins the bishop-pair and leaves White somewhat better.

9 ♗c4! ♕d6 10 d4 cxd4 11 ♞b5 ♕b8 12 cxd4

Once more d5 is threatened and so Tsesarsky tries to develop by attacking the powerful e1–rook, but Sutovsky is more than happy to sacrifice it to prevent Black from castling.

12...♗b4

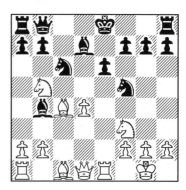

13 d5! ♗xe1 14 ♕xe1 ♞ce7 15 d6! ♗xb5

Now the d-pawn continues to be a real nuisance for Black, but 15...♞xd6 16 ♗f4 ♗xb5 17 ♗xb5+ ♔f8 18 ♕b4 was also rather good for White.

16 ♗xb5+ ♞c6 17 d7+! ♔f8 18 ♗xc6 bxc6 19 ♗g5 ♕c7 20 ♖d1 ♞e7 21 ♕e5! ♕d8 22 ♕d6 f6 1-0

That's been some performance from the IQP and here Black gave up without waiting for the crushing 23 ♞d4.

Game 62
S.Rublevsky-P.Eljanov
Russian Team Ch. 2005

1 e4 c5 2 ♞f3 ♞c6 3 ♗b5 e6 4 0-0 ♞ge7 5 c3 a6 6 ♗a4

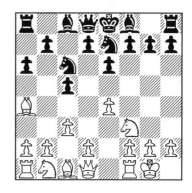

6...c4!?

Despite Kasparov's losing to Rublevsky with this approach, interest in it has soared in the past six months, although Black does usually opt for the move order 6...b5 7 ♗c2 c4. Then 8 b3 ♘g6 9 ♕e2 is our main game here, while we also deal with 9 bxc4 below under 6...c4 7 ♗c2.

Black should though avoid 6...d5?! due to 7 exd5 ♕xd5

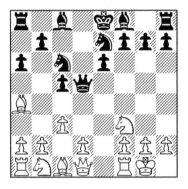

8 d4 when 8...b5? is strongly rebuffed by 9 c4! as 9...♕xc4 10 ♗b3 ♕b4 11 ♗d2 traps the black queen. Instead 8...♘g6 9 ♗e3 also leaves White with the initiative, while 9...♕h5?! 10 dxc5! held on to the c5-pawn after 10...♗d7 11 b4 in M.Adams-G.Sarthou, Moscow 2001 as 10...♗xc5? 11 ♗xc6+! bxc6 12 ♕a4 ♗d7 13 ♕a5 would have won a piece due to the pin along the fifth.

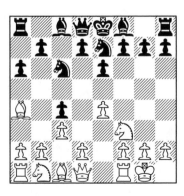

7 ♕e2

Despite being Rublevsky's choice, not everyone has yet raced to follow in his footsteps. However, Black appears to be holding his own after 7 d4 cxd3 8 ♕xd3 b5 9 ♗c2 ♘g6 with a reasonable Taimanov set-up, albeit one that normally comes about via 6...b5 7 ♗c2 c4 8 d4 cxd3 9 ♕xd3 ♘g6. White must try and play on the queenside here, but after 10 a4 b4! 11 c4 ♗e7 12 b3 d6 13 ♗e3 0-0 14 ♘bd2 ♗b7 15 ♖ad1 ♕c7 16 ♗b1 ♖ad8 17 ♖fe1 ♗f6 he hadn't really achieved anything in D.Schneider-A.Moiseenko, Dallas 2004.

A more promising try against 6...c4 is the prophylactic 7 ♗c2!? when White appears to hold the edge after 7...d5!? 8 d4! cxd3 9 ♕xd3. Instead 7...b5 8 b3 (of course this also often arises via 6...b5 7 ♗c2 c4 8 b3) 8...♘g6 (or 7...♘g6 8 b3 b5) reaches an important and unclear position.

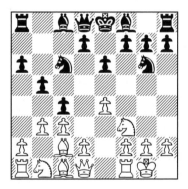

Then 9 bxc4! (9 a4 ♗b7 10 ♘a3 cxb3 11 ♗xb3 b4! 12 ♘c4 ♘a5 13 ♘xa5 ♕xa5 saw Black manage to hold his own on the queenside in J.Plachetka-T.Oral, Czech Team Ch. 1998) 9...bxc4 10 ♕e2 ♘a5 11 d4! cxd3 12 ♗xd3 ♕c7 13 ♗e3 was the critical course of I.Morovic Fernandez-G.Milos, Sao Paulo 2002. The white bishops are pointing left and the key question is whether he can gain the queenside advantage. This position deserves further exploration and, while 13...♗b7 14 ♘bd2 ♗e7 15 ♖ab1 ♘c6 16 ♘c4 favours

White, the game wasn't so clear after 13...♘f4! 14 ♗xf4 ♕xf4 15 ♘bd2 ♗e7 16 ♖ab1. Milos did now stray with 16...0-0?! when 17 e5! ♗b7 18 ♘d4 left his queen a little offside, but Black appears to be fine after Finkel's 16...♕c7 17 e5 ♗b7 when that c3-pawn is starting to look a little tender, although the position remains quite unclear after 18 ♘e4!?.

7...b5 8 ♗c2 ♘g6 9 b3

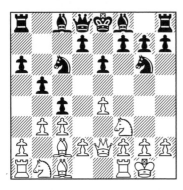

9...♗c5

Khalifman's choice, although this may well be inferior to Kasparov's 9...♕c7. However, 10 bxc4 ♘f4 11 ♕e3 bxc4 12 ♗a3! was still awkward for the world no.1 as 12...♗xa3 13 ♘xa3 ♘a5 14 ♖ab1 would have left White in control of the queenside and c4 quite weak. That pawn still was though after 12...♗e7 13 ♗xe7 ♘xe7 14 ♘a3 when Rublevsky had also weakened Black's dark squares and the straightforward 14...0-0 15 ♖ab1 gave White the edge after 15...f5!? 16 ♕b6! ♕xb6 17 ♖xb6 fxe4 18 ♗xe4 d5 19 ♗c2 in Rublevsky-Kasparov, Izmir 2004. Then 19...♘eg6 20 ♗xg6! ♘xg6 21 ♘c2 favoured White due to his active rook and to his ability to target the vulnerable black centre, while Rublevsky went on to impressively convert a tough rook ending. Kasparov should thus possibly have tried 19...♘h3+!? 20 ♔h1 e5 21 ♘xe5 ♖xf2 22 ♖xf2 ♘xf2+ 23 ♔g1 ♘g4 24 ♘xg4 ♗xg4, although Rublevsky's 25 ♗a4, intending ♘c2 and then ♘d4 or ♘e3, would have retained

an edge due to the weaknesses of a6 and d5.

10 bxc4!

Once again the plan is to weaken Black on the dark squares and to target c4, whereas previously 10 e5 d5! 11 d4 cxd3 12 ♗xd3 0-0 13 ♗xg6 fxg6 14 ♗a3 b4! 15 cxb4 ♘xb4 had given Black sufficient counterplay in Zhang Zhong-A.Khalifman, Shanghai 2001.

10...♘f4 11 ♕e1 bxc4 12 ♗a3 ♕a5 13 ♗xc5 ♕xc5 14 ♕e3!

This is why the queen retreated to e1 and now Eljanov is left struggling to cover his advanced c-pawn.

14...♕xe3 15 dxe3 ♘g6 16 ♘a3

16...a5!?

No doubt familiar with Rublevsky-Kasparov, Eljanov opts for active defence although Rublevsky now again demonstrates excellent technique. However, 16...♘a5 17

Ξab1 d5 18 Ξfd1 would have been rather unpleasant for Black with 18...♗b7 19 exd5 exd5 20 ♗a4+ ♔e7 21 Ξb6 continuing to see the white pieces dominating the board.

17 ♘xc4 ♗a6 18 ♘b6! Ξb8

18...♗xf1 19 ♘xa8 ♔e7 20 ♔xf1 Ξxa8 21 Ξb1 would also have left Black unable to gain play down the b-file, while Rublevsky now brings his king over to support his centre.

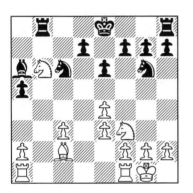

19 Ξfb1 ♔e7 20 ♘d4 ♘ge5 21 f4 ♘c4 22 ♘xc4 ♗xc4 23 ♔f2! f6 24 ♔e1 g6 25 ♔d2 e5 26 ♗b3!

Fine technique and now White begins to use the support of his extra e-pawn to attack on the kingside.

26...♗a6 27 ♘f3 d6 28 g4!

28...♘d8 29 ♗d5 ♘e6 30 f5 ♘c5 31 c4 g5 32 h4 h6 33 ♔c2 a4 34 hxg5 hxg5 1-0

Perhaps Eljanov lost on time, although by sinking his bishop into d5, Rublevsky has ensured that a blockade isn't a problem for him. After 34...hxg5 White should exchange all the rooks with 35 Ξxb8 Ξxb8 36 Ξh1! a3 37 Ξh7+ ♔d8 38 Ξh8+ ♔c7 39 Ξxb8 ♔xb8 before picking off the a-pawn after 40 ♘d2 (Barsky) which should be enough to win.

Game 63
A.Morozevich-I.Smirin
Russia v World Rapidplay, Moscow 2002

---

1 e4 c5 2 ♘f3 ♘c6 3 ♗b5 e6 4 0-0 ♘ge7 5 c3 a6 6 ♗a4 b5 7 ♗c2 ♗b7 8 Ξe1

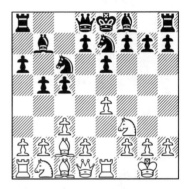

8...Ξc8

Black gets ready to meet 9 d4, although he can also advance with 8...d5!?. Due to the queenside space gained, 9 exd5 is no longer especially effective and 9...♘xd5 10 d4 cxd4 11 cxd4 ♗e7 12 ♘c3 ♘cb4! gave Black a perfectly acceptable IQP position in R.Kasimdzhanov-E.Bacrot, Cannes (rapid) 2001. White should thus prefer 9 e5 d4 10 ♗e4 when the critical try is 10...♘f5!? (covering d4 whereas 10...♘g6?! 11 cxd4 cxd4 12 d3 ♗e7 13 ♘bd2 0-0 14 ♘b3 ♕b6 15 h4! instructively left Black tied to the defence of d4 and White making good kingside progress in J.Timman-M.Cebalo, Taxco Interzonal 1985) 11 a4 ♗e7 when the strong e4-prelate supports play on both flanks, but 12 axb5 axb5

---

13 ♖xa8 ♕xa8 14 ♘a3 ♘a7! (exchanging off the strong bishop and freeing his position) 15 ♗xb7 ♕xb7 16 cxd4 cxd4 17 d3 ♕d5 18 ♘c2 ♘c6 19 ♖e4 h5! was about equal in I.Glek-E.Gausel, Recklinghausen 1999 as Black could hold his own on the all important kingside.

9 a4

Striking out on the queenside only now that the black rook has left the a-file. Instead practice has shown that 9 d3 g6! gives Black a good set-up, while 9 d4 should be met by 9...cxd4 10 cxd4 ♘b4! 11 ♗b3 ♖xc1 12 ♕xc1 ♘d3 13 ♕d2 ♘xe1 14 ♕xe1 ♘g6 which isn't completely clear, but Black appears to have sufficient play with his bishop-pair and against the white centre.

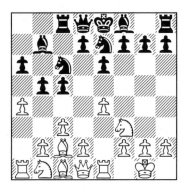

9...♕b6

Now White gets to advance in the centre, which isn't so bad for Black but he does have two playable alternatives:

a) 9...b4!? 10 d4!? (previously 10 d3 ♘g6 11 ♗e3 ♗e7 12 ♘bd2 0-0 13 d4?! bxc3 14 bxc3 cxd4 15 cxd4 ♘b4 16 ♗b3 f5! had made excellent use of the black set-up and especially the b7-bishop in E.Miroshnichenko-M.Krasenkow, European Team Ch., Ohrid 2001) 10...bxc3 11 d5 is energetic, but the gambit should be declined and 11...♘b4 12 ♘xc3 ♘g6 13 ♗d3 c4 14 ♗f1 ♗c5 15 ♗e3 0-0 gave Black an active position in B.Damljanovic-A.Goloshchapov, Topola 2004.

b) 9...♘g6 10 ♘a3 b4

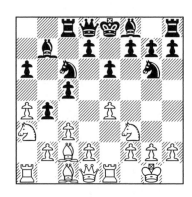

11 ♘c4 sees the white knight reach a good square and has been tried by Smirin; presumably impressed by the queenside undermining plan after his defeat in our main game. Then 11...♕c7 12 h4!? ♗e7 13 h5 ♘ge5 14 ♘fxe5 ♘xe5 15 ♘xe5 ♕xe5 16 d4 still gave White his centre in I.Smirin-A.Moiseenko, European Team Ch., Plovdiv 2003. Thus Black should prefer Erenburg's suggestion of 13...♘f4!? when White must sacrifice his h-pawn. Now 14 h6 gxh6 15 d4 ♖g8 gives Black counterplay, but Black also doesn't appear to be worse after 14 d4 cxd4 15 cxd4 ♘xh5 16 d5! ♘a5 17 ♘xa5 ♕xa5 18 ♘d4 ♘f6 19 ♗f4 ♕b6! (Erenberg) although White's central grip gives him reasonable compensation.

10 ♘a3! ♘g6 11 axb5 axb5 12 d4 cxd4 13 cxd4 ♗b4 14 ♖e2

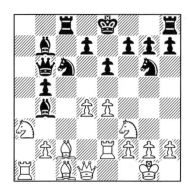

The rook isn't greatly inconvenienced here and play soon takes on a French feel.

14...0-0 15 ♗e3 d5! 16 e5 ♗e7 17 ♗d3 b4 18 ♘c2 ♖a8 19 g3 ♗a6!

Swapping off his bad bishop and beginning to make queenside progress, which White must quickly counter on the other flank.

20 ♖xa6 ♖xa6 21 ♗xa6 ♕xa6 22 h4! ♖a8?

Black doesn't really need the rook here just yet, whilst he shouldn't allow the h-pawn to run all the way. Instead he should have challenged on the kingside with 22...f6! when 23 h5 fxe5 is possible as the f3-knight is loose, while 23 exf6 ♗xf6 24 h5 ♘ge7 25 h6 g6 (Rabinovich), followed by ...♘f5, gives Black counterplay against d4 and a much better kingside defence than he obtains in the game.

23 h5! ♘f8 24 h6 g6 25 b3 ♕c8 26 ♗g5!

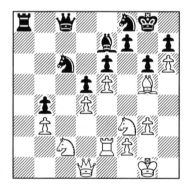

Crippling Black on the dark squares and it doesn't take Morozevich long to exploit this.

26...♘d7 27 ♘e3 ♗xg5 28 ♘xg5 ♕d8 29 ♘f3 ♘e7 30 ♖c2! f6

Hastening the end, although Smirin was in huge trouble in any case.

31 ♘g4 fxe5 32 dxe5 ♖c8?! 33 ♘g5! ♖xc2 34 ♕xc2 ♕b6 35 ♘f6+ 1-0

Here 35...♘xf6 36 exf6 ♘c6 37 f7+ ♔f8 38 ♘xe6+! ♔xf7 39 ♕xc6 would have won a piece and so Smirin gave up; a graphic illustration of the dangers of weakening the kingside dark squares.

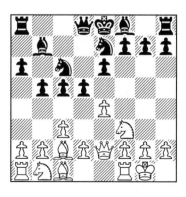

Game 64
S.Gross-A.Goloshchapov
Austrian Team Ch. 2002

1 e4 c5 2 ♘f3 ♘c6 3 ♗b5 e6 4 0-0 ♘ge7 5 c3 a6 6 ♗a4 b5 7 ♗c2 ♗b7 8 ♕e2

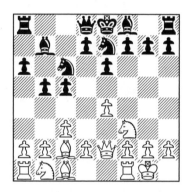

8...g6!?

Black prepares to complete his development with a fianchetto; a plausible plan given that the white queen no longer supports d4. This approach is fairly interesting but is also quite rare. A number of different set-ups have been tried, but Black has been coming under some pressure of late after his two most popular options (these being the moves 8...d5 and 8...♘g6):

a) 8...d5

9 e5 d4 10 ♗e4 is very similar to a position

we considered in our last illustrative game. Black has here been trying to play actively with 10...♘d5!? (10...♘g6 is again an inferior option when 11 cxd4 cxd4 12 d3 ♗e7 13 ♘bd2 ♕c7 14 ♘b3 0-0 15 ♗d2! indirectly defended e5 in I.Smirin-M.Krasenkow, Dos Hermanas 2001; 15...♖fc8 16 ♖ac1 ♕b6 17 h4 gave White the initiative, but 15...♘gxe5? would have lost material after 16 ♖ac1 ♘xf3+ 17 ♕xf3 ♖ac8 18 ♘a5)

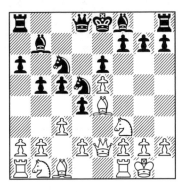

11 d3 (and not 11 cxd4?! ♘xd4! 12 ♘xd4 cxd4 when the exchange of knights frees the black position and reveals an important point behind 10...♘d5; 13 a4 b4! 14 d3 ♕c7 15 f4?! ♖c8 16 ♘d2 ♘e3 17 ♖f3 ♗xe4! 18 dxe4 d3! 19 ♕xd3 ♘c2 then forced the win of an exchange in A.Grischuk-G.Kasparov, Moscow (rapid) 2002) 11...dxc3 12 ♘xc3 ♕d7!. This approach deserves serious consideration, although 13 ♖d1 ♗e7 14 d4! ♘xd4 15 ♘xd4 cxd4 16 ♘xd5 exd5 17 ♖xd4 0-0 18 ♗d3, whilst not fully clear, did appear to favour White due to his kingside chances in S.Rublevsky-A.Moiseenko, Moscow 2003.

b) 8...♘g6 9 d4 cxd4 10 cxd4 ♘h4?! was a strategy initially praised for Black, but the exchange of knights is no longer seen as assuring him of sufficient counterplay. After the continuation 11 ♘bd2 ♖c8 12 ♗b1!? it's not so easy for Black to continue as 12...♗e7 13 ♘xh4 ♗xh4 14 ♘f3 leaves the white pieces well coordinated and those bishops already

eyeing up the kingside. Instead 12...♗d6!? 13 a4! bxa4 14 ♖xa4 ♘xf3+ 15 ♘xf3 ♘b4 gave Black some play in M.Adams-A.Shirov, Linares 2002, although after 16 ♗d2 a5 17 ♖d1 0-0 18 ♗c3 White was slightly better due to his centre and kingside prospects.

c) 8...♖c8!?

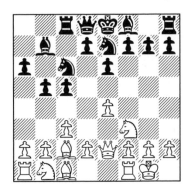

sees Black wait for 9 d4 before breaking with 9...cxd4 10 cxd4 d5 and this approach deserves attention as it's been employed by Lautier. 11 e5 ♘b4! would then remove a key bishop and so Gallagher-Lautier, French Team Ch. 2005 saw 11 ♘c3 ♘b4 12 ♗b1 dxe4 13 ♗xe4 ♗xe4 14 ♕xe4 ♘ed5 15 ♗d2 ♘xc3 16 bxc3 ♘d5, but this was fine for Black. Instead 9 ♖d1 is well met by 9...♕c7 which prevents d4, but striking on the queenside a la Morozevich with 9 a4!? merits attention, meeting 9...b4 with 10 d4 bxc3 11 d5.

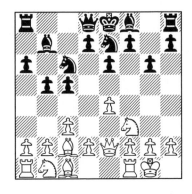

9 a4

Black doesn't mind pushing on in advance to this as, with ♘c3 ruled out, it's not so easy for White to quickly complete his queenside development. Critical must be 9 d4!? cxd4 10 cxd4 ♗g7 when 11 d5 appears to be well met by 11...♘b4. Instead 11 ♖d1!? 0-0 12 ♘c3 d6 13 ♗f4 gave White his centre in R.Felgaer-A.Ramirez Alvarez, Havana 2001, although after 13...♖c8 Black had a reasonable Hippo set-up and queenside counterplay. As we've seen before, making use of the strong centre isn't always so easy and here 14 ♖ac1 ♖e8 15 e5!? ♘d5 should have been met by 16 ♘xd5!? exd5 17 ♗b3, despite the pin down the e-file, as 16 ♗g3?! ♘xc3! 17 bxc3 dxe5 18 dxe5 ♕c7 19 h4 ♘e7 gave Black a good version of the c3 Sicilian with at least sufficient counterplay against c3 and e5.

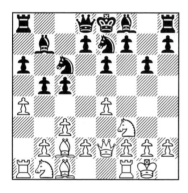

9...b4! 10 d4 cxd4 11 cxd4 ♗g7 12 d5?!

Rather committal, although after 12 ♗e3,

Goloshchapov notes that 12...0-0 13 ♘bd2 f5! gives Black sufficient counterplay.

12...♘a5 13 ♖d1?

Now the d-pawn becomes a problem for Gross and, with 13 d6 ♘ec6 14 ♘bd2 0-0 15 e5 ♕b6! 16 ♖e1 ♘d4 17 ♘xd4 ♕xd4 also leaving him overextended, he should have simply exchanged on e6.

13...exd5 14 exd5 0-0 15 ♗g5 ♖e8!

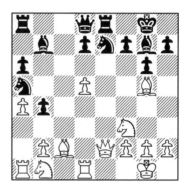

The unfortunate position of the white queen allows Black to sidestep the pin and White is already in some trouble, although he does now collapse rather quickly as all the black minor pieces spring to life.

16 d6 ♘d5 17 ♗xd8 ♖xe2 18 ♗d3 ♘b3 19 ♗xe2 ♖xd8! 20 ♗c4

Now Goloshchapov wins material, although he also would have done so with 20 ♖a2 ♖c8 21 ♘bd2 ♘c1.

20...♘xa1 21 ♗xd5 ♗xd5 22 ♖xd5 ♖c8! 0-1

Summary

This leads to some of the most fascinating positions in this book and must be worth seriously considering as Black if one is at all creative. However, Black, but also White, must handle the early phases carefully. 4 ♗xc6 doesn't promise White an advantage, but this approach does require accurate handling from Black. Currently 5 d3 ♘e7 6 ♕e2 looks like a more promising course for White than 5 0-0 or 5 b3, although Black can deviate at move five, while both players must always avoid drifting!

Opting for early piece play is possible in a few ways for White. 5 b3 certainly deserves further attention as Black has struggled a little of late with both 5...♘g6 and 5...a6, although at least the former should be enough to equalise. Instead the once popular plan of ♗xc6, ...♘xc6, d4 retains some bite, but is more promising when White has omitted ♘c3. A quick ...♘d4 is though a good option for Black against an early ♘c3, whilst he should also give some thought to 5 ♖e1 ♘d4!?.

The Rublevsky-favoured 5 c3 approach is the current main line. Black may be able to make 5...d5 work due to 6 exd5 ♕xd5 7 ♖e1 a6, while he should also look to the lesser played options after 5...a6 6 ♗a4 b5 7 ♗c2 ♗b7 8 ♕e2. Indeed a ♕e2 set-up both there and with 7...c4 8 b3 b5 9 ♕e2 is White's best, while Black needs an improvement to maintain ...c4 as a valid choice.

1 e4 c5 2 ♘f3 ♘c6 3 ♗b5 e6 *(D)* **4 0-0**

    4 ♗xc6 bxc6
       5 d3
               5...♘e7 – *Game 52*; 5...d6 – *Game 53*
       5 0-0 – *Game 54*; 5 b3 – *Game 55*

4...♘ge7 5 c3

    5 b3
              5...♘g6 – *Game 56*; 5...a6 – *Game 57*
    5 ♖e1 a6
       6 ♗f1 – *Game 58*
       6 ♗xc6 ♘xc6 7 d4 cxd4 8 ♘xd4 *(D)*
               8...♕c7 – *Game 59*; 8...d6 – *Game 60*

5...a6 (5...d5 – *Game 61*)
6 ♗a4 b5 (6...c4 – *Game 62*)
7 ♗c2 ♗b7 *(D)*

    8 ♖e1 – *Game 63*; 8 ♕e2 – *Game 64*

    3...e6   *8 ♘xd4*   *7...♗b7*

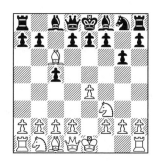

CHAPTER NINE

3...g6 4 ♗xc6: The Modern Treatment

1 e4 c5 2 ♘f3 ♘c6 3 ♗b5 g6 4 ♗xc6

3...g6 remains the main line of the Rossolimo and the choice of many of the world's elite. Some 3...g6 experts like Vasilios Kotronias, Peter Leko and Luke McShane generally stick with one approach as Black against 4 ♗xc6, but others, and especially Vladimir Kramnik and Loek Van Wely, have employed a number of different set-ups. Indeed here lies one of Black's problems after 4 ♗xc6; the play isn't especially forcing and the general plans for each side are at least as important as specific move orders. However, we are talking about modern chess here and so some of Black's options have unsurprisingly built up a body of theory, albeit a smaller one than many Sveshnikov lines possess.

4...dxc6

In the past five years this has been roughly three times as popular as the alternative recapture, 4...bxc6. However, fashion isn't always logical and this approach shouldn't be neglected as an option by either side when preparing 4 ♗xc6. Here 5 0-0 ♗g7 6 ♖e1 is White's best move order as 6 c3 reduces his options against an immediate 6...♘f6. After 6 ♖e1, Black should avoid 6...d6?! 7 e5!, while we consider 6...♘f6 in Game 65 and 6...e5 in Game 66. His main option is though 6...♘h6

7 c3 0-0 when Black intends to regroup with ...f6 and ...♘f7 (he can also begin with 6...f6), after which he is fairly solid and will hope to later exploit the bishop-pair.

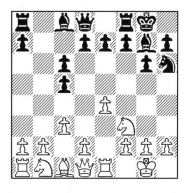

As we'll see in Game 67 White's space advantage does still often grant him a small edge, whilst there White opts for 8 h3. Then 8...d5?! isn't too good due to 9 d3! when 9...f6 10 ♗e3! c4!? 11 exd5 cxd3 12 ♕xd3 cxd5 13 ♗c5 generated strong pressure in S.Rublevsky-Z.Hracek, Polanica Zdroj 1996. Instead 8 d4 is a move popular move order, but here Wells is correct that this is less accurate as it gives Black a useful extra option. Yakovich has favoured 8...cxd4 9 cxd4 d5!? (9...f6 10 b3 ♘f7 11 ♗b2 d6 is Game 67) 10 e5 f6!, rather than the more popular 10...♗g4, when White has tried just about every approach, but without finding an edge, such as 11 exf6 exf6 12 h3 g5! 13 b3 ♗f5 14 ♗a3 ♖e8 15 ♖xe8+ ♛xe8 16 ♘bd2 ♘f7 17 ♛f1 ♘d8 saw Black cover c6 when White struggled to pose any real problems in M.Ulibin-Y.Yakovich, Maikop 1998.

5 d3

White used to prefer 5 h3, but he hasn't been worried by 5...♗g4, due to 6 ♘bd2 followed by recapturing on f3 with the knight, for a number of years. After 5 h3, Black should though be aware that he doesn't have to let White transpose back to normal 5 d3 lines after 5...♗g7, but can prefer 5...e5! 6 d3 f6. In its few recent outings this has continued to score well for Black whether he chooses, after 7 c3 ♘h6 8 0-0 ♘f7 9 ♗e3, the solid 9...♗d6, Kramnik's promising 9...g5!?, or even 9...f5!? when 10 exf5 ♗xf5 11 ♛b3 (11 d4 cxd4 12 cxd4 ♗g7 with good play down the diagonal is the tactical justification behind Black's ninth) 11...♛b6! which was already quite promising for Black in C.Bauer-M.Mchedlishvili, European Team Ch., Batumi 1999; already d3 was weak and Black had solved the problem of his often slightly bad light-square bishop, which is here rather well-placed.

5...♗g7

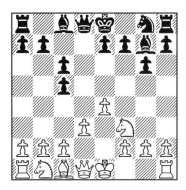

6 h3

This appears to be White's best move order as after 6 ♘c3, Black can consider 6...♗g4 with White no longer able to harmoniously recapture with the knight on f3. Also possible is 6...c4!?, as well as 6...♘f6 when 7 h3 returns to normal lines. Instead 7 ♗e3 ♘g4! was an inspired over the board novelty from the Italian IM, Carlo Rossi. White should still then take the opportunity to reach normal lines with 8 ♗d2 0-0 9 h3 ♘f6 10 ♗e3, whereas 8 ♗xc5? ♛a5 9 d4?! b6 10 ♗a3 ♗a6 11 h3 c5! 12 hxg4 cxd4 already netted a piece in D.Fernando-C.Rossi, Istanbul Olympiad 2000 as 13 ♘xd4 is met by 13...♖d8.

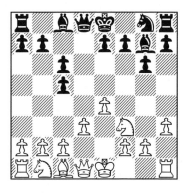

6...♘f6

Black keeps his options open, although an immediate 6...e5 is still sometimes seen these days, but after 7 ♗e3 Black usually now opts for 7...b6, transposing to our next note rather than the older 7...♛e7 when the accurate 8 ♛d2! ♘f6 9 ♗h6 gives White a small edge and an improved version of Game 70.

An intriguing option for Black, which has been championed by Kotronias, is the prophylactic 6...b6!? after which he can develop his king's knight to e7 or to h6 as well as to f6, and we'll discuss such an approach in Game 68. An immediate 6...♘h6!? is somewhat rarer when White's best try is probably 7 ♘c3 b6 8 ♗e3 f6 9 ♛d2 ♘f7 10 0-0 0-0 11 ♘h2, although after 11...e5 12 f4 f5! 13 fxe5 ♘xe5 14 ♗h6 fxe4 15 ♖xf8+ ♛xf8 16 ♗xg7 ♛xg7 17

♘xe4 ♗f5 Black was pretty solid and no more than a fraction worse in V.Bologan-L.Van Wely, European internet Ch. (blitz) 2004, which just shows how much fertile ground remains to be explored after 4 ♗xc6.

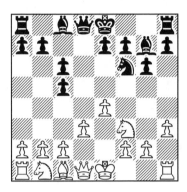

7 ♘c3

One reason behind the large amount of interest in this variation for White of late has been that he can develop flexibly like this, retaining the option of going long. However, an immediate 7 0-0 remains a valid alternative and is the subject of Game 69.

7...♘d7

Black immediately prepares to bring his knight around to e6 via f8, while supporting 8...e5. However, another very popular option is 7...0-0 8 ♗e3 b6 9 ♕d2 e5 10 ♗h6 ♕d6 which can quickly lead to rather sharp play after opposite-side castling as we analyse in Game 70. As the e-pawn is immune (10 ♘xe5 runs into 10...♘xe4!), this is now much more popular than the older 9...♖e8, although that does allow Black to preserve his bishop with 10 ♗h6 ♗h8. White is though doing fairly well here after 11 0-0 and a3 or with the more aggressive 11 e5 ♘d5 12 ♘e4 ♘c7 13 0-0-0.

An enterprising approach which surprisingly hasn't caught on more is Shvedov's 7...c4!?, hoping to activate all of the black pieces after 8 dxc4 ♕xd1+ 9 ♔xd1 ♗e6. Instead 8 d4!? (8 0-0 cxd3 9 cxd3 c5 10 ♗e3 b6 11 d4! cxd4! 12 ♗xd4 0-0 13 ♕a4 ♕d7 14

♕b4 only gave White a tiny edge in A.Grischuk-L.Van Wely, Wijk aan Zee 2003) 8...b5 9 e5 ♘d5 10 ♘e4 ♗f5 11 ♘g3 ♕d7 12 0-0 c3 13 bxc3 ♘xc3 14 ♕e1 ♘a4 saw Black holding his own in this unclear position in P.Wells-E.Lawson, Hastings Challengers 2002/3.

8 ♗e3 e5 9 ♕d2

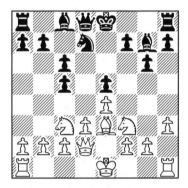

9...h6!?

The modern approach which preserves the black dark-square bishop, and that piece can become fairly useful so long as Black meets f4 with an essential trade on that square. However, the older and very solid 9...♕e7 remains a playable alternative as we witness in a battle between two British Rossolimo experts in Game 71.

10 0-0 ♕e7

and now White is at a crossroads and there isn't yet any general consensus as to which road to prefer. Game 72 shows that some life remains in 11 a3, while there we also discuss White's tenth move alternatives. Instead in Game 73 White prefers the more popular approach of arranging f4 with 11 ♘h2.

Game 65
M.Ferguson-T.Hisler
European Club Cup, Chalkidiki 2002

---

1 e4 c5 2 ♘f3 ♘c6 3 ♗b5 g6 4 ♗xc6 bxc6 5 0-0 ♗g7 6 ♖e1 ♘f6

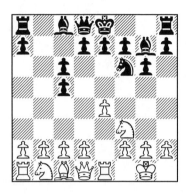

7 e5 ♘d5 8 ♘c3

A rare move, but a reasonable alternative to the critical line. However, unlike if the exchange on c6 hadn't been made, the black knight is defended and so it doesn't now have to exchange or retreat, although Black must find a good follow-up if he wishes to keep his knight on d5. The critical choice is thus the more aggressive 8 c4!? ♘c7 9 d4! cxd4 10 ♕xd4 when White logically intends to put his extra space to some good use, especially by beginning a kingside attack. Black does though have the strong e6-square for his knight and so can continue with 10...♘e6!? when 11 ♕h4 gives him a choice:

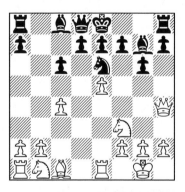

a) 11...h6 keeps the bishop out, but now Black can't castle and 12 ♘c3 d6 13 ♖d1 ♗b7 14 ♗e3 c5 15 exd6! exd6 16 ♕g3 has been shown to clearly favour White, partly due to

16...♗xf3 17 ♖xd6! ♕b8 18 ♖xe6+! (Pedersen).

b) 11...d6!? is superior and could really do with another outing or two. White probably shouldn't rush here with 12 ♘c3 as 12 ♗h6?! ♗xe5! 13 ♘xe5 dxe5 14 ♘c3 f6 15 ♖ad1 ♕c7 was a fairly reasonable pawn grab in E.Miroshnichenko-Bu Xiangzhi, Bled 2000; White had some compensation after 16 f4!, but by offering to return the pawn with 16...exf4 17 ♖e4 ♖b8! 18 b3 ♖b7 Black got a good game.

8...0-0 9 ♘e4!

Preparing c4, while the knight is well-placed to support White's central play and also any kingside ambitions he might have.

9...d6?!

A standard central break, but Black must be more precise for he can quickly stand worse as the game demonstrates. Thus Rabinovich's suggestion of 9...♕b6! is much better when the queen observes the b2- and d4-squares, while Black intends ...f5, especially in response to 10 c4.

10 c4! ♘c7?!

Trying to reach e6, but a better try is 10...♘b6!?, although White is slightly better after 11 d3 dxe5 12 ♘xc5 ♕d6 13 ♗e3, despite the backwards d-pawn. However, Black could then gain some counterchances with 13...f5, although further advancing the pawns isn't easy as Black must beware losing control over the e4-square.

11 exd6 exd6 12 d4!

This may appear to play into the hands of the g7-prelate, but a more important feature of the position is the pressure against the c6 and d6 hanging pawn duo.

12...cxd4 13 ♘xd4 ♕d7?! 14 ♗f4

Black should have preferred 13...f5 14 ♗g5 ♕d7 15 ♘c3, although that is still a pleasant edge for White, as here Ferguson also had the strong 14 ♗h6! (Rabinovich) when 14...d5 15 ♗xg7 ♔xg7 16 cxd5 cxd5 17 ♘c5 leaves White with two very well-placed knights.

14...♘e8 15 ♕d2 ♗a6 16 ♖ac1 ♖d8 17 ♘f3

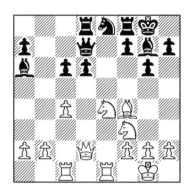

Hisler has been completely outplayed and soon collapses, but 17...f5 18 ♘g3, intending c5 and also quite possibly h4-h5, would still have left White clearly better.

17...♕g4?! 18 h3 ♕f5 19 b3 d5 20 ♘c5 ♕c8?

Losing material, although White was superbly coordinated in any case and 20...♗c8 21 ♘d4 would have been pretty strong.

21 ♕a5! ♗b7 22 ♘xb7 1-0

Game 66
V.Nevednichy-P.Nikac
Niksic 2000

---

1 e4 c5 2 ♘f3 ♘c6 3 ♗b5 g6 4 ♗xc6 bxc6 5 0-0 ♗g7 6 ♖e1 e5

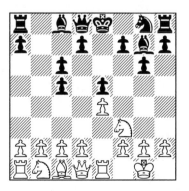

This is much less popular than the ...♘h6 and ...f6 plan, but we've now have reached an important position which also arises via 4 0-0 ♗g7 5 ♖e1 e5 6 ♗xc6 bxc6.

7 c3

Preparing to advance in the centre and again to generate pressure against d6 and c6. These positions should be compared with the variation 3...d6 4 ♗xc6+ bxc6, but here the black dark-square bishop, although more actively placed, doesn't provide any support to a pawn on d6. Indeed it's that which is often the route of Black's problems as we saw Hisler discover.

White also has a promising alternative here in 7 b4!? cxb4 8 a3! which looks a little strange at first glance. However, a b-pawn sacrifice is an important positional motif after the exchange on c6; it gives White good queenside pressure and he can quickly gain strong central play:

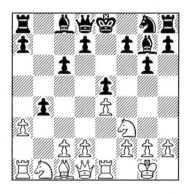

a) 8...bxa3 9 ♗xa3 d6 10 d4 exd4 11 e5! gives White the initiative, while 9...♘e7 10 ♗d6 f6 11 c3 0-0 12 ♕b3+ ♖f7 13 ♘a3 (Timman) supplies promising compensation for White.

b) 8...c5 9 axb4 cxb4 10 d4! exd4 11 ♗b2 d6 12 ♘xd4 left Black struggling to develop and to cover his many weaknesses with ♘d2-c4 on the way in R.Fischer-B.Spassky, Sveti Stefan 1992.

c) 8...♘e7?! tries to return the pawn to develop, but after 9 ♗b2 d6 10 axb4 0-0 11 d4! ♗g4 12 dxe5 ♗xf3 13 ♕xf3 dxe5 14 ♖a5 Black didn't even have a pawn to show for his weaknesses in J.Degraeve-S.Renard, Bethune 2001.

7...♘e7 8 d4 cxd4 9 cxd4 exd4 10 ♘xd4 0-0 11 ♘c3

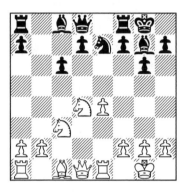

11...♖b8

Counterattacking against b2 is probably the best try, but Black is worse in any case. The d4-knight is well-placed, whilst White can simply increase the pressure after 11...d6 with 12 ♗g5 and then ♕d2-f4. Instead 11...d5?! 12 exd5 cxd5 13 ♗g5 was positionally awful for Black in M.Oratovsky-G.Draghici Flutur, Mondariz Balneario 2002, while 11...♗b7 12 ♘b3! (heading for c5) 12...d5 13 ♗g5 f6 14 ♗e3 dxe4 15 ♘xe4 ♘d5 16 ♗c5 gave White a clear positional edge in H.Hunt-M.Ankerst, Bled Olympiad 2002.

12 ♘b3 d5 13 ♗g5!?

Nevednichy succeeds in forcing a further weakness before bringing the bishop to e3, but it can also go there immediately. However, after 13 ♗e3 dxe4 Pedersen is correct that Kasparov's 14 ♗c5!? ♖b7 15 ♘xe4 ♗xb2 16 ♘d4 isn't so clear, but the simple 14 ♘xe4 does favour White. After 14...♗xb2 15 ♗xa7 White is better because of his outside passed pawn and the weakness of c5, while 15...♖a8 can be countered by 16 ♗d4! when 16...♗xa1? 17 ♘f6+ ♔g7 18 ♕xa1 ♘f5 19

♗c5 regains the exchange and maintains a strong attack. Instead 14...♕xd1?! 15 ♖axd1 ♗e6 16 ♗xa7 ♖b7 17 ♗c5! ♗xb3 18 axb3 ♖a8 19 ♘d6 ♖c7 20 ♘c4 left White clearly better, as his extra doubled pawn was quite useful with c6 vulnerable, in B.Predojevic-I.Saric, Bosnjaci 2005.

13...f6

Black could try 13...h6 when his bishop-pair offers reasonable play for the pawn after 14 ♗xe7 ♕xe7 15 exd5, but simply 14 ♗e3 retains an edge. Black has though scored well with 13...d4!?, but here Nevednichy probably intended to improve over 14 ♘e2 with 14 ♘a4!, heading for c5 with a useful bind on the position, while d4 can easily become weak or thoroughly blockaded.

14 ♗e3 dxe4 15 ♘xe4 f5?!

Reopening the bishop's path, but this does deprive the knight of a square and indeed that piece quickly turns out not to be too comfortable on e7.

16 ♘c3

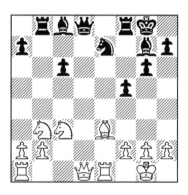

16...♕c7?

16...♕xd1 17 ♖axd1 would also have been strong with even 17...♘d5 failing to help Black unravel due to 18 ♗xa7 ♘xc3 19 bxc3 ♖a8 20 ♗c5! when the black back rank is again the decisive factor. However, Black could have grovelled grimly with 16...♕xd1 17 ♖axd1 ♖b7, whereas now White wins at least an exchange on the dark squares.

17 ♗c5! ♖d8 18 ♖xe7! ♖xd1+ 19 ♖xd1 1-0

Netting a clear piece as Black cannot both maintain his queen and defend his vulnerable back ranks.

Game 67
S.Fedorchuk-M.Oleksienko
Ukrainian Ch., Kharkov 2004

---

1 e4 c5 2 ♘f3 ♘c6 3 ♗b5 g6 4 ♗xc6 bxc6 5 0-0 ♗g7 6 ♖e1 ♘h6 7 c3 0-0

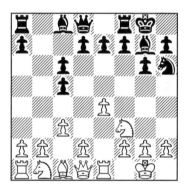

8 h3

As we've already noted, 8 d4 allows Black the option of 8...cxd4 9 cxd4 d5 10 e5 f6!, although he often declines that and 9...d6 10 h3 f6 11 b3 ♘f7 transposes to our main game.

8...f6

White is now ready to meet 8...d5, but Black can try to exploit the absence of 8 d4 with 8...e5!?. However, after 9 d4! Black must be careful that his h6-knight doesn't become misplaced and 9...exd4 10 cxd4 cxd4 11 ♘xd4 f5!? (rather ambitious, but 11...f6 12 ♘c3 ♘f7 13 ♗f4 would have given White a small, but pleasant edge) 12 ♗xh6! ♗xh6 13 e5 closed the position against the bishops in S.Rublevsky-K.Sakaev, St Petersburg (rapid) 2003. After 13...♕b6 14 ♘a3 ♗a6 15 ♕a4 ♖ae8 16 ♖ad1, intending ♘c4 White had kept control well thus far and was beginning to increase the pressure.

Oleksienko prefers to build-up more slowly and this method of combating 4 ♗xc6 for Black, by bringing the knight to f7, was fairly popular in the mid-nineties, but has now fallen out of favour, although Ponomariov has made some use of it

9 d4 cxd4 10 cxd4 ♘f7 11 b3

Fedorchuk wants to create an ideal set-up with his queen's knight on d2 not blocking his fianchettoed bishop. Instead 11 ♘c3 d6 reaches an important position:

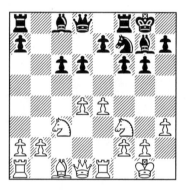

Nunn assessed this as being equal in *NCO*, but White is probably slightly better or at least more grandmasters appear to be happier on the white side here. They are attracted by White's space advantage and his ability to pressurise the black queenside. Black's position is though quite playable, but he must be patient and aim to find a way to activate his bishops which is usually achieved through ...c5 or ...f5. Once again White must now choose whether or not to fianchetto:

a) 12 ♗e3 is the more popular choice and this aims to prevent ...c5, while Black usually covers c6 with 12...♗d7 and this appears to be his best set-up. Here 13 ♕d2 is often seen, but that takes away a useful square from the f3-knight and so White can prefer 13 ♖c1, although 13...♕a5 14 ♘d2 f5!? 15 e5 (White's ideal response to ...f5) 15...dxe5 16 ♘c4 ♕b4 17 ♘xe5 ♘xe5 18 dxe5 f4! gave Black good counterplay in R.Ruck-P.Acs, Hungarian

Team Ch. 1999, as even 19 ♗c5!? ♕xc5 20 ♕xd7 f3! 21 g3 ♔h8 wouldn't have allowed White to defend e5 and to maintain full control over the position.

b) 12 b3 f5!? (critical, whereas 12...♗d7 gives White pretty reasonable chances for an edge and 13 ♗b2 ♖e8 14 ♕c2 ♕a5 15 ♖ad1 ♕h5 16 ♘e2! kept Black's counterplay fully under control in M.Turov-R.Ponomariov, Kharkov 2001) 13 exf5?! (or 13 e5 dxe5 14 dxe5 ♕xd1 15 ♘xd1 c5! 16 ♗b2 ♗b7 which activated one bishop and 17 e6 ♘d8! 18 ♗xg7 ♔xg7 was fine for Black due to the weakness of e6 in E.Lobron-Y.Yakovich, European Ch., Saint Vincent 2000) 13...♗xf5 14 ♕e2 e5! 15 dxe5 ♘xe5 saw the black pieces sprang to life in I.Leventic-D.Pavasovic, Zadar 2004 and so White should prefer the older 13 ♗b2! fxe4 14 ♘xe4, transposing to our main game.

11...d6 12 ♗b2 f5!?

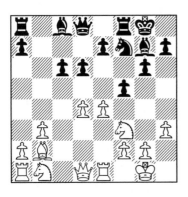

13 ♘bd2

Instead 13 e5!? dxe5 14 ♘xe5 was also fairly critical when 14...♘xe5 15 dxe5 ♗a6 16 ♘c3 heads for c5 and appears to give White an edge, but 14...♗b7!? may be possible.

13...fxe4 14 ♘xe4 c5!?

This position had been thought to be good for White prior to this game and indeed it may be. However, this active move does further open up the black bishops and enables the central white knights to be disturbed.

15 ♕d2 cxd4 16 ♘xd4 ♕b6 17 ♖ad1 e5!? 18 ♘c2 ♗b7 19 ♘c3 ♘g5 20 ♘d5

The queen can still join the attack from d8 and instead White shouldn't have rushed to occupy d5, but should have offered some key support to his kingside with 20 ♘e3!, still retaining an edge.

20...♕d8 21 f4?

White wants to exploit his d5-knight to open the position and to attack the black monarch, but this actually gives Black the attack as he is happy to give up an exchange to reactive his light-square bishop.

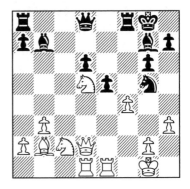

21...♖xf4! 22 ♘xf4 exf4 23 ♗xg7 ♘xh3+! 24 ♔h2??

Shocked by the sacrifices Fedorchuk blunders into mate, and he had to try 24 gxh3 ♕g5+ 25 ♔f1 when Notkin analysed several lines for *Chess Today*, but White appears to be able to escape with a draw, such as with 25...♗a6+ 26 ♖e2 ♖e8 27 ♘d4 ♕g3 28 ♘b5 ♕f3+ 29 ♔e1 ♕g3+ when it's perpetual.

24...♕h4! 25 ♗f6 ♕g3+ 26 ♔h1 ♘f2+ 0-1

Game 68
V.Bologan-V.Kramnik
Wijk aan Zee 2004

---

1 e4 c5 2 ♘f3 ♘c6 3 ♗b5 g6 4 ♗xc6 dxc6 5 d3 ♗g7 6 h3 b6!?

Kotronias' favoured line with which Black

takes the sting out of ♗e3, as c5 is covered, and thus he can play ...e5 without having to follow-up with ...♕e7.

7 ♘c3

Preparing to develop the bishop, although there is no clear consensus yet as to White's best course of action or even move order if he wishes to go short. He can begin with 7 0-0 when Black must choose where to develop his knight to:

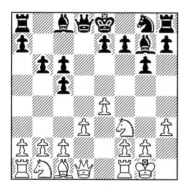

a) 7...e5?! 8 a3! exploits the omission of ♘c3 and aims to seize the queenside initiative. After 8...a5 9 ♗e3 ♘e7, 10 ♘bd2 appears even better than the also promising 10 ♕d2 of Zhang Zhong-P.Svidler, Wijk aan Zee 2004. Black must then avoid the loose 10...f5? 11 exf5! ♘xf5 12 ♗g5 when e5 is weak, while 10...f6 11 ♘c4 ♗e6 12 b4! was a typical sacrifice for the queenside initiative in I.Glek-R.Kleeschaetzky, Berlin 1994. After 12...axb4 13 axb4 ♖xa1 14 ♕xa1 b5 15 ♘a5 cxb4 16 ♘b7 ♕b8 17 ♘c5 Glek had created a superb outpost for his knight and stood better after regaining the pawn on b4.

b) 7...♘f6, racing the knight round to e6 now that White is committed to going short, is thus correct and was used by Kramnik just two days after our main game here. However, White may be able to get a little something with 8 ♗d2!? 0-0 9 ♗c3 ♘e8 (heading for e6 and then probably onwards to d4) 10 ♘bd2 ♘c7 11 ♗xg7 ♔xg7 12 a3 f6 when Shirov

opted for the sharp 13 e5!? in A.Shirov-L.Van Wely, Bundesliga 2004, but the more consistent 13 b4 cxb4 14 axb4 e5 15 ♕b1 ♗e6 16 ♕b2 (Barsky) would have given White the edge due to his pressure down the a-file and to the possibility of a d4-break.

7...e5

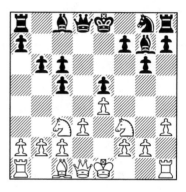

8 0-0

If White intends to play on the queenside after this, then he's probably better off with 7 0-0 as the knight is already here committed to c3. The main alternative is 8 ♗e3 when 8...♘e7 forces White to decide on a plan:

a) 9 ♕d2 is flexible and White's main choice, although 9...h6! is again a good response, especially as here the light-square bishop can be easily developed after which Black will go long. Then 10 g4!? ♗e6 11 0-0-0 ♕d7 12 ♖hg1 0-0-0 13 ♔b1 might have prevented ...f5, but Black is very solid here and wasn't especially troubled after 13...f6 14 ♘a4 ♔b8 15 ♕c3 ♘c8!, bringing the knight to d6, in L.Nisipeanu-S.Halkias, European Ch., Silivri 2003.

b) 9 0-0 h6 10 ♘h2 prepares f4, but allows Black to demonstrate one of the strengths of his set-up and 10...♗e6 11 f4 exf4 12 ♗xf4 g5! 13 ♗g3 ♕d7 14 ♔h1 0-0-0 15 ♘f3 f5 gave Black good kingside prospects in V.Sanduleac-A.Kotronias, European Ch., Silivri 2003.

c) 9 a3!? shouldn't overly worry Black as

the e7-knight enables him to gain quick counterplay and 9...h6 10 b4 cxb4 11 axb4 f5! 12 exf5 gxf5 13 d4 f4 14 ♘xe5 0-0 15 ♗c1 c5! gave him a promising initiative for his pawn in N.McDonald-P.Wells, Hastings Challengers 2002/3.

8...♘e7

Sticking with the ...f5 plan, but Kotronias prefers 8...f6 and ...♘h6-f7 once White has gone short and so can't begin a rapid kingside attack. White then has his usual choice between queenside play and f4:

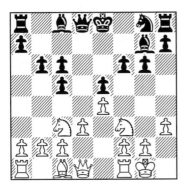

a) 9 a3 ♘h6 10 b4 cxb4 11 axb4 ♘f7 was the course of A.Cherniaev-V.Kotronias, Hastings 2003/4 in which Black began to advance with 12 ♗e3?! f5! 13 ♕b1 f4. Instead 12 b5! has been suggested by several sources as an improvement, but Kotronias is incredibly well prepared and had probably already examined this. After 12...c5!? 13 ♘d5 f5 14 c4 f4 (Rowson) the d5-knight is a strong piece, but Black has reasonable chances to play around it. Indeed I'm far from certain that Black's kingside play isn't at least the equal of any pressure which White can gain against a7.

b) 9 ♘h2 ♘h6 10 f4 exf4 11 ♗xf4 ♘f7!? (retaining more flexibility than his earlier 11...0-0 when 12 ♕d2 ♘f7 13 ♘f3 ♗e6 14 a4! a5 15 ♖ad1 ♕d7 16 ♔h1 ♖ae8 17 ♕f2 ♖e7 18 d4! gave White the edge in M.Oratovsky-V.Kotronias, Lisbon 2001) 12 ♘f3 ♗e6 13 a4 a5 was the course of

R.Berzinsh-V.Kotronias, EU Ch., Cork 2005. This ended quickly with 14 ♔h1 ♕d7 15 ♕e2 0-0 16 ♖ad1 f5! and ½-½, but the key question is how would Black have responded to 14 ♕d2? Perhaps Kotronias even intended 14...♕d7 15 ♖ad1 g5!? which is rather double-edged, but appears playable.

9 a4

As Black can prevent ♘d2-c4 with ...♗e6, this may well not be the most testing plan. However, 9 a3 a5 10 ♗e3 a4!? is a notable idea to prevent the intended ♘a4 and b4. Then it's logical for White to switch plans with 11 ♘h2, but 11...h6! appears to be fine for Black who is happy to exchange on f4 which serves to open up the g7-bishop. However, the aggressive 12 h4?! 0-0 13 ♕d2 ♔h7 14 h5 didn't fully convince, with White having gone short, after 14...gxh5! 15 f4 f5! 16 fxe5 ♘g6 when Black had the better attacking prospects in Zhang Pengxiang-Bu Xiangzhi, Yongchuan Zonal 2003.

9...a5 10 ♘d2 ♗e6! 11 ♘e2 0-0 12 f4 f5

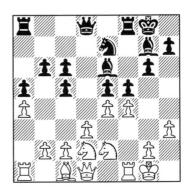

Black appears to have solved all his problems here; he has good central counterplay and has got his light-square bishop into the game. Bologan has meanwhile already felt the need to try and improve his knight from c3 and thus future attention after 6...b6!? may well focus on 7 0-0.

13 fxe5 fxe4 14 ♘xe4 ♗xe5 15 ♗g5 ♕c7 16 ♕d2 ♘f5 17 ♖ae1 ♗d5

Now all the black pieces are on good squares, but White remains very solid and can make some exchanges and so the game shortly ended.

18 ♗f4 ♘d4 ½-½

Game 69
M.Adams-L.Van Wely
French Team Ch. 2003

---

1 e4 c5 2 ♘f3 ♘c6 3 ♗b5 g6 4 ♗xc6 dxc6 5 d3 ♗g7 6 h3 ♘f6 7 0-0 ♘d7 8 ♘c3

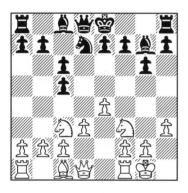

8...♘f8!?

With White having gone short, there's no need for Black to hurry to castle and instead Van Wely gives priority to bringing his knight to the favoured e6-square. However, Black has usually preferred 8...e5 when White has two options:

a) 9 ♗e3 is the standard move when 9...♕e7 10 ♕d2 h6 transposes into the topical 9...h6 line (see Games 72 and 73). It's worth noting that the position after 10 ♕d2 can also arise from the 7 ♘c3 ♘d7 8 ♗e3 e5 9 ♕d2 ♕e7 of Game 71 after 10 0-0, while here Ivanchuk has shown another way for Black: 10...♘f8 (there's no hurry to castle and so Black, as in our main game, first improves his pieces and even retains the option of going long) 11 ♗h6 ♘e6!? 12 ♗xg7 ♘xg7 (this looks a little strange, but is very logical as Iv-

anchuk wants to advance on the kingside and so first covers f5) 13 ♘e2 f6 14 ♘h2 g5! 15 a3 a5

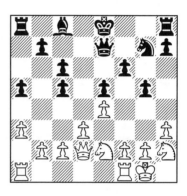

and Black had deprived White of his two main plans and was fine in V.Anand-V.Ivanchuk, Prague (rapid) 2002, especially after 16 c3 0-0 17 ♘g4?! ♗xg4! 18 hxg4 h5 when he was already slightly for choice due to his kingside prospects and to the potential weakness of d3.

b) 9 ♗g5!?

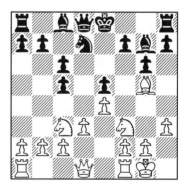

aims to gain an improved version after 9...f6 10 ♗e3 when White can break with d4 more easily. That occurred in A.Naiditsch-A.Skripchenko, Pulvermuehle 2004 after 10...♕e7 11 a3 ♘f8 (playing as Kramnik did against Ponomariov, as we saw in the Introduction, is tempting, while 11...0-0 is the alternative when the plan is ...♖d8 and ...♘e6;

an immediate 12 b4 doesn't fully convince, but 12 ♖b1 ♖d8 13 b4 cxb4! 14 axb4 is probably a small edge, although Black is pretty solid after 14...♘b6 15 ♕e2 ♗e6 when it's not so easy for White to advance with either b5 or d4) 12 b4 ♘e6 13 ♘a4 b6 14 bxc5 b5! 15 ♘c3 ♘xc5 16 d4!

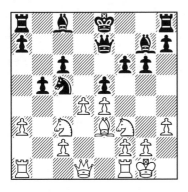

16...exd4 17 ♘xd4. However, Naiditsch's idea hasn't yet spawned many imitators, quite possibly because Black is fairly active and not worse here. 17...♗b7 is sensible, while Skrip-chenko was hit by a bolt from the blue after 17...♗d7 18 a4 b4 in the shape of 19 ♘db5!. She was massacred after 19...cxb5? 20 ♘d5 ♕d6 21 ♗f4 ♕c6 22 axb5 ♕b7 23 ♘c7+, but even declining the sacrifice would still have been acceptable enough for Black; Ora-tovsky's 19...0-0! 20 ♗xc5 ♕xc5 21 ♕xd7 cxb5 22 ♘xb5 f5! activates the bishop and supplies counterplay.

9 ♘e2

White might do better with 9 ♗e3!?, al-though Black may then still have time for 9...b6 before ...e5 and ...♘e6. In practice he has though opted for 9...♘e6 when 10 ♘d2 ♘d4 11 f4 f5! is fine for him, while 10 ♘h2!? ♘d4 11 f4 should probably just be met by 11...f5 12 ♘a4 b6 13 c3 ♘b5 14 ♘f3 as now Black can consider 14...♘d6!? and if 15 e5, 15...♘b5 heading for c7.

9...e5 10 ♗e3 ♘e6 11 ♕d2 h6! 12 ♘h2 b6 13 ♖ad1 g5!

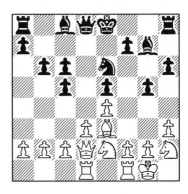

Playing a la Ivanchuk to stop White's breaks. Adams can only counter the knight's strong arrival on f4 by pushing d4, but that doesn't trouble Van Wely and only really leads to exchanges:

14 ♘g3 ♘f4 15 c3 0-0 16 ♘f3 ♗e6 17 d4 cxd4 18 cxd4 exd4 19 ♘xd4 c5! 20 ♘xe6 fxe6 21 ♕c2 ♕e7 22 ♖d2 ♖ad8 23 ♖fd1 ½-½

Game 70
V.Bologan-P.Leko
Dortmund 2003

---

1 e4 c5 2 ♘f3 ♘c6 3 ♗b5 g6 4 ♗xc6 dxc6 5 d3 ♗g7 6 h3 ♘f6 7 ♘c3 0-0 8 ♗e3 b6 9 ♕d2 e5!

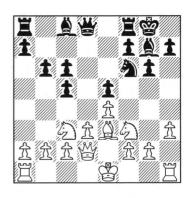

10 ♗h6

Standard, although with the aggressive cas-

---

tling long lines running into some problems of late, White has been trying 10 a3!? a little. However, it turns out that 10...♕d6! is still a good move, covering b4 and e5 when 11 ♖b1 a5 12 a4 ♘h5! 13 g3 ♗e6 14 ♕e2 c4!? 15 dxc4 ♕b4 gave Black good compensation for the pawn in A.Rustemov-E.Najer, Sochi (rapid) 2004.

Of course White shouldn't though test the tactical point behind 9...e5 with 10 ♘xe5?! ♘xe4 which is already pretty comfortable for Black and after 11 ♘xc6 (or 11 ♘xf7 ♘xd2 12 ♘xd8 ♘f3+! 13 gxf3 ♖xd8 with at least sufficient compensation due to the bishop-pair and the split white kingside – D.Gurevich) 11...♘xd2 12 ♘xd8 ♘c4! 13 dxc4 ♖xd8 14 0-0 ♗e6 15 ♖fd1 ♗xc4, Black had regained her pawn with an edge in H.Al Tamimi-V.Cmilyte, Gibraltar 2005.

10...♕d6

This has pretty much fully superseded the older 10...♕e7 as the queen is more active here; she supplies cover to the d4- and f4-squares, while sometimes Black is even able to attack with ...c4 and ...♕b4.

11 g4!?

Trying to delay the once very popular queenside castling, but that isn't White's only alternative:

a) 11 0-0-0 is the sharpest approach and has received a fair amount of high level testing when Black must choose how to counter:

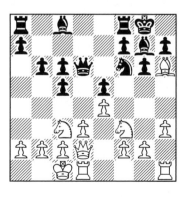

a1) 11...♗e6?! 12 ♗xg7 ♔xg7 13 ♕g5! ♘d7 14 ♕g3! left the queen well-placed to support 15 d4! as well as the h-pawn and attack in A.Grischuk-A.Shirov, Dubai (rapid) 2002.

a2) 11...b5!? might transpose to our main line, whereas 12 g4 a5 13 ♖dg1?! a4 14 ♘e2 b4 15 ♗xg7 ♔xg7 16 ♘g3 b3! 17 a3 bxc2 18 ♕c3 ♘d7 19 ♘d2 ♗a6 gave Black the faster attack in M.Brodsky-A.Shirov, Tallinn (rapid) 2004.

a3) 11...a5 has been Black's preferred route to counterplay and helped to put Shirov off 11 0-0-0, whilst here we have a further split:

a31) 12 ♗xg7 ♔xg7 13 g4 (13 ♘h2 a4 14 ♘g4 is also possible, but Leko's 14...♘g8! is a good response when the play becomes rather sharp after 15 ♘e2!? ♗xg4 16 hxg4 ♕e6! 17 ♔b1 ♕xg4 18 f3 ♕e6 19 g4 f6 20 f4 and White had some play for his pawn in A.Grischuk-R.Ponomariov, Moscow [rapid] 2002, but 20...a3 21 f5 ♕d7 22 b3 g5! 23 ♕e3 h6 was a solid and good defence) 13...a4 14 ♘e2 b5 15 ♘g3 b4 was A.Shirov-P.Leko, Dortmund Candidates 2002. This isn't fully clear, but Black does appear to hold slightly the more promising attacking chances and he went on to win a fine game.

a32) 12 ♘h2!? is less direct,

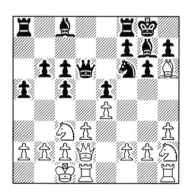

while Oratovsky has shown that 12...a4?! 13 ♘g4 favours White after 13...a3 14 b3. Black has thus preferred to prepare 13 ♘g4

②h5 with 12...♖e8!? when 13 ②g4 ②h5 14 ♗xg7 ♔xg7 15 ②e2 f6 16 ♖hf1 ②f4! was fine for him in M.Oratovsky-J.Ivanov, Mondariz Balneario 2003. Rublevsky thus tried 13 ♗xg7 ♔xg7 14 ♖df1! ♗e6 15 f4 exf4 16 ♖xf4 ②d7! 17 ♖h4 h5 18 ②f3 ②e5 in S.Rublevsky-A.Korotylev, Tomsk 2004 which was rather unclear, although Black appeared to be solid enough.

The world's elite have generally since moved on from this sharp line, while 12 ②h2!? looks likes White's best hope if he wants to continue using 11 0-0-0, although it's a little surprising as to why 11...b5!? isn't seen more. There's certainly no obvious reason as to why it might be bad with 12 ②h2 allowing Black to push on with 12...b4 13 ②e2 c4.

b) 11 0-0

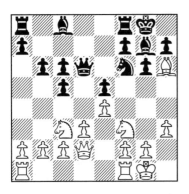

11...②h5! immediately brings the knight to its best square once White has gone short. This helps to take some of the sting out of f4, while even allowing Black to consider also playing on the queenside with ...♗e6, ...♖ad8 and ...c4. After 12 ②e2 (or 12 ②h2 ♗e6 13 ②e2 f6! 14 ②g4 – D.Howell-J.Shaw, British Ch., Edinburgh 2003 – and now Black should have consistently begun counterplay with 14...♗xh6 15 ♕xh6 c4) 12...f6! (keeping the white pieces out of ...g5, whilst Black can even consider ...g5 himself should White play too slowly) 13 a3 a5 14 ②h2 ♖a7 15 ♖ad1 ♗e6 16 ♗xg7 ♖xg7 17 ②g4 ♖d7 Black had his

ideal set-up and White clearly hadn't got anywhere when M.Vachier Lagrave-J.Lautier, French Ch., Val d'Isere 2004 was agreed drawn here.

11...♗e6

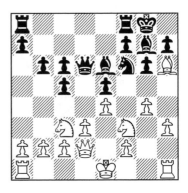

12 ②e2

Bringing the knight over to the kingside as 12 ♗xg7 ♔xg7 13 0-0-0 still doesn't appear too scary for Black. He should rely on trying to get ...c4 in, and 13...♖ad8 14 ♖hf1 b5! 15 ②g5 h6 16 ②xe6+ ♕xe6 17 ♔b1 c4 assured him of sufficient counterplay in A.Shirov-P.Leko, Monaco (rapid) 2002 after which Shirov switched to 11 0-0-0.

White has also tried 12 ♕e3, but then 12...a5! is a useful move whichever side White castles and 13 ②e2?! a4! 14 a3 b5 15 ②g3 ②e8 16 0-0 f6 17 ②d2 ♖d8!, preparing ...c4, left Black solid on the kingside and already slightly for choice in R.Ponomariov-P.Leko, Linares 2003.

12...♖ad8 13 ♗xg7 ♔xg7 14 ♕c3!

Forcing the knight backwards to defend e5 and refusing to allow Leko anywhere near as free a reign to improve his position as Ponomariov did.

14...②d7 15 ②g5 h6

Preventing 16 f4 and now after the exchange on e6, Black maintains control of the f4-square which is rather more important than the doubled e-pawns.

16 ②xe6+ fxe6!

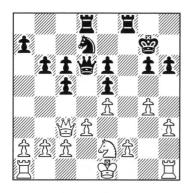

17 ♔f1!

White is just in time to put his king on g2 and to defend f2 after which neither side can really do anything.

17...♖f3 18 ♔g2 ♖df8 19 ♖af1 ½-½

Game 71
G.Quillan-J.Shaw
Gibraltar 2005

---

1 e4 c5 2 ♘f3 ♘c6 3 ♗b5 g6 4 ♗xc6 dxc6 5 d3 ♗g7 6 h3 ♘f6 7 ♘c3 ♘d7 8 ♗e3 e5 9 ♕d2 ♕e7

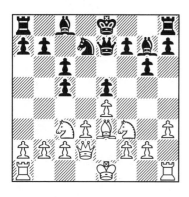

Rogozenko's suggestion in his *Anti-Sicilians: A Guide for Black*, this remains a rather solid choice for Black.

10 ♗h6

White wants to weaken the black kingside before advancing with f4, while it's also useful

to deprive Black of the chance to later get his bishop-pair to operate in harmony. This isn't forced, but 10 0-0 ♘f8!, transposing to the note to Black's 8th move in Adams-Van Wely, is fine for Black as Ivanchuk demonstrated.

10...f6

Black faces a move order dilemma here and Shaw opts for Rogozenko's preferred choice. The problem with the older 10...♗xh6 11 ♕xh6 f6 is the active 12 ♘h4!, whereas 12 ♘d2 ♘f8 13 f4 exf4 14 ♕xf4 ♘e6 reaches Quillan-Shaw, but with both sides having used up a move less. However, Rowson has instead essayed there the ambitious and quite interesting 14 0-0!?, although after his suggested 14...♘e6 15 ♖ae1 ♕f8 16 ♕h4 g5 17 ♕f2 ♗d7 it would be surprising if White had more than enough compensation. Black is fairly solid and that extra pawn does supply a bit of a bind, although his king isn't overly happy and 18 e5 0-0-0 certainly isn't clear with a b4-break on the cards.

After 12 ♘h4!

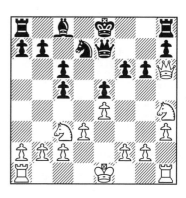

12...♕f8 (12...♘f8 13 0-0 prevents the knight from coming to e6 and White is doing well here, such as after 13...♗e6 14 f4 exf4 15 ♖ae1! 0-0-0 16 ♕xf4 c4 17 d4, with the greater pressure and better structure, of A.Shirov-B.Predojevic, Sarajevo 2004) 13 ♕d2 ♕e7 14 0-0-0 f5 15 g3 f4 16 ♘g2 fxg3 17 fxg3 ♘f8 18 h4 saw White retain the initiative and a small advantage in V.Ivanchuk-V.Filippov, Chalkidiki 2002, while even after Filippov's improvement of 14...♞f8!?, White still has a small but pleasant edge with 15 ♕h6 ♗e6 16 g3.

11 ♗xg7 ♕xg7

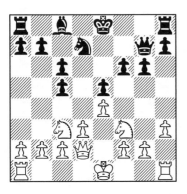

12 ♕e3

Preventing ...♞f8 for a move, whereas 12 ♞h2 ♞f8! 13 f4 exf4 14 ♕xf4 ♞e6 15 ♕d6 ♕e7 16 ♕xe7+ ♚xe7 17 ♞f3 ♞d4 fully equalised in D.Pikula-Z.Lanka, Bundesliga 2002 as after an exchange on d4, Black could support the d4-pawn after which his bishop on e6 was no worse than the white knight.

Moving the queen to e3 isn't though especially problematic for Black and so future investigations may well focus on 12 a3!? ♕e7 13 ♞e2. However, it's not clear that Black must prevent 14 b4, and 13...♞f8 14 b4 ♞e6 looks like a reasonable option with White unable now to increase the pressure on c5 with ♞a4, whereas 13...a5?! 14 ♞h2! ♞f8 15 f4 exf4 16 ♕xf4 ♞e6 17 ♕e3 left Black unable to bring his knight to d4 or to develop his bishop, and he was worse after 17...♞g7 18 ♞f3 0-0 19 0-0 ♗d7 20 ♖f2 ♖ae8 21 ♖af1 in D.Gormally-S.Gordon, British Ch., Scarborough 2004.

12...♕e7 13 ♞d2 ♞f8 14 f4 exf4

Black must exchange on f4, but he remains solid after it and can bring his knight to d4. Instead allowing White to exchange on e5 has

been known to be mistaken ever since L.Psakhis-F.Roeder, Vienna 1991 which saw 14...♞e6?! 15 fxe5 fxe5 16 0-0-0 ♞f4 17 ♖hg1 ♗d7 18 ♞f3 0-0-0?! 19 ♞b1! g5 20 ♞bd2 h6 21 ♞c4 when, having regrouped against e5, Psakhis then opened the queenside with 21...♞g6 22 b4!.

15 ♕xf4 ♞e6

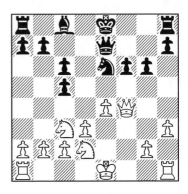

16 ♕h4

Keeping an eye on f6, but now Black can equalise with ...f5 and thus White has usually preferred an alternative square for the queen, although the strong d4-knight always gives Black good chances to fully equalise:

a) 16 ♕h6 ♞d4 17 0-0-0 ♗e6 18 ♖hf1 0-0-0 19 ♚b1 f5! 20 ♖de1 ♖de8 fully equalised and was soon agreed drawn in I.Smirin-A.Shirov, Sarajevo 2002.

b) 16 ♕f2 ♞d4 17 ♞f3!? (challenging the black knight is probably the best try for the advantage, although White can also do that with 17 ♞b3 ♕e5 18 0-0 0-0 when 19 ♞xd4 cxd4 20 ♞e2 c5 21 ♞f4 saw White hoping to prove that his was the superior minor piece in this closed position in M.Rose-R.Palliser, Oxford 2003; Black was only a touch worse after 21...♗e6, but 21...♗d7!? improves, intending ...♗c6 and ...f5 to open the position for the bishop) 17...♕d6 18 0-0-0 ♗e6 19 ♞e2 ♞xe2+ 20 ♕xe2 0-0-0 21 ♚b1 ♕g3 22 ♖hf1 was the course of M.Illescas Cordoba-P.San Segundo Carrillo, Spanish Ch., Cala Mendia

2001. This sort of position is equal, although the white position is slightly the easier to improve due to his f-file pressure, while Black especially must be careful not to drift. San Segundo now began to, but it was important for him to try and improve his bishop and Rogozenko's 22...♖hf8, intending ...♖de8 and ...f5, would have been fine for him.

C) 16 ♕e3 ♘d4 17 ♖c1 ♗e6 18 ♘d1 aims to evict the knight from d4 with c3, but is rather ambitious and probably not a great plan; after 18...0-0-0 19 0-0 ♖he8 20 c3 ♘b5 21 b3 f5! White was a little weak down the central files and Black had good counterplay in V.Bologan-V.Filippov, Russian Team Ch. 2003.

16...♘d4 17 0-0-0 ½-½

White offered the draw he needed for a norm, but Black should again be able to fully equalise here with a couple of accurate moves, such as 17...♗e6 18 ♖hf1 ♖f8 and only then after 19 ♖f2, 19...f5.

Game 72
M.Adams-C.Philippe
French Team Ch. 2004

---

1 e4 c5 2 ♘f3 ♘c6 3 ♗b5 g6 4 ♗xc6 dxc6 5 d3 ♗g7 6 h3 ♘f6 7 ♘c3 ♘d7 8 ♗e3 e5 9 ♕d2 h6

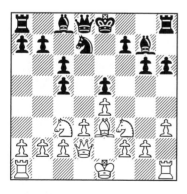

10 0-0

The main choice, although White has toyed

with the alternatives on occasion:

a) 10 0-0-0 appears rather risky as here it's not so easy for White to advance on the kingside, while the Black king is quite happy in the centre for the time being. Black should seriously consider 10...♕a5 or Wells' 10...a5!? to punish White's last, although he often just opts for the solid 10...♕e7 11 ♘h2 ♘f8 12 f4 exf4 13 ♗xf4 ♘e6 14 ♗e3 ♘d4, intending ...♗e6 and ...0-0-0.

b) 10 h4!? tries to show Black's last up as a weakness, but is well met by 10...h5 11 a3 ♕e7 12 ♖b1 ♘f8 when 13 b4 ♘e6 14 ♘a4 b6! borrowed an idea from Kramnik (see the note to White's thirteenth) in D.Gormally-P.Wells, Halifax (rapid) 2004 and 15 ♘g5?! ♘f4! 16 ♗xf4 exf4 17 ♕xf4 cxb4 18 axb4 b5 19 ♘c5 ♗c3+ 20 ♔e2 a5 gave Black promising activity.

c) McShane later switched to giving f4 the immediate priority with 10 ♘g1!? when White can recapture on f4 with his knight and thereby doesn't disrupt his coordination. This approach deserves to be more popular as 10...♕e7 11 ♘ge2 ♘f8 12 f4 exf4 13 ♘xf4 ♘e6 14 0-0 ♘d4!? 15 ♖ae1 0-0 16 ♘d1! ♔h7 17 ♕f2 b6 18 b4! undermined the d4-knight and favoured White in C.Bauer-P.Tregubov, Belfort 2002.

10...♕e7

11 a3

Beginning queenside play, whereas we'll

consider White's main choice of 11 ♘h2 and f4 next in Akopian-Van Wely.

11...♘f8

Recently Black has also begun to exploring 11...b6!? and after 12 ♖fe1 (prophylaxis against a rapid ...f5), he should probably just opt for the solid 12...♘f8 which doesn't appear too problematic for him. Instead the risky 12...♗b7?! 13 ♘a4! 0-0-0 didn't convince after 14 ♘h2! (preparing to slow down the black attack) 14...f5 15 f3 ♘f6 16 ♗f2 f4 17 b4 c4 18 ♗xb6! axb6 19 ♘xb6+ and the three pawns for the piece supplied White with a strong attack in S.B.Hansen-T.Nedev, Calvia Olympiad 2004. Despite that game, 11...b6 may become a reasonable alternative to 11...♘f8, while instead 12 ♖fb1 ♘f8 13 b4 ♘e6 14 bxc5 f5! gave Black good play and the initiative for his pawn in M.Bezold-P.Wells, Pulvermuehle 2000.

12 b4 ♘e6

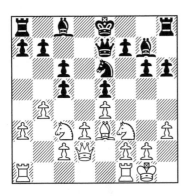

13 bxc5!?

Declining to increase the pressure on c5 and thereby not allowing Philippe to employ Kramnik's ingenious concept of 13 ♘a4 b6!. Then, as we saw in the Introduction, 14 ♘h2?! f5! 15 f3 f4 16 ♗f2 h5 favoured Black in R.Ponomariov-V.Kramnik, Linares 2003. However, White has improved with 14 ♖aee1!? when 14...♗a6?! 15 bxc5 b5 16 ♘b2 ♖d8 17 a4! saw him gain his desired queenside initiative after all in N.Delgado-L.Schandorff, Cal-

via Olympiad 2004. Thus Black had to bite the bullet and still meet 14 ♖ae1 with 14...f5! when there's no clear way for White to increase the central pressure, although he could try 15 exf5 gxf5 16 ♕e2, as instead 16 ♗xc5!? bxc5 17 ♘xe5 ♘xe5 18 ♖xe5, whilst dangerous, doesn't fully convince.

13...♘xc5

Best, whereas 13...f5?! is rather risky and 14 exf5 gxf5 15 ♕e1! 0-0 16 ♖b1 ♕f6 (or 16...f4 17 ♗d2 ♕xc5 18 ♕c1, followed by ♘e4 with an edge) 17 ♘a4 ♔h7 18 ♗d2 ♖g8 19 ♔h2 ♗h8 20 ♖g1 held the rather useful extra pawn and defended the kingside without too much difficulty in E.Miroshnichenko-V.Rogovski, Alushta 2003.

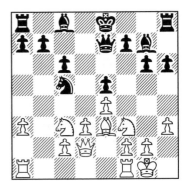

14 ♘e2

Threatening 15 ♕c3, whilst there doesn't seem to be any need to try and prevent ...f5 with 14 ♖fe1 here when 14...♘e6 15 a4 ♔f8! 16 a5 ♔g8 17 ♘a4 ♔h7 18 ♕c3 ♖d8 19 ♖ab1 ♘d4 left Black very solid, while White was unable to get anywhere on the queenside, and P.Svidler-A.Grischuk, Russian Ch., Moscow 2004 was shortly drawn.

14...♘e6 15 ♖ab1!?

Possible partly relying on his 300+ point rating advantage, Adams allows Black the double-edged ...f5 advance, whereas in the later game S.Rublevsky-A.Grischuk, Mainz (rapid) 2004 the players simply repeated with 15 ♕b4 ♕c7 16 a4 ♗f8 17 ♕b2 ♗g7 18

♕b4 ♗f8.

15...f5!?

It's worth noting that Rublevsky didn't copy Adams' approach; quite possibly because this isn't at all bad for Black. However, Philippe could also have opted for 15...♔f8, playing very solidly a la Grischuk and meeting 16 ♕a5, not with 16...♕d6 when 17 ♗xa7! is on, but with 16...♕c7!. Black is still pretty solid after an exchange of queens, but White might well try that exchange and then perhaps aim for ♘e2-c3-a4-c5, as 17 ♗b6 ♕b8 18 ♕b4+ ♔g8 19 ♗e3 ♔h7 doesn't lead anywhere for him.

16 exf5 gxf5 17 ♕b4

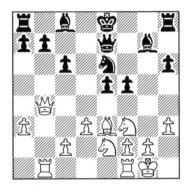

17...♕f6?

Too optimistic as now White has d4-ideas and can quickly build up against e5. Instead the queen exchange would have led to a complex position, but one in which Black should be holding his own, especially with 17...♕xb4 18 axb4 (or 18 ♖xb4 b6! and ...c5 to get the light-square bishop into play) 18...♗d7 19 ♗d2 (trying to attack e5) 19...e4! 20 ♘h4 exd3 21 cxd3 0-0 when Black's weaknesses don't appear to be much worse or easier to exploit than White's.

18 ♖fe1 ♔f7? 19 ♘g3!

Suddenly, but in true Adams style, the white pieces are very well coordinated and the end is already nigh for the hanging black pawns.

19...a5 20 ♕c4

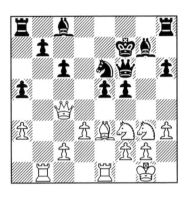

20...e4

Black now sheds a number of pawns before giving up, but his position had already gone by this point as 20...♖d8 21 ♗d2 would have brought the bishop round to c3 to pick off the e5-pawn.

21 dxe4 b5 22 ♕xc6 ♖a6 23 ♕xb5 f4 24 ♘h5 1-0

Game 73
V.Akopian-L.Van Wely
Wijk aan Zee 2004

---

1 e4 c5 2 ♘f3 ♘c6 3 ♗b5 g6 4 ♗xc6 dxc6 5 d3 ♗g7 6 h3 ♘f6 7 ♘c3 ♘d7 8 ♗e3 e5 9 ♕d2 h6 10 0-0 ♕e7 11 ♘h2 ♘f8 12 f4 exf4

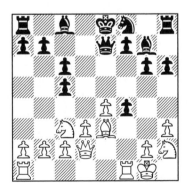

13 ♖xf4

Preparing to double on the f-file against f7, although this does allow Black to gain a tempo with his knight. Thus 13 ♗xf4 is also seen, albeit somewhat less often but it has recently been used by Shirov. After 13...♘e6 14 ♗g3 ♕g5 15 ♕e1 ♘d4? 16 ♕f2! 0-0 17 ♗d6! ♗xh3 18 ♗f4 Black did manage to scramble three pawns for the piece, but he was always worse with the white pieces fairly actively placed in A.Shirov-L.Van Wely, Monaco (blindfold) 2005. 14...♘d4 avoids Shirov's devious tactics and improves, while after 15 ♘d1 Black can then consider 15...♕g5!?, intending 16 ♕f2 ♘e2+!.

13...♘e6

Driving the rook backwards, but rushing the knight to d4 can be considered a little ambitious. Black, however, has an important alternative in 13...♗e6, intending ...♘d7-e5 to fully neutralise any pressure down the f-file, while here White usually still retreats his rook:

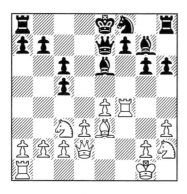

a) 14 ♖ff1 aims to play on the queenside and in the centre, but Black isn't badly compromised here and does enjoy a powerful prelate bearing down the a1–h8 diagonal. After 14...♘d7 15 ♕f2 (or 15 ♘f3 when Black can choose between the solid 15...b6 16 a4 a5, challenging White to find a good plan, and the more ambitious 15...0-0-0 16 ♘e2 f5!?, improving over 16...♘e5 17 ♘xe5 ♗xe5 18 ♖ab1 which gave White reasonable queenside play in D.Adams-A.Muir, British Ch.,

Edinburgh 2003) 15...b6 16 a4 a5! 17 ♘f3 0-0 18 ♕g3 g5! 19 ♖ae1 ♖ae8 20 ♔h1 ♕d8 and Black was fine and very solid in T.Oral-L.McShane, Qaqortoq (rapid) 2003.

b) 14 ♖f2 remains White's main try when 14...♘d7 15 ♘e2 0-0-0 16 ♖af1 sees him encouraging Black to grab a risky queenside pawn or to weaken his kingside with an inopportune advance:

b1) 16...f6 had been considered to be about equal, but then Svidler popped up on the white side and 17 ♕a5!? (this appears promising, while previously 17 ♘f3 b6 18 ♗f4 h5 19 ♗h2 ♗h6 20 ♘f4 ♗f7 21 ♘h4?! ♖dg8 hadn't led anywhere for White, who was soon to be impressively be pushed back on the kingside, in S.Rublevsky-L.McShane, European Ch., Silivri 2003, but Shipov's 18 b4!? would have been somewhat more dangerous, intending 18...cxb4 19 ♘d4) 17...♔b8 18 b4! f5 19 bxc5! fxe4 20 d4 ♗c4 21 ♕a4 ♗xe2 22 ♖xe2 ♕e6 23 c4 saw the b-file and mobile centre give White the advantage in P.Svidler-A.Grischuk, Wijk aan Zee 2005.

b2) 16...♘e5!? is less weakening and deserves serious attention. After 17 ♕a5 b6 18 ♕a6+?! ♔b8 the weakness to the black queenside isn't too severe, while 19 ♘f3 g5!

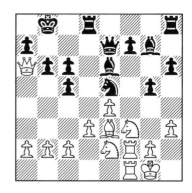

20 ♕a3 ♘xf3+ 21 ♖xf3 f5 gave Black good play in A.Shchekachev-P.Wells, Austrian Team Ch. 2003. White now tried to seize the initiative with 22 exf5 ♗d5! 23 ♖g3!?, but

after 23...♗e5 24 ♗f2 ♗xg3 25 ♘xg3 one way for Black to retain his advantage was 25...♖he8!?, making it as hard as possible for White to improve his minor pieces.

14 ♖f2 ♘d4 15 ♖af1 ♗e6

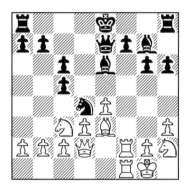

16 b3

Defending the b-pawn so that the c3-knight can be improved, while a critical path is 16 ♘g4 0-0-0! 17 ♘xh6?! (probably too ambitious, although 17 ♘f6 ♗xf6 18 ♖xf6 ♗f5! is a neat trick which fully equalised after 19 ♗xh6 ♕xf6 20 ♗g5 ♕d6 21 exf5 ♘xf5 22 ♗xd8 ♖xd8 in D.Fernandez-A.Lesiege, Philadelphia 2003) 17...f6 18 ♘d1 (or 18 ♘a4 when Black doesn't have to double rooks, but can prefer 18...b5!? 19 ♘c3 ♕f8!? 20 ♘g4 ♗xg4 21 hxg4 ♕g8 with serious threats and 22 g3 ♕h7 23 ♖h2 ♕xh2+ 24 ♕xh2 ♖xh2 25 ♔xh2 ♘xc2 26 ♗xc5 ♖xd3 should be fine for him) 18...♖h7 19 c3 ♘b5 20 ♘g4 ♗xg4 21 hxg4 ♘d6! and Black, who had ideas of ...c4 as well as ...♖dh8, had more than enough

compensation in M.Turov-P.Maletin, Moscow 2005.

16...0-0-0 17 ♘e2 b6!

Preventing 18 ♕a5 and maintaining the d4-knight, thereby making it harder for White to organise his pieces and to build up some pressure.

18 ♘f4 ♖d7 19 ♘xe6 ♕xe6 20 ♘f3!

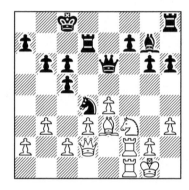

Now White is happy to exchange on d4 when Black would be left with a static structure and would lack counterplay. Van Wely thus wisely opts for the dynamic choice of preparing ...f5.

20...♘b5! 21 ♕e1 ♖e7 22 a4 ♘d6 23 ♗f4 f5 24 ♖e2

White hasn't got anywhere on the queenside, while Black doesn't mind an exchange on d6 as then his bishop can easily contain the white knight. Exchanges are now imminent and peace soon breaks out.

24...fxe4 25 ♗xd6 ♕xd6 26 ♖xe4 ♖he8 ½-½

Summary

This tricky capture leads to positions which, even if equal, are often a little more pleasant for White to play. However, this approach, after peaking in popularity in 2002 and 2003, has now seen 4 0-0 overtake it once again as the more popular choice in grandmaster play. That can be partly attributed to Black's 9...h6 concept which appears to be fully holding its own and which leads to some fairly complex and challenging positions.

White is also struggling for an advantage after 4...dxc6 5 d3 ♗g7 6 h3 ♘f6 7 ♘c3 0-0 8 ♗e3 b6 9 ♕d2 e5 which is a fairly good try for the more dynamic Black player, whilst those happy to play solidly should prefer 7...♘d7 8 ♗e3 e5 9 ♕d2 ♕e7. Elsewhere, 6...b6!? deserves further exploration when an immediate 7 0-0, followed by queenside play, looks like being White's best try. White is though certainly doing well after 4...bxc6, although 5 0-0 ♗g7 6 ♖e1 f6 7 c3 ♘h6 has been neglected a little of late and that isn't so easy for White to handle as we saw Fedorchuk discover.

1 e4 c5 2 ♘f3 ♘c6 3 ♗b5 g6 4 ♗xc6 *(D)*

4...dxc6

       4...bxc6 5 0-0 ♗g7 6 ♖e1

              6...♘f6 – *Game 65*; 6...e5 – *Game 66*; 6...♘h6 – *Game 67*

5 d3 ♗g7 6 h3 ♘f6

       6...b6 *(D)* – *Game 68*

7 ♘c3

       7 0-0 – *Game 69*

7...♘d7

       7...0-0 – *Game 70*

8 ♗e3 e5 9 ♕d2 h6

       9...♕e7 – *Game 71*

10 0-0 ♕e7 *(D)*

       11 a3 – *Game 72*; 11 ♘h2 – *Game 73*

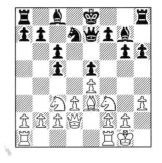

    4 ♗xc6   *6...b6*   *10...♕e7*

CHAPTER TEN

3...g6: The Main Line Rossolimo

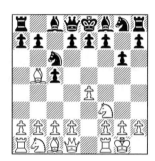

1 e4 c5 2 ♘f3 ♘c6 3 ♗b5 g6 4 0-0

This doesn't have to lead to sharper positions than 4 ♗xc6, but it can lead to fairly complex play and to a more open position. Thus it has appealed to the likes of Sutovsky and Svidler, whereas Adams and Rublevsky have generally preferred the immediate exchange on c6. However, 4 0-0 isn't White's only alternative to the exchange and we will deal with 4 c3 in the notes to Game 79.

White can also try 4 ♘c3 when 4...♗g7 5 0-0 reaches a position that also arises via 4 0-0 ♗g7 5 ♘c3. Here 5...♘d4 is possible, but White is ready for it and gains reasonable chances for an edge with 6 ♘xd4 cxd4 7 ♘e2 a6 8 ♗a4, while 5...d6!? 6 e5!? reveals one idea behind White's ♘c3 concept, but the unbalanced position arising after 6...dxe5 7 ♗xc6+ bxc6 8 ♖e1 f6 doesn't appear to be bad for Black and 9 b3 ♘h6 10 ♗a3 ♘f7 11 ♗xc5 f5 12 d4 e4 13 ♘d2 ♘g5! 14 ♕e2 ♘e6 gave him good play in A.Ansell-A.Greet, British Ch., Edinburgh 2003.

Black usually prefers the solid 4 0-0 ♗g7 5 ♘c3 e5, intending to develop harmoniously with ...♘ge7 and ...0-0 and so here 6 d3 is a little slow. However, Black shouldn't feel that 5...e5 instantly solves his problems as Carsten Hansen observed in *New in Chess Yearbook*.

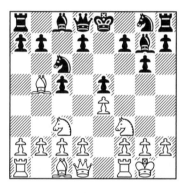

Black must be aware that 6 ♗xc6 dxc6 gives him a slightly inferior version of Game 69 as he can't race his knight straight to d7. However, with White committed to ♘c3, 6...bxc6! becomes a promising recapture when 7 a3 a5 8 b3 ♘e7 9 d3 d6 10 ♗b2 0-0 11 ♘d2 f5 12 exf5 ♘xf5 saw Black's centre give him quite a reasonable position in E.Shaposhnikov-S.Ionov, St Petersburg 2004. White has thus instead tried 6 ♗c4, when 6...♘f6!? 7 d3 0-0 8 a3 d6 9 ♖b1 a6 10 b4 b5 11 ♗a2 cxb4 12 axb4 ♗g4 was a sensible response and was fine for Black in M.Al Modiahki-A.Motylev, Bermuda 2003, and 6 a3!? ♘ge7 7 b4, but this shouldn't be enough for an edge without there being any doubled black c-pawns and after 7...d6 Black has a reasonable set-up and maintains his central bind on the d4-square.

4...♗g7

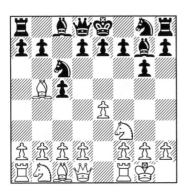

5 c3

White has an important alternative here in 5 ♖e1 when we'll examine 5...e5 in Games 74 and 75, but Black's main response is 5...♘f6 after which White usually transposes back to c3 lines with 6 c3 or with 6 e5 ♘d5 7 c3. However, he can also opt for 6 e5 ♘d5 7 ♘c3 or for 6 ♘c3 and we'll examine those approaches in Game 76.

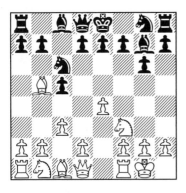

5...♘f6

5 ♖e1 e5 might be playable, but 5 c3 e5 is a rather risky choice for Black, and White has then scored well with three different approaches. Surprisingly 6 b4!? cxb4 7 d4 remains rather rare but it certainly deserves consideration, while White often opts for simply

6 d3 ♘ge7 7 ♗e3. However, Black shouldn't fear that so long as he selects 7...d6 8 d4 exd4! 9 cxd4 ♗g4!? or 9...0-0 10 ♘c3 ♕b6!. Probably best, as well as the most popular, option for White is 6 d4!?, quickly opening the centre and beginning an assault on the dark squares.

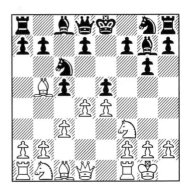

Now 6...cxd4 7 cxd4 ♘xd4 8 ♘xd4 exd4 is very promising for White after either 9 ♘a3!? a6 10 ♗f4! or the more established 9 f4 ♘e7 10 f5! and thus Black usually opts for 7...exd4 when 8 ♗f4 (the rare 8 ♗g5!? might be even better when White has excellent compensation after 8...♘ge7 9 e5! 0-0 10 ♖e1 as he also had with 8...♕b6 9 ♘a3 ♘ge7 10 ♘c4! ♕c7 11 e5! in J.Perez-J.Garcia Baez, Cuba 2003) 8...♘ge7 9 ♗d6! transposes to a position we considered in Game 40 in Chapter Six. There White gained promising compensation and so Black might prefer 8...a6!? when 9 ♗c4 d6 10 ♕b3 ♘a5! may favour White, but it is quite complicated. However, there are some good alternatives, such as 9 ♗a4!? b5 10 ♗b3 d6 11 a4! with the initiative when 11...b4 12 ♘bd2 ♘a5?! 13 ♗d5 ♖a7 14 ♘b3 ♘e7 15 ♘xa5 ♕xa5 16 ♘xd4 regained the pawn with a large advantage in A.Ardeleanu-A.Arandjelovic, Bucharest 2001.

6 ♖e1

Defending the e-pawn like this is White's main choice, but he has a number of alternatives. 6 ♕e2 was popular in the sixties and has recently been used by Peter Svidler as we'll see in Game 77, where we also discuss the sharp but slightly dubious gambit 6 d4. Another way to defend the e-pawn is the subject of Game 78; the enterprising 6 ♕a4!? with which Ramil Hasangatin and Leonid Totsky have enjoyed some success. The most obvious move for White is though probably 6 e5 when 6...♘d5 7 d4 cxd4 8 cxd4 0-0 9 ♘c3 reaches a sharp position. However, this advance isn't especially fashionable, although Sutovsky has made good use of it as we'll see in Game 79.

6...0-0

The contours of play are already becoming clear with Black being happy, in true hypermodern style, to allow White an advanced pawn centre which he will hope to undermine. We discuss 7 e5 in Game 80, but such a handling of the position isn't especially popular. Instead 7 d4 also hasn't enjoyed a promising reputation for some time, as Black can advance with ...d5, and so it was surprising to see Kasparov pop up on the white side as he did in Game 81. The fashionable choice remains the useful waiting move, 7 h3!?; a fairly crafty idea with which we'll complete our coverage in Game 82 of the often subtle Rossolimo.

Game 74
J.Benjamin-K.Dolgitser
New York Ch., Kerhonkson 2002

1 e4 c5 2 ♘f3 ♘c6 3 ♗b5 g6 4 0-0 ♗g7

5 ♖e1 e5

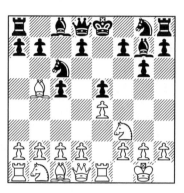

6 b4!?

A dangerous gambit with which White hopes to justify ♖e1 and to gain a strong central initiative. This idea hasn't ever fully caught on though, unlike the 6 ♗xc6 of our next game, but it certainly deserves further analysis and serious consideration. Another tricky idea for Black to face is 6 c3 ♘ge7 7 d4, although this is a poor relation of 5 c3 e5 6 d4 where White usually manages without ♖e1. Here 7...cxd4 8 cxd4 exd4 9 ♗f4 prepares ♗d6 and gives White some compensation, but 9...a6 10 ♗a4 b5! 11 ♗b3 d6 leaves him struggling for enough, whereas 9...0-0 10 ♗d6 b6 11 ♘bd2 ♗b7 12 ♘b3 ♖e8 13 ♗c4! forced 13...♘c8 and was quite unclear in M.Novikov-V.Vasiliev, Tula 2001.

6...♘xb4

Maintaining his bind on d4 for the time being at least, but now White does get to drum up a fair initiative. The alternative is 6...cxb4 7 a3 and then:

a) 7...♘ge7 8 axb4 ♘xb4?! 9 ♗a3 ♘bc6 10 ♗d6! is awkward for Black, while 8...0-0 was recommended by Rogozenko, but White may well be a little better here. After 9 ♗b2 (or 9 ♗xc6!? bxc6 10 ♗b2 d6 11 d4 f6 12 ♘bd2 ♗e6 13 c4 with a rather useful advancing pawn wall in D.Stellwagen-M.Carlsen, Wijk aan Zee 2005, although Black then gained some essential counterplay with 13...g5 14

♕c2 ♘g6 15 ♘f1 g4! 16 ♘3d2 f5) 9...d6 10 ♗xc6 ♘xc6 11 b5, Black should consider the 11...♘a5!? 12 d3 a6 13 ♘c3 ♗d7 of S.Brynell-Y.Yakovich, Stockholm 1999. That was fairly unclear and saw Black successfully battling on the queenside, whereas 11...♘d4?! 12 ♘xd4! exd4 13 ♖a4! ♕b6 14 ♘a3 ♗d7 15 ♕a1 favoured White in A.Ashton-M.Devereaux, British Ch., Torquay 2002.

b) 7...b3!? is a sensible choice, on both practical and theoretical grounds, and has been the focus of some recent attention. Then 8 cxb3 ♘ge7 9 ♗b2 0-0 is relatively critical and there doesn't seem to be any way to an advantage for White. Black is fine after 10 d4 exd4 11 ♘xd4 ♕b6!, while 10 b4 d5 11 exd5 ♕xd5 12 ♘c3 ♕d6 is also acceptable enough for him, although White should prefer that to the 11 ♗xc6?! ♘xc6 12 b5?! dxe4! 13 bxc6 exf3 14 ♕xf3 bxc6 15 ♕xc6 ♖b8, with the bishop-pair and superior structure for Black, of A.Helstroffer-E.Prie, Montpellier 2004.

7 ♗b2

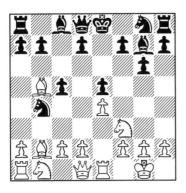

7...a6

Putting the question to the bishop, but now White can open further lines on the queenside. Instead returning the pawn with 7...♘c6!? appears sensible and is probably the best option. This deserves further attention and 8 ♗xc6 dxc6 9 ♘xe5 ♕c7 10 ♘c4 ♗xb2 11 ♘xb2 ♗e6 was quite acceptable for Black in Qin Kanying-E.Pigusov, Shanghai 2000

with the white knight not being too happy on b2, whilst it was also hard for White to utilise her central advantage. Instead preparing ...♘c6 with 7...♕c7 is rather risky for Black and 8 c3! ♘c6 9 d4! exd4 10 cxd4 ♘ge7 11 ♘c3 cxd4 12 ♘d5 ♕d8 13 ♗a3 0-0 14 ♗d6 gave White a great position in I.Foygel-B.Kreiman, US Ch., Seattle 2003.

8 a3 axb5 9 axb4 ♖xa1 10 ♗xa1 c4?!

This fails to convince as now White gets to favourably capture on b5 or e5, while Black lags in development. More testing is 10...cxb4 11 ♗xe5 ♗xe5 12 ♘xe5 ♘e7 when Pedersen points out that 13 d4 d5! is roughly equal. However, White shouldn't rush as Black's weaknesses along the b-file will remain for some time and 13 d3 0-0 14 ♘d2 d6 15 ♘ef3 ♗e6 16 ♕a1! ♘c6 17 ♕b2 ♕b6 18 ♘b3 ♖a8 19 h4! was pretty pleasant for White, due to his prospects right across the board, in M.Okkes-L.Van Wely, Dutch Team Ch. 2003.

11 ♘a3 d6

11...♕b6 12 ♘xe5 ♘f6 13 d3 d6 14 ♘f3 ♗e6 15 ♘d4 is also pretty good for White, but the opening of the centre isn't good news for the black monarch.

12 d4! f6?! 13 dxe5 dxe5 14 ♘xb5

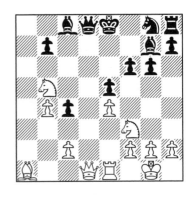

Simply threatening to remove another pawn with 15 ♘d6+ and Black is powerless to prevent that. Dolgitser tries to, but just lands up allowing an even worse blow.

14...♕xd1 15 ♖xd1 ♗f8? 16 ♘xe5! ♗e6

17 ♘c7+ ♔e7 18 ♘xe6 ♔xe6 19 ♘xc4

That's two extra pawns, while Black is still to get his kingside out and already the game has been a clear success for 6 b4!?.

19...♘h6 20 ♖d8 ♘f7 21 ♖e8+ ♔d7 22 ♖a8 ♗xb4 23 ♖xh8 ♘xh8 24 ♗xf6 ♘f7 25 ♔f1 ♔e6 26 ♗d4 ♘d8 27 ♔e2 ♘c6 28 ♗e3 1-0

Game 75
P.Svidler- P.Leko
Wijk aan Zee 2004

---

1 e4 c5 2 ♘f3 ♘c6 3 ♗b5 g6 4 0-0 ♗g7 5 ♖e1 e5 6 ♗xc6 dxc6!

The main recapture here and also the best one, whereas 6...bxc6?! was seen in Game 66. After that White can put the e1–rook to good use by expanding with c3 and d4, but doing so after 6...dxc6 isn't usually possible. White must thus play instead on the queenside, but the consensus appears to be that this is less challenging than the more flexible 4 ♗xc6.

7 d3

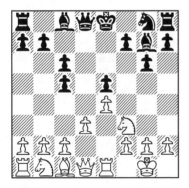

7...♕e7

Covering c5 and e5 and thereby again facilitating ...♘f6, although this isn't the only way to handle the position:

a) 7...♘e7!? remains a reasonable alternative, even though it's not so easy to play an ambitious ...f5 with the rook on e1. As Black's counterplay isn't always thus as fast as in the 4

♗xc6 dxc6 5 d3 ♗g7 6 h3 b6 and ...♘e7 variation, he should meet 8 a3 with 8...a5 to prevent b4, while 8 ♗e3 b6 9 a4 a5 10 h3 0-0 11 ♘a3 ♕c7 12 ♕c1 ♗a6! (forcing ♘c4 to be prefaced by b3; thus c3 and b4 looses some of its strength with d3 weakened, as does f4 with White then vulnerable down the long diagonal after ...exf4) 13 b3 ♖fe8 14 ♘c4 ♖ad8 15 ♗h6 f6 16 ♗e3 ♘c8! 17 ♘h2 ♘d6 was quite comfortable for Black and didn't see White getting anywhere in I.Sofronie-A.Motylev, Sovata 2001.

(b) 7....♗g4 is though a move White is fairly happy to see and 8 ♘bd2 ♘f6 9 ♘c4 ♗xf3 10 ♕xf3 ♕e7 11 ♗d2 0-0 12 a3! ♕e6 13 b4 cxb4 14 axb4 ♘d7 might have left Black quite solid in M.Adams-R.Kasimdzhanov, Bundesliga 2002, but 15 ♕e3 a6 16 ♖a5 still left White with a pleasant edge and control over the position.

(c) The ...♘h6 plan isn't especially recommended here with a rook on e1 and 7...f6 8 c3! ♘h6 9 h3 ♘f7 10 ♗e3 b6 11 d4 cxd4 12 cxd4 0-0 13 ♘c3 exd4 14 ♘xd4 gave White the edge in J.Plaskett-R.Burnett, Hampstead 1998.

8 ♘bd2

Bringing the knight to c4 to place some pressure on e5 and the black queenside, but White can also opt for 8 a3, aiming to open the queenside:

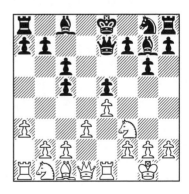

a) If 8...♘f6 then 9 b4! gives White a useful

initiative, while the white dark-square bishop can enter the game with effect, such as with 9...♘d7 10 bxc5 ♘xc5 11 a4! 0-0 12 ♗a3 (J.Watson). Instead 9...♗g4 10 ♘bd2 0-0 11 h3 ♗xf3 12 ♘xf3 ♖fd8 13 ♗d2 ♘h5 14 ♕b1 ♘f4?! 15 bxc5 ♕xc5 16 d4! saw White take over the centre in N.Sedlak-D.Velimirovic, Subotica 2002.

b) 8...a5!, keeping the queenside closed, is much better when after 9 a4 ♘f6 10 ♘a3 0-0 11 ♘c4, Black can settle for just the solid 11...♘d7, intending ...b6, ...♖d8, ...♗b8 and ...♘f8 (Rogozenko), as it's hard for White to do much on the queenside, while the active 11...♘h5!? 12 ♗d2 ♕c7 13 ♗e3 b6 14 b4! b5! 15 axb5 cxb5 16 ♖xa5 ♖xa5 17 ♘xa5 cxb4 18 ♘b3 ♗g4 gave Black good counterplay in D.Svetushkin-M.Sorokin, Linares 1999.

Instead White would of course like to play an immediate 8 b4!?, but here Black has done quite well with 8...cxb4 9 a3 b3, which is the sensible approach, keeping the queenside relatively closed, and even with 9...bxa3!? 10 ♗xa3 ♕c7, intending 11 ♘bd2 ♘e7 12 ♘c4 c5!.

8...♘f6

With the white knight on d2, 8...♘h6 becomes a viable option, but this is simple and effective when it's tough for White to make progress.

9 ♘c4 ♘d7 10 a3

White can also play more flexibly with 10 ♗d2!? when Black often castles, but that leaves him less flexibly placed to respond after 11 a3. However, the accurate 10...b6! 11 a4 0-0 12 ♕c1 ♖e8 13 ♖b1 ♘f8 14 ♗c3 f6 15 b4 ♗e6 16 ♘e3 ♗f7 17 bxc5 bxc5 18 ♗b2 ♘e6 was fine for Black in M.Adams-P.Leko, Bled Olympiad 2002; the doubled c-pawns were then actually quite useful, covering d4 and d5, while the white knights lacked any good outposts to advance to.

10...b6 11 ♗d2 ♗a6

11...a5 was also an option, but Leko doesn't fear b4 when he has the option to exchange on c4. Svidler delays that break and, although the players stop a little prematurely, it's very hard for White to really achieve anything, especially with ...f6, ...♖fd8 and ...♘f8-e6 set to give Black easy play.

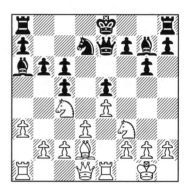

12 ♗c3 ♗xc4 13 dxc4 0-0 14 ♕e2 ½-½

Game 76
Xu Yuhua-T.Stepovaia Dianchenko
China-Russia Summit, Shanghai 2001

1 e4 c5 2 ♘f3 ♘c6 3 ♗b5 g6 4 0-0 ♗g7 5 ♖e1 ♘f6

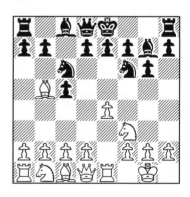

6 e5

White's main alternative to 6 c3 whereas 6 ♘c3 transposes back after 6...0-0 7 e5 ♘e8 8 ♗xc6 (8 d3 ♘c7 9 a4 b6! holds White up on the queenside and 10 ♗xc6 dxc6 11 a5 ♗g4 12 h3 ♗xf3 13 ♕xf3 ♘e6 14 ♗e3 ♕c7 was pretty equal when J.Timman-A.Khalifman, Hoogeveen 2000 was agreed drawn here) 8...dxc6 9 d3 ♘c7 10 ♘e4 ♘e6 to our main game here.

A much more aggressive option is the rare 6 d4; a favourite of Artur Kogan's. Then 6...cxd4 7 e5 ♘d5 8 ♗xc6 dxc6 9 ♕xd4 is similar to White's play in the note to White's 8th move in Game 65 except that Black is much better off here with his knight still on d5. Furthermore, although ♕h4 will put some pressure on the kingside, e7 is now fairly easy to cover. Black should though avoid 9...♗f5 10 ♘a3 0-0?! 11 ♕h4!, but 10...♕b6! 11 ♕h4 ♕b4 12 c4 ♘b6 gave him good counterplay in J.Becerra Rivero-D.Mieles Palau, Guayaquil 2001 when after 13 b3, Becerra Rivero recommends 13...0-0-0!, intending 14 ♘b1 ♗xe5!.

6...♘d5 7 ♘c3

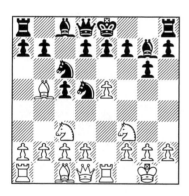

7...♘c7

Retreating is definitely best; 7...♘xc3?! 8 dxc3 sees the pressure down the d-file outweigh the doubled pawns and 8...0-0 9 ♕d5! b6 10 ♗g5 ♕c7 11 ♖ad1 a6 12 ♗c4 ♖a7 13 ♕e4 b5 14 ♗d5 ♗b7 15 ♕h4 gave White a strong attacking platform in M.Pavlovic-A.Liebergesell, Biel 2002. Meanwhile it's worth knowing that the position after the knight retreat also occurs via 3...♘f6 4 e5 ♘d5 5 0-0 g6 6 ♖e1 ♗g7 7 ♘c3 ♘c7.

8 ♗xc6 dxc6

Once again Black must be careful and 8...bxc6 9 d4! cxd4 10 ♕xd4 is an improved version of 6 d4 for White; 10...♘e6 11 ♕h4 gives White some pressure, while 10...d6? 11 ♕c4! was already superb for him in V.Iordachescu-R.Hoffman, Vlissingen 2004.

9 ♘e4

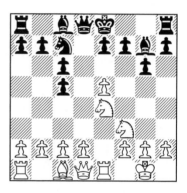

9...♘e6

Defending c5 and against 10 ♘f6+, but 9...b6 is a very reasonable alternative. As in our main line the position is roughly level, but both sides have chances to outmanoeuvre the other, while recent practice has confirmed that 10 ♘f6+ ♔f8 11 ♘e4 ♗g4 12 d3 ♘e6! is fine for Black. Thus 10 d3 0-0 11 h3 has started to gain attention and White isn't so unhappy to see Black castle as he then has some chances to launch a kingside attack. However, Black is very solid here and 11...♘e6 12 ♗e3 ♘d4! 13 ♘xd4 cxd4 14 ♗f4 a5 15 a4 ♕d5 16 ♘d2 c5 was evenly balanced in V.Anand-T.Radjabov, Benidorm (rapid) 2003. White has been known to surprisingly often prefer 9 h3 on his last turn, but there's no need for that as here 9 ♘e4 ♗g4 10 ♘xc5! ♕d5 11 d4 doesn't give Black enough compensation. Atalik has now supplied a lot of analysis to show that 11...♗xf3?! 12 ♕xf3 ♕xd4 13 ♘xb7 ♕d6+ 14 ♘d6+! is too dangerous for Black, while in R.Janssen-S.Atalik, Wijk aan Zee 1997 White switched to a kingside attack with 11...0-0 12 c3 ♘e6 13 ♘e4

♖fd8 14 h3 ♗f5 15 ♘g3 c5 16 ♘h4!.

10 d3 0-0 11 ♗e3 b6 12 ♕d2 f5!

Claiming some useful space whereas we saw in the Introduction that 12...♘d4?! 13 ♘xd4 cxd4 14 ♗h6 is rather pleasant for White.

13 exf6 exf6 14 ♗h6 a5!

Taking further space and thus enabling a3 to be meet by ...a4, while this also prepares to develop the rook along the second. It is though quite easy for both sides to drift in this variation and 14...♕d7?! 15 ♗xg7 ♔xg7 16 a3! ♘d4 17 ♘xd4 cxd4 18 b4 ♗b7 19 ♕f4 ♖ad8 20 h4! favoured White in E.Rozentalis-M.Carlsen, Copenhagen 2004.

15 ♘g3?!

Now Black can recapture on g7 with the rook and White is left struggling a little for a plan. However, 15 ♗xg7 ♔xg7 is fine for Black although the strong e4-steed remains, while 16 ♖e2 ♖a7 17 ♖ae1 ♖af7 18 ♘c3 ♘c7! 19 ♕f4 ♘d5 20 ♘xd5 cxd5 21 h4 h6! prevented White from getting anywhere on the kingside in F.Eid-R.Kasimdzhanov, Bled Olympiad 2002.

15...♖a7!

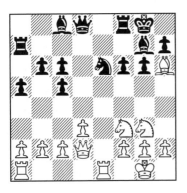

16 ♗xg7 ♖xg7 17 ♖e4?!

The knight is doing little on g3 and so Xu Yuhua should probably have accepted her earlier error by simply returning it here to e4 when White remains very solid and can meet ...f5 with ♘g5. Encouraging Black forwards

on the kingside is rather misguided, while White soon compounds her error by getting her rook stuck on e5.

17...f5! 18 ♖e5 f4 19 ♘e4?! g5! 20 ♕c3 g4 21 ♘fd2 ♘d4 22 ♔h1 ♕h4 23 ♘f1 ♖g6!

White simply hasn't got out of the blocks and already the end is nigh.

24 g3 fxg3 25 ♘fxg3 ♖h6 26 ♖g5+ ♔h8 0-1

Game 77

P.Svidler-A.Shirov

Leon Rapidplay Knockout 2004

---

1 e4 c5 2 ♘f3 ♘c6 3 ♗b5 g6 4 0-0

White often prefers to reach our main game via 4 c3 ♘f6 5 ♕e2 ♗g7 6 0-0 0-0, but with that move order he should avoid the overly greedy 6 e5 ♘d5 7 ♕c4? when 7...♘c7 8 ♗xc6 dxc6 9 ♕xc5 ♕d3! 10 ♕e3 ♗f5 11 ♕xd3 ♗xd3 12 ♔d1 ♘e6 13 ♘e1 ♘f4 was already very good for Black in R.Fischer-M.Matulovic, Palma de Mallorca Interzonal 1970.

4...♗g7 5 c3 ♘f6

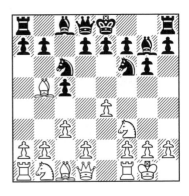

6 ♕e2

Defending e4, while a more aggressive course is 6 d4!?, although this gambit has been out of favour for some time. However, Svidler and Volokitin both used it in 2004, but unfortunately for us their opponents responded feebly. If the gambit is to be rejuvenated then White must find something against 6...cxd4 7 cxd4 (although 7 e5 does transpose to Game 79) 7...♘xe4 8 d5 ♘d6!. After 9 ♗d3 ♘b4 10 ♘c3 0-0 his d-pawn cramps the black position, but Black can unravel without too much difficulty with ...b6. Instead Morozevich and Motylev have both tried, albeit on just the one occasion each, 9 ♘a3!? a6 10 ♕a4, but 10...♘e5! 11 ♘xe5 ♗xe5 12 ♖e1 ♗f6 13 ♗h6 (and not 13 ♗f4 0-0 14 ♗e5?? ♗xe5! 15 ♖xe5 ♘xb5 16 ♘xb5 d6 17 ♖e3 ♗d7 which cost a piece in O.Nikolenko-O.Gladyszev, Tula 2003) 13...♘f5 14 ♕f4!, despite preventing castling and being quite complex, wasn't especially convincing in A.Motylev-O.Lemmers, Rotterdam 1998 and after 14...axb5 15 ♘xb5 Black should have opted for 15...♘xh6!? 16 ♘c7+ ♕xc7 17 ♕xc7 0-0 or for 15...d6 16 ♖ac1 ♗e5! (Motylev) with a clear advantage in both cases.

6...0-0 7 d4

This isn't forced, but 7 e5 ♘d5 8 ♕c4?! is again too greedy after 8...♘c7, while White often prepares d4 with 7 ♖d1 when Black must decide how to respond:

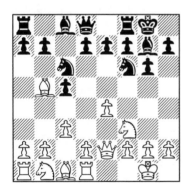

a) 7...a6 isn't quite active enough and 8 ♗xc6 dxc6 9 h3 ♕c7 10 d4 cxd4 11 cxd4 c5 12 d5 ♘d7 13 a4! b6 14 ♘a3 ♗b7 15 ♗g5 saw White's centre give him the edge in I.Smirin-D.Rogozenko, Istanbul Olympiad 2000.

b) Rogozenko later endorsed 7...e5!? and this remains a good alternative for Black due to the tactical points 8 d4 cxd4 9 cxd4 exd4 10 ♘xd4 ♘xd4 11 ♖xd4 ♕b6! and 8 ♗xc6?! dxc6 9 ♘xe5? ♖e8 10 d4 cxd4 11 cxd4 ♘xe4! when Black was already much better in A.Dueckstein-P.Wells, Vienna 1998.

c) 7...d5 is the logical counter, although after 8 e5 ♘e8 9 ♗xc6 bxc6 10 h3 Black must be careful as his compromised structure could make it difficult to obtain counterplay. Thus he should opt for 10...c4! when 11 d3 cxd3 12 ♕xd3 ♕b6 13 ♗e3!? was an enterprising gambit in E.Djingarova-J.Campos Moreno, Andorra 2004. After 13...♕xb2 14 ♘bd2 ♘c7 15 ♗c5! ♗f5 16 ♕e3 White gained good play, but 14...♗f5! improves, although White still retains some compensation due to the weaknesses of c6 and e7.

7...d5

Not the only move order and if White can force an early exchange on d4 in any case, so that he can develop with ♘c3, then Black could just begin 7...cxd4 8 cxd4 d5 9 e5 ♘e4 when 10 ♗e3 transposes to our main game. However, White shouldn't there be too ambitious with his queen's knight as 10 ♘c3 ♗g4 11 ♘xe4? ♘xd4! 12 ♕e3 ♘xb5 13 ♘c5 ♗xf3 14 gxf3 ♕b6! was awful for him G.Klompus-A.W.Martin, correspondence 1990.

8 e5 ♘e4 9 ♗e3 cxd4

It's not so easy for Black to maintain the tension as 9...♗d7 10 ♗xc6! bxc6 11 dxc5! ♕b8 12 ♖e1 ♗xe5? 13 ♘xe5 ♕xe5 14 ♗d4 leaves him vulnerable on the dark squares and especially down the e-file. Instead P.Svidler-V.Ivanchuk, Monaco (blindfold) 2004 saw 12...♖e8 13 ♗d4 ♗g4 14 ♘bd2! ♕xb2 15 ♘xe4 ♕xe2 16 ♖xe2 dxe4 17 ♖xe4 ♗e6 when Black had some compensation, but Svidler demonstrated that his central bind and the not terribly active g7-bishop gave White the advantage.

10 cxd4 ♗d7 11 ♘c3

Trying to improve on his earlier 11 ♗d3 when 11...♖c8 12 ♘bd2 ♘xd2 13 ♕xd2 ♕a5 14 a3 ♕xd2 15 ♘xd2 f6! didn't give White anything in P.Svidler-P.Leko, Monaco (rapid) 2004.

11...♘xc3 12 bxc3 ♘a5!

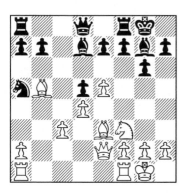

Eyeing up the weakened c4-square and also preparing to target c3. This already seems quite comfortable for Black as White is a long way from breaking with e6 or doing anything on the kingside, and Svidler hasn't repeated this line since.

13 ♗d3 ♖c8 14 ♖ac1 ♘c4 15 ♗f4 ♖c6 16 ♖b1 ♕c8 17 ♗g5?!

White hasn't got anywhere, but provoking ...f6 just helps Black by activating his kingside pieces. Thus White should have objectively grovelled for a draw with 17 ♖fc1 ♗f5 18 ♘d2 (Avrukh).

17...f6 18 ♗c1?!

18 exf6 exf6 19 ♗c1 ♖e8 would have favoured Black, but Svidler's slightly desperate pawn sacrifice shouldn't have sufficed.

18...fxe5 19 ♘xe5 ♘xe5 20 dxe5 ♖xc3 21 ♗g5 ♗f5 22 ♗xf5 ♖xf5 23 f4 e6?

Shirov has forced the exchange of his bad bishop and is just a clear pawn up, but this lets White back into the game whereas he surely would have found 23...♗xe5! with more time when 24 fxe5 ♖xg5 25 ♕f2 ♕c5! should be sufficient.

24 ♗f6! ♗xf6 25 g4 ♖c2 26 ♕f3 ♖c3

Shocked by the turnaround Shirov forces the draw, although he would still have been somewhat better after Avrukh's 26...♗xe5 27 gxf5 ♗d4+ 28 ♔h1 gxf5.

27 ♕e2 ♖c2 28 ♕f3 ♖c3 29 ♕e2 ½-½

Game 78
R.Hasangatin-P.Smirnov
Russian Team Ch. 2004

---

1 e4 c5 2 ♘f3 ♘c6 3 ♗b5 g6 4 0-0 ♗g7 5 c3 ♘f6 6 ♕a4!?

An intriguing idea after which Black must be careful about advancing his d-pawn as White might well grab on c6. Furthermore, ...a6 isn't now going to be too effective, while the queen's location especially enables White to play a d4-gambit.

6...♕b6

The black queen covers d4 from here, while she also ensures that ...a6 will put the question to the b5-bishop, but 6...0-0 is Black's main choice and after 7 d4! cxd4 8 cxd4 he must decide how to respond to White's concept:

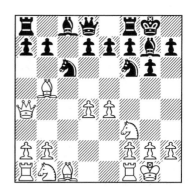

a) 8...d6!? is one critical test of the white set-up as Anand has demonstrated and 9 ♘c3 (White can take up the challenge as Svidler and Movsesian have done, although 9 ♗xc6 bxc6 10 ♕xc6 ♗g4 certainly supplies compensation; the key question is whether it's fully enough and White needs to do better than the 11 ♘bd2 ♖c8! 12 ♕a4 ♕b6 13 ♖e1 ♕b7 14 ♕b3 ♕xb3 15 ♘xb3 ♖c2 of E.Alekseev-A.Ramirez, Santo Domingo 2003 when Black certainly had sufficient activity for the pawn; 9...♗d7 10 d5 ♘b8 11 ♗e3 a6 12 ♗xd7 ♘bxd7 13 ♕b3 ♕a5! 14 ♗d4 b5 began counterplay in A.Morozevich-V.Anand, Frankfurt (rapid) 2000. However, White later improved with 11 e5! when 11...dxe5 12 ♘xe5 ♗xb5 13 ♕xb5 ♕c7 14 ♖e1 ♘e8 15 ♗f4 ♘d6 16 ♕e2 gave him a good position in R.Hasangatin-B.Furman, Marianske Lazne 2005.

b) 8...d5 9 e5 ♘d7 10 ♗xc6 ♘b6 11 ♕a5 bxc6 12 b3 is also strategically unbalanced, but White's structural advantage appears to slightly outweigh the bishop-pair, and after 12...♗g4 13 ♘bd2 ♘d7, as well as Wells' 14 ♕xd8 ♖xd8 15 ♗a3, White can gain a small advantage with 14 ♕c3 ♖c8 15 ♗a3. Now 15...f6 is well met by 16 e6!, but 15...c5!? didn't fully convince after simply 16 ♗xc5 ♘xc5 17 dxc5 in L.Totsky-D.Lopushnoy, St Petersburg 1997.

c) 8...a6 can be met by 9 d5, but simple and effective is 9 ♘c3 ♘a5 10 ♗d3 b5 11 ♕d1 ♗b7 12 a3 ♖c8 13 ♖e1 ♘c4 14 ♕e2 ♕c7 15 ♗g5! when the c4-knight didn't supply enough counterplay in A.Kovalev-J.Isaev, Calvia Olympiad 2004.

d) 8...♘xe4!?

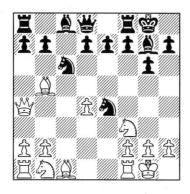

is the acid test of 6 ♕a4 when 9 d5 ♘c5 10

♕a3 ♕b6 saves the piece and a key position occurs after 11 ♘c3 ♘d4 12 ♘xd4 ♗xd4 13 ♗h6 when White's better development clearly grants him reasonable compensation. Due to Kovalev's 13...♗g7 14 ♗xg7 ♔xg7 15 b4! I would have said pretty good compensation, but then Kotronias came up with 13...d6!. Now the black light-square bishop easily gets out, while the other black bishop becomes rather strong and 14 ♗xf8 ♔xf8 15 ♖ad1 ♗e5 16 ♗e2 ♗f5 17 g3 a5! left Black now with the promising compensation in G.Hernandez-V.Kotronias, Calvia Olympiad 2004.

7 ♖e1 0-0

Black can also follow his last move up with 7...a6, but 8 ♗f1 e5 9 d4! was another promising d-pawn sacrifice in R.Tischbierek-H.Ellers, Bundesliga 2005 and White stood well after 9...cxd4 10 cxd4 exd4 11 ♗f4 0-0 12 ♗d6 ♖e8 13 ♘bd2 ♕d8 14 ♗c4.

8 d4 cxd4

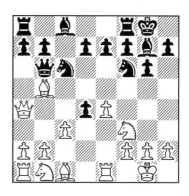

9 e5

Now we reach a version of the 6 ♖e1 0-0 7 e5 variation, but with the white queen a little offside on a4. Thus White should prefer 9 cxd4 as Hasangatin later did and 9...d5 10 e5 ♘e4 11 ♗xc6 bxc6 12 ♘bd2 ♘xd2 (or 12...♗f5 13 ♘b3 c5 14 dxc5 ♘xc5 15 ♘xc5 ♕xc5 16 b3 with an edge) 13 ♘xd2! c5 14 dxc5 ♕xc5 15 ♕h4 ♗f5 16 ♘b3 ♕c7 17 ♗h6 slightly favoured White due to his superior minor piece in R.Hasangatin-D.Sharma, Alushta 2005.

9...♘d5 10 cxd4 d6 11 ♘c3 ♝e6 12 ♝d2?!

Black already enjoys a fairly harmonious position, but this is simply too submissive and White had to play more actively, such as with 12 ♝g5.

12...♜ac8 13 ♜ac1 a6!

Exploiting his pressure down the b-file to net the bishop-pair and Smirnov is quick to put his extra light-square bishop to good use.

14 ♝xc6 ♜xc6 15 ♕a3 ♘xc3 16 bxc3 ♜fc8 17 exd6 exd6 18 ♘g5 ♝c4 19 h4?!

A little late in the day White goes on the offensive, but this actually only serves to weaken his own kingside and Hasangatin is soon finished off by a neat rook lift.

19...h6 20 ♘e4 d5! 21 ♘c5 ♕d8 22 ♘xb7?! ♕xh4 23 g3 ♕h3 24 ♘a5 ♜f6! 25 ♘xc4 ♜f5! 0-1

Game 79
E.Sutovsky-V.Filippov
Aeroflot Open, Moscow 2005

---

1 e4 c5 2 ♘f3 ♘c6 3 ♝b5 g6 4 c3

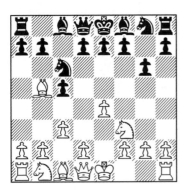

4...♘f6

Black's main response, but 4...♝g7 is also possible. This was considered dubious due to an immediate 5 d4 when Black is advised to steer clear of the likes of Bronstein's 5...♕b6

6 a4 cxd4 7 0-0! and especially 5...cxd4 6 cxd4 ♕b6 7 ♘c3! ♘xd4 8 ♘d5 ♘xf3+ 9 ♕xf3 ♕d8 10 ♝f4 e5 11 ♕c3! (Motwani). However, Pedersen drew attention to Black's best option of 5...♕a5! and this has subsequently received a few more tests, although it remains surprising that this aggressive queen move isn't a lot more popular. If now 6 ♕b3 then Black can force a useful exchange with 6...♘xd4! 7 ♘xd4 cxd4, while 6 ♕e2 ♘xd4 7 ♘xd4 cxd4 8 0-0 a6 9 ♝c4 d3! 10 ♝xd3 d6 11 c4 ♘f6 12 ♘c3 0-0 (Grigore) leads to an acceptable Maróczy position for Black. Thus practice has focused on 6 ♝xc6 dxc6 7 0-0 when 7...♝g4 8 dxc5! ♕xc5 9 ♝e3 ♕b5 10 ♕b3, as De la Riva Aguado has employed, is slightly awkward for Black. However, instead 7...cxd4! 8 cxd4 ♝g4 9 ♝e3 ♘f6 10 ♘bd2 0-0 11 ♕c2 ♘d7! and ...e5 gave Black fully sufficient counterplay in Kr.Georgiev-G.Grigore, Istanbul Olympiad 2000.

5 e5 ♘d5

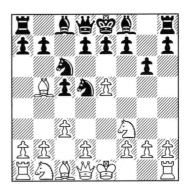

6 0-0

Sutovsky is happy to return play to a fairly normal line and we soon reach a position that often arises via 4 0-0 ♝g7 5 c3 ♘f6 6 e5 ♘d5 7 d4 cxd4 8 cxd4 0-0. However, White can also keep play in more independent channels as Krum Georgiev has liked to do with 6 d4 cxd4 7 ♕b3!?. This is a tricky option, but there are a number of ways for Black to gain a fairly reasonable position and 7...♘c7 8 ♝c4

♘e6 9 cxd4 ♘a5 10 ♕c3 ♘xc4 11 ♕xc4 sees Black bag the bishop pair. White does though have an imposing-looking centre for it, but Black has a useful resource in 11...♕c7 and then 12 ♕c3 d5 13 0-0 ♗d7 can be recommended for those happy to play fairly solidly as Black. However, a more dynamic option is also available in 11...b6!? when 12 d5 ♘c5 13 b4 ♗a6 14 b5 ♗b7 and ...e6 supplies counterplay, whereas 12 ♘c3 ♗b7 13 d5 ♖c8 was seen in Kr.Georgiev-V.Kotronias, Yugoslav Team Ch. 1999. Now Krum Georgiev has analysed 14 ♕d3 (protecting d5 from an exchange sacrifice on c3) 14...♘c5 15 ♕d4 ♗a6 16 ♗g5 ♘d3+ when the position is rather unclear after 17 ♔d2; White might not be able to castle, but his impressive and dangerous centre remains.

6...♗g7 7 d4 cxd4 8 cxd4 0-0 9 ♘c3

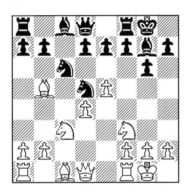

9...♘xc3

Now the position takes on certain c3 Sicilian characteristics as Black aims to undermine the white centre by pressurising e5 and c3. However, he can also opt for 9...♘c7 when practice has repeatedly shown that 10 ♗a4 d6! offers Black sufficient counterplay, but he has begun to come under some pressure after 10 ♗f4. After 10...♘xb5 11 ♘xb5 a6 12 ♘c3 d6 13 exd6 Black can't recapture any longer with his queen and so White hopes that his knight-pair will find good roles in this symmetrical structure. Filippov had thus previously tried

13...♗g4!?, but 14 d5 ♘d4 15 ♕e1! ♘xf3+ 16 gxf3 e5 17 dxe6 ♗xe6 18 ♕d2 left the extra white d6-pawn as the most important feature of the position in Y.Quezada-V.Filippov, Merida 2003. Thus Black must fall back on 13...exd6 14 h3 ♖e8 when he's still to fully equalise and he didn't manage to after 15 ♕d2 d5 16 ♖fe1 ♖xe1+ 17 ♖xe1 ♗e6 18 ♘e5! ♖c8 19 ♘xc6 ♖xc6 20 ♗e5! in A.Kornev-A.Bakutin, Tula 2004.

10 bxc3 d6 11 exd6

Clarifying the central situation, although White has an important alternative in 11 ♖e1, transposing into our next game.

11...exd6

Covering e5, although 11...♕xd6!? is a reasonable alternative for Black when White usually tries to bring his bishop to a3 and 12 a4! a6 13 ♗a3 ♕c7 14 ♗xc6 ♕xc6! 15 ♗xe7 ♖e8 16 d5 ♕xc3 was the sharp continuation of L.Fressinet-C.Paci, Montpellier 2001. After 17 ♖c1 ♕a5 18 d6 ♗d7 19 ♕b3 the position was rather tense, although Black shouldn't be worse after Rogozenko's 19...♗c6.

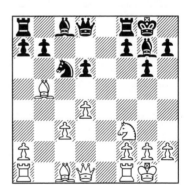

12 ♗g5!

As Sutovsky explains in his notes to this game in *New in Chess* White has numerous options here, but his aggressive choice does appear to be best.

12...♕c7 13 ♖e1 h6

Black later deviated with 13...♗d7 and obtained a reasonable position after 14 h3 ♖fe8

15 ♕b3 a6 16 ♗d3 ♗e6! 17 ♕a3 ♗d5 in P.Svidler-P.Leko, Monaco (rapid) 2005. Sutovsky suggests 14 ♕d2!? as an improvement, whilst it's noticeable that in the game he doesn't rush to commit his queen to d2 and is soon able to employ her better elsewhere.

14 ♗f4 ♘e7

Black could also have tried to defend actively on the kingside with 14...g5?! 15 ♗g3 f5, but then Sutovsky's brilliant 16 ♗c4+ ♔h7 17 ♖e8!! ♖xe8 18 ♘xg5+ gives White a very strong attack.

15 ♕b3 g5?! 16 ♘xg5! hxg5 17 ♗xg5

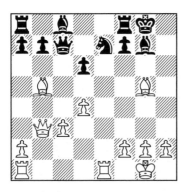

17...♗e6

Sutovsky doesn't need any invitation to add further wood to the fire, although White had dangerous compensation in any case, such as with 17...♘g6 18 h4! ♗g4 19 ♗d3 ♔h8 20 f3 ♗d7 21 h5 ♕a5 22 f4! f6 23 ♗xg6 fxg5 24 ♖e7 (Notkin).

18 ♖xe6! fxe6 19 ♕xe6+ ♖f7 20 ♖e1 a6 21 ♗a4 ♘c6 22 ♗b3 d5

White has superbly judged that he has time to calmly bring his rook into the attack and Filippov never had a satisfactory defence, such as here 22...♔f8 would have allowed a neat finish with 23 ♗f4 ♖d8 24 ♗xd6+!. However, giving up his d-pawn fails to save him and Sutovsky h-pawn's pawn soon decides this superb game for him:

23 ♗xd5 ♔f8 24 ♕g6 ♖e8 25 ♖xe8+ ♔xe8 26 h4! ♔f8 27 h5 ♕d7 28 ♗e6

♘e5!? 29 dxe5 ♕d1+ 30 ♔h2 ♗xe5+ 31 f4! ♗xf4+ 32 ♗xf4 ♖xf4 33 ♕h6+ ♔e7 34 ♕xf4 ♔xe6 35 ♕e4+ ♔d6 36 ♕d4+ ♕xd4 37 cxd4 ♔e7 38 d5 1-0

Game 80
J.Shaw-L.McShane
British League 2003

---

1 e4 c5 2 ♘f3 ♘c6 3 ♗b5 g6 4 0-0 ♗g7 5 c3 ♘f6 6 ♖e1 0-0 7 e5 ♘d5 8 d4 cxd4 9 cxd4 d6

Here the modern white player is happy to cede the bishop-pair and so 9...♘c7 appears to be slightly inferior due to 10 ♘c3! when 10...♘xb5 11 ♘xb5 a6 12 ♘c3 d6 13 exd6 ♕xd6 14 d5 ♘e5 15 ♗f4 gave White a pleasant edge in I.Glek-V.Ikonnikov, Belgian Team Ch. 2001, while after 15...♘xf3+ 16 ♕xf3 ♕b4 17 ♖e2! e6 18 ♖ae1 (Kaufman) White has some useful extra space and will aim to weaken the black kingside with ♗e5.

10 ♘c3

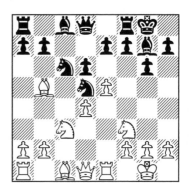

10...♘xc3

Once again retreating is a fairly common option, but White can convert his extra space into the advantage with 10...♘c7 11 exd6! ♕xd6 (or 11...exd6 12 ♗g5 f6 13 ♗e3 ♘xb5 14 ♘xb5 a6 15 ♘c3 and the knights enjoyed a slightly favourable structure, while here e6 has been badly weakened) 12 ♗g5 ♗e6 13 ♗xc6 bxc6 14 ♕d2. This is a pleasant IQP position as White should be able to exploit his control over e5 and c5, whilst also depriving Black of the bishop-pair and 14...罝fe8 15 彙f4 豐d8 16 彙e5! 彙d5 17 彙xg7 含xg7 18 ②e5 ②e6 19 罝e3 ②f8 20 罝c1 retained a clear edge with good prospects on both flanks in I.Glek-J.Karr, French Team Ch. 2003. Likewise Glek has demonstrated that 10...dxe5 11 彙xc6! bxc6 12 ②xe5, followed by ②e4-c5 is also fairly pleasant for White.

11 bxc3

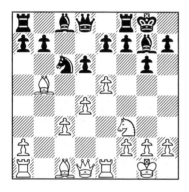

11...a6

Black has done quite well by encouraging an exchange on c6 with this, although it's by no means his only playable option:

a) 11...彙g4 12 exd6 豐xd6 13 h3 彙xf3 14 豐xf3 is seen surprisingly often, but it's hard for Black to target the white centre here, while the bishop-pair is quite useful and promises White the edge, such as with 14...e5!? 15 a4! 罝fd8 16 彙g5 f6 17 彙e3 exd4 18 罝ad1 f5 19 cxd4 (Yakovich).

(b) 11...豐a5 has been used by Wells and appears to be a valid alternative to McShane's choice, while Tkachiev's 12 彙xc6 bxc6 13 exd6 exd6 14 彙f4!? should be met by Rogozenko's 14...罝d8! 15 彙g5 f6 16 彙d2 豐d5!. Here White cannot easily exploit the weakness of e6, while we find a common potential problem for him in this variation; namely that he can easily become rather weak on the light squares and here ...彙f5 or ...彙g4 will give

Black comfortable play.

c) Rogozenko has also drawn attention to the rare 11...豐c7!? which keeps c6 and e7 covered and it's surprising that this hasn't been seen more. M.Dzhumaev-M.Taleb, Abu Dhabi 2000 continued 12 exd6 exd6 13 彙f4 and now Black opted for the ambitious but playable 13...②e7!? 14 豐b3 h6 15 罝ac1 g5, whereas 13...彙f5 (Rogozenko) seems quite comfortable for him; White can't easily increase the pressure, while Black plans to play down the c-file with ...②a5 and ...罝ac8.

12 彙xc6 bxc6 13 exd6

Kaufman prefers 13 彙f4!?, but here Black should be fine so long as he can find a role for his light-square bishop as he did with 13...彙e6! 14 豐d2 彙d5 15 ②g5 dxe5 16 dxe5 豐c8 which was roughly level in J.Clavijo Usuga-V.Ikonnikov, Sants 2003.

13...exd6 14 彙g5 豐c7

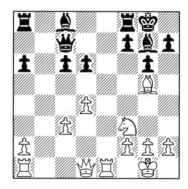

15 豐d2

It's a little surprising that this variation isn't more popular considering Glek's successes with it, although it did though gain a high-level test in Zhang Zhong-L.Van Wely, Wijk aan Zee 2004 where White improved with 15 罝e7!. Then 15...豐a5 16 彙e3 彙g4!? 17 彙e7 罝fe8 18 彙xd6 罝xe3 19 fxe3 豐xc3 20 豐c1 gave him the edge, although Van Wely was to exploit the presence of opposite-coloured bishops and his strong light-square play to fairly comfortably hold the draw a pawn down after 20...♕d3 21 ♘e5 ♗xe5 22 ♗xe5 ♗e6 23 ♕e1 f6! 24 ♗xf6 ♖b8.

15...♗e6! 16 ♗h6 ♖fe8 17 ♗xg7 ♔xg7 18 ♘g5 ♗d5

Shaw has deprived Black of the bishop-pair, but McShane enjoys a small edge here due to his strong bishop. White thus sensibly hunts it down, although Black retains the edge by transferring his queen instead to d5.

19 ♘h3 ♕a5 20 ♘f4 h6 21 ♘xd5 ♕xd5 22 h3 a5

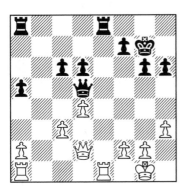

23 a4?

Now White becomes even weaker on the light-squares and the active 23 ♖xe8 ♖xe8 24 ♕d3, intending c4 and counterplay down one of the open files would have kept the disadvantage to a minimum.

23...♕c4! 24 ♕c2 ♖ab8 25 ♖xe8 ♖xe8 26 ♖b1 ♖e2 27 ♕b3 ♕d3! 28 d5?

Allowing McShane to force a winning queen ending and so Shaw had to continue defending solidly for at least a move with 28 ♖f1. This appears grim after 28...♖c2, but then 29 ♕b8! offers reasonable counterplay and chances to draw, such as with 29...♕xc3 30 ♕xd6 ♖e2 31 d5! cxd5 32 ♕xd5 ♖e5 33 ♕d7, although Black can clearly continue to grind for some time here after 33...♕b4 34 g3 ♖e4 35 ♖a1 ♕b2.

28...cxd5 29 ♕b5 ♕d2 30 ♖f1 ♖e1! 31 g3 ♖xf1+ 32 ♔xf1 ♕xc3 33 ♕xd5 ♕a1+ 34 ♔g2 ♕xa4 35 ♕xd6 ♕e4+! 36 ♔h2

a4 37 h4 h5 38 f3 ♕e2+ 39 ♔g1 ♕b2 0-1

Game 81
G.Kasparov-A.Shirov
Linares 2002

1 e4 c5 2 ♘f3 ♘c6 3 ♗b5 g6 4 0-0 ♗g7 5 c3 ♘f6 6 ♖e1 0-0 7 d4 cxd4

It's slightly surprising that Shirov opted to release the tension as most attention in recent years has focused on 7...d5. White then gains some central options, but his inability to smoothly develop his queenside has been considered for some time to give Black equality:

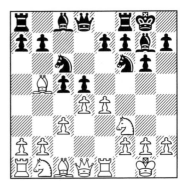

a) 8 exd5 has all but been abandoned as 8...♕xd5 9 c4 ♕d6 10 dxc5 ♕xc5 11 ♗e3 ♕h5 is fine for Black, while 10 d5?! ♘d4! 11 ♘xd4 cxd4 has only caused White problems; 12 ♕xd4? ♘g4! must be avoided, but 12 h3 a6 13 ♗a4 b5! 14 cxb5 axb5 15 ♗xb5 ♕xd5 decimated the white centre and left Black much better in H.Al Hadarani-M.Carlsen, Dubai 2004.

b) 8 e5 ♘e4 has seen many recent grandmaster games in this line when we have another fork:

b1) 9 ♘bd2 cxd4 10 cxd4 is fairly rare and allows Black to possibly even consider 10...♗d7!?, although Black has continued to do fairly well with 10...♕b6 11 ♗xc6 ♕xc6.

However, then 12 ♕e2!? is a rare response when Black should opt for 12...♘xd2 13 ♗xd2 ♗f5 as 12...♗f5 13 ♘h4! ♗e6 14 ♘xe4 dxe4 15 ♕xe4 ♗d5 16 ♕e2 didn't give him enough compensation in A.Lanin-A.Shariyazdanov, Togliatti 2003.

b2) 9 ♗xc6 bxc6 10 ♘bd2 reaches a critical and fairly fashionable position when Black has two promising options:

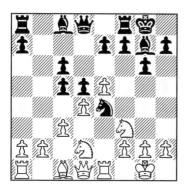

b21) 10...cxd4 11 cxd4 c5! 12 dxc5! ♘xc5 13 ♘b3 ♘xb3 14 ♕xb3 d4!? (those looking for an easier life can consider 14...♗g4 15 ♘d4 ♕b6! when practice has shown that Black gains enough play on the queenside and with a timely ...f6 to offset the white knight's ideal current home) opens the long diagonal, while the d-pawn is often a bit of a nuisance for White and 15 ♕d3 (White has tried a number of alternatives here, albeit without finding an advantage, such as 15 ♖d1 ♗e6! 16 ♕a3 ♕b6 17 ♘xd4 ♗xe5 was pretty comfortable for Black in A.Volzhin-A.Motylev, Dubai 2002) 15...♗b7 16 ♕xd4 ♕xd4 17 ♘xd4 ♖fd8 18 ♘f3 ♖d3 regained the pawn with full equality in A.Grischuk-P.Leko, Dubai (rapid) 2002.

b22) 10...♗f5!? is an important alternative when Black can consider, after the critical 11 ♘h4 e6 12 ♘xf5 exf5 13 ♘f1, the rare but sharp 13...cxd4!? 14 cxd4 ♕b6 when 15 f3 ♗xe5 16 fxe4 ♗xd4+ 17 ♔h1 fxe4 gives him three pawns and a strong centre for the piece,

while 15 ♖e3 c5! 16 ♖b3 ♕c7 17 f3 cxd4 18 fxe4 dxe4 19 ♕xd4 ♗xe5 20 ♕a4 ♖fe8 21 ♗d2 f4 gave Black pretty reasonable compensation in J.Houska-V.Kotronias, Hastings 2004/5.

8 cxd4

Kasparov is happy after Shirov's last to keep play within 7 d4 boundaries, whereas 8 e5 would have transposed to our last illustrative game.

8...d5 9 e5 ♘e4

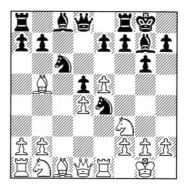

The best try as 10 ♗xc6 bxc6 11 ♘bd2 c5 would transpose to a key position we just considered after 7...d5.

10...♗f5!?

Supporting the knight and sharpening the struggle, whereas 10...♘xc3 11 bxc3 isn't quite enough for Black to gain equality, despite White's weaknesses down the c-file, when 11...♗g4 (or 11...♘a5 12 ♘g5! h6 13 ♘f3 ♗g4 14 h3 ♗xf3 15 ♕xf3 when White had forced a weakness and thereby threatened a strong e6-advance in J.Stocek-V.Volodin, Pardubice 2003) 12 ♗xc6! (preventing ...♘a5-c4, while 12 h3 ♗xf3 13 ♕xf3 is well met by 13...♕a5 with sufficient counterplay for Black) 12...bxc6 13 h3 ♗xf3 14 ♕xf3 ♕a5 15 ♗g5 provoked 15...f6 and gave White a clear edge after 16 exf6 exf6 17 ♗f4 ♖fe8 18 ♖e3, with the better bishop and prospects down the e-file and on the kingside, in D.Campora-R.Cifuentes Parada, Calvia Olympiad 2004.

11 ♘h4 ♗e6! 12 ♗xc6 bxc6 13 ♘a4!

Shirov retreated his bishop to the best square so that after 13 ♘xe4 dxe4 14 ♖xe4 he would have gained plenty of counterplay with 14...c5 and 15...♗d5.

13...g5 14 ♘f3

The game has sprung to life and it's noticeable that Kasparov avoided the sharpest continuation of 14 f3!? when 14...gxh4 15 fxe4 h3! leaves both sides with weakened kingsides. White's problem is that 16 ♘c5 hxg2 17 ♔xg2 dxe4! pretty much forces him to give up the well-placed knight when 18 ♘xe6 fxe6, followed by ...♕d5 or ...♕e8, gives Black sufficient activity.

14...f6

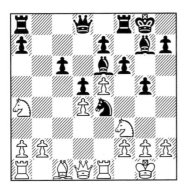

15 ♗e3?!

Kasparov clearly wasn't fully on the ball on this day, despite playing his favourite customer and in his favourite event. Now play quickly fizzles out to a draw and McShane later improved with 15 exf6!? when 15...♗xf6 16 ♘xg5! ♗xg5 17 ♖xe4 dxe4 18 ♗xg5 is a reasonable exchange sacrifice for two strong minor pieces and kingside chances. However, Black should perhaps contest that as 15...exf6 16 ♘d2! f5 17 ♘b3 ♗f7 18 ♗d2 ♘xd2 19 ♕xd2 f4 20 f3 ♕d6 21 ♘ac5 ♖fe8 22 ♘d3 saw the knights outclass the bishops in L.McShane-D.Jakovenko, Goa 2002.

15...g4 16 ♘d2 fxe5! 17 ♘xe4 dxe4 18 ♘c5 ♗f5 19 dxe5 ♕xd1 20 ♖axd1 ♗xe5

21 ♘d7!

Forcing the draw as, despite being a pawn up, Black can't cover all of his wrecked structure.

21...♗xd7 22 ♖xd7 ♗xb2 23 ♖xe7 ♖fe8 24 ♖c7! ♖ec8! 25 ♖e7 ♖e8 26 ♖c7 ½-½

Game 82
N.Short-J.Pierrot
Najdorf Memorial, Buenos Aires 2000

---

1 e4 c5 2 ♘f3 ♘c6 3 ♗b5 g6 4 0-0 ♗g7 5 c3 ♘f6 6 ♖e1 0-0 7 h3

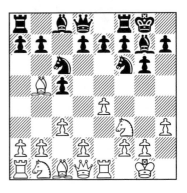

7...e5

White's h3 is a useful move in many different positions and Black must now try to find a good role for his bishop. Pierrot opts to clamp down on the d4-square, but Black has tried a number of other set-ups:

a) 7...♕b6!? 8 ♘a3 and:

a1) Not 8...d5 when 9 e5! ♘e8 10 d4 (Smyslov's 10 d3!? ♘c7 11 ♗a4 ♘e6 12 ♘c2 also offers reasonable chances for a small edge) 10...cxd4 11 cxd4 ♘c7 12 ♗xc6 is slightly more pleasant for White after both 12...bxc6 13 ♖e3 and Ponomariov's 12...♕xc6 13 ♕b3!

a2) 8...d6 once again sees the black queen being actively and well placed on b6, and this looks like quite a reasonable choice. White hasn't got anywhere with 9 ♗f1 or with 9 d3 when Black quickly advances with ...e5, while 9 d4 cxd4 10 cxd4 d5 11 e5 ♘e4 12 ♗e3 ♗f5

13 ♖c1 ♖fc8 was also fine for Black, with White continuing to suffer from his not especially well-placed queenside pieces, in P.Svidler-V.Kramnik, Monaco (blindfold) 2005.

b) 7...d6?! is a little too compliant and 8 d4 cxd4 9 cxd4 a6 10 ♗f1 b5 11 ♗g5 ♗b7 12 ♘c3 ♖c8 13 ♕d2 ♘a5 14 d5! favoured White in R.Ponomariov-T.Dovramadjiev, internet blitz 2004.

c) 7...♕c7 leaves the queen well-placed to assist Black's queenside play after 8 d4 cxd4 9 cxd4 d5 10 e5 ♘e4, but 8 ♘a3! d5 9 e5 ♘d7 10 d4 a6 11 ♗f1 cxd4 12 cxd4 b5 13 ♗f4 e6 14 ♘c2 gave White the edge in M.Palac-F.Yacob, Cap d'Agde 2003.

d) 7...♘e8 doesn't wait for e5 before heading around to c7 to challenge the b5-bishop.

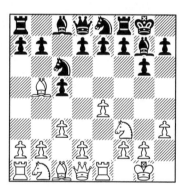

This has received a number of tests, but still looks a little artificial and 8 d4 cxd4 9 cxd4 ♘c7 10 ♗a4 d5 11 e5 ♗f5 12 ♘c3 ♖c8 13 ♗xc6! bxc6 14 ♘a4 ♘e6 15 ♘g5! left the black knight having not actually achieved very much after all in D.Campora-M.Agopov, Andorra 1999.

e) 7...d5 is a central break White is happy to see as after 8 e5 the knight must retreat and 8...♘e8 9 d4 cxd4 (or 9...♕b6 10 ♗f1 cxd4 11 cxd4 ♗f5 12 ♘c3 and White's kingside prospects give him the edge, especially after 12...♘b4?! 13 ♘h4! – Collinson) 10 ♗xc6! (the bishop lacks a good role elsewhere, while this again helps to later cement a knight on

c5) 10...bxc6 11 cxd4 ♘c7 12 ♘c3 ♘e6 13 ♘g5 ♘xg5 14 ♗xg5 f6 15 ♗f4 saw White's superior minor piece give him the edge in M.Turov-D.Goldenberg, Montreal 2001.

8 a3!?

With Black having blocked in his bishop, Short logically forgoes the d4-advance for queenside play. Instead Black has a number of good responses to 8 d4, such as 8...exd4 (or 8...cxd4 9 cxd4 d5!? when 10 ♗xc6 bxc6 11 ♘xe5 ♘xe4 12 ♘c3 c5 fully equalised in V.Zvjaginsev-E.Sutovsky, Russian Team Ch. 2005) 9 cxd4 cxd4 when 10 ♘xd4 is well met by 10...♕b6!, while 10 e5 ♘d5 11 ♗g5 ♕c7 has been shown not to give White more than enough compensation. However, Black might prefer an old suggestion of Joe Gallagher's which continues to hold up well and 10...♘e8 11 ♗g5 f6 12 exf6 ♗xf6 13 ♗xf6 ♕xf6 14 ♘bd2 ♘d6 15 ♗d3 b6 16 ♘e4 ♘xe4 17 ♗xe4 ♗b7 was pretty equal in V.Belov-V.Kotronias, Kavala 2004.

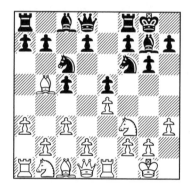

8...a6?!

White doesn't mind damaging the black structure, whilst it's not then so easy for Black to gain central and light-square counterplay. The ...a6-pawn rules out ...♗a6 ideas, while Pierrot could really do with his king's knight being on the more harmonious e7-square which would enable ...f5. Black thus later preferred to improve his knight with 8...♘e8! 9 b4 ♘c7 when the exchange on c6 has lost much of its effectiveness, while 10 ♗f1 d6 11 d3 ♘e6 12 ♘bd2 ♗d7 13 ♗b2 didn't really give White much in A.Shabalov-J.Echavarria, Cali 2001 and Rogozenko's 10...d5!? would have been at least as effective.

More often though Black has opted for 8...d6, but then 9 b4 ♗d7 10 d3 ♖e8 11 ♗e3 still gives White reasonable chances for an edge and after 11...b6 12 ♘bd2 ♘h5 13 ♖c1 ♘f4 14 ♗xf4! exf4 15 ♗xc6! ♗xc6 16 d4 the knight-pair was in the ascendancy in G.Sarakauskas-K.McPhillips, Isle of Man 2004, especially after 16...d5?! 17 e5 c4 18 ♘h2!.

9 ♗xc6 dxc6

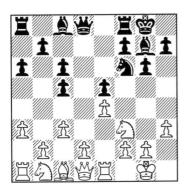

10 d3 ♕c7

A later game saw 10...♖e8, but 11 ♕c2 a5 12 ♘bd2 ♘h5 13 ♘f1 ♘f4 14 d4! cxd4 15 cxd4 ♘e6 16 dxe5 ♘d4 17 ♘xd4 ♕xd4 18 ♘d2 ♖xe5 19 ♘c4! maintained control and White's advantage in S.Movsesian-M.Jirovsky, Czech Team Ch. 2004. Indeed the tactical d4-advance is a little awkward for Black as he would like to double on the d-file after 10...♕d6!?, but 11 d4! cxd4 12 cxd4 ♖d8 13 ♗d2 doesn't fully solve his problems, although this might still be his best bet.

11 ♕c2 h6 12 ♗e3 b6 13 b4!

Thematically striking out against the black

queenside and Short is soon allowed to also favourably advance in the centre.

13...cxb4 14 axb4 ♗e6?! 15 d4 exd4 16 cxd4 ♕b7 17 ♘c3 ♖fe8 18 ♗f4

Black might possess the bishop-pair, but he is struggling for a plan and must just defend solidly and as best he can, although Short's impressive technique is unlikely to let him off the hook.

18...♘d7 19 ♗d6 ♗c4 20 e5!

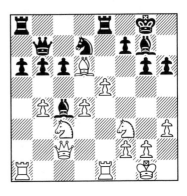

20...♖e6?!

Underestimating White's ideas and now Short gets to force the exchange of the black light-squared bishop, to take the c-file and to usefully mobilise his f-pawn.

21 ♘d2! ♗d5 22 ♘xd5 cxd5 23 ♖ec1 ♗f8 24 ♗xf8 ♘xf8 25 ♘f1!

Beginning to target the weakened black kingside and Short now supplies an excellent demonstration of how to completely undo Black on that side of the board.

25...♖ee8 26 ♘e3 ♖ec8 27 ♕a2 ♖d8 28 f4 ♘e6 29 ♕d2 ♘g7 30 ♖f1 ♕e7 31 ♖f3

Remaining alert to ...♕g5 ideas and now the attack quickly breaks through, while Black's counterplay is too little, too late.

31...♖a7 32 f5 ♕g5 33 ♕f2! a5 34 h4 ♕e7 35 f6 ♕xb4 36 fxg7 ♕xd4 37 ♖f1 1-0

Summary

This should suit the ambitious white player more than 4 ♗xc6, although it isn't a route to a clear edge. 5 ♖e1 is probably best met by 5...♘f6 when the ♘c3 systems don't impress so long as Black knows what he's doing. Instead 5 ♖e1 e5 is also playable when 6 b4 deserves further attention instead of the more popular trade on c6, as after 6...dxc6! White is struggling to show anything at all.

5 c3 ♘f6 6 ♕a4!? continues to deserve further exploration, although Black may well then gain as much fun as White. Instead it's puzzling as to why 6 ♖e1 ♘f6 7 d4 continues to be seen so often when 7...d5 is a good counter. 7 h3 has also been popular, but both 7...e5 8 a3 ♘e8! and 7...♕b6 are currently looking quite reasonable for Black. If that remains so then Glek's preferred 6 ♖e1 ♘f6 7 e5 and the Sutovsky endorsed 6 e5 might well be set for a return to centre stage.

1 e4 c5 2 ♘f3 ♘c6 3 ♗b5 g6 4 0-0 *(D)*
4...♗g7 5 c3
> 5 ♖e1
>> 5...e5
>>> 6 b4 – *Game 74*; 6 ♗xc6 – *Game 75*
>> 5...♘f6 – *Game 76*

5...♘f6 6 ♖e1
> 6 ♕e2 – *Game 77*; 6 ♕a4 *(D)* – *Game 78*; 6 e5 – *Game 79*

6...0-0 *(D)*
> 7 e5 – *Game 80*; 7 d4 – *Game 81*; 7 h3 – *Game 82*

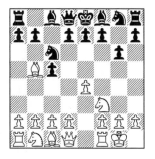

4 0-0

6 ♕a4

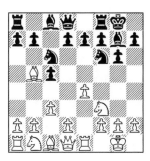

6...0-0

INDEX OF COMPLETE GAMES